SISTERS IN CRISIS

Ann Carey

Sisters in Crisis, Revisited

From Unraveling to Reform and Renewal

IGNATIUS PRESS   SAN FRANCISCO

First edition
Sisters in Crisis: The Tragic Unraveling of Women's Religious Communities
© 1997 by Our Sunday Visitor Publishing Division
Our Sunday Visitor, Inc.

Cover images (from left to right)

Sisters of St. Francis, including Mother Marianne Cope (far right), serving
at the Branch Hospital for Lepers in Hawaii, 1886

Sister Simone Campbell, executive director of Network, speaking in Ames, IA,
during a nine-state Nuns on the Bus tour, Monday, June 18, 2012
AP Photo/Charlie Neibergall

A Sister of Life visiting with two children outside the Basilica of St. John the Evangelist
in Stamford, CT, after a profession of vows ceremony, August 6, 2012
Photo by Amy Mortensen

Cover design by John Herreid

© 2013 by Ignatius Press, San Francisco
ISBN 978-1-58617-789-8
Library of Congress Control Number 2012953858
Printed in the United States of America ⊗

To my teachers, the Sisters of Loretto and the Sisters of Saint Joseph of Carondelet

CONTENTS

III. Where Do Sisters Go from Here?

PREFACE

The situation for women religious in the United States has changed considerably since the first edition of *Sisters in Crisis* was published in 1997. Some of the new as well as some of the established orders of sisters who live the classic, traditional style of religious life have been thriving and attracting vocations. An apostolic visitation of US sisters was approved by Pope Benedict XVI and was conducted between 2009 and 2011. An assessment of the Leadership Conference of Women Religious (LCWR) carried out by the Congregation for the Doctrine of the Faith from 2008 to 2012 found that the conference had serious doctrinal problems. Prominent sisters have taken public positions, contrary to those of the United States Conference of Catholic Bishops, in support of legislation that allows funding for abortion and denies the conscience rights of those who object to immoral medical procedures.

This new edition of *Sisters in Crisis* covers all of these important developments while retaining most of the original content in order to provide in one book a history of US sisters since the Second Vatican Council closed in 1965. The historical background in the first edition sheds considerable light on the events that have occurred since 1997, for many of the subsequent developments were foreshadowed by and built upon previous ones. This history reflects the forbearance of the Vatican, which had tried for more than forty years to reform religious life and the conference of women superiors before it initiated the apostolic visitation and doctrinal assessment.

ACKNOWLEDGMENTS

I wish to acknowledge the valuable contribution of the many sisters who have shared their experiences, prayers, and suggestions for this work. These sisters belong to a variety of religious institutes, including those of the Benedictines, Carmelites, Daughters of Charity, Dominicans, Franciscans, Holy Cross, Immaculate Heart of Mary, Little Sisters of the Poor, Loretto, Mercy, Notre Dame, Saint Joseph, Sisters of Charity, Sisters of Christian Charity, and Sisters of the Holy Names of Jesus and Mary. Most of these sisters have asked not to be named, as they did not want to be perceived as criticizing their religious institutes to which they are unfailingly loyal. Some of them wanted to remain anonymous because they feared retribution from leaders who hold views different from their own. Some sisters who were not named in the first edition are named here, as they have passed on to their eternal reward and I wish to honor them by acknowledging their names.

I also am indebted to the staff of the University of Notre Dame archives, who graciously and patiently helped me access material in their holdings. Among the collections at Notre Dame were the records of the Leadership Conference of Women Religious (LCWR), the National Assembly of Religious Women (NARW), and the Consortium Perfectae Caritatis. Much of the material gathered from primary sources in those collections, such as correspondence and meeting minutes, was published for the first time in the first edition of this book.

INTRODUCTION

For more than 150 years, religious sisters have been the backbone of the Catholic Church in the United States. Sisters built the parochial school system as well as the Catholic health care and social-service systems. Sisters helped dioceses and parishes spread the Catholic faith to the unchurched while ministering to the spiritual needs of the Catholic people. Perhaps most important, sisters dedicated their lives to giving visible witness to the transcendence of God and to the spiritual aspect of our humanity.

The US Church had 180,000 sisters in 1965, but by 2012, that number had dropped to 55,000, with the median age in most orders being over seventy. Sisters have nearly disappeared from many Catholic institutions, and some of the sisters who are still visible seem to be very angry with the Church in general and with the male hierarchy in particular. Within many orders, the sisters themselves seem to be divided about how religious life should be lived: Some wear religious garb and continue to work in Catholic institutions while others in the same community wear regular clothes, live alone in apartments, and work in secular occupations.

Journalists are trained to ask questions referred to as the five *W*s and the *H*. During the thirty-plus years that I have worked as a journalist in the Catholic press, I have often pondered these questions: *Who* led the changes in religious life, and *who* were most affected by them? *What* events and ideas influenced these changes? *When* did the philosophy of religious life change? *Where* have all the sisters gone? *Why* was the renewal of religious life interpreted so differently by so many sisters? And *how* did religious life for sisters evolve into its current state of crisis? For this new edition of *Sisters in Crisis*, I would add one more question to those original ones: *Why* are the orders that have embraced the classical model of religious life attracting the most vocations? My research and experience have helped me find the answers to these questions, which I detail in the following pages.

In order to simplify a complex topic, I have used consistent terms throughout the book. Strictly speaking, there are some canonical differences between the terms *institute, community, congregation* and *order*. In general usage, however, these terms are used interchangeably, as they are in this book. Similarly, the term *nun* refers canonically to a woman who belongs to a cloistered or contemplative order and remains behind convent or monastery walls, while *sister* is the canonical term for women religious who belong to congregations that are engaged in apostolic work. Most laypeople are not aware of this distinction, so these terms also will be used interchangeably in this book, although the topics covered refer only to sisters who are members of apostolic communities and do not apply to the approximately four thousand nuns who belong to contemplative institutes.

An additional matter of clarity involves the four-hundred-plus religious institutes of women in the United States. Some of these institutes are provinces of international orders that have headquarters in other countries. For example, the motherhouse of the Sisters of Saint Francis of Perpetual Adoration is in Olpe, Germany. There are two American provinces: the Eastern, or Immaculate Heart of Mary, Province in Mishawaka, Indiana; and the Western, or Saint Joseph, Province in Colorado Springs, Colorado. On the other hand, some US religious institutes, such as the Dominican Sisters of Hawthorne, were started in this country. The larger institutes of women religious, whether they are international or domestic, usually are divided into several provinces in this country. The province of a particular order, however, should not be confused with an autonomous order. Many of these diverse institutes of women religious were founded on the same tradition or rule, and the names of their institutes are very similar. Hence, many laypeople think that institutes founded under the same rule are somehow connected. This is not the case except for provinces of the same institute.

The charism—the spirituality that guides the institute's way of life and approach to the apostolate—is also distinct in each institute. For example, the Dominican Sisters of Saint Cecilia in Nashville, Tennessee, founded in 1860, is a very traditional order whose primary ministry is education in Catholic schools. The Dominican Sisters of the

Congregation of the Most Holy Rosary in Sinsinawa, Wisconsin, founded in 1847, is a very diverse order with multiple ministries.

The title *mother* was always used in pre–Vatican II days to designate a sister who was superior general of an order or superior of a province. In some institutes, the title *mother* was retained after a sister went out of office, but this was not always the case. After Vatican II, the title *mother* was dropped by many institutes of women religious. For consistency, the title *sister* is used throughout this book for all sisters, even though they may have been superiors with the title *mother* at the time they are referenced.

Another possible source of confusion is that prior to Vatican II most orders required their sisters to take a religious name, quite often prefixed by *Mary* in honor of the Blessed Mother. Following Vatican II, and with the Vatican's approval, however, many orders allowed their sisters to use their baptismal and family names if they so desired. Thus, some of the sisters mentioned herein were known by their religious names at one time then later resumed the use of their given names. An effort has been made to indicate in parenthesis the alternate name of the sister where there is the possibility of confusion.

Additionally, there is some confusion over the name of the Congregation for Institutes of Consecrated Life and Societies of Apostolic Life. This is the Vatican Curia administrative department that has authority to establish and give general direction to religious and secular institutes, to oversee renewal and adaptation of the institutes, to review and approve their constitutions, and to set up and communicate with conferences of major superiors. This congregation had three names during the years covered in this book. Before 1967, it was the Congregation of Religious; from 1967 until 1988, it was the Congregation for Religious and Secular Institutes; since 1988, the title has been Congregation for Institutes of Consecrated Life and Societies of Apostolic Life. To simplify matters, this congregation will be referred to throughout the book as the Congregation for Religious.

Likewise, the United States Conference of Catholic Bishops (USCCB) has changed its name during the years this book covers. To simplify matters, I refer to the bishops' conference throughout (except in footnotes) as the USCCB, even if it was using its former title of National Conference of Catholic Bishops during the time it was cited.

Finally, I am uncomfortable with using the terms *liberal* and *conservative* for religious orders because of the political connotations of the terms and also because they carry negative images for many people. Therefore, I follow the example of sociologist Helen Rose Fuchs Ebaugh by using the term *change-oriented* to describe sisters or religious institutes inclined to seek a new definition of religious life by expanding the boundaries usually associated with the religious state. I use the term *traditional* to describe sisters or institutes that adhere to the traditional understanding of religious life as contained in Vatican II documents and other Church teachings. Neither term should be construed as inherently negative.

CHRONOLOGY

Important Events for US Sisters

1950   Pope Pius XII calls for the updating of women's religious institutes.

1956   The US Conference of Major Religious Superiors of Women's Institutes (CMSW) is founded.

1959   Pope John XXIII announces that he will convene a Second Vatican Council and that the 1917 Code of Canon Law will be revised thereafter.

The CMSW receives canonical status.

1962   The CMSW's statutes are approved by the Vatican.

The Second Vatican Council opens on October 11.

1964   Sisters attending a meeting in Grailville, Ohio, to study preliminary drafts of Vatican II documents decide to publish a book about renewing religious life, and they propose that the CMSW research possible resources for the renewal of sisters.

1965   In June *The Changing Sister* is published with essays by nine sisters who set forth their ideas about the impact of the upcoming renewal of religious. This book heavily influences the content of the 1967 Sisters' Survey.

October 28: *Perfectae Caritatis*, the *Decree on the Appropriate Renewal of Religious Life*, is issued.

Vatican II closes on December 8.

1966   Pope Paul VI issues *Ecclesiae Sanctae*, the motu proprio with specific directives for implementing *Perfectae Caritatis*.

1967   In the spring, the Sisters' Survey is sent to 140,000 US sisters by the CMSW.

In July, a group of Catholic educators meets at Land O' Lakes, Wisconsin, to discuss the role of the Catholic university. It issues the "Land O' Lakes Statement", which declares that Catholic universities "must have a true autonomy and academic freedom in the face of authority of whatever kind, lay or clerical, external to the academic community itself".

1968   *Catholic Institutions in the United States: Canonical and Civil Law Status*, by Monsignor John J. McGrath, is published, contending that schools and hospitals separately incorporated from the religious institutes that own them are not subject to canon law.

1970   A group of women and men superiors compose and circulate the "Statement on American Religious Life in the Seventies", calling for American religious to function democratically and determine their own course of renewal.

1971   Pope Paul VI issues the apostolic exhortation *Evangelica Testificatio*, setting forth his observations about positive and negative developments in the renewal of religious life.

The CMSW approves new statutes, admits sisters who are not major superiors, and changes its name to the Leadership Conference of Women Religious (LCWR).

The Consortium Perfectae Caritatis is founded.

1974   The LCWR responds to *Evangelica Testificatio* with *Widening the Dialogue*, a critique of the papal document.

1975   The LCWR refuses a Vatican request to dissociate itself from the first Women's Ordination Conference (WOC), and the LCWR liaison sister to the WOC becomes coordinator of the organizing task force for the WOC.

1978   The LCWR publishes "Patterns in Authority and Obedience", which cites tensions between sisters and the hierarchy over "different expectations of authority".

1979   LCWR president Sister Theresa Kane, RSM, is chosen to represent women religious in greeting John Paul II on his first papal visit to the United States. She uses the occasion to tell the pope that "all ministries in the Church" should be open to women.

1983   January 25: Pope John Paul II promulgates the new Code of Canon Law for the Latin Rite of the Church.

   May 9: Sister Agnes Mary Mansour, RSM, requests dispensation from her vows after she is told she cannot remain a religious and still hold the position of director of social services for the state of Michigan and oversee Medicaid payments for abortion.

   June 22: It is revealed that Pope John Paul II has appointed Archbishop John Quinn to conduct a study of religious life in the United States. The pope directs the Congregation for Religious to issue *Essential Elements on Church Teaching in Religious Life* as a guideline for bishops performing the study.

1984   January 19: Sister Arlene Violet, RSM, resigns from her order to run for state attorney general in Rhode Island. (The 1983 Code of Canon Law prohibits religious from holding public office.)

   October 7, Respect Life Sunday: A display ad published in the *New York Times* claims that the Catholic Church's condemnation of abortion is not the only "legitimate Catholic position" on abortion and includes the signatures of twenty-six women religious.

1985   The LCWR publishes *Claiming Our Truth*, which includes a claim to a right to "loyal dissent".

1986   In October the Quinn Commission gives its final report to the Vatican, concluding that "in general religious life in the United States is in good condition."

1987   The Forum of Major Superiors is established within the Institute on Religious Life (which eventually will participate in forming a new superiors' conference for women).

1989   Pope John Paul II writes to US bishops about the results of the Quinn Commission and expresses concern about the "polarization" of US sisters. He reminds bishops to work with religious "to remain faithful to the church's mission and teaching".

The pope appoints Cardinal James Hickey as official liaison to the Vatican for sisters who are not affiliated with the LCWR.

The LCWR adopts five-year goals that include "to develop structures of solidarity with women in order to work for the liberation of women through transformation of social and ecclesial structures and relationships".

The LCWR and the Consortium Perfectae Caritatis hold their first dialogue session at the request of Cardinal Hickey.

1991   The sisters in the Consortium Perfectae Caritatis and the Forum of Major Superiors decide to disband their organizations to form a new, combined organization and request canonical status.

1992   The Vatican recognizes the Council of Major Superiors of Women Religious (CMSWR) as an alternative US superiors' conference.

1993   The LCWR national board issues the statement "Concerning the Rights of Gay and Lesbian Persons", charging that "recent Church documents invoke religious principles to justify discrimination against homosexual persons."

1994   The Congregation for Religious issues *Fraternal Life in Community*, reiterating that life in common is a crucial element of religious life.

The World Synod of Bishops convenes on the topic of consecrated life.

1996   Pope John Paul II issues the apostolic exhortation *Vita Consecrata*, his reflections on the synod.

1999   The Congregation for the Doctrine of the Faith (CDF) tells Sister Jeannine Gramick and Father Robert Nugent to stop all ministry to homosexual persons because some of their positions were incompatible with Church teaching. The LCWR protests the CDF action.

2001   During their spring visit to the Vatican, LCWR leaders are alerted by the CDF that doctrinal concerns have been raised by their statements regarding the 1994 apostolic letter *Ordinatio Sacerdotalis*, the 2000 declaration *Dominus Jesus*, and "the problem of homosexuality".

2002   The Congregation for Religious issues *Starting Afresh from Christ: A Renewed Commitment to Consecrated Life in the Third Millennium*.

2003   The Congregation for Catholic Education issues *Consecrated Persons and Their Mission in Schools: Reflections and Guidelines*.

2007   LCWR assembly keynote speaker Sister Laurie Brink, OP, says that some groups of sisters are "no longer ecclesiastical" and are "Post-Christian".

2008   April 8: LCWR leaders are told by the CDF that since the doctrinal errors cited in 2001 had not been corrected, a doctrinal assessment of the organization would be undertaken, but no public announcement is made.

        May 11: The Congregation for Religious issues *The Service of Authority and Obedience*.

        September 27: Cardinal Franc Rodé, prefect of the Congregation for Religious, speaks at a symposium on consecrated life at Stonehill College. Two sisters there ask him for an apostolic visitation of US women religious.

2009   January 30: An apostolic visitation of US women religious is announced by the Congregation for Religious. Mother Mary Clare Millea, ASCJ, is named apostolic delegate to conduct the visitation.

        A February 18 CDF letter to the LCWR confirms the decision to undertake the doctrinal assessment. Bishop Leonard Blair of Toledo is named apostolic delegate to conduct the assessment.

        An April 14 article in the *National Catholic Reporter* reveals that the Vatican had started the doctrinal assessment of the LCWR.

2010   The LCWR, Network, and the Catholic Health Association endorse the Patient Protection and Affordable Care Act (Obamacare) in opposition to the US bishops, who had rejected the bill because it contained funding for abortion and lacked protection for conscience rights.

2012   In January Mother Mary Clare Millea submits the final reports of the apostolic visitation to the Vatican. The Vatican commences its study of the visitation findings.

April 18: The CDF releases the doctrinal assessment of LCWR, calling for sweeping reform of the organization and appointing Archbishop J. Peter Sartain as apostolic delegate to conduct the reform over a five-year period.

In August the LCWR annual assembly considers whether to cooperate with the doctrinal assessment and concludes that LCWR leaders should continue to dialogue with Archbishop Sartain.

2013   The CDF prefect informs LCWR leaders on April 15 that Pope Francis has affirmed the findings of the doctrinal assessment and the program of reform for the LCWR.

ABBREVIATIONS

CDF	Congregation for the Doctrine of the Faith
CHA	Catholic Health Association
CMSW	US Conference of Major Religious Superiors of Women's Institutes
CMSWR	Council of Major Superiors of Women Religious
CPC	Consortium Perfectae Caritatis
FORUS	*Future of Religious Orders in the United States*
IHM	Immaculate Heart of Mary Sisters
LCWR	Leadership Conference of Women Religious
NAM	New Age Movement
NARW	National Assembly of Religious Women
NAWR	National Assembly of Women Religious
NCAN	National Coalition of American Nuns
NCEA	National Catholic Educational Association
PPACA	Patient Protection and Affordable Care Act
SFC	Sister Formation Conference
USCCB	United States Conference of Catholic Bishops
WOC	Women's Ordination Conference

PART I

POST–VATICAN II SISTERS:
READY FOR RENEWAL OR REVOLUTION?

I

Sisters Encounter the 1960s

I have not come here to preach peace, but to call for a revolution, a revolution in the life of active nuns.[1]

—Cardinal Léon Joseph Suenens

Cardinal Léon Joseph Suenens attracted attention in 1963 when he made the above proclamation on a trip to the United States. He was not the first high-ranking churchman to call for reform in convents, but he was the first to use the terms *revolution* and *war*. During his papacy, from 1939 to 1958, Pius XII had tried repeatedly to move women religious to modernize but in terms less flamboyant than those of Cardinal Suenens, who had a flair for the dramatic.

The leaders of women religious generally had resisted reform partly out of comfort with the status quo and partly because the needs of the Catholic Church in the United States kept the sisters so occupied that they had little time to sit back and evaluate their own situation. Most priests and bishops also were reluctant to encourage change because sisters were key workers in parishes and dioceses that were burgeoning with Catholic families after the post–World War II baby boom. These Church leaders did not want to encourage any changes in convents that would restrict the number of sisters available to staff Catholic institutions. Thus, like most revolutions, the one in American convents took place because leaders failed to implement desperately needed reforms.

[1] Cardinal Leon Joseph Suenens, "The Nun in the World of Today", *Catholic Herald*, January 17, 1964.

The Need for Renewal

Customs and daily schedules for sisters often were based on a European lifestyle that was hundreds of years old and rooted in an uneducated, rural society. Even in the 1950s, many American convents still followed schedules that had been devised before the widespread use of electricity. Thus, the sisters' day began at dawn to take advantage of the daylight, and their activities outside convent walls—and often inside, too—ceased at sunset.

While contemplative orders devote the majority of their time to prayer, active orders engage in outside works, or apostolates. Yet, before the Second Vatican Council, many of the active communities of women lived a monastic lifestyle and spent up to four hours a day in prayer. Often that prayer time was devoted to a recitation of routine devotions, with little consideration given to spiritual enrichment, Scripture study, liturgically related prayer, or personal prayer. Such a lengthy prayer schedule could be quite taxing for sisters holding down full-time jobs, particularly teachers, who needed evening hours to plan classes and grade papers. (Some retired sister-teachers readily admit that they regularly threw student papers in the trash because they simply did not have time to look at them.) Sisters also had little time for personal enrichment or even reading a newspaper or news magazine to keep up with current events. In many convents, reading of such outside materials was strictly controlled by the superior, and many sisters, even those who taught social studies, had no idea about what was going on in the outside world.

Custom and rule books that hadn't been revised in modern times usually controlled the day-to-day lives of sisters and were sometimes so detailed that they even described how certain foods should be consumed. Horariums prescribed a sister's activities for each hour of the day and even dictated bedtime. Mail usually was censored, and some orders restricted the number of letters a sister could write, even to her own family. Little courtesies, such as offering a cup of coffee to a visitor, had to be cleared through the superior in some communities, and most orders did not allow a sister to venture outside the walls without a sister companion.

Some of the changes proposed by Pius XII and the Congregation for Religious included putting more flexibility into the convent schedule, discarding outmoded acts of devotion or penance, updating religious garb, providing better professional training, improving religious formation, and teaching a stronger theology of the vows.[2] In his apostolic constitution *Sponsa Christi*, released on November 21, 1950, the pope wrote, "And so, while fully maintaining all the basic and principal elements of the venerable institute of nuns, we have decreed, in relation to other elements, which are to be regarded as extrinsic and accessory, to introduce cautiously and prudently those adaptations to present-day conditions, which will be able to bring not only greater dignity but also greater efficacy to this institute."[3]

Again, on September 15, 1952, Pius XII brought up the matter of updating when superiors general of women's institutes were meeting in the Vatican: "In this crisis of vocations, be watchful lest the customs, the way of life or the asceticism of your religious families should prove a barrier or be a cause of failures. We are speaking of certain usages which, if they had once a certain significance in a different cultural setting, do not possess it nowadays." The pope gave the example of the habit, saying it should be "suitable and meet the requirements of hygiene". He also warned the superiors to give their sisters the necessary education to put them on equal footing with their lay colleagues and to give them the means to keep their professional knowledge up-to-date.[4]

In a 1958 radio message, Pius XII observed, "Let monasteries and orders of nuns have esteem for their own special character ... but they must not defend it in a narrow, inflexible spirit, and still less with a certain stubbornness which is opposed to any form of timely development and would not lend itself to any form of adaptation, even when the common good demands it."[5]

At the September 1952 meeting of mothers general in Rome, Claretian Father Arcadio Larraona, secretary of the Congregation for Religious, had advised that custom books and some convent practices be updated: "Notwithstanding all their good qualities, it is undeniable

[2] Elizabeth Kolmer, ASC, *Religious Women in the United States* (Wilmington, Md.: Michael Glazier, Inc., 1984), 35.

[3] Pius XII, quoted in Abbé Gaston Courtois, ed., *The States of Perfection* (Westminster, Md.: The Newman Press, 1961), 154.

[4] Ibid., 216, 218.

[5] Ibid., 349.

that custom books, because of their detailed regulating of many aspects of daily life, can and do become oppressive, or at least embarrassing. There are superiors of all types and temperaments, and some of them are unduly attached to the letter of the prescription, without considering the spirit." [6]

Still, change was resisted by most women's orders, which continued to follow practices needing reform. For example, in many orders, even in the early 1960s, sisters were required monthly to ask their superiors for permission to perform routine tasks such as bathing, obtaining toothpaste and soap, doing assigned work, and even praying. Some sisters needed permission for normal adult activities such as using the telephone, even when doing so was an implicit part of their job. Behind this practice of requesting permission was an interpretation of the vow of obedience in which everyday activities didn't have merit unless they were done as acts of obedience. Thus, all actions, even daily routines that every adult must perform, came under the authority of the superior.

The chapter of faults was another common monthly practice, convened under the direction of the mother superior, in which members publicly confessed their faults to the rest of the community. Faults might include common accidents such as breaking a dish or spilling food on one's clothing. In some orders, if a sister neglected to accuse herself of a fault, the other sisters were obliged to accuse her.

Many orders also had rules that were unusually restrictive, such as the rule limiting exercise to a weekly walk or the one that prohibited sisters from eating in the homes of laypeople. Some orders prevented their sisters from visiting their family, even to see a seriously ill parent or to attend the wedding of a sibling. The basis for this restriction was that each sister embraced a new way of life and a new family—her community—when she made the decision to enter the convent. Visits to the outside could undermine a sister's dedication to her vows or to her community. Still, Pius XII and other members of the hierarchy began to realize that families might be more supportive of their daughters' religious vocations if those daughters weren't expected to sever family connections and obligations entirely. The daughters would be happier sisters if they were permitted to have an ongoing relationship

---

[6] Arcadio Larraona, CMF, "Address to Mothers General", *Review for Religious* (November 1954): 298.

with their families and to be given freedoms more appropriate for a rational adult.

Another area greatly in need of reform was the tyranny of some mother superiors. Often these women were superiors for life who ruled their subjects with an iron hand and sometimes with very little Christian charity. Although they exhorted others to practice the virtue of obedience and claimed to be acting in the name of the Church, some of the most authoritarian superiors strongly resisted the directives of the pope and the Congregation for Religious to shed outdated customs.

Even in congregations with moderate, loving superiors—and certainly there were many—life could be very difficult and stifling with little possibility for personal growth or responsible decision making. So-called recreation time often consisted of sisters being required to chat with the other members of the community, even if their own idea of recreation was to read a book or to take a walk or simply to be alone. All the duties of daily life, such as caring for one's habit, doing household chores, and participating in community prayer often left little time for any other activity or any possibility to expand one's horizons.

The lifestyles, customs, and rules of sisters varied from congregation to congregation, and even from convent to convent, and some sisters found their routines more difficult or repressive than did others. What might have been comforting and spiritually uplifting to one sister might have been stifling and humiliating to another. One former sister reported that her order accepted aspirants as young as twelve years of age. Many of the sisters in her order had been in the convent since preadolescence, and having gone from the authority of their parents to the authority of their superiors without ever making decisions on their own, they never learned to function as independent adults. Regulations that seemed overly restrictive to more mature sisters were perfectly acceptable to those who had been in the convent practically since childhood.

In addition to accepting girls at a young age, many orders did not carefully screen candidates. Some of the women entering the convent were not well suited for religious life, and some entered for the wrong reasons: fear of marriage, a failed romance, escape from an abusive home, the opportunity for a free education, etc. Yet, with dioceses begging for more sisters to staff their institutions, congregations were not inclined to turn away possibly unsuitable candidates.

Inadequate screening of aspirants was noted by Dr. J. T. Nix, a medical doctor who surveyed women religious and reported on his findings in 1961. In religious communities, Dr. Nix found other, and from a doctor's point of view more serious, problems:

1. Health education, health counseling, periodic health examination, and health records are nonexistent or inadequate.
2. Psychological screening as part of the preadmission examination is the exception rather than the rule.
3. Overwork is the rule rather than the exception, and in many communities retreats and attendance at conventions are synonymous with vacation.
4. Half of the community infirmarians have no nursing training.
5. Two-thirds of religious communities have no hospital insurance.
6. Admission requirements vary with every community, and many communities apparently have none at all.
7. Catholic medical and hospital care is not always available to Negro sisters in certain sections of the country.[7]

Clearly, many elements of religious life were in need of reform, but most orders of nuns were like Tevye, the fictional main character in *Fiddler on the Roof,* who clung to tradition simply because that was how things always were done. Even though many nuns had no idea why their communities practiced many of their traditions, they adhered to those traditions tenaciously. While tradition is important to any institution or society, traditions that no longer promote the good of the community should be reevaluated, as Tevye found out when the modern world intruded into his village and family.

Addressing this issue, Jesuit Father Joseph Gallen wrote in 1961 that "any custom, practice or observance that is queer, odd, peculiar, or artificial is evidently wrong, simply because you will never find such a quality in the model of all sanctity, Jesus Christ." Father Gallen's examples of outdated practices included "kneeling on meeting or leaving a superior, bowing from the waist when encountering him, kneeling

---

[7] Mary Florence Wolff, SL, ed., *Religious Life in the Church Today: Prospect and Retrospect.* Proceedings of the Women's Section of the Second National Congress of Religious in the United States, under the auspices of the Conferences of Major Religious Superiors (Notre Dame: University of Notre Dame Press, 1962), 222.

when talking to him, and kissing the hand of a superior". What concerned Father Gallen was the possibility that such customs, which dated back to the days of European aristocracies, might be identified with sanctity, thus leading to their "multiplication and obstinate retention". The unfortunate result of this misidentification, he pointed out, is that a religious might cling to these actions at the expense of the real source of holiness, an interior life.[8]

As one Dominican sister observed, many outdated customs were simply done by rote and no one could explain the reasons for them. Many sisters didn't understand the meaning behind the essential customs and traditions either, she said. Thus when orders undertook renewal and began discarding their unnecessary customs, many of them moved too quickly and without adequate planning. As a result, meaningful practices that served the spiritual life of the community, such as periods of silence and times for prayer, were also thrown out. As a Franciscan sister related, "It was like removing tiles from a mosaic. At first, removing a few small tiles didn't hurt the big picture. But we kept going, and when we took away some of the essential pieces, the whole thing collapsed."

The Habit of Habits

The habit was another aspect of religious life that needed reform, and Pope Pius XII also approached this topic, telling the sisters to modernize their dress.

Most habits had been modeled after clothing that was typical at the time religious institutes were founded, as long ago as several hundred years. But what might have been suitable attire for sixteenth-century sisters who rarely set foot outside the stone walls of cool, damp European convents, might not have been appropriate for twentieth-century American women in active apostolates. Yet many communities pegged their identity on their distinctive habit, and some sisters were reluctant to modernize for fear their community might lose this identity. Sisters were aware that as cumbersome as their habits might be, they made a clear statement that one had devoted her life to God and

---

[8] Joseph Gallen, SJ, "Femininity and Spirituality", *Review for Religious* (November 1961): 453.

to service to the Church. Because of this symbolism, the habit garnered respect from both clergy and laypeople, and helped to attract
new vocations. Many sisters also feared the effect that modernizing
the habit would have on them, making them too worldly not only in
appearance but also in their attitude. As one sister put it, "I knew that
if the habit went, all the other stuff would come in, like beauty par-
lors and permanents."

Ill-prepared Professionals

Perhaps even more important than the lifestyle of the sisters was the
issue of education. Even into the 1960s, it was common practice for
sisters to be sent into the classroom or the hospital without completing
their professional training. A 1952 study by Franciscan Sister M. Brideen
Long looked at the educational background of 1,286 teaching sisters.
Sister Brideen found that only 18 percent had finished three or more
years of college education before they began teaching in elementary
schools. Nearly 50 percent of them had less than two years of college.[9]

Pius XII addressed this problem repeatedly, saying that religious working in Catholic institutions should have the same professional training
as their lay counterparts. The pope's concern was not only for the wel-
fare of young sisters who were placed into professional positions without adequate preparation, but also for the people served by them. In his
1951 remarks to teaching sisters, the pope called on religious orders to
give their teaching sisters professional preparation and support.[10] A 1951
circular from the Congregation for Religious instructed superiors to
give their sisters "pedagogical and technical training", stating that sending a young teacher into the classroom without proper preparation was
"rash".[11] Yet it was common practice for sisters to be on what was
often referred to as "the twenty-year plan", with many of them taking
twenty to thirty years to complete their education because they could
attend school only during the summers, when they weren't teaching.

The teaching orders were in a real quandary. The superiors wanted
their young sisters to have a good education, but they were under

[9] M. Brideen Long, OSF, *Sister Formation Bulletin* (Autumn 1966): 2.
[10] Pope Pius XII quoted in Courtois, *The States of Perfection*, 199.
[11] Courtois, 218, footnote 8.

great pressure from pastors and bishops to provide teachers for the record numbers of children enrolled in parish grade schools and parochial high schools. In 1940, there were just over two million students in parochial and diocesan grade schools.[12] By 1955, that number had jumped to over three million, and by 1965, it had more than doubled to about 4.5 million. Diocesan and parochial high school enrollments also increased, from under 300,000 students in 1945 to more than 500,000 in 1960 and nearly 700,000 in 1965. Some orders even cut short the spiritual formation for young sisters to prepare them more quickly for the classroom, a practice condemned by the Vatican. The practice was shortsighted, for many young sisters didn't receive the formation they needed to cope with the challenges of religious life, particularly during an era of profound change.

Why didn't the women's religious institutes heed the Holy See's pre–Vatican II counsel to give their sisters a better education? While the need for this reform was acknowledged by at least some women religious, the methods for actually achieving it were elusive. In addition to the lack of time young sisters had to attend college for four years, many orders were strapped for money. Without a college of their own, they could not come up with the tuition fees to educate sisters who were drawing no income. It was easy for the Vatican to say that sisters should have the same professional training as their lay counterparts, but to make that happen was another matter indeed.

An Overworked, Underappreciated Work Force

Probably the greatest abuse in need of reform was the way the clergy and laypeople took sisters for granted. The Church in America expected so very much from her sisters but gave little in return. American Catholics simply assumed that the sisters would always be there to educate the children and nurse the sick for wages that barely covered their living expenses—and sometimes didn't cover them at all. Parents appreciated the music and art lessons the sisters gave in their spare time, but few laypeople realized that sisters often worked those long hours to

---

[12] Unless otherwise indicated, all such statistics are from the appropriate year of the *Official Catholic Directory* (New Providence, N.J.: P.J. Kenedy & Sons in association with R.R. Bowker, a Reed Reference Publishing Co.).

supplement their income, which in 1957 averaged $25 to $50 a month.[13] Author George Stewart observed in his comprehensive history of American sisters, *Marvels of Charity*, that in spite of such limited incomes, sisters lived so frugally that they still managed to save money to invest in their institutions, indeed even to construct buildings and, at times, to loan money to pastors who got into dire financial straits.[14]

Still, Catholics expected after-school tutoring—and a myriad of other services—to be provided for free. Little thought was given to the sisters' retirement needs or the needs of the elderly sisters who were being supported by the working sisters. And it was simply assumed that the sisters should do menial tasks that could have been done quite easily by lay parishioners. Many Catholics had little consideration for the sisters' need for recreation, vacation, cultural enrichment, family visits, or even just a little time to themselves. On top of this, meddling pastors often tried to tell sisters how to do their jobs in the parish schools, even though the priests knew far less about education than the sisters.

As Jesuit Father Michael Caruso observed in his 2012 book, *When the Sisters Said Farewell: The Transition of Leadership in Catholic Elementary Schools*: "Most people would have been shocked to learn of the sacrifices being made by the sisters. Again, there was a legitimate spirituality that spoke to making sacrifices, and the sisters embraced these challenges with earnestness and ardor, but sometimes the degree of severity was not healthy."[15]

Vocations Flourish

In spite of these difficulties in religious life, vocations flourished. In 1965, there were about 180,000 sisters, the largest number the American Church had ever seen. Experts point to several reasons for this phenomenon. The most obvious explanation is that in the mid-1960s, the children born in the post–World War II baby boom would have

[13] Neil G. McCloskey, SJ, "How to Find and Pay Teachers," *America*, April 27, 1957, 122.

[14] George Stewart, *Marvels of Charity* (Huntington: Our Sunday Visitor Publishing Division, Our Sunday Visitor, Inc., 1994).

[15] Michael Caruso, SJ, *When the Sisters Said Farewell: The Transition of Leadership in Catholic Elementary Schools* (Lanham, Md.: Rowman & Littlefield Education, 2011), 32.

been in their late teens, the age at which most women entered religious life in that era. But there were other factors, too. The sisters were role models to the millions of children they saw every day in the classroom, and they inspired many of their students to join them in dedicating their lives to God. For many orders, the largest source of new vocations were the high schools operated by their sisters.

Furthermore, prior to 1960, there were few opportunities for women to engage in social service outside of Church structures, and many young women saw the sisterhood as a way to serve mankind. Religious life also gave women an opportunity to serve the Church, a possibility not open to laywomen before Vatican II. Some young women also perceived religious life as a means to obtain an education and professional stature that was not otherwise attained by many laywomen before the 1960s. In fact, Catholic sisters were probably the only women managing large institutions prior to the women's movement of the 1960s. And certainly many young women entered the convent because they had a calling from God to sanctify themselves in a lifestyle that specifically attempted to imitate the life of Jesus, who himself was poor, chaste, and obedient as he spread the good news about God's love.[16] They were "people who are consumed by God, people who are on fire", as sociologist Sister of Charity Patricia Wittberg put it.[17] They were women who wanted to serve the Church and live in community with other like-minded individuals who supported each other in pursing the vocation of every Christian to achieve union with Christ.

In 1965, when the Second Vatican Council ended, more than 104,000 nuns were teaching in Catholic schools in this country. Over 13,000 sisters staffed some 808 hospitals that were owned and operated by religious orders.[18] Sisters also operated most of the 250-plus Catholic orphanages that sheltered nearly 25,000 children. But these numbers were to be short-lived, for the revolution in the convents was already underway, and as we shall see in the following chapters, the revolution had a dramatic impact on vocations and the Catholic institutions the sisters staffed.

[16] See Pope John Paul II, *Vita Consecrata*.

[17] Patricia Wittberg, SC, cited in Ann Carey, "Why 'People on Fire' Fizzled Out", *Our Sunday Visitor*, May 7, 1995, 5.

[18] Christopher J. Kauffman, *Ministry and Meaning: A Religious History of Catholic Health Care in the United States* (New York: The Crossroad Publishing Co., 1995), 273.

The Tumultuous Sixties

The 1960s was a turbulent decade in the United States, and women religious were just as profoundly affected as the rest of American society by the cultural, political, and social turmoil of those years. Author Jules Archer observed in *The Incredible Sixties* that the period from 1963 to 1968 was the stormiest chapter in American history, with the exception of the Revolutionary and Civil Wars.[19] When many Americans were experimenting with radical new lifestyles and questioning authority— hardly the most stable time to undertake a transformation process—the Catholic Church convened the Second Vatican Council and required religious to rewrite their constitutions. As some scholars have pointed out, the impact of the Council on American sisters would no doubt have been quite different if it had taken place in any other decade.

According to Passionist Father John Kobler, the revolutionary movements of the 1960s influenced how religious understood the Council's call to renew their orders; some interpreted their task as being more political than spiritual.

> It should come as no surprise, then, that an unreflective incarnation of the spirit of Vatican II in the secular, social concerns and values of the '60s often resulted in a "religious" product somewhat resembling "Rosemary's Baby": e.g., the urge to change The System, the push for People Power in the Church, more Participatory Democracy in governance, greater opportunities for women and racial minorities, and advocacy for the laity to assume positions of responsibility in the Church. However worthy these intentions may have been, this radically "prophetic" stance has often been hard to distinguish from empowerment as a political movement.[20]

During the 1960s, the feminist movement greatly influenced American sisters. They were especially affected by a brand of feminism that went beyond the reasonable agenda of "equality feminists", who simply sought equal compensation for women in the workplace and respect for women's contribution to society. Many sisters bought into the militant "gender feminism", as described by Christina Hoff Sommers

---

[19] Jules Archer, *The Incredible Sixties: The Stormy Years That Changed America* (San Diego: Harcourt Brace Jovanovich, 1986).

[20] John Kobler, CP, *Passionist.* 27 (1994): 83.

in her book *Who Stole Feminism?* Gender feminists, Sommers explained, seek not merely just wages for women, but a confrontation that sets women against men in all areas of life.[21]

Sisters had legitimate cause to complain about the insulting, paternalistic attitude toward them that they often experienced in the Church. The clergy assumed that sisters were the workforce of Catholic institutions, yet priests and bishops seldom consulted sisters about their opinions, ideas, needs, or desires. Often clergy enjoyed a plush lifestyle at the expense of sisters. For example, some chaplains for religious orders who were provided a comfortable salary and room and board by the sisters they served also collected stipends for Masses for the deceased or ill of the order. Some priests and bishops expected to be treated like royalty by sisters who often worked longer hours and had fewer financial resources than they did. Even though many sisters thought clergy should be treated with admiration and respect, their situation bred resentment and anger, and some sisters saw in feminism a way to redress their grievances.

The Vanishing Sister

The turmoil of the 1960s profoundly affected renewal in religious institutes. The orderly reform of religious life envisioned by the Second Vatican Council succeeded in some convents, but it failed miserably in those where Council documents were misunderstood or misinterpreted and changes were not intelligently planned or were introduced at a pace too rapid to allow for adequate evaluation. The result was that many sisters left religious life. Some left because their reformed communities bore no resemblance to the ones they had entered. Others left because they felt reform wasn't happening fast enough and going far enough. And during this exodus, fewer young women chose to commit themselves to religious life. In 1965 there were 165,000 sisters in the United States. During the next five years, that number declined by 19,000. By 2000, there were 81,000, fewer than half the original number. In 2012, there were only about 55,000 sisters, with the median age creeping into the seventies.

[21] Christina Hoff Sommers, *Who Stole Feminism? How Women Have Betrayed Women* (New York: Simon & Schuster, 1994).

This dwindling number of women religious began depriving Catholic schools of the sisters they depended on for their workforce. Also depleting the number of teaching sisters was the new policy of "open placement", which allowed women in many orders to select their own jobs and living arrangements. Catholic schools that had enjoyed over 104,000 teaching sisters in 1965 lost almost half of those in just ten years; by 1975, there were approximately 56,000 sisters teaching in Catholic schools. By 1985, the number of teaching sisters had declined to just over 30,000; by 2012 only about 4,000 sisters were teaching in Catholic schools.

The loss of these teaching sisters, along with other demographic and economic factors, caused the demise of many Catholic schools. In 1965 there were 10,500 Catholic elementary schools serving about 4.5 million children. By 2012 the number of these schools had been cut by almost half, with 5,378 schools serving 1.3 million children. Catholic high schools didn't fare any better. There were more than 1,500 in 1965, enrolling around 698,000 students. By 2012, there were 327,345 students in 721 parochial high schools. Private Catholic high schools declined from about 900 with about 390,000 students in 1965 to 595 schools with approximately 296,268 students in 2012.

Catholic colleges also decreased in number during this period. In 1965, there were 295 Catholic colleges and universities. In 2012, there were 233. Some of these schools closed, while some, such as Webster College in Saint Louis—founded and operated by the Sisters of Loretto— remained open but ceased to be identified as Catholic institutions.

Catholic hospitals were also dramatically affected by the loss of sisters in their workforce, and many have closed or have lost their Catholic identity. Although the reasons for closing or selling hospitals are complex and include finances, mergers, government regulations, insurance implications, and a number of other issues, the declining number of nursing sisters surely contributed to the trend. From 1965 to 2012, more than 200 Catholic hospitals were closed or gave up their Catholic identity, in some cases because they were sold to or merged with non-Catholic corporations. In 1965, there were 808 Catholic general hospitals. The 2012 figure was 605.

With fewer and fewer sisters working in Catholic hospitals or sitting on hospital boards, there was growing pressure for hospitals to forfeit their Catholic identity. Dr. Alan Sager, an associate professor at the Boston University School of Public Health, reported in 1994 that some nursing orders were requested by their lay boards and physicians to diminish the Catholic mission of their hospitals.[22] By the early twenty-first century, some of the few remaining women religious were freely willing to relinquish the Catholic identity of their hospitals because they did not want to abide by the *Ethical and Religious Directives for Catholic Health Care Services* written by the US bishops.

One of the casualties of the diminished identity of Catholic hospitals is the Catholic tradition of caring for the poor, which has become an economic disadvantage in the competition for contracts with secular health maintenance organizations and health networks. The mission of Catholic hospitals has also been compromised by government regulations that infringe on the conscience rights of Catholics.

Ironically, in the years between 1965 and 2012, when Catholic institutions were closing their doors at an alarming rate, the Catholic population needing those institutions grew by over twenty million people. The Catholic schools and hospitals that do remain are staffed predominantly by laypeople, and many of those laypeople do an outstanding job of teaching the Catholic faith and preserving the Catholic identity of their institutions. But as Pope John Paul II pointed out in his 1996 apostolic exhortation *Vita Consecrata* (On Consecrated Life), the religious vocation is at the heart of the Church as a manifestation of every Christian's calling to be united with Jesus, and its diminishment harms the identity of the Church. "Jesus himself, by calling some men and women to abandon everything in order to follow him, established this type of life which, under the guidance of the Spirit, would gradually develop down the centuries into the various forms of the consecrated life. The idea of a church made up only of sacred ministers and lay people does not therefore conform to the intentions of her divine founder, as revealed to us by the Gospels and the other writings of the New Testament" (29).

The decline of American sisters is therefore an important issue for the whole Church. The following chapters examine many of the circumstances that have contributed to the unraveling of women's religious communities in the United States and perhaps offer some clues about the way forward.

---

[22] Alan Sager quoted in Ann Carey, "Recalling All Religious", *Our Sunday Visitor*, November 20, 1994, 16.

2

The Vatican Calls for Renewal

I think it would be safe to say that all communities have suffered greatly
during this post-Conciliar period. Sufficient time was not taken to read
and absorb the documents.[1]

—Sister M. Claudia Honsberger, IHM

The documents issued by the Second Vatican Council and subsequent
related documents called upon religious orders to renew themselves
by modernizing their habits, eliminating meaningless rules and regulations, enriching their spiritual and liturgical practices, and applying
their apostolates to contemporary needs. But none of the documents
called for a complete transformation of religious life; rather they reaffirmed the rich heritage of the religious orders, praised the teaching
and health care apostolates, stressed community life, designated religious habits as important signs of consecration to God, and emphasized the importance of communal prayer.

Why, then, did many well-intentioned sisters sincerely believe that
they were following the teaching of the Council by living alone in
apartments, wearing secular clothing, interacting only rarely with members of their community, and engaging in occupations totally unrelated
to the Catholic Church? Why did those sisters who began stressing
missions to serve "marginalized people" also begin ignoring Church
authority? This chapter examines how the content of the Council

[1] M. Claudia Honsberger, IHM, "Women Religious and Church Authority", *Homiletic
and Pastoral Review* (December 1984): 21.

documents was misinterpreted, transposed, and even disregarded by religious and their advisers. Thus, the renewal of religious institutes foreseen by the Council fathers did not resemble what really happened in many American convents.

The Decree on the Renewal of Religious Life

Perfectae Caritatis, the Council decree on religious life, was issued toward the close of Vatican II, on October 28, 1965. Canonist Sister Elizabeth McDonough, OP, observed that Perfectae Caritatis expands on chapter 6 of another Vatican II document, Lumen Gentium, the dogmatic constitution on the Church. She explained that Lumen Gentium specifies consecrated life as "a distinct, different, and identifiable manifestation of the holiness to which all Christians are called and, as such, is integral to the life and holiness of the church itself".[2]

A relatively short document, Perfectae Caritatis dealt with general principles for renewal and directed religious institutes to return to their original inspiration and to adapt those principles to the changed conditions of contemporary times. In doing this, the religious institutes were to retain their heritage while adapting the life, prayer, work, and government of their institutes to the needs of their members. The institutes also were urged to be more aware of cultural circumstances and to respond to contemporary apostolic needs. To achieve this end, Perfectae Caritatis directed religious institutes to employ community-wide consultation to revise their rules and constitutions. Perfectae Caritatis was so important that entire portions were incorporated into the Code of Canon Law of 1983.

Regarding the vows, Perfectae Caritatis reaffirmed chastity as a special symbol and effective means for fostering service (12). The document urged new forms of poverty, material as well as spiritual (13). Obedience was emphasized as both the member's cooperation and "the superior's obligation to foster mature and responsible expressions of obedience in consecrated life" (14). Perfectae Caritatis also affirmed the "importance of common life as expressed in prayer, in the sharing of the same spirit, in living together, and in bearing one another's

---

[2] Elizabeth McDonough, OP, "The Conciliar Decree Perfectae Caritatis", Review for Religious (January/February 1994): 142.

burdens" (15). The habit was described as a symbol of consecration that should be "simple, modest, poor, and becoming as well as in keeping with the requirements of health and adapted to various times and places and apostolic needs" (17).

In order to implement *Perfectae Caritatis* and three other Council decrees, Pope Paul VI issued *Ecclesiae Sanctae* in August 1966. *Ecclesiae Sanctae* is a *motu proprio*—a document written by the pope on his own initiative that applies as legislation to the entire Church. Both *Perfectae Caritatis* and *Ecclesiae Sanctae* were widely misunderstood, however, and American religious for the most part misinterpreted or simply ignored them.

Ecclesiae Sanctae directed that all religious institutes hold a special general chapter (meeting) on renewal by October 11, 1969, in order to approve changes in their constitutions that would allow for experiments in religious life that would respond to the mandates of Vatican II. A general chapter determines the important business of a religious institute and is convened every three to ten years. Rather than mandating certain changes in religious institutes, the Vatican wanted to preserve the unique charisms of the various religious institutes by having each institute make changes appropriate for its own specific spirituality and way of life. The experiments were supposed to safeguard the purpose, nature, and character of the institute and were to be temporary. Then the experiments were to be evaluated at the next regular chapter meeting of the institute. The beneficial experiments were to be incorporated into the institutes' constitutions, and the experiments that were not helpful were to be discontinued. If further experimentation was deemed necessary at that first regular chapter meeting that followed the special renewal chapter, that experimentation could continue, but it was to be evaluated at the next chapter meeting and then either incorporated into the constitution or discontinued.

Experimentation Gets Out of Hand

Since religious institutes had chapter meetings at various intervals, the period of experimentation lasted from a few years to as many as twenty years, until the promulgation of the revised Code of Canon Law in 1983. Thus, since the period of experimentation was somewhat fluid, experiments tended to go on much longer than the Council fathers or the pope had intended. Some religious institutes purposely expanded the years between general chapters so that experiments could be stretched out. Others purposely incorporated items into their constitutions that they knew would never be approved by the Vatican so they could continue experimenting endlessly.

Certainly the Council and the Holy Father intended that the experiments would address some needed reforms, but the reforms were to be made to the incidentals of religious life, not to the essentials. Examples of appropriate experimentation were given by Holy Cross Father Edward Heston, a canon lawyer and soon-to-be secretary of the Vatican Congregation for Religious, in a 1967 presentation at the summer Institute for Local Superiors at the University of Notre Dame: modifying and modernizing the habit; eliminating the separation between novices and professed sisters; extending the period of temporary vows beyond the maximum of six years; modifying the length of the canonical year of the novitiate; doing away with the regular appointment of ordinary and extraordinary confessors; changing the term of office for a superior; changing the method for designating local, provincial, and general superiors; and altering other details of the administrative structure of the congregation.[3]

Father Heston further explained that during the experimentation period, the Holy See would not approve constitutions. The whole idea was for the religious institutes to try out the new ways of doing things and then determine after ten years or so what worked and what didn't. After this period of trying out the new, when an institute knew what worked well, its constitution could then be sent to the Vatican for approval.

However, almost prophetically, Father Heston also warned of the dangers of experimentation:

> It should be borne in mind in every community that this period of experimentation, when no texts of constitutions will be definitively approved by the Holy See, does not mean that a religious institute remains completely without constitutions or without concrete norms for its life and activities. Every special general chapter should make it

[3] *Proceedings for the Institute for Local Superiors 1967* (Notre Dame: University of Notre Dame Press, 1968), 23–24.

clear to all members that the constitutions presently in force remain binding until the next definitive approval of the Holy See, except in those parts which may have been changed by this same special general chapter. Thus there will be no grounds for claiming that everything is lawful because the constitutions are to be regarded as being in a state of abeyance.[4]

Unfortunately, some religious institutes acted as if they indeed had no constitutions during the period of experimentation. Furthermore, some institutes ignored or did not realize that *Ecclesiae Sanctae* required that any experimentation that was contrary to the Code of Canon Law had to be specifically approved by the Vatican. The Code of Canon Law then in effect had been approved in 1917, and there were several canons on religious life that eventually would be dropped or updated in the 1983 revised code. For example, the 1917 code required a period of postulancy for nonclerical members of religious institutes, whereas the 1983 code does not even mention postulancy. The 1917 code had about 200 canons pertaining to religious, and the 1983 code has 173 canons covering consecrated life, including new forms such as secular institutes.

During the experimentation period, religious knew that the Code of Canon Law was being updated, and some of them saw this as an opportunity simply to abrogate the old code without bothering to get the permission of the Vatican. The National Assembly of Women Religious (NAWR)—a small, independent organization of sisters from a variety of orders—declared, "Continued insistence on observance of the Code of Canon Law is anachronistic, the Sisters insist, since the Code itself is being totally revised."[5]

Immaculate Heart of Mary Sister Sandra Schneiders observed: "Much of what developed in the life experience of religious was either actually contrary to the [canon] law or so original as to have no real relationship, positive or negative, to it.... Superiors found themselves challenged to lead their congregations into an uncharted future for which present law was inadequate; individual religious experienced the call to venture beyond the limits of what was permitted by common

---

[4] Ibid., 31–33.
[5] NAWR press release, undated, titled "Re: American Religious—Sacred Congregation", Records of the NAWR/NARW (hereafter cited as CARW), 10/14, UNDA.

[canon] or particular [congregational] law and often into conflict with superiors."[6]

Some of the old canons were indeed outdated, but *Ecclesiae Sanctae* did not give religious institutes the carte blanche many of them assumed in implementing experiments and rewriting their constitutions. Rather, it stated that any deviation from the 1917 Code of Canon Law was to receive special permission from the Vatican, but apparently this permission was not always sought. Understandably, American religious grew impatient waiting for responses from the slow-moving Vatican bureaucracy, and, as with any bureaucracy, paperwork very likely did get lost occasionally. But in any event, religious institutes did not have authority to put into effect any decrees that deviated from canon law without that specific Vatican permission, even if it was slow in coming.

Complicating the picture was the fact that a good deal of erroneous information circulated about the canons governing religious life. Many sisters confused the rules or customs of their own congregations, such as the chapter of faults, with canon law, when in fact such practices were not even mentioned in canon law. Part of this confusion resulted because English translations of canon law were not widely available to sisters, and women were not admitted to study in canon-law departments until after the Second Vatican Council.

Many religious institutes went far beyond the boundaries for experimentation set by *Ecclesiae Sanctae*. These communities radically transformed the purpose, nature, and character of their institutes, all under the guise of obedient renewal. Some communities gave their members total freedom in deciding when and how they would pray, where they would live, what work they would do, what hours they would keep, and what they would wear—freedom that led to excesses, such as miniskirted nuns smoking, drinking, and dating. And some sisters simply took it upon themselves to change religious life. Sister Elizabeth Kolmer of the Adorers of the Blood of Christ wrote that "frequently enough individual sisters did not wait for those in authority to make the first move or, faced with reluctance on the part of the superior, made their own decision."[7] Many sisters left religious life because of this rapid

---

[6] Sandra M. Schneiders, IHM, "Towards a Theology of Religious Obedience", in *Starting Points*, ed. Lora Quinonez, CDP, (Washington, D.C.: LCWR, 1980), 73.

[7] Kolmer, *Religious Women*, 53

transformation in their lifestyle, since their communities no longer resembled in any way the communities they had entered.

Archbishop Augustine Mayer, OSB, secretary of the Congregation for Religious, observed in 1973:

> Now it is bewildering to see some constitutions. . . .
>
> We cannot have all the forms of committed life in our institutes. A great source of confusion in many institutes is that now they want to live all the forms of consecrated life at the same time. . . . That is not possible. . . . If, in the end, some communities think they want the life of a secular institute, then they should say it. . . . Then Mother Church will find a category for them but they shouldn't try under the name of religious life to put in everything. That doesn't go; that only makes for confusion.[8]

In her book *Out of the Cloister*, Helen Rose Fuchs Ebaugh, a former Sister of Divine Providence and a sociologist, presented case studies of three orders. One of those orders, which she described as "change-oriented", had already made the following changes by 1970:

- Regarding government: "While president administers, all sisters cooperate in discovering and serving the needs of man. . . . Spirit speaks in all members, not just superiors."
- In job assignments: "Open placement puts responsibility for job on the individual. The order is to assist the person; the person herself is to discern where the Spirit is directing her."
- On prayer: "Frequency, place, and type of communal prayer [is] to be determined by the local group."
- On dress: "Each individual may wear what she wishes in regard to dress, veil and any external symbol of her religious consecration."[9]

As early as September 1967, at the annual assembly of the CMSW, Holy Cross Father Bernard Ransing, a staff member of the Congregation for Religious and adviser to the CMSW, alluded to defective experimentation that was already taking place just one year after *Ecclesiae Sanctae*:

---

[8] Archbishop Augustine Mayer at October 18, 1973, meeting of provincial superiors, CCPC 5/38, UNDA.

[9] Helen Rose Fuchs Ebaugh, *Out of the Cloister* (Austin: University of Texas Press, 1977), 37.

But it is unfortunately true, also, that a considerable amount of unauthorized experimentation has been initiated, due to misunderstandings or wrong interpretations of the "mind of the Holy See". Because these experiments have been premature, they have lacked that wise preparation desired by the Holy See and the prudent deliberation of the General Chapter itself. Worst of all they have caused confusion among the Communities, and have led to unrest and disquiet among certain individual religious who are eager for change.[10]

Christian Brother Bernard M. Ryan observed in 1969 that some experiments in religious communities were really not experiments, for they had no preparation, premise, method, or evaluation.[11] And one group of sisters wrote the Congregation for Religious in 1972 that "five years of well-meant but illogical experimentation in unlimited adaptation have all but destroyed religious life in our country."[12]

Redefining Poverty, Chastity, and Obedience

The meaning of the vows underwent a radical redefinition in many communities. In a matter of just a few months, some sisters found themselves rocketed from a life of burdensome and meaningless restrictions and regulations to a lifestyle that was hardly recognizable as religious. Obedience was often redefined as "response to the Spirit". Poverty was considered to consist of open dialogue and availability to people. Chastity was probably the least changed of the vows, but many religious felt it was perfectly acceptable to date. Some Jesuits even invented a lifestyle situated between the married state and the priestly or religious state, which they called the "third way".[13]

One Franciscan sister recalled that her congregation wanted the young sisters to learn to be more comfortable in the company of men, so

[10] Bernard Ransing, CSC, letter to CMSW assembly in *Proceedings of the Annual Assembly, 1967* (Washington, D.C.: Conference of Major Religious Superiors of Women's Institutes of the United States of America, 1968), 150.

[11] Bernard M. Ryan, FSC, A Critique of *Experience in Community: Should Religious Life Survive?*, Papers of Sister Rose Eileen Masterman, CSC (hereafter cited as CMAS), 4/1, UNDA.

[12] Letter from Administrative Board of the Consortium Perfectae Caritatis to the Congregation for Religious regarding topics for the October 23, 1972, plenary assembly in Rome, CMAS 2/11, UNDA.

[13] Joseph M. Becker, SJ, *The Re-Formed Jesuits* (San Francisco: Ignatius Press, 1992), 72.

social occasions with priests and brothers were arranged for them. At first, the sister said, she didn't notice that couples were pairing up, but the message became clear when some sisters left the order to marry the brothers or priests they had met at those community-sponsored events. Holy Cross Sister Gerald Hartney told the author that she left early from a three-day regional meeting of priests and nuns in Chicago when the evening entertainment was a "mixer" at which the priests and nuns were invited to dance together.

Some examples from chapter decrees demonstrate how the Vatican directives were interpreted—or misinterpreted—by some of the renewal chapters. In June 1969 the Franciscan Sisters of Perpetual Adoration of La Crosse, Wisconsin, approved their interim statement of renewal, "Unity in Diversity". Regarding their apostolate of education, the statement reaffirmed their "commitment to Catholic education". On the other hand, the statement broadened "the term 'education' to include the involvement of Sisters in parish, ecumenical and civic organizations, and in public schools and universities." The document also permitted sisters to "be open to serve in whatever apostolate seems most beneficial to the Church and within the limits of available personnel", which was a departure from the original purpose of the institute.

Regarding prayer life, the statement urged sisters to "esteem" the Mass and "cherish" the privilege of participating in it daily. As for the habit, "sisters shall be free to wear a black habit and veil or to continue in further experimentation in appropriate contemporary dress." The only specific requirement for dress was that the sister should retain her medal of the Blessed Sacrament and her ring.[14]

In the 1967 chapter of the Medical Missionary Sisters, "the habit of the society was retained, but liberty was given to each Sister to determine whether or not it would be more beneficial for her service to the Church to wear lay clothes."[15] Indeed, canon law did allow for lay clothing in exceptional circumstances, but those circumstances were to be unusual and determined by the superior, not by the individual religious themselves. Of course, the role of superior also was diluted by many congregations. For example, the Franciscan Sisters of the

---

[14] "Unity in Diversity", Interim Statement of Renewal of Franciscan Sisters of Perpetual Adoration, Saint Rose Convent, LaCrosse, Wis., CLCW 172, UNDA.

[15] Report on the Medical Missionary Sisters' Sixth General and Special Chapter, November 15, 1967, CLCW 158/19, UNDA.

Poor in Brooklyn, New York, changed the title of superior general to community service coordinator, whose primary responsibility was leadership.[16] Many other communities followed suit.

The July 9, 1969, issue of the *National Catholic Reporter* noted that the Sisters of Charity of the Blessed Virgin Mary "have gone all the way from a typically monarchial and authoritarian form of government to complete democracy" in which "there are no 'superiors' named from on high. Each local group of sisters is asked to designate a community representative to handle official correspondence and serve as contact person for the house. Apart from this, each house is free to set up whatever structures the sisters want." And "instead of being assigned to a teaching or other kind of job by a superior's fiat, each sister can now apply for whatever work position she thinks she is qualified for, and she can work out her own living arrangements as long as they are financially feasible." The orders' Kinetics of Renewal also provided that "each sister is now free to make her own decisions about the details of her life—whether she goes to mass today, the clothes she wears, the amount of time she spends with friends outside the community."

The impact of this kind of radical change has been enormous, and many sisters have been very disturbed about what has transpired in their orders. A survey of a Detroit province of sisters taken around 1972 indicated the concerns of some of these sisters regarding their "renewed" order. Respondents to the survey cited many problems. Self-determination of where a sister would live fostered selfishness, with sisters selecting only their peers as housemates. Convents built by parishioners were being abandoned by sisters who preferred living in apartments with a select group. Some sisters indulged themselves in leisure, travel, and recreation, while talking of the poor only in broad terms. One sister expressed her concern about a laissez-faire lifestyle, noting: "Failure to observe the vows, lack of external expression of prayer and growing secularization appear to be condoned by the governing board as an individual's right of self-expression." Because sisters self-selected their work, some works of the order were overstaffed, while others were understaffed. There was no single authority figure,

---

[16] Proceedings of 1971 General Chapter of the Franciscan Sisters of the Poor, Brooklyn, New York, CLCW 172, UNDA.

and the governing board was top-heavy, with too many coordinators who had too much power. "We need guidelines, just like Boy Scouts or a union", a sister wrote.[17]

How Good Was the Expert Advice?

Adding to the confusion of unlimited experimentation was the fact that religious institutes, in trying to respond enthusiastically to the reforms of Vatican II, sought advice from many sources. It was not uncommon for "experts" to be consulted about renewal chapters and new constitutions. Many of these people no doubt gave their best advice, but even experts who were priests or religious were not always familiar with the unique charism or spirituality of an institute and sometimes not very familiar with the relevant Church documents.

In her book *Climb along the Cutting Edge*, Benedictine Sister Joan Chittister (president of the LCWR in 1976), described her order's 1968 chapter. She wrote that normally chapters had one consultant present during a general chapter—a Benedictine priest who was a canon lawyer. However, for the 1968 renewal chapter, fourteen consultants were invited to be present—a mixture of lay, religious, and clergy. In 1969, there were sixteen consultants. These consultants included canonists, theologians, a Scripture scholar, a philosopher, an anthropologist, a sociologist, a psychologist, an attorney, and a parliamentarian.[18]

Many religious institutes thought they could solve structural problems by applying successful business models. Hence, management consulting firms such as Booz, Allen, and Hamilton were frequently called in to help with constitutional changes and reorganizations. These secular firms no doubt were conscientious in advising sisters on efficient management techniques, but they did not always have a firm grasp of canon law or a clear understanding of the meaning of religious life or of the charism of a particular institute. Nor did management advice based on industry always work well in religious institutes, which are not oriented toward producing and selling goods in the marketplace.

[17] Results of Detroit Province Government Survey, undated, CMAS 2/8, UNDA.

[18] Joan Chittister, OSB, et al., *Climb along the Cutting Edge* (New York: Paulist Press, 1977).

Canon law itself was variously interpreted for the sisters, who had to rely on canon lawyers who were priests. Another source of misinformation was faulty or hasty unofficial translations of Vatican II documents. Even before the documents were officially translated and promulgated, private translations often were made and given to religious, who were understandably eager to see what the Council had to say about the consecrated life.

Even with official translations, religious often paid more attention to commentary on the Council documents than they did to the documents themselves. And many so-called Council experts warned against literal interpretation of the documents, as if understanding these contemporary works requires the same kind of background information that is helpful in interpreting Sacred Scripture. The idea that the documents should be interpreted by experts rather than taken literally by the sisters themselves encouraged subjective analyses on the part of experts with a change-oriented agenda. When sisters got hold of a faulty translation or commentary—or heard a talk by a so-called expert who substituted opinion or speculation for fact—misinformation was often the unfortunate result.

The Congregation for Religious was so concerned about this problem that in January 1967 it asked Cardinal Egidio Vagnozzi, apostolic delegate to the United States, to discuss the matter with Sister Mary Luke Tobin, president of the CMSW. The CMSW was the official organization recognized by the Vatican as representing women religious in the United States, and part of its role was to act as a communications link between them and the Vatican. Cardinal Vagnozzi wrote Sister Mary Luke that unqualified people should not be invited to lecture the sisters about Vatican II or the renewal of religious life. He stressed that communities of sisters should not be addressed by anyone not previously approved by the local bishop.[19]

At the September 1967 assembly of the CMSW, Father Ransing, again addressed this issue:

> There are so many forces working against the proper understanding and execution of the texts of the Decrees and the will of the Church.
> Frequently, "the mind of the Church" is quoted as authority for certain changes that are suggested. Superiors are told that if they do

[19] Cardinal Vagnozzi letter to Sister Mary Luke, January 12, 1967, CLCW 1/9, UNDA.

not adopt this or that innovation they are not acting according to this mind. But where is the mind of the Church to be found, if not in these documents that we have quoted?

We have had reason to remark before, a number of times, on the self-constituted authorities who are giving their own personal interpretation of the religious life and how it is to be lived, and on how much harm they are doing in speaking or writing about something of which they have only superficial knowledge or no knowledge at all. . . . Quantities of books and articles are still being published, that propose personal views, and that, unfortunately, seem to be read and accepted by a certain class of religious much more readily than the official documents of the Church. And most unfortunate it is that some preachers, retreat masters, and spiritual directors plant erroneous ideas in the minds of religious, or encourage them in false concepts of their own. The main difficulty is always that they do not know or refer to the sources. They overlook and neglect the documents of the Church in elaborating their theories. And, of course, there is always that articulate minority within the religious family itself, which agitates for its own ideas and which not infrequently either undertakes on its own to start a trend, or forces the hand of the superiors to permit practices that have not been properly authorized.[20]

But how many sisters actually were able to obtain and read *Perfectae Caritatis* and other documents on religious life in those pre-Internet days? Apparently, many sisters did not have access to the recent Church documents or to correct translations of them. On July 8, 1966, Monsignor Joseph T. V. Snee, assistant vicar for religious of the Archdiocese of New York, wrote Sister Mary Luke Tobin, asking to be placed on the conference mailing list and observing, "I think that some of our [religious] communities are not being properly briefed on the various directives coming from the Holy See."[21]

The Vatican had assumed that superiors would conscientiously pass along pertinent information to their sisters, as is their duty according to Canon Law: "The moderators of every institute are to promote knowledge of the documents of the Holy See which affect members entrusted to them and be concerned about their observance of them"

[20] Bernard Ransing, CSC, in *Proceedings of Annual Assembly, 1967*, 148–49.
[21] Msgr. Joseph T. V. Snee letter to Sister Mary Luke, July 8, 1966, CLCW 158/20, UNDA.

(Can. 592 §2). Certainly, many leaders of women's religious institutes adhered faithfully to this canon, but there is plenty of evidence that a good number of sisters in local convents never came into contact with the Vatican documents and thus relied on someone else's interpretation of Church teaching, which was not always accurate.

While lack of access to good information is partly to blame for the renewal going astray, often religious communities were ignoring or defying Vatican pronouncements due to resentment that women were not in decision-making positions in the Church. Indeed, it seems that a good number of sisters took the advice that Jesuit Father John Haughey gave at the 1970 assembly of the CMSW:

> We should make two things perfectly clear. That whatever ecclesiastical authority does not have the common courtesy to communicate directly to you, those directives and decisions that have been made about your lives; that such directives and decisions will be treated by you as if they do not exist; and secondly, if there is not clear proof that subsequent directives and decisions have had the benefit of consultation with representatives of those most immediately affected by these, that you have absolutely no intention of complying with them.[22]

Much of the misinformation about the Church's renewal of religious orders was promulgated by the very people who were responsible for directing that renewal—the leaders of some religious institutes who perhaps were misinformed themselves or who simply put their own interpretation on documents and teachings emanating from the Vatican. And certainly some responsibility for misdirecting the renewal belongs to pseudo-experts who created their own concept of what Vatican II intended for the renewal of religious life and then sold that concept to religious institutes. Thus, many women's religious institutes in the United States proceeded along a precipitous path that was directed more by the politics of women's liberation than by the official documents of the Second Vatican Council.

The next chapter reports on efforts by the Church to get the renewal of religious communities back on track.

---

[22] John C. Haughey, SJ, "Where Has Our Search Led Us?", delivered at CMSW National Assembly, September 9–13, 1970, CCPC 8/32, UNDA.

3

Alarm in the Vatican

Rome and America simply do not share the same value systems: they do not speak the same renewal language. American religious men and women no longer look to Rome for regulations and directives. They operate from a milieu that encourages the responsible freedom of the individual within the framework of her personal commitment to Christ and his church.[1]

— National Assembly of Women Religious

As the process of renewal proceeded in religious communities, Church officials became alarmed about experimentation that exceeded canon law, a secularized lifestyle, rejection of authority, unprecedented numbers departing consecrated life, declining numbers of new vocations, and the abandonment of community life and prayer as well as the traditional apostolates of health care and education. During the 1970s and the 1980s, the Holy See consequently undertook several initiatives to refocus the renewal of religious life on the proposals laid out by the Second Vatican Council. Some of these initiatives were directed to religious all over the world, and some were focused on religious in the United States. But, as with the mixed reception of the Vatican II documents, these initiatives by the Holy See often were met with resistance by some religious who were determined to pursue their own version of renewal. And this inclination to reject the Vatican's guidance

[1] NAWR press release, "Re: American Religious—Sacred Congregation", undated, CARW 10/14, UNDA.

and authority was supported by some bishops, priests, and laity who wanted more independence for the American Catholic Church.

Pope Paul's Evaluation

The motu proprio about the renewal of religious institutes had been out for about five years when, on June 29, 1971, Pope Paul VI issued the apostolic exhortation *Evangelica Testificatio*, in which he set forth his observations about renewal efforts.

Paul VI praised religious for their dedication and generosity. But he also mentioned "certain arbitrary transformations", an "exaggerated distrust of the past", "too hardy" experimentation, and "a mentality excessively preoccupied with hastily conforming to the profound changes which disturb our times" (2). Paul VI reminded religious of the necessity and dignity of work, the centrality of the liturgy, the primacy of an interior life, and the importance of the religious habit, communal sharing, obedience, faithfulness to prayer, and silence. The pope's rather gentle criticism of renewal in religious institutes was not what some religious desiring a more radical renewal wanted to hear, and some even claimed that Paul VI was trying to undo the renewal called for by the Second Vatican Council.

In 1972 the Theology Committee of the LCWR launched a project to elicit responses to the exhortation, which in reality was an attempt to refute the papal document. Directing the project was Sister Sandra Schneiders, who later would write in her book *New Wineskins* that *Evangelica Testificatio* was, "in general, a theological step backward toward preconciliar understandings of religious life".[2]

The LCWR's *Evangelica Testificatio* project soon thereafter published the book *Widening the Dialogue*, a collection of essays on the papal document. The book questioned the authorship of the apostolic exhortation (even though Pope Paul VI had signed it) and impugned the validity of the Latin translation. One essay by Franciscan Sister Francis Borgia Rothluebber (LCWR vice president in 1972, president in 1973) reveals the origin of the title of the sisters' book. In her essay, she wrote that *Evangelica Testificatio* was ambivalent and rooted in the past

[2] Sandra M. Schneiders, IHM, *New Wineskins: Re-imagining Religious Life Today* (New York: Paulist Press, 1986), 23.

rather than the future, and she invited "a searching dialogue" on the exhortation.[3] The essays from this book were then used by the superiors' conference in workshops for sisters. Thus the LCWR interpretation of, and challenge to, *Evangelica Testificatio* was spread to sisters all over the country.

A Reminder from the Congregation for Religious

Less than a year after *Evangelica Testificatio* had been issued, the Congregation for Religious issued *Experimenta Circa* on February 5, 1972. This decree reiterated that purely democratic forms of government were unacceptable in religious institutes, for a superior must exercise personal authority. Then, on July 10, 1972, the Congregation for Religious sent a letter to all mother superiors stating that the Congregation had asked (in 1967) to see the acts of special general chapters in order to be aware of experiments and to be certain that chapters stayed within the limits of *Ecclesiae Sanctae*. The letter explained that the decrees from chapters that had been seen thus far had some common problems and that, to address these, the Congregation was making observations and suggestions.

The letter reminded sisters that the purpose, nature, and character of their institutes must be preserved, and that "every derogation from common [canon] law must have a dispensation explicitly granted." The letter also admitted that, in some cases, the Congregation may have overlooked some change that was contrary to canon law, but "this would have been due to an oversight and may not be interpreted as an explicit concession."

Among the observations made by the Congregation for Religious about problematic chapter decrees are these:

1. Chapter decisions that dispense with any kind of dependence or accountability are not acceptable.
2. The obligation and right of the superior to exercise personal authority must be respected.
3. The formula for religious profession should be based on *Ordo Professionis* and approved by the Congregation for Religious. This formula is to be the same for each sister in the institute.

---

[3] Francis Borgia Rothluebber, OSF, in *Widening the Dialogue* (Ottawa: Canadian Religious Conference and Washington: LCWR, 1974), 245–46.

4. Sisters in temporary vows may not hold positions of authority.

5. Small communities are acceptable if the lifestyle is that of a religious community, with a person in authority. Small communities should not be composed of only peer groups or according to personal choice.

6. Chapters should not hesitate to prescribe a minimum of time for daily prayer.

7. "The religious, not as a private individual but as a member of her Institute, engages in apostolic work which is according to the end of her Institute."

8. Chapter decisions on habit should follow *Perfectae Caritatis*, which states that the religious habit is an outward mark of consecration to God and should be simple, modest, and poor.

9. Some chapters leave to the individual all decisions about recreation, vacations, etc. In these matters, superiors cannot totally abdicate their authority.

10. The spirit of the foundress should permeate the constitution.

11. Constitutions should include juridical matters, such as eligibility for active and passive voice, practice of poverty, manner of admittance to profession, etc.[4]

Later in 1972, French Cardinal Jean Danielou, in an interview on Vatican radio, observed that religious life in the Western world was in crisis. He blamed the crisis on false interpretations of Vatican II found in conferences, journals and other theological publications. Cardinal Danielou cited "a false concept of liberty which brings in its wake contempt for constitutions and rules, and exalts the whim of the moment and improvisation". He called for an end to experiments and decisions that were contrary to the directives of the Council, and he suggested that in institutes where this was not possible, religious who wanted to be faithful to their constitutions should be allowed to set up their own distinct communities.[5]

As the 1970s passed, the direction of renewal in many religious institutes continued to trouble the Vatican, and some American sisters made

[4] Archbishop Augustine Mayer letter to "Dear Reverend Mother", July 10, 1972, provided to the author by Father Bernard Ransing, CSC.

[5] "Interview with Cardinal Danielou" by Vatican Radio, October 23, 1972, CLCW 2/25, UNDA.

it very clear that they had no intention of submitting their reforms to the Holy See.

The Essentials of Religious Life

In 1983 many religious were still either ignoring or failing to grasp the directives of *Perfectae Caritatis* (1965) and *Ecclesiae Sanctae* (1966). Additionally, some communities were continuing to experiment widely with their lifestyle and governance some seventeen years after *Ecclesiae Sanctae* authorized temporary, limited experimentation. Meanwhile, the numbers of American priests, brothers and nuns were plummeting.

On May 31, 1983, the Congregation for Religious issued a summary of canonical norms for religious life called *Essential Elements in the Church's Teaching on Religious Life as Applied to Institutes Dedicated to Works of the Apostolate*. This document had been requested by Pope John Paul II prior to announcing a study of American religious life to be headed by Archbishop John Quinn of San Francisco. The pope wrote the US bishops that he requested this study because of the unprecedented number of American men and women leaving the priesthood or religious life and the rapidly diminishing number of vocations to replace them. *Essential Elements*, he wrote, would help the US bishops perform the study needed to understand these trends and remedy them.

Essential Elements simply restated and clarified Church teaching and canon law regarding religious life. The document repeated Pope John Paul II's 1979 call for religious "to evaluate objectively and humbly the years of experimentation so as to recognize their positive elements and their deviations" (2). *Essential Elements* also signaled an end to the period of experimentation mandated by *Ecclesiae Sanctae*, for the new Code of Canon Law, which was promulgated by the pope on January 25, 1983, would become effective on November 27, 1983.

Essential Elements stressed the importance of religious vows, which included the following: putting all gifts and salaries in common as belonging to the community; obedience to superiors and the Holy Father; community living, which involves sharing prayer, work, meals, leisure, and a common spirit; directing the works of all members to a common apostolate; wearing "a religious garb that distinguishes them as consecrated persons"; and placing personal authority in a superior, not a group (16, 19, 25, 34).

While the more traditional religious praised *Essential Elements*, some very vocal change-oriented sisters, who were beginning to relish a certain independence from the Vatican, expressed disapproval of the Holy Father's interference. Some religious were angry at the pope for his study of religious life in the United States, regarding his action as an insulting inquisition that singled out American sisters. Some religious argued that the Vatican was trying to reverse the mandates of the Second Vatican Council, even though *Essential Elements* referenced Vatican II documents. Unfortunately, too many religious were unfamiliar with those documents, so they accepted and even joined the Vatican-bashing undertaken by some outspoken and high-profile religious and laity.

In her introduction to the 1985 book she edited, *Midwives of the Future*, Loretto Sister Ann Patrick Ware wrote: "One of the reasons for publishing this book at this time is that ominous signs are in the air. In 1983, the Congregation of Religious and Secular Institutes (SCRIS) issued a document, *Essential Elements of Religious Life*, which in effect would undo the work of renewal that religious communities of women have carried out." [6]

Dorothy Vidulich, a Sister of Saint Joseph of Peace and a comember of the Loretto Sisters who was a columnist for the *National Catholic Reporter*, made it clear that some American religious considered their "lived experience" as having more authority than the pope or Vatican II to define authentic religious life. She wrote: "The 1983 SCRIS [Congregation for Religious] *Essential Elements of Religious Life* is a feeble recall to a lukewarm monastic style completely divorced from Vatican II theology. Its critique by so many United States women and men religious is a healthy and encouraging sign that our lived experience is basic to the emerging new theology of religious life." [7]

Anita Caspary, who had been superior of the Los Angeles Immaculate Heart of Mary sisters before she and the majority of her order became laicized in 1971 rather than follow the Vatican's directives on renewal, wrote in the *National Catholic Reporter* on March 2, 1984, that some sisters were quite right in ignoring *Essential Elements*, and she issued a veiled threat. She wrote that some nuns "have set the

---

[6] Ann Patrick Ware, SL, ed., *Midwives of the Future* (Kansas City: Leaven Press, 1985), 3.
[7] Dorothy Vidulich, CSJP, "Finding a Founder", in *Midwives*, 170.

whole matter aside to go on with the work at hand rather than using time to readdress questions they have settled for themselves. But among a sizable group of sisters of various communities, there is emergent anger, a growing frustration with the system. The more outspoken predict another exodus of sisters like that of the 1960's should the Vatican intervention be carried out to the letter." Caspary further lamented that the Vatican was directing bishops to "lead the sisters back into a pre-Vatican mode of life".

Essential Elements did not sit well with some members of the LCWR either. Former executive directors of the conference, Mary Daniel Turner, a Sister of Notre Dame de Namur, and Providence Sister Lora Ann Quinonez (who was executive director in 1983), reported that at their 1983 assembly, forty-three LCWR members publicly repudiated "the characterization of religious life in *Essential Elements* as alien to the experience of American sisters". They were particularly disturbed that *Essential Elements* offended "American cultural sensibilities—the voice of the people is conspicuously absent from the document; its approach is ahistorical, nonexperimental; it is an attempt to quell what Rome sees as rebellion; it is an anonymous document, produced in secret; its fuzzy, ambiguous legal force leaves the door wide open for unchecked administrative abuse." Sisters Mary Daniel and Lora Ann called this reaction "a clear demonstration of the growing acknowledgment of the legitimate role of culture in shaping religious identity".[8]

Not all American sisters disapproved of *Essential Elements*. Sister Claudia Honsberger, a former superior of the Servants of the Immaculate Heart of Mary, Immaculata, Pennsylvania, wrote a lengthy defense of the document in 1984. A former regional chairwoman in the CMSW, Sister Claudia had parted company with official conference positions several times before. She wrote that religious communities had not taken sufficient time to read and absorb the Vatican II documents, resulting in many misinterpretations and subsequent confusion. She suggested that some disputed the content of *Essential Elements* because they were living a lifestyle totally different from the lifestyle for religious described by the pope in the document.

---

[8] Lora Ann Quinonez, CDP, and Mary Daniel Turner, SNDdeN, *The Transformation of American Catholic Sisters* (Philadelphia: Temple University Press, 1992), 62, 86–87.

Sister Claudia struck a poignant note when she recalled the turmoil caused by unlimited and unevaluated experimentation in religious communities: "Every religious knows what a time of anxiety and confusion it was, and still is, for many of the outgrowths of the period, and the Chapters have been a source of pain, if not real agony." [9]

Collapsing Community Life

Most change-oriented orders did not apply *Essential Elements* to their lifestyle and governance, but rather they continued to define religious life in their own terms. One result was that many of these orders began having more sisters living away from their community than living with the community.

Since the 1970s, even in cities where a motherhouse is located, it has not been uncommon for sisters to live alone, with only one other sister, or with laypeople, in apartments or houses. In its 1994 document *Fraternal Life in Community*, the Congregation for Religious observed that the emphasis of mission over community "has had a profound impact on fraternal life in common to the point that this has become at times almost an option rather than an integral part of religious life" (59).

Fraternal Life in Community also noted that among women religious a culture of individualism has weakened commitment to community life and projects (4); a lay mentality stresses the material over the spiritual (46); some religious have become consumers, not builders, of community (24); authority is misunderstood to the point that no one is in charge; and adequate time for prayer is not set aside. The document stated that religious should not live alone or away from community without serious reason, nor should religious live with laity. Communities in which the majority of the members live apart, it cautioned, "would no longer be able to be considered true religious institutes" (65). This warning was not a new ruling from the Vatican; it was merely a reiteration of the definition of religious life already in existing Church documents.

Again the Vatican provided clear directions about religious life, and again many American sisters rejected them, with some arguing that

[9] Honsberger, "Women Religious and Church Authority", 19–27.

there can be many definitions of community, including "community without walls". And the result of not heeding the call to community life has been quite detrimental. Studies over several years by the Georgetown University Center for Applied Research in the Apostolate (CARA), including the 2009 *Recent Vocations to Religious Life*, consistently showed that religious institutes whose members live in community are much more successful in attracting new vocations than those that permit members to live on their own. The comprehensive 1992 *Future of Religious Orders in the United States* (FORUS) study also reached this conclusion.

A Synod on Religious Life

During the entire month of October 1994, the World Synod of Bishops took up the topic of consecrated life. But many American sisters were not happy that a body of bishops would be discussing the religious vocation and making recommendations to the pope. Furthermore, some religious superiors saw no reason even to make the members of their institutes aware of the synodal topic, even though the Vatican wanted all religious to be involved.

The synod followed an agenda set forth in a working paper that had been previously developed. Since a synod is advisory and not legislative, propositions for future action were sent to Pope John Paul II for his consideration in preparing his apostolic exhortation on the synod. The propositions were not made public, but reportedly they included the requirements that religious adhere to Church teaching as part of their witness and discuss with their bishops the importance of the Magisterium and their relationship with the local church.[10]

The interventions of the bishops generally were not publicized either, but press sources reported on a few of these presentations. Bishops from various countries were full of praise for the contributions of consecrated persons to the Church, and they emphasized that consecrated life was vital to the Church; but many bishops also indicated that they shared some of the same concerns that had appeared in the synod's working paper.

[10] McDonough, "The Concluding Message of the 1994 Synod on Consecrated Life", *Review for Religious* (May / June 1995): 462–66.

Archbishop Augusto Vargas Alzamora of Lima, Peru, called for a return to distinctive garb for religious, saying that one reason for a decline in vocations was that religious cannot be distinguished from laypersons.[11] Archbishop Oscar Andres Rodriguez Maradiaga of Tegucigalpa, Honduras, a member of the Salesians of Don Bosco, pleaded for religious to return to the traditional apostolate of education. He defined education as "a new aspect of the Gospel's preferential option for the poor", saying that religious orders that had left educational institutions in favor of other ministries for and with the poor should reconsider their decision in light of the potential of education to bring people out of poverty.[12]

The bishops from the United States espoused a variety of views among themselves. For example, Cardinal Joseph Bernardin of Chicago counseled against premature judgments about new ways of living consecrated life. He noted that tensions are inevitable in an era of change, and he called for "a broad scope for legitimate diversity".[13] Bishop Francis George, a member of the Missionary Oblates of Mary Immaculate who then headed the diocese of Yakima, recognized the "diversity of charisms" in consecrated life, but he voiced some concern that individualism sometimes eclipsed the call to holiness. He noted that "consecrated persons too trustful of their own experience can begin to assimilate uncritically the imperatives of their culture and gradually lose their ability to be a source of spiritual strength for other men and women struggling to achieve the generosity needed to found Christian families, to defend life in a culture of death, to be faithful to the Gospel in business, the arts and politics."[14]

Bishop James Timlin of Scranton acknowledged "many wonderful, beautiful and necessary changes" in religious life since the Second Vatican Council, but he was the most outspoken of the American bishops, saying that "the last twenty-five years have been devastating to religious life", particularly in the United States. While leaving ample

[11] Cindy Wooden, "Bishops Ask That Religious Wear Habits, Teach in Schools", Catholic News Service, October 4, 1994.

[12] Archbishop Rodriguez Maradiaga, SDB, "Education: The Way out of Poverty", Origins, October 20, 1994, 334.

[13] Wooden, "Chicago Cardinal Says Societal Changes Lead to Religious Crisis", Catholic News Service, October 5, 1994.

[14] Bishop Francis George, OMI, "Crises Are Calls to Convert", Origins, October 20, 1994, 333.

room "for a rich diversity in religious life", Bishop Timlin called for a return to the traditional interpretation of the vows. Apparently alluding to some sisters who do not attend Mass or receive the sacraments because women are excluded from ordination, he contended that "at the very least, for one to be considered a religious, he or she must be what we euphemistically call a 'practicing Catholic'." The bishop maintained that "we must still be clear about what is expected by the church of those who publicly profess to be vowed sons and daughters of the church. We must be determined to chart a clear course for consecrated life.... We have dialogued enough. We have experimented enough.... The era of experimentation, or whatever we want to call it, has not been all that successful, and we should honestly and humbly admit it." [15]

As a copresident of the synod, Cardinal John O'Connor of New York submitted to the synod secretariat a written intervention to be included in the published papers of the meeting. In it he explained that, as with other reforms initiated by the Second Vatican Council, the renewal of religious institutes had been lacking proper guidance from the bishops of the Church. He added:

> The result was the creation of unfulfillable expectations. On the part of religious, many changes they introduced sincerely believing them to be faithful to Vatican II were ultimately rejected, and, indeed, sincere religious themselves were even criticized for introducing such changes. Obviously, at the same time, some religious abused the occasion for true reform and renewal, in order to accomplish their own objectives, quite different from the objectives of Vatican II. [16]

John Paul II Speaks about Religious Life

When John Paul II's apostolic exhortation on consecrated life, *Vita Consecrata*, was released on March 28, 1996, it was greeted with enthusiasm—and relief—by virtually all the religious in the United States. This warm reception no doubt was due to the fact that the

[15] Bishop James Timlin, "Devastating Years for Religious Life", *Origins*, October 20, 1994, 331–332.

[16] Cardinal John O'Connor, written intervention at World Synod of Bishops, October 27, 1994, copy provided by him to the author.

exhortation was extremely positive, and rather than chastising religious for any deviation from the norms established by the Church, the pope expounded on the reasons behind them.

The few negative comments made by the pope were not readily apparent in the predominantly positive exhortation, but he did note the following:

- The desire of religious to become closer to laity can lead to the adoption of a secularized lifestyle. (38)
- While Church authority should be "fraternal and spiritual" and involve community members in decision-making, "it should still be remembered that the final word belongs to authority and consequently that authority has the right to see that decisions taken are respected". (43)
- Allegiance of mind and heart to the Magisterium "must be lived honestly and clearly testified to before the people of God by all consecrated persons, especially those involved in theological research, teaching, publishing, catechesis and the use of the means of social communication". (46)
- Institutes "should grow and develop in accordance with the spirit of their founders and foundresses, and their own sound traditions", and each should "follow its own discipline to keep intact its spiritual and apostolic patrimony". (48)
- Pastoral initiatives of consecrated persons should be "determined and carried out in cordial and open dialogue between bishops and superiors". (49)
- Conferences of superiors should "maintain frequent and regular contacts" with the Congregation for Religious as "a sign of their communion with the Holy See". (53)
- Consecrated persons should "foster respect for the person and for human life from conception to its natural end." (83)

Its pastoral, patient tone was perhaps the exhortation's greatest strength, but at the same time, its greatest weakness. The exhortation was directed to the entire world, and certainly religious life was not in crisis everywhere. But because the exhortation was so positive and so acceptable, it was interpreted by many as an affirmation of the religious who ignored, even belittled, Church documents. Mercy Sister Doris Gottemoeller, a past president of the LCWR and a synod auditor, reacted to the exhortation in this way: "Each congregation serves the church and the world in its own distinct way. The exhortation recognizes and affirms this diversity as a testament to the dynamism and vitality of religious life and its ability to change to meet the needs of the people and the times." [17]

What Went Wrong?

The Council's directive to religious institutes to experiment with their way of life and to rewrite their constitutions during the upheaval of social revolution was as an invitation to disaster in the United States.

Making the task of renewal even more confusing for American sisters was the fact that canon law was also being revised. Even when religious institutes dutifully wrote to the Vatican for permission to set aside a canon that could possibly be deleted from the new code, the Vatican took years to reply. By then, an innovation in a given community might be fixed. The Holy See had been unrealistic to expect that sisters, lacking timely answers, would be able to reverse years-long experiments if later they were found to be contrary to the new Code of Canon Law.

Another complicating factor was that most American bishops did not involve themselves sufficiently in the renewal process, probably because they did not want to interfere with the autonomy of religious institutes. Many of the bishops did not even familiarize themselves with the new authoritative documents about religious life and as a result failed to recognize deviations from Church teaching occurring among sisters in their own dioceses.

Even if the bishops had been more involved, some sisters would have ignored them as they did the Vatican. The chief agent for promoting a version of renewal independent of the Magisterium was the women superiors' conference, which had been established by the Vatican to be the official communications link between it and the sisters in the United States. As the next three chapters detail, the superiors' conference eventually evolved into an autonomous body of sisters disinclined to cooperate with Rome.

---

[17] Undated LCWR news release obtained by the author, c. April 1996.

4

The Radical "Rethink"

As you well know, the Conference of Major Superiors of Women has
undergone a radical process of rethink in the past two years.[1]

—Sister Joan de Lourdes Leonard, CSJ,
LCWR executive committee, 1970

Two influential organizations created in the 1950s initiated many needed
reforms for sisters, but they also generated much of the chaos and
confusion that thinned the ranks of women religious, stifled the growth
of new vocations, and instigated the revolution in the convents. These
organizations were the Sister Formation Conference (today called the
Religious Formation Conference), which will be discussed in chapter 9, and the Conference of Major Religious Superiors of Women's
Institutes (CMSW), today called the Leadership Conference of Women
Religious (LCWR). Both groups were established with very noble
purposes, and they effectively served women religious and the Church
for a number of years. Unfortunately, as the reform movement progressed, both organizations led sisters far beyond the renewal that was
envisioned by the Second Vatican Council.

In 2008, the Congregation for the Doctrine of the Faith initiated
a doctrinal assessment of the LCWR and in 2012 issued the results
of that assessment, which found "serious doctrinal problems that affect
many in Consecrated Life". The document stated that the LCWR
had distorted the role of Jesus in the salvation of the world and

[1] Sister Joan de Lourdes letter to LCWR members, May 2, 1970, CLCW 34/33, UNDA.

undermined "the revealed doctrines of the Holy Trinity, the divinity of Christ, and the inspiration of Sacred Scripture". It noted the group's rejection of Church authority and its unacceptable positions on the centrality of the Eucharist, the nature of religious life, women's ordination, human sexuality, and ministry to homosexual persons. The CDF also found the LCWR's presentation of the life issues to be inadequate.[2] Given the gravity of the situation, the Vatican appointed Archbishop J. Peter Sartain of Seattle as apostolic delegate to oversee the reform of the LCWR. What had brought the leadership group to this point?

In the 1960s, activist sisters in the superiors' conference introduced at the group's annual assemblies programs that promoted a form of religious life different from that envisioned by Vatican II. These activists shaped implementation of the renewal in convents all over the country by conducting a conference-sponsored survey that presented the activists' agenda. This survey reached every sister in the United States. Some change-oriented members of the conference also employed questionable political tactics to rewrite the conference's membership requirements and constitution, eventually leading to a split in the organization and repeated conflict with the Vatican.

In 1971, the conference of women superiors renamed itself the Leadership Conference of Women Religious and began to function as a professional organization of women who were determined to set their own definition of religious life, based not on spiritual and theological truths, but rather on political and sociological issues.

Early Years of the Conference of Superiors

During the early 1950s, the Vatican began to encourage superiors of religious institutes to come together in national conferences for the purpose of exchanging information, giving each other support, and building up religious life. The groups were also intended to work with local bishops, national bishops' conferences, and the Holy See itself. These conferences were specifically mentioned in the 1965 Vatican II document *Perfectae Caritatis* and later incorporated into the

---

[2] Congregation for the Doctrine of the Faith, *Doctrinal Assessment of the Leadership Conference of Women Religious*, April 18, 2012. See appendix.

1983 Code of Canon Law. The statutes of these organizations need the approval of the Holy See, which alone has the power to give the conferences canonical status. By 1995, over one hundred countries had these national conferences of religious,[3] and in his 1996 apostolic exhortation *Vita Consecrata*, Pope John Paul II cited the "significant contribution to communion" made by these groups, whose principal purpose is "the promotion of the consecrated life within the framework of the church's mission" (53).

Originally, when the CMSW and its counterpart for men, the Conference of Major Superiors of Men (CMSM), were being organized in 1956, it was planned that the two groups would be combined as a single Conference of Religious of the United States (as has been done in many countries). Each side was to have its own officers, but the president of the men's group was also to be president of the combined conference. The permanent secretary of the joint conference also was to have been a male religious. The women religious, however, decided they wanted to have their own separate organization not led by men, so the two groups organized into separate conferences. The women's conference was canonically established in 1959, and its statutes were approved by the Holy See in 1962, the same year the Second Vatican Council convened. According to article 1 of the statutes:

> The purpose of the Conference, which is to be accomplished through close contact and common endeavor, is: (a) To promote the spiritual welfare of the women religious of the United States of America; (b) To insure an ever-increasing efficacy in their apostolate; (c) To effect an ever-closer fraternal cooperation with all religious of the United States of America, with the venerable Hierarchy, with the Clergy, and with Catholic associations; (d) To provide a proper and efficient representation with constituted authorities.[4]

The patroness of the organization was "Our Lady under the title of the Immaculate Conception".

Article 4 of the statutes pledged "perfect allegiance" to Church hierarchy and "perfect submission" to diocesan authority "as to serve as

---

[3] Felician A. Foy, OFM, and Rose M. Avato, eds., *1996 Catholic Almanac* (Huntington: Our Sunday Visitor Publishing Division, Our Sunday Visitor, Inc., 1995), 523.

[4] Bylaws of the Conference of Major Religious Superiors of Women's Institutes, CCPC 8/23, UNDA.

an example to all". Membership was open only to major superiors who were superiors general or provincial superiors. The conference was broken down into seven geographic regions, each with its own regional chair, vice chair, and secretary-treasurer elected by the members of that region. The regional officers then formed the twenty-one-member national executive committee, which in turn elected from its membership the three national executive officers. Terms of executive officers were three years, with the right of re-election for a consecutive term. The national executive committee was charged with managing the affairs of the conference and arranging national meetings. The statutes also allowed for permanent committees made up of conference members.

The early records of the CMSW reflect activities such as vocations surveys and discussions of catechetics and common governing issues such as health and finance. As the 1960s progressed, it became apparent that the Second Vatican Council was going to ask religious institutes to renew and update their constitutions and rule books. Anticipation of these reforms, along with the social, political, and cultural changes of the 1960s—especially the rise of feminism—prompted many women religious to reevaluate their role in the Church, and the CMSW was both agent and catalyst for this evaluation.

The superiors' conference expanded the scope of its original mandate and went on to engage in nonreligious activities such as seeking membership in the United Nations as a nongovernment organization; issuing statements on matters such as women's rights, labor disputes, the death penalty, ecology, homosexual rights, and the Equal Rights Amendment; and pursuing a strong social-justice agenda almost to the exclusion of spiritual issues.

The evolution of the CMSW can be demonstrated rather dramatically by looking at its annual assemblies between 1965 and 1971, when the conference adopted new bylaws and changed its name to the LCWR. Until 1965, the annual assemblies of the women superiors had a predominantly spiritual tone, and much of the assembly time was dedicated to networking between the various institutes of women religious and addressing issues of common concern to the sisters.

But, as the Second Vatican Council progressed during the early 1960s, it became clear that the Council would call for renewal of religious life. It also became clear that the Code of Canon Law approved in

1917 was going to be updated for modern times and revised to reflect many of the decisions of Vatican II. Thus, the leaders' national assemblies began to reflect the anticipation of change, and the sisters grew increasingly eager for renewal. Adding to the excitement was the fact that the chairwoman of the women's superiors—Loretto Sister Mary Luke Tobin—had been the only American woman invited to be an observer at Vatican II.

The 1965 Assembly: Sisters and the Council

The 1965 annual assembly of the women superiors took place just a couple of months before the close of Vatican II, and the prospect of updating canon law and rewriting the constitutions of religious institutes surely influenced the choice of speakers for the meeting. Speakers included Passionist Father Paul Boyle, president of the Canon Law Society of America; Redemptorist Father Bernard Haring, an expert consultant to the Second Vatican Council; Jesuit Father Bernard Cooke, a theologian; and Maryknoll Father Eugene Kennedy, a psychologist. (Fathers Cooke and Kennedy eventually left the priesthood, and Cooke went on to become a member of the board of the Church-reform organization Call to Action.)

Father Boyle raised some eyebrows when he told the assembly that "whenever an observance of the letter of the law will hinder the attainment of the purpose or spirit of the law, then the letter must fall. The letter is merely a means to an end." He also observed that "in the past sixty years we have witnessed a progressive denuding of religious constitutions, to the point where they are nothing more than cold canonical prescripts." And he said that the "doctrine of experimentation" should be incorporated into revised canon law "as another essential principle which has already been canonized by the Conciliar document".[5]

The proceedings of the assembly published by the major superiors included the main addresses, but the sisters intentionally did not obtain an imprimatur for the book—as they had done in past years—causing

---

[5] Paul Boyle, CP, in *Proceedings of the Annual Assembly, 1965* (Washington, D.C.: Conference of Major Religious Superiors of Women's Institutes of the United States of America, 1966), 19–22.

considerable consternation at the Vatican, which was accustomed to docile sisters who followed proper procedures.[6]

The 1965 assembly also approved a petition to be sent to the Congregation for Religious, the pope, and all US bishops, asking that sisters "serve as permanent consultative or acting members of the Sacred Congregation for Religious, of the commission for the revision of canon law and of any post-conciliar commission that may be set up for the implementing of acts of Vatican II in regard to religious".[7] This request eventually was granted for the most part, but in 1965 it was considered to be a very bold statement, especially for women religious.

The 1966 Assembly: Rebuke from the Vatican

In 1966 Father Bernard Haring again addressed the CMSW national assembly, along with Archbishop William Cousins of Milwaukee; Bishop Gerald V. McDevitt, auxiliary bishop of Philadelphia; sociologist Sister Marie Augusta Neal; and Philip Scharper, who was editor-in-chief of Sheed and Ward publishers. The Vatican considered some of these speakers to be uncomfortably progressive on Church-related issues, and about six months after the meeting, Father Bernard Ransing, an American staff member of the Congregation for Religious and the Vatican's religious adviser to the CMSW, sent a letter to the conference's executive director, Sister Emmanuella Brennan of the Holy Names of Jesus and Mary. The apostolic delegate was unhappy with the content of their annual assembly, wrote Father Ransing, and the conference needs to "control" their speakers.[8]

In addition, Cardinal Antoniutti, prefect of the Congregation for Religious, wrote the conference's president regarding the assembly speakers, pointing out the "necessity of choosing carefully the persons who are to address the Conference". He wrote that "a number of doctrinal inaccuracies (if not errors) have been noted in four of the discourses, along with some tendentious attitudes and a marked superficiality in

[6] Sister Mary Rose Emmanuella Brennan letter to Sister Mary Luke Tobin, May 17, 1966, CLCW 158/20, UNDA.

[7] National Catholic Reporter, September 1, 1965.

[8] Father Bernard Ransing letter to Sister Emmanuella, April 23, 1967, CLCW 1/12, UNDA.

some parts of these same discourses." He pointed out the necessity of selecting speakers who were real authorities in their fields and noted for the soundness of their doctrine, and he again reminded the sisters to request an imprimatur from the local bishop for publication of future proceedings.[9]

The Vatican seemed to react with surprise that the formerly docile sisters were interested in an agenda that had not been dictated to them by Rome. Yet Vatican authorities were apparently puzzled over how to handle the increasingly independent American sisters. As the sisters gradually began to assert themselves more and more, the Vatican fell into the mode of reacting after the fact, a role that would continue for many years.

The 1967 and 1968 Assemblies: The Sisters' Survey

The topic of the 1967 and 1968 CMSW assemblies was their Sisters' Survey, an extensive questionnaire allegedly designed to determine the readiness of American sisters for renewal. The survey's critics, however, charged that it also was an indoctrination tool used to introduce radical renewal concepts into convents all over the country. Unlike most surveys that obtain accurate data by questioning a sample of a population, the Sisters' Survey was sent to nearly every active sister in the United States—some 157,000 of them. Chapter 8 of this book examines the survey in depth and reports the controversial nature of its statements and questions about theology, authority, governance, and lifestyle.

At the 1967 assembly, the survey was big news, as the results were just becoming available and being distributed to superiors. These results were then used by change-oriented sisters to promote reorganization of the conference. Sister Mary Daniel Turner, who was chair of the committee that had prepared and conducted the survey, recommended that the organization's statutes be revised to reflect the growing desire of sisters for shared decision-making—a conclusion reached

[9] Cardinal Antoniutti letter to Mother Mary Omer, February 16, 1968, CLCW 34/07, UNDA. The letter indicates that the doctrinal inaccuracies in talks at the annual assemblies cited in the CDF 2012 doctrinal assessment had been noted by the Vatican some forty-six years earlier.

by the creators of the Sisters' Survey.[10] (What Sister Mary Daniel didn't tell the assembly was that the eventual revision of the statutes actually would give more power to an elite executive committee.)

The planning committee for the 1967 assembly included Sister Mary Daniel; Sister Mary Luke Tobin, conference president from 1964 to 1967; Sister Marie Augusta Neal, a sociologist who prepared the survey; and Sister Humiliata (Anita) Caspary, who as superior of the Immaculate Heart of Mary community in Los Angeles was engaged in a dispute with their archbishop, Cardinal James McIntyre, about changes in their constitution.

The planning committee revealed something about their own philosophy regarding renewal and relationships with the Vatican through their lineup of invited speakers. They asked Father Paul Boyle to return and invited sociologist Father Andrew Greeley. Invited to speak, but not attending, was Christian Brother Gabriel Moran, who eventually would make headlines in the 1970s by declaring that religious orders and Catholic parishes should be dismantled and replaced by "something that is more human, and that builds on qualities other than geography or sexual segregation and institutionalization".[11]

Appearing on the program in Brother Moran's place was Jesuit Father Carroll Bourg (who eventually left the priesthood). In his talk, Father Bourg encouraged the sisters' independence from the Vatican, saying: "You need to realize that the greatest gift you can give to the Church, the greatest measure of your loyalty, is to become American, to be the religious of the Church as modern American women. To achieve this high and lofty purpose, I think you must become more autonomous, you must be an independent body of women in authority, women of responsibility, more ready to lead than to follow; more disposed to represent to Rome than to be represented by Rome."[12]

At the same 1967 assembly, giving advice quite contrary to Father Bourg's, was the conference's religious adviser and staff member of the Congregation for Religious, Father Bernard Ransing. He expressed

[10] Mary Daniel Turner, SMDdeN, in *Proceedings of the Annual Assembly, 1967* (Washington, D.C.: Conference of Major Religious Superiors of Women's Institutes of the United States of America, 1967), 193–94.

[11] *National Catholic Reporter*, February 2, 1973, 2.

[12] Carroll Bourg, SJ, in *Proceedings of the Annual Assembly, 1967*, 158.

concern that renewal among religious was getting off track, and he reminded the superiors that the Vatican II documents placed the following limitations on experimentation: (1) the purpose, nature and characteristics of the Institute must be preserved intact; and (2) any experiments "contrary to the Common Law" require the permission of the Holy See before they are put into execution.[13]

The 1968 assembly also took up the topic of the Sisters' Survey, even though some members had requested a more spiritual program. Sister Mary Daniel noted in a 1968 letter to the conference's executive committee that perhaps she should resign from the program committee since many members had wanted the assembly to have a more spiritual tone instead of devoting more time to the Sisters' Survey. But she went on to criticize an alternate spiritual program that had been drawn up by other conference officials while she was out of the country, saying it was "so 'other-worldly' in character". She added that, "in a period of 'new humanism' I wonder if the program is not too contrived in order to bring in 'the faith dimension'."[14]

A conference official responded by letter to Sister Mary Daniel, explaining that the best-attended assemblies had been on the subject of prayer, and the program planners were caught between what the members wanted and what Sister Mary Daniel recommended. She suggested that as a compromise, the titles of some of the talks could be changed to reflect the "new humanism" and speakers could be asked to avoid an overemphasis on the spiritual.[15]

The program finally presented at the 1968 assembly included talks by Jesuit Father Ladislas Orsy, a canon lawyer, and Marist Father Thomas Dubay, a theologian and popular retreat master who went on to become a regular contributor on EWTN. But also speaking was militant feminist Mary Daly, author of *The Church and the Second Sex*. In that book Daly had expounded on the second-class status of women in the Church, symbolized by their exclusion from the priesthood. When Mary Daly was in Rome during the Second Vatican Council, she had told nuns that their veils were signs of submission

---

[13] Bernard Ransing, CSC, ibid., 151.

[14] Sister Mary Daniel letter to CMSW executive committee, April 8, 1968, CLCW 34/09, UNDA.

[15] Sister Cecilia Abhold letter to Sister Mary Daniel, April 13, 1968, CLCW 34/09, UNDA.

to men.[16] Also on the program was a discussion on "new govern-ment structure in religious communities" led by Sister Francis Bor-gia Rothluebber, Mercy Sister Thomas Aquinas (Elizabeth) Carroll, Sister Angelita Myerscough of the Adorers of the Blood of Christ, and Sister Margaret Brennan, all change-oriented sisters who would become presidents of the superiors' conference in the early 1970s.

A good deal of time at the 1968 assembly was spent on the Sisters' Survey and the proposal by the survey committee to restructure the conference. The conference vice president and chair of the statutes committee reported to the assembly that a draft of revised statutes had been circulated to the total membership of six hundred, but only forty-one members had returned it with comments. In spite of this appar-ent lack of interest by the membership in making changes in the statutes, she proposed that the conference hire consultants Booz, Allen, and Hamilton to do a study for the conference and recommend changes. She told the assembly that proposed revisions would be submitted to the membership at large for "approval, amendment, etc., prior to any formal vote or decision respecting change".[17] This process did not occur exactly as proposed, for new bylaws eventually were introduced and actually enacted before the assembly had a chance to vote for-mally on them.

Resolutions introduced at the 1968 assembly reflected the growing interest of the organization in social action. The resolutions included a proposal that the conference issue a press release supporting the Amer-ican Civil Liberties Union's call for a study of events surrounding the 1968 Democratic National Convention (defeated 194 to 122) and a proposal that the conference invite volunteer representatives to be present at the Baltimore trial of Father Daniel Berrigan, who had been arrested in May for burning draft files at Catonsville, Maryland (defeated 215 to 80).[18]

In February of 1969, the conference's executive committee voted to commission Booz, Allen, and Hamilton to do a study of the

---

[16] Mary Luke Tobin, SL, "Doors to the World", in *Midwives*, 185.

[17] *Proceedings of the Annual Assembly, 1968* (Washington, D.C.: Conference of Major Reli-gious Superiors of Women's Institutes of the United States of America, 1969), 87, CLCW 10/14, UNDA.

[18] CMSW notes on resolutions from 1968 assembly, dated October 21, 1968, CLCW 1/23, UNDA.

organization, at a cost of $42,000 to $45,000.[19] To pay for the study, each member was to be assessed fifty cents for every working sister in her community. Then, in August, just prior to the 1969 assembly, Sister of Charity Mary Omer Downing, conference president, wrote members and told them that the executive committee had decided at its February meeting that regions should not hold regional elections until the Booz, Allen, and Hamilton study was finished and the reorganization of the conference had taken place.[20] Thus, reorganization of the conference proceeded even though there had been no clear mandate for change from the membership.

The 1969 Assembly: Reorganization of the Conference

The September 1969 national assembly in Saint Louis was a stormy meeting. The Booz, Allen, and Hamilton report was presented at a general session of the assembly but not voted on at that time. Causing considerably more controversy was an address by Father Edward Heston, an American canon lawyer and newly appointed secretary of the Congregation for Religious. He presented six key points for the sisters to consider in renewing their congregations: the religious habit, collaboration with the local bishop, community prayer, shared community life, a primacy of the spiritual, and a corporate witness.[21] Sister of Notre Dame Mary Elise Krantz, who was present at that meeting, told the author that Father Heston's talk simply was a reminder of the essentials of religious life as defined by Vatican II, and it seemed to be a discreet effort to correct some communities that were going beyond the renewal desired by the Council.

But many of the more change-oriented superiors did not take kindly to Father Heston's advice, as they saw it as an attempt to slow down the renewal process. Some sisters also thought Father Heston's remarks were designed to gather support for the Congregation for Religious in an ongoing dispute with the Immaculate Heart of Mary Sisters (IHM) of Los Angeles, who had been criticized by their archbishop,

---

[19] Vote cited in Sister Emmanuella memo, March 17, 1969, and cost cited in Sister M. Rose McPhee letter to CMSW members, July 24, 1969, CLCW 1/24, UNDA.

[20] Mother Mary Omer letter to members, August 19, 1969, CLCW 1/24, UNDA.

[21] *National Catholic Reporter*, October 1, 1969.

Cardinal James McIntyre, about radical changes to their constitution and lifestyle that went beyond Vatican decrees and Council documents (see chapter 12). Indeed, the same six points made by Father Heston had also been made by the Congregation for Religious in a letter to the IHM Sisters. Their case had been appealed to the Congregation for Religious, which came down on the side of Cardinal McIntyre, thus upsetting many of the superiors.

At the end of the assembly, twenty-two resolutions were presented for voting. The first four passed quickly. But resolution number 5 proposed that "the CMSW publicly offer support to the IHM Sisters by requesting [that] the Sacred Congregation for Religious allow them to follow their chapter decisions during an extended period of experimentation".

Father Heston warned the assembly that a vote for the resolution would be a vote against the congregation. But Sister Angelita Myerscough (who would be elected president in 1970) and Sister Thomas Aquinas (Elizabeth) Carroll (who would be elected vice president in 1970) called the priest's intervention inappropriate and resumed arguing in support of the resolution.[22] After lengthy debate, during which many members left for home because the hour was late, the resolution garnered a majority of the votes of the 278 sisters still present: 166 voted yes; 90 voted no; and 22 abstained. However, the statutes required 60 percent approval of those present, which would have required 167 votes in favor, so the motion failed by one vote.[23]

The events of the 1969 assembly did not go unnoticed in the outside world. In an *Ave Maria* editorial, Holy Cross Father John Reedy criticized the interventions of both the Congregation for Religious and Father Heston. The Congregation for Religious, Father Reedy wrote, had shown "truly extraordinary insensitivity to the exciting progress being made by many communities of American sisters". He went on to note that the Congregation for Religious was overreacting to what Father Heston described as "stacks of mail we have been receiving from very good religious who are complaining about the excesses of renewal programs". Father Reedy observed, "It seems a mistake, almost always, to offer leadership by reaction to complaints." Instead,

[22] Quinonez and Turner, *Transformation*, 153.
[23] Sister Corita Kemble letter to Mother Paulita, September 23, 1969, CLCW 5/18, UNDA.

Father Reedy wrote, the Congregation for Religious and Father Heston should have offered "a rousing, encouraging vote of confidence in the tremendously exciting progress which the American sisters have made during the past decade".[24]

The executive director of the superiors' conference, Sister Mary Claudia, wrote Father Reedy, thanking him for the editorial. She also wrote about the "havoc" caused by Father Heston's remarks. After the "painful meeting", she wrote, no one left without feeling "hurt, anxious and demoralized".[25]

Three days later, Father Reedy responded to Sister Mary Claudia, writing that several priests at the University of Notre Dame had argued strongly with Father Heston against his planned presentation, but "it was like bouncing rocks off the walls of the Vatican." Father Reedy recommended that the sisters not allow confrontation on the issues but rather "apply to this authoritative statement [by Father Heston] the same kind of evaluation that a great many conscientious, reverent married couples are using in examining *Humanae Vitae*" (which was to ignore it). He went on to explain:

> It seems to me that the situations facing our communities and the conscience of individual religious are so grave today that we simply must evaluate positive 'legislation' in terms of the total demands of charity, justice, reverence for personal dignity of the religious, the state of conscience of the members of our communities.... For myself, simple survival and sanity impose on me the obligation to exercise some critical judgment over actions by church authorities which I regard as absurdities.[26]

After the 1969 assembly, a committee was appointed by Sister Mary Omer to recommend a structure based on the findings of the Booz, Allen, and Hamilton study. That committee recommended a five-member task force to prepare for a special assembly in February of 1970 and to carry out the recommendations of the consulting firm.[27]

[24] John Reedy, CSC, editorial, *Ave Maria*, October 25, 1969.

[25] Sister Mary Claudia letter to Father John Reedy, October 24, 1969, CLCW 158/22, UNDA.

[26] Father John Reedy letter to Sister Mary Claudia, October 27, 1969, CLCW 158/22, UNDA.

[27] Members of that task force were Mercy Sister Maurita Sengelaub, Mercy Sister William Joseph Lydon, Sister Claudia Zeller (conference executive director), Sister of Charity

So, as the eventful 1960s drew to a close, the stage was set for restruc-turing the superiors' conference, a reorganization that was of little interest to the general membership. Yet an elite group of change-oriented sisters who were in positions of influence was determined to liberate the conference from the Vatican's control and create a corpo-rate entity that could exercise the power of women in the Church and in society. As we shall see in the next chapter, they were able to manip-ulate procedures to change the nature of the superiors' conference, but they also caused the conference to rupture.

Josephine Marie O'Brien, and Sister Mary Daniel Turner, as related in CMSW letter to membership, July 21, 1971, CLCW 11/4, UNDA.

5

The Coup

The newly-adopted bylaws and title [of the superior's conference] signaled a transformed understanding and appreciation of the *raison d'être*
of the conference; not only was it to be a forum for enabling leadership, it was also to become a corporate force for systemic change in
Church and society.[1]

—Sister Mary Daniel Turner, SNDdeN,
and Sister Lora Ann Quinonez, CDP

As the 1970s dawned, the Conference of Major Religious Superiors
of Women's Institutes (CMSW) was about to be transformed from a
national group of superiors organized to exchange ideas and to facilitate communication with the Vatican to an organization headed by
activist sisters exercising the corporate power of the conference to influence the Church and society at large.

The majority of members of the conference had shown little interest in reorganization, but change-oriented sisters were intent on promoting a new structure that would distance the conference from the
Vatican's control. As we shall see in this chapter, these activist sisters
were successful in their quest, for they employed sophisticated political maneuvering and questionable constitutional manipulation to achieve
their goal, while the majority of the membership of the conference
seemed quite unaware of what was actually transpiring. Nor was the

[1] Lora Ann Quinonez, CDP, and Mary Daniel Turner, SNDdeN, "From CMSW to
LCWR: A Story of Birth and Transformation", *Review for Religious* (March / April 1990):
207.

Vatican aware. Although conferences of superiors depend upon the authority of the Congregation for Religious for their existence, Church authorities were not consulted about the reorganization, but merely informed after the fact. In the end, the LCWR emerged as a new entity asserting independence from the Vatican and openly challenging the Church in many areas.

The February 1970 Special Assembly

An unprecedented special assembly of the conference was scheduled for February 23–25, 1970, to consider the Booz, Allen, and Hamilton report on reorganizing the conference. But many busy superiors didn't have the time or the money for more than one annual assembly, and interest in restructuring the conference had not been high. Even Father Ransing canceled plans to attend. Nevertheless, the assembly convened and adopted sweeping changes, including: a new purpose for the conference; expanded general membership criteria; expanded geographic regions; a new five-member executive committee of the national board; restructuring of the annual assembly; approval of non-superior sisters' serving on special committees; election of officers by membership rather than by the national executive committee; and increased dues.[2]

The actions of this 1970 special assembly grew to be quite confusing and controversial, for the official conference interpretation of the meeting was that the organization had voted to dissolve all old structures and build up a new one from scratch. There was considerable controversy, however, over whether the organization had the authority simply to dissolve its old statutes without consulting the Vatican. The 1962 statutes provided that their interpretation was reserved to the Holy See and that they "may be amended, subject to the subsequent approval of the Holy See, by a two-thirds vote of the members of the National Executive Committee" (article 15, sections 1 and 2). The 1962 statutes also allowed for the implementation of bylaws, but those bylaws were to be "not inconsistent with these statutes" (article 16, section 1).

The confusion among members was so great that many members simply did not understand what they supposedly had approved at the

---

[2] Sister Mary Omer letter to US bishops, April 20, 1970, CLCW 10/16, UNDA.

special assembly. Adding to the confusion and concern of some members was the fact that a new five-member executive committee—made up of the three conference officers and two other sisters appointed by the national board—apparently had assumed sweeping new powers. For example, one of the motions passed at the special assembly directed that a task force on credentials should be appointed by the chairwoman and "recommend a definition of membership criteria and should present its recommendations to the executive committee prior to registration for the September [1970] annual assembly. This special assembly empowers the executive committee to act on recommendations of this Task Force on Credentials." [3]

In other words, the 1970 special assembly allegedly turned over all decisions about who could join the organization to the new five-member executive committee. And this premise was used to expand membership in the conference beyond major superiors, although expanding membership beyond major superiors was the opposite of what the Booz, Allen, and Hamilton report had recommended. The management consultants hired by the conference had recommended that since the organization was for major superiors, membership should be limited to canonically defined major superiors if the organization was to have any significance. The report also found that there was too much responsibility in the national executive committee, which isolated members from active participation. [4]

Nevertheless, the task force on organization and coordination of the conference went to work after the February special assembly and reported on April 2, 1970, that it had finalized an interim organization chart, determined the size and composition of ad hoc and special committees, and appointed chairwomen for all committees. [5] The next day, the task force met with the chairwomen of all interim committees. The report of that meeting indicates new bylaws replacing the 1962 statutes would be formulated and presented to the membership. Also, the new election procedures supposedly approved by a resolution at the 1970

[3] Minutes of CMSW national board meeting, September 4, 1971, CLCW 11 / 1, UNDA.
[4] Booz, Allen, and Hamilton, "Summary of Survey of Objectives, Programs, Organization, Administration and Financing, Conference of Major Religious Superiors of Women's Institutes in the U.S.A.", September 19, 1969, 27–28, CLCW 10/15, UNDA.
[5] Report of Task Force on Organization and Coordination of CMSW, April 2, 1970, CLCW 10/17, UNDA.

special assembly would be implemented, and new membership criteria would be approved and adopted by the national board prior to registration for the annual 1970 assembly in September.[6]

The 1962 statutes had directed that each region elect its own chair, vice chair, and secretary-treasurer. Then those three officers from each of the seven regions would make up the twenty-one-member national executive committee. The national executive committee then elected from its own members the three national officers: a chair, vice chair, and secretary-treasurer. But the new election procedure approved by resolution at the special assembly and put into effect by the national board for the 1970 election provided for popular election of national officers. This change in method of electing national officers was very significant in light of the fact that the new membership criteria being developed included members from leadership teams in the more change-oriented congregations, which had moved to a team concept rather than the traditional one-superior model. These new members were admitted to the 1970 and 1971 annual assemblies before the national assembly could vote on this change. The official conference explanation was that the special assembly had authorized these actions, but many members remained confused and suspected they had witnessed a coup d'état. Thus, when the 1970 regular assembly rolled around in September, there was plenty of commotion and downright ill will, which would be exacerbated at the assembly.

The 1970 Annual Assembly: A New Image

The statutes committee reported on the progress of the new bylaws, and election of officers took place—the first popular election of officers using new election methods and new membership criteria allegedly established by the February 1970 special assembly. Elected were the following: chair, Sister Angelita Myerscough, who had been chair of the conference's Canon Law Committee; vice chair, Sister Thomas Aquinas (Elizabeth) Carroll, who had been chair of the conference's National Sister Formation Committee; and secretary-treasurer, Sister

[6] Report of meeting of CMSW Task Force on Organization and Coordination with chairmen of all interim committees, April 3, 1970, CLCW 10/18, UNDA.

Margaret Brennan, who had been vice chair of the conference's Sister Formation Committee.

The September 18, 1970, *National Catholic Reporter* described the new officers as a "'with it' administration", compared with outgoing president Sister Mary Omer, who the *Reporter* said "has a reputation as a conservative". Attending the assembly for the first time were observers invited from organizations such as the National Coalition of American Nuns (NCAN) and the National Assembly of Women Religious (NAWR). Sister Adrian Marie Hofstetter of NCAN was quoted by the *Reporter* as saying that "Sister Luke [Tobin, president of the conference from 1964 to 1967] was ahead of her time, that now many members of the conference are thinking with her and want to move, not only here, but in their own orders".

The September 17, 1970, *Southern Cross* of San Diego, California, called the election a clear victory for progressive forces.

An address at the 1970 assembly by Father John Haughey seemed to set the tone for the meeting. Father Haughey, associate editor of *America*, speculated about hypothetical articles he could write based on different interpretations of what he saw at the sisters' assembly. One article would encourage the superiors' conference to dissolve itself since it was created by the Congregation for Religious as "a device for prolonging the kind of directive authority which has become *passé* for all but a few benighted souls—those under you who need a mother, and you who need a father to obey or be in tension with". The sisters, he said, had been ignored by bishops and the Vatican. "To put it bluntly," he told them, "you are being made fools of. Until you declare in no uncertain terms that legislation without representation is intolerable, you are still light years away from 1776." If the superior's conference were to be dissolved by the Vatican, Father Haughey advised, the sisters should "join hands with the Women's Liberation movement". He also said an expected encyclical on religious life "will be sprung on you from its surreptitious lair, indistinct origins, fashioned by unknown architects ... determining for you, what your life as a religious is without benefit of your experience ... [and will] subjugate charism to institution and ... women to men". He asked, "Are you ready for a *Humanae Vitae* of the religious life?" [7]

---

[7] Haughey, "Where Has Our Search Led Us?"

Father Haughey did indeed go on to write articles similar to the ones he described in his talk. In the September 26, 1970, issue of *America* he wrote:

> This year's assembly marked a sharp turning of the corner for CMSW. I have not personally attended anything in the last three years more fraught with significance for the whole American Church. In a word, directive authority is no longer acceptable, unless it comes as a result of having heard out those who are being directed.
>
> There are several indices of the swift change that has come over this conference in the past year. The national board of officers voted in at this session represented some of the most progressive voices heard from the floor in the past couple years; they are youngish and heavy with postgraduate degrees.

Father Haughey also noted that an encyclical on religious life was in the works (which turned out to be not an encyclical, but the apostolic exhortation *Evangelica Testificatio*). He warned that the document "had better reflect something of the understanding of religious life articulated by these 450 major superiors, or there'll be hell to pay".[8]

Father Haughey's remarks at the assembly and his subsequent September 26 article in *America* caused quite a stir among women religious, and several superiors complained to the conference about them.

Sister of Charity Ruth Marion McCullough wrote conference executive director Sister Claudia Zeller, asserting that some sisters did not feel they were represented by the conference described by Father Haughey. She went on to list principles formulated by the sisters of her congregation that she said more accurately defined the attitude of sisters, including: "assent without reservation to the teaching, the spirit, and the directions of the Second Vatican Council for renewal"; "filial and joyful submission to the Holy Father"; and "fidelity and respect for our Bishop as a concrete expression of our vow of obedience". She also wrote that the "role as religious is distinct from that of the laity" and that renewal does not imply "the indiscriminate introduction of lay customs into religious life".

She continued, "We are bewildered by those religious who question the need for vows. . . . We desire in the matter of religious teaching

---

[8] John Haughey, SJ, "CMSW Takes a Sharp New Turn", *America*, September 26, 1970, 208.

to hold fast to the integrity of the Catholic Faith which we receive from Scripture, from Tradition and from the Magisterium.... We believe that personal opinions are not the fundamental teachings of the faith, and we depend upon the hierarchy to be vigilant and decisive when the personal opinions of some theologians threaten to weaken the faithful."[9]

The Statement on American Religious Life

Another controversy surrounding the 1970 assembly was the "Statement on American Religious Life in the Seventies", which became a major cause of division when sisters proposed that the conference endorse it. The statement declared that the Vatican was not sufficiently open to some of the creative styles of religious life that allowed American sisters to govern themselves democratically and to determine their own course of renewal.

The story behind the statement began in 1969. According to a conference memo to the membership, a group of men and women major superiors had been meeting for a year to discuss "the pros and cons of experimentation in small group living". At one of these meetings at the Passionist Retreat House in Warrenton, Missouri, "an atmosphere of real hope and a sense of purpose surfaced among the group in an almost tangible fashion", and the group decided to share their findings. Father Paul Boyle, then president of the Conference of Major Superiors of Men, was contacted, and forty-eight men and women superiors were invited to participate in a seminar in Saint Louis from September 3 to 5, just days before the CMSW had its 1970 assembly. This group of superiors wrote a statement that, the memo reported, "may give American Religious some sign of the 'new life' that is developing in the Church".[10] The statement, appended to the memo, read in part:

> We believe in the primacy of the human person and we affirm that each man or woman has a dignity and freedom that are inviolable....Therefore

[9] Sister Ruth Marion McCullough letter to Sister Mary Claudia Zeller, October 7, 1970, CLCW 158/21, UNDA.

[10] Memo to CMSW Membership with appended Statement, undated, c. September 5, 1970, papers of Sister Rose Eileen Masterman, CSC, in University of Notre Dame Archives (hereafter cited as CMAS), 2/5 UNDA.

we deem it destructive if a religious congregation is required to ask a
brother or sister to depart, or the congregation itself is asked to abandon
its public ecclesial character for the reason that a particular style of life is
deemed, a priori, incompatible with religious life.

. . . It may well happen that the broad ecclesial role of religious communities will necessitate a revision of the priorities of service within
the ecclesiastical institutions of the American Catholic Church. . . .

Mission and apostolate as expressed in the ecclesial life of religious
men and women necessarily require that we increasingly engage in secular occupations as we search out the "pressure points of power" that
control and direct vital areas of human life. . . .

We feel that the Church which terms itself catholic is capable of
assimilating broad developments within religious life. We look for the
opportunity to speak our views to all our fellow Christians, especially
those who are called to positions of prominent service within the Church.
We feel the times are critical and issues are urgent. Because we believe
the Spirit is truly alive within religious life, we must state that American religious must be consulted on any directives that purport to deal
with them. . . . We shall follow the paths that seem most in harmony
with adult Christian living of the Gospel and suitably responsive to
religious living in our age and nation.

Among the fifty religious—and former religious—whose names were
appended to the statement were all three women who were elected to
national office for the superiors' conference in 1970 under the evolving bylaws and wider membership criteria that had not yet been voted
on by the national assembly.[11] A conference press release on the 1970

[11] Several of these individuals supporting the statement were past or future presidents of
the Conference of Major Religious Superiors of Women's Institutes, including Sister Mary
Luke Tobin (1964–1966); Sister Angelita Myerscough (1970); Sister Thomas Aquinas (Elizabeth) Carroll (1971); Sister Margaret Brennan (1972); Sister Frances Borgia Rothluebber
(1973); Franciscan Sister Francine Zeller (1974); and Sister of Charity Helen Flaherty (1982).
Other prominent names were Sister Mary Daniel Turner, a member of the Sisters' Survey
committee and Conference executive director, 1972–1978; Precious Blood Sister Anthonita
Hess, chair of the Conference's East Central Region as well as the Conference's Vocation
Committee; Loretto Sister Helen Sanders, president of the Loretto Sisters, 1970–1978;
Anita Caspary, former president of the Immaculate Heart of Mary Sisters of Los Angeles,
who in early 1970 had led more than three hundred IHM sisters in requesting dispensation
from their vows rather than agree to follow the directives of Rome for renewal; Father
Paul Boyle, president of the Conference of Major Superiors of Men, 1969–1974, a past
president of the Canon Law Society of America (1964–1965) and canonical advisor to
many orders of sisters; Father Francis Gokey of the Society of Saint Edmund, executive

assembly indicated disappointment that the statement had not been approved:

> The smooth surface of consensus and unity was ruffled in the final session of the meeting when a statement relative to the CMSW's role in effecting direct communication between American religious and the SCR [Congregation for Religious] was brought to the floor. The position paper, signed by fifty major superiors of men and women who had met prior to the CMSW assembly, was introduced. After a brief, heated discussion, the statement was tabled indefinitely.
>
> In opposition to the several sisters who supported the statement and asked that the CMSW indicate reaction to its philosophy, a number of members rejected any consideration of the statement on the basis that they had not had sufficient time to study it.
>
> One pro-statement speaker summarized the assembly's reaction as suggesting that to this group "structure is more important than the Spirit".[12]

Some conference members opposing the statement thought it was a thinly disguised attempt to gather support for the group of Los Angeles IHM Sisters who had decided to become laicized rather than follow Vatican mandates on renewal and also for the School Sisters of Saint Francis, who were engaged in a similar struggle with the Vatican over their renewal efforts (see chapter 12). Sister Francis Borgia Rothluebber, one of the signers of the statement, was superior of the School Sisters of Saint Francis and would go on to become president of the women superiors' conference in 1973.

Following the 1970 assembly, Sister of Mercy Eucharia Malone, chair of the conference's western region, wrote a letter to several fellow conference members, telling them she had made the original objection to having the statement voted on at the assembly because there had been insufficient time to discuss it. She suggested a revised statement that would indicate clearly the conference's relationship with the Church. She wrote:

---

secretary of the Superiors of Men; and Brother Gabriel Moran, president of the Long Island / New England province of the Christian Brothers, whose 1970 book, *The New Community*, called for dissolution of religious orders.

[12] CMSW press release, undated, CLCW 16/3, UNDA.

Whatever Statement, if any, issues from CMSW must include a clear statement of our relationship as religious with the Church. Otherwise, I simply cannot be a part of CMSW. This relationship with the Church seems to be the point on which we are divided. I respect sincerely those who hold another view but I do not see how we can constructively work together for the true renewal of religious life if we hold fundamentally different views on one of the essentials of religious life.[13]

Even though the statement had not gathered enough support to pass the conference's September 1970 assembly, promoters did not wish to see it die, and they were in positions influential enough to see that this did not happen. The November 14, 1970, meeting of the liaison committee for the two conferences of superiors of men and women religious took up the topic of the statement. The names of all five of the male representatives at that liaison meeting had been appended to the statement: Father Paul Boyle; Mission Father James Fischer; Capuchin Father Finian Kerwin; Jesuit Father Gerald Sheahan; and Christian Brother Augustine Loes. Five of the seven representatives of the women's conference had their names attached to the statement: Sisters Angelita Myerscough, Margaret Brennan, Thomas Aquinas (Elizabeth) Carroll, Francis Borgia Rothluebber, and Rosalie Murphy.[14]

The minutes from the liaison committee meeting report a motion that the statement be sent to all members of the US Conference of Catholic Bishops (USCCB) as "a formulation of a representative trend in American Religious Life today". That motion failed, but the liaison committee agreed to send the statement anyway to the bishops on the USCCB Liaison Committee with Religious[15] (later named the Commission on Religious Life and Ministry). A cover memo dated November 14, 1970, from the liaison committee of the men's and women's conferences of superiors that was sent to the USCCB Liaison Committee with Religious made clear that the committee members were not acting for all religious or all superiors. But it explained that the committee of superiors had discussed the advisability of sharing

---

[13] Sister M. Eucharia Malone letter to Dear Sister, November 13, 1970, CMAS 2/5, UNDA.

[14] The other two women Religious attending the liaison meeting were Mercy Sister Inviolata Gallagher and Dominican Sister Leo Vincent Short.

[15] Minutes of CMSM/CMSW liaison committee meeting, November 14, 1970, CLCW 6/8, UNDA.

the statement with the bishops to "make known to the Bishops a sample of the thinking of many religious men and women in the United States today". The memo said that "the sentiment of this statement was in part prompted by deep concern that the Congregation for Religious and Secular Institutes is not sufficiently aware of the needs and the strengths of the religious life in the United States and that definite reforms in the constitution and functioning of the Congregation are seriously needed." [16]

The December 1970 issue of *Searching*, the newsletter of the CMSW, confirmed that the statement had been discussed by the liaison committee of the two conferences of superiors, and "after much debate it was decided to share the statement with the bishops who are on the Men and Women's Liaison Committee. The Major Superiors felt that it would give the Bishops a sampling of some of the thinking concerning Religious Life in the United States." [17] So, even though the national assembly refused to endorse the statement, the leaders of the superiors' conferences used the authority of their offices to promote the statement that they personally endorsed.

This action caused considerable confusion for the bishops, too. Bishop James Hogan, chair of the Bishops' Liaison Committee with the superiors' conferences, originally thought that the statement had come from the two conferences. He wrote in a January 20, 1971, report to the bishops: "As a reaction to the statement 'American Religious Life in the Seventies,' formulated by a group of men and women superiors and furnished to us in November. It did not stem from the CMSW or CMSM—as I felt it did. For me, it contains serious flaws that should not go unchallenged." [18]

Even after the 1970 assembly closed, an effort was made within the women's conference to promote the philosophy in the statement and somehow rally the endorsement of the conference. Newly elected conference president Sister Angelita Myerscough informed Bishop Joseph Breitenbeck of the USCCB Liaison Committee that the statement had

---

[16] CMSW / CMSM Liaison Committee letter to members of Bishops' Liaison Committee with CMSW / CMSM, November 14, 1970, CLCW 6/8, UNDA.

[17] *Searching*, newsletter of the CMSW, December 1970, 3, CLCW 1/25, UNDA.

[18] Report from chairman of the Liaison Committee with Religious Women to NCCB Administrative Board, January 20, 1971, 4, papers of the Consortium Perfectae Caritatis in University of Notre Dame Archives (hereafter cited as CCPC), 5/45, UNDA.

been distributed at the conference meeting to make it available to all present. She wrote that some members wanted it to be a statement of the conference, but others feared an effort to railroad it through. "I believe many regions may use it for study and for affirmation, and it may be the basis of some future position of CMSW", Sister Angelita wrote.[19]

Indeed, the conference of women's superiors eventually would go on to embrace many of the ideas contained in the statement, as this chapter reports. But the debate over the statement on the floor of the 1970 assembly was a major factor in the splintering of the conference, for it was after the statement was introduced that several mother superiors got together and decided to form a separate organization of sisters because they thought that the superiors' conference was adopting a flawed vision of religious life. That organization, the Consortium Perfectae Caritatis, is discussed in chapter 7.

The Coup Is Completed

After the 1970 regular assembly, the services of Booz, Allen, and Hamilton were terminated by the national board, apparently in a dispute over how many of the firm's recommendations should actually be incorporated into the new bylaws of the conference. The statutes committee then compiled a draft of the proposed statutes, taken from suggestions of the members, the 1970 annual assembly, and the Booz, Allen, and Hamilton report.

But after the statutes committee presented its recommendation to the board, the committee was dissolved by the new national board in early 1971. The new board took charge of the bylaws and named an ad hoc committee to incorporate its suggestions. Named to that ad hoc committee were the following: Sister of Saint Joseph Joan de Lourdes Leonard, Sister Bernadine Pieper of the Congregation of the Humility of Mary; Sister of Notre Dame Rosalie Murphy; and conference executive director Sister Claudia Zeller.[20] (Both Sisters Bernadine and Rosalie had been signers of the controversial statement prior to the 1970 assembly in Saint Louis.)

[19] Sister Angelita Myerscough letter to Bishop Joseph Breitenbeck, September 20, 1970, CLCW 84/08, UNDA.

[20] CMSW letter to membership, July 21, 1971, CLCW 11/4, UNDA.

The suggestions of the Booz, Allen, and Hamilton team evidently were not widely accepted by the national board in its new version of the bylaws. A January 25, 1971, report of the conference's executive director to the national board noted that "the proposed revision of bylaws and handbook is a complete departure from the tight compartments envisioned by the B.A.H. [Booz, Allen, and Hamilton] Report." [21] The executive director had observed earlier, "I am steadily losing respect for the B.A.H. Report. Its greatest service is that it has brought groups together to share, discuss, and in some cases, dialogue." [22] Indeed, the conference acknowledged later that year that some sisters had complained that Booz, Allen, and Hamilton had received $40,000 to guide revision of the statutes, but "an incredible number of changes have been made in their work".[23]

The national board not only dissolved the statutes committee, but all other standing committees, too. The February 1971 issue of the conference newsletter *Searching* reported that "in the process of reorganization, the CMSW temporarily discontinued its committee structure in order to begin to build up a new organization." [24]

But this action was not well received by all members of the conference, and some members simply didn't understand what was going on. The chairwoman of the defunct statutes committee was so incensed that her committee had been dissolved that she resigned from the conference. Sister of Saint Joseph Alice Anita Murphy, also a member of the dissolved statutes committee, wrote conference president Sister Angelita in July of 1971, pointing out that her committee's version of the bylaws retained their ecclesial character as a pontifical institute, whereas the newly proposed bylaws that had been "chiseled to its present form" by the ad hoc committee did not. She expressed "deep concern" over the evolving "sociological and civil character" of the conference, with power invested in the national board, executive director, credentials committee, and national executive committee. Sister Alice Anita wrote that few busy superiors had time to

[21] Report of the executive director to the national board of CMSW, January 25, 1971, CLCW 2/9, UNDA.

[22] Sister Mary Claudia Zeller letter to Sister Angelita Myerscough, January 2, 1970, CLCW 158/22, UNDA.

[23] CMSW memo to members, June 17, 1971, 7, CLCW 1/27, UNDA.

[24] *Searching*, No. 5, February 1971, 6, CLCW 1/28, UNDA.

figure out what was really happening in the evolving version of the bylaws. She particularly objected to setting a quorum for the national assembly at just one-third of the membership, which would mean that only two-ninths of the members could adopt new bylaws. Sister Alice Anita called for an open discussion of the ad hoc committee's revisions because of the "incredible number of changes" made by that committee.[25]

Other conference members also wrote to express their belief that the new bylaws were unconstitutional because the old statutes were still in effect. Some also pointed out that the juridical existence of the conference depended on approval of the Holy See, and the Holy See would not approve of the conference's removing every vestige of dependence on the Church. Yet this is exactly what happened; the new bylaws constructed by the ad hoc committee defined the conference as more of an independent corporation than an entity created through the authority of the Vatican.

The new bylaws omitted any reference to the conference's connection to the Congregation for Religious, let alone any dependence on, or allegiance to, the Holy See or the hierarchy. Also conspicuously absent was any mention of our Lady, named the conference patroness in the 1962 statutes. The new bylaws declared that the national executive committee, made up of the three officers and two additional members elected by and from the national board, would "provide the on-going leadership of the work of the LCWR between National Board meetings".

The basic objectives of the conference listed in section 3 of the new bylaws included the following:

- To strengthen the leadership service of its members within their congregations and the Church;
- To provide mutual support to one another;
- To develop and further understanding of the essential character and meaning of the existential role of women religious in a constantly evolving world;
- To initiate and strengthen relationships with groups concerned with the needs of contemporary man and to exercise the potential

[25] Mother Alice Anita Murphy letter to Sister Angelita, July 2, 1971, CLCW 10/21, UNDA.

of the conference for effecting constructive attitudinal and structural change.[26]

A June 17, 1971, conference memo to members summarized the content of letters received from members regarding concerns about the changes being implemented in the conference. Some of those concerns included these: "If [the] Statutes of 1962 are not in effect, who has [the] right to invalidate them? Certainly not the CMSW, whose juridical existence depends upon approval of Holy See"; "Putting By-laws into effect before they are approved by the Assembly is invalid"; and "Powers vested in the National Board, Executive Committee, Executive Director, Credentials Committee cause great concern."[27]

Former executive directors Sisters Mary Daniel Turner and Lora Ann Quinonez admitted that reassurances by the conference officers about the sweeping changes "did not totally eliminate tensions within the conference. These tensions remained throughout the process of revision and after its completion."[28]

The 1971 Assembly: The LCWR Is Born

Plans for the 1971 assembly had begun in January with a seminar in Chicago that featured several resource persons, including progressive theologians Father Gregory Baum (who later left the priesthood), Father Richard McBrien from the University of Notre Dame, and Father Henri Nouwen of Holland, discussing the assembly topic "The Church Is for the World".[29] Then each region of the conference was to hold a workshop to discuss the material from the Chicago seminar in order to prepare for the annual assembly.

Fathers Baum, McBrien, and Nouwen also were scheduled to speak at the 1971 assembly. Whether by accident or by design, the choice of speakers for the assembly—as well as the topic itself—discouraged attendance by members who did not accept the change-oriented theology / ecclesiology of the speakers. Sister Eucharia Malone, a conference board

---

[26] Bylaws of the Leadership Conference of Women Religious in the United States, CLCW 11/4, UNDA.

[27] CMSW memo to members, June 17, 1971, 7, CLCW 1/27, UNDA.

[28] Quinonez and Turner, "From CMSW to LCWR: A Story of Birth and Transformation".

[29] Sister Regina Kelly, OP, letter to members of the CMSW, January 26, 1971, 1, CLCW 1/26, UNDA.

member, wrote Sister Angelita Myerscough, conference president, about her concerns regarding the program as well as concerns that too many decisions were being made by the five-member executive committee: "I think the content of the September program has disturbed many Sisters. . . . And I think this program is potential for a break within the CMSW." Sister Eucharia further commented, "I think the Executive Committee is making decisions that should first be discussed at the National Board level. We must give serious consideration to the powers of the Executive Committee, those of the National Board and those areas that belong to the membership as a whole."[30] Sister Claudia Honsberger wrote to Sister Angelita, suggesting that it was time to focus on sisters as religious women in the Church, and she suggested revamping the program to meet the needs of all superiors.[31]

Dominican Sister Mary Dominic wrote to Sister Angelita that after seeing the proposed program, she would not be attending. The treatment of the assembly theme in the preliminary seminar as well as in questions proposed for regional discussions failed to offer a basis for "fruitful searching" in faith, Sister Mary Dominic concluded.[32]

But the program was not changed, so the stage was set for considering controversial new conference bylaws at an assembly that was being boycotted by many of the traditional members, because they could not approve of the program or the speakers. Perhaps it was a tactical error for the sisters who were disturbed by the transformation of the conference to stay away from the 1971 meeting, for it was their last chance to influence the direction of the conference.

Like the 1970 assembly, the 1971 assembly also would have additional voting members present under new credentials criteria that had not yet been approved by the national assembly. In a memo to members of the credentials committee, Immaculate Heart of Mary Sister Ann Virginia Bowling explained that the national board had accepted recommendations for changes in credentials in January, so additional members would be allowed to join under the new credentials.[33] The

[30] Sister M. Eucharia Malone letter to Sister Angelita, April 20, 1971, CLCW 158/22, UNDA.

[31] Sister Claudia Honsberger letter to Sister Angelita, April 5, 1971, CLCW 10/22, UNDA.

[32] Mother Mary Dominic letter to Sister Angelita, March 22, 1971, CLCW 10/22, UNDA.

[33] Sister Ann Virginia Bowling letter to members of the CMSW Credentials Committee, February 2, 1971, CLCW 5/2, UNDA.

more change-oriented communities surely benefited by this amendment in membership requirements, for traditional communities were
holding to the one-superior model of authority urged by the Vatican,
while the more change-oriented communities were moving to a team-
leadership concept. This change made several sisters from one community eligible for conference membership and eligible to vote under
the new rules, enabling the change-oriented sisters to outnumber the
traditional superiors.

But this decision didn't sit well with some members. Sister of Christian Charity Virgina Janson wrote the credentials committee on February 25, 1971, that it was "strange" and "invalid" to be using new
membership criteria that had not yet been approved by the general
membership. And, she noted, "the present criteria leave the field wide
open for some communities and close it to others", because even small
provinces or congregations that were headed by leadership teams had
several voting members at the 1970 annual assembly, while larger congregations, such as her own, that retained the one-superior model had
only one voting member.[34]

In response to Sister Virgina Janson, Sister Ann Virginia Bowling
wrote that there had not been time at the 1970 assembly to complete deliberations on the credentials. Since so many inquiries were
being received about membership, the committee went ahead and
expanded the criteria for membership and accepted new members
"with genuine confidence that the assembly would agree with their
tentative position".[35] The national board also had approved associate
membership—voice without vote—for leaders of noncanonical groups
such as NCAN and NAWR, organizations that are profiled in chapter 14 of this book.

Even the Vatican could not prevail upon the conference's executive
committee—Sisters Angelita Myerscough, Thomas Aquinas (Elizabeth) Carroll, Francis Borgia Rothluebber, Margaret Brennan, and Rosalie Murphy—to change the assembly program. On July 21, 1971, Bishop
Luigi Raimondi, apostolic delegate to the United States, wrote to the
conference president regarding Pope Paul VI's June 29, 1971, apostolic

[34] Mother Virgina Janson letter to Sister Ann Virginia Bowling, February 25, 1971,
CLCW 5/1, UNDA.
[35] Sister Ann Virginia Bowling letter to Mother Virgina Janson, March 3, 1971, CLCW
5/1, UNDA.

exhortation, *Evangelica Testificatio*. In the exhortation, the pope reflected on the strengths and weaknesses of renewal in religious institutes since the close of Vatican II. Bishop Raimondi wrote the sisters that the Congregation for Religious "urges that national conferences of Religious make this pontifical document the object of particular consideration at their forthcoming assemblies in order to effect the practical application of the teachings of the Holy Father to assure authentic renewal in their institutes".[36]

The conference's executive committee, however, did not schedule a general discussion of *Evangelica Testificatio* at the upcoming assembly. Instead, according to their meeting minutes, the committee decided that the apostolic exhortation would be dealt with in panel reports.[37] The executive committee failed not only to add the pope's exhortation to the assembly agenda, but also to let their members know that the Vatican had made such a request.

The bishops who represented the USCCB to the superiors' conference wrote in their report on the conference's 1971 assembly that "since there was scant reference in the assembly to the Apostolic Exhortation to Religious, our Committee injected the message during the liturgy and again at our [liaison committee] meeting."[38]

Just before the 1971 assembly, the superiors' conference national board met on September 4. Minutes of that meeting reveal that the board was very much aware that some members of the conference were questioning the legality of the methods used to expand the membership and implement new bylaws, so the leaders discussed how to handle possible dissent. The minutes reported that "Sister Charitas Marcotte raised the question of the authority of the National Board to approve new CMSW members under criteria not yet accepted by the assembly at large and the possibility of illegal action in the Board's operating under Bylaws which had not received approval of the national assembly. Everyone agreed that the topics should be given serious consideration to avoid delay and possible unpleasantness during the Assembly."

Then Sister Thomas Aquinas (Elizabeth) Carroll read the motion that had been passed at the February 1970 special assembly, which

[36] Bishop Raimondi letter to Sister Angelita, July 21, 1971, CLCW 56/02, UNDA.

[37] Minutes of executive committee meeting, July 21, 1971, CLCW 56/02, UNDA.

[38] Report to the U.S. bishops by the NCCB liaison committee with the CMSW, c. November 17, 1971, CLCW 6/21, UNDA.

directed the task force on credentials to recommend a definition of membership criteria and empowered the national board to act on those recommendations. So the conference officers concluded that they could use the sweeping mandates of the 1970 special assembly as the rationale for their actions. The minutes continue: "Everyone concurred that the acceptance of this motion cleared up any possible misunderstandings regarding the procedure of the National Board and the Credentials Committee." [39]

The board also was concerned that sisters attending the assembly might attempt to discuss a document titled "History of the CMSW" that had been circulated widely to major superiors and members of the hierarchy. The "History" traced what the anonymous sister-writer called a drastic reversal of policy in the conference and radical restructuring of the statutes, thus leading the conference away from reliance on the Holy See. The document also charged that the new bylaws shifted power away from the superiors and invested that power in the conference secretariat.

But the "History" was not brought up at the 1971 assembly, and the officers attempted to defuse further criticism of their actions in their speeches at the assembly. In her presidential address opening the assembly, Sister Angelita explained, "We have with us at this assembly some members who have come in under the credentials which were approved" by the credentials committee and the national board at its January 1971 meeting. She acknowledged that there "has been some question . . . as to the legality of this". But she explained that the 1970 special assembly had authorized the credentials committee to continue its work, and that the executive committee was authorized "to proceed on the basis of those credentials for the registration for the Assembly".[40]

Roberta Kuhn, a Sister of Charity of the Blessed Virgin Mary and a member of the credentials committee, further explained in her report to the assembly that "the membership proposal which had been presented and accepted tentatively at the September meeting last year did not seem to provide adequately for the very rich diversity which is so evident among our membership." Since "broader

[39] Minutes of CMSW national board meeting, September 4, 1971, CLCW 11/1, UNDA.

[40] Angelita Myerscough, ASC, presidential address in Official Minutes of Business Meeting No. 3, September 6, 1971, CLCW 11/1, UNDA.

guidelines were imperative", she said that the credentials committee made proposals to the executive committee, which then incorporated those broader guidelines into the proposed bylaws.[41]

Then Sister Angelita explained away the bylaws crisis by assuring the members that they didn't really have any rights anyway, for all the power of the organization was at the national level: "Strictly, legally as of yet, according to the 1962 statutes, it is only the National Committee, the National Board which has any kind of authority in the conference and until we get those Bylaws voted in by which the Assembly does have authority, this assembly really doesn't have it."[42] So, even though the national board had been operating for over a year under the proposed new bylaws for important matters such as elections and membership, the board invoked a convoluted explanation of the 1962 statutes as justification for its action.

The 1971 assembly went on to ratify the bylaws, though there is some question about the numbers voting. Adoption of the bylaws required approval by a two-thirds vote of those present, which would have been 400 in favor, if a CMSW press release claiming 600 members in attendance was correct.[43] The vote reported was 356 in favor, 39 opposed, 2 abstaining.[44] There is no explanation as to where the other 203 members supposedly in attendance were during that vote. And there is no breakdown as to how many of the members voting at the assembly were new members brought in under the broad new membership criteria accepted by the executive committee and implemented before the assembly.

Sister Mary Elise Krantz, a conference member who objected to the direction being taken by the conference, wrote the Congregation for Religious after the assembly, pointing out that of the 710 total members of the conference, 520 were in attendance at the 1971 assembly. Of those 520, she claimed that 220 were new members.[45]

[41] Credentials Committee report in Official Minutes of Business Meeting No. 3, September 8, 1971, CLCW 38/20, UNDA.

[42] Myerscough, ASC, presidential address.

[43] Undated CMSW press release reporting on 1971 national assembly that ended September 11, 1971, CLCW 11/1, UNDA.

[44] Official Minutes of Concluding Business meeting, September 11, 1971, CLCW 38/20, UNDA.

[45] Sister Mary Elise Krantz letter to Cardinal Antoniutti, September 19, 1971, CCPC 5/23, UNDA.

Sister Mary Elise was head of a coalition of major superiors and other sisters who believed that the conference was straying too far from the authority of the Church and the renewal intended by Vatican II. Calling themselves the Consortium Perfectae Caritatis, after the Council document on religious life, *Perfectae Caritatis*, the group already had been in touch with the Vatican about their concerns. Jesuit Father John Hardon, a theologian who had often consulted for the Consortium, tried to convince the sisters—and others unhappy with the direction the conference was taking—to confront the leadership at the 1971 assembly. Sister Mary Elise told the author, however, that the Congregation for Religious advised the Consortium sisters not to have a public confrontation with conference leaders at that time. Apparently the Congregation for Religious and the traditional sisters thought it would be too unseemly for sisters to be airing their differences in public, but this reticence simply made it easier for the progressives to push through their agenda.

Some moderate members of the conference did try to insert into the bylaws more references and connections to the Congregation for Religious and the authority of the pope, but these motions were defeated. A last-minute amendment passed 186 to 165, with five abstentions, changing the name of the organization to the Leadership Conference of Women Religious.[46] (The parliamentarian ruled that since the name of the organization was a minor matter, only a simple majority vote was required rather than the two-thirds vote required to ratify the bylaws.)

This new name had been suggested at the July 21, 1971, meeting of the conference executive committee, consisting of Sisters Angelita Myerscough, Thomas Aquinas (Elizabeth) Carroll, Francis Borgia Rothluebber, Margaret Brennan, and Rosalie Murphy. Sister Ann Virginia Bowling, conference executive director at the time, told the authors of *The Transformation of American Catholic Sisters* that "the whole emphasis was to share power and part of the sharing of power was to get rid of the title 'major superiors'."[47] Sisters Mary Daniel Turner and Lora Ann Quinonez, subsequent executive directors, noted that the former name "communicated a negative image to the public: its militaristic

---

[46] Official Minutes of Business Meeting No. 5, September 10, 1971, CLCW 11/1, UNDA.
[47] Quinonez and Turner, *Transformation*, 77.

and hierarchic connotations needed dispelling".[48] Whatever one's opinion of the titles, the new name of the organization was a much more
accurate reflection of the new makeup of the organization, for under
the new membership criteria, many members of the conference clearly
were not major superiors, but rather were members of "leadership
teams".

The Congregation for Religious, however, withheld approval of the
name for about three years. Sister of Notre Dame de Namur Mary
Linscott, a canon lawyer who was a staff member of the Congregation
for Religious for several years, explained that the congregation was
reluctant to approve the name change because there was more involved
than simple terminology. First of all, the national conferences were
supposed to be made up of only major superiors. Secondly, the term
leader has implications in other languages that it does not have in English
(e.g., *leader* being *führer* in German and *duce* in Italian). Sister Mary
explained:

> For the congregation [for Religious], "major superiors" and "leader-
> ship" were not synonymous terms; the use of the one for the other
> could create confusion and even lead to changes of a more substantial
> kind, notwithstanding the likelihood that the sisters intended the words
> to denote the same reality.... SCRIS [Congregation for Religious] felt
> that the substitution of "leadership" for "major superiors" could raise
> problems in an area where clarity was needed. Permission for the change
> came only after long reflection and on condition that the interpretation
> of the name was in accord with the provisions and intention of the
> Second Vatican Council.[49]

Indeed, the Congregation for Religious as well as the USCCB continued to refer to the conference by its original name in official documents until the change was finally approved in 1974. Even then, the
Vatican approved the new name only on the condition that it be followed by this sentence: "This title is to be interpreted as: the Conference of Leaders of Congregations of Women Religious of the United

---

[48] Quinonez and Turner, "From CMSW to LCWR: A Story of Birth and Transformation", 207.

[49] Mary Linscott, SNDdeN, "Leadership, Authority, and Religious Government", *Review
for Religious* (March / April 1993): 166–167.

States of America." [50] However, the LCWR did not abide by that requirement.

The Congregation for Religious also insisted on some changes in the new bylaws, including acknowledgment of the authority of the bishops and the Holy See, the relationship of the conference to the Congregation for Religious, and the conference's responsibility to the apostolic delegate. [51] However, the conference executive committee did not tell its membership that there were any problems with the Vatican about the new bylaws. President Sister Thomas Aquinas (Elizabeth) Carroll wrote members on April 24, 1972, "Up until this time we have not mentioned to you the fact that after Sister Margaret Brennan [conference vice president] and I presented our Bylaws of the LCWR to Archbishop Mayer and Cardinal Antoniutti [in October of 1971], we had received some negative criticism [from the Congregation for Religious]." Sister Thomas Aquinas wrote that the executive committee had been engaged in correspondence with the Congregation for Religious about several disputed points, including the name change and the fact that the bylaws must be approved by the Holy See before being put into effect. She also wrote that the committee had met twice with the apostolic delegate and continued to communicate by mail. "You may feel that the whole membership should have known of all these proceedings. Really, there were points so delicate that I felt knowledge of the proceedings by only a few would accomplish more", Sister Thomas Aquinas concluded. [52]

Sister Claudia Honsberger, chairwoman of the conference's Region III, fired a letter back to Sister Thomas Aquinas, saying that her region had met on May 16 and discussed the Congregation for Religious' points of concern. Sister Claudia wrote that it was the unanimous decision of Region III that "all future cases, documents or recommendations from the Sacred Congregation should be communicated to the entire membership." [53]

[50] Quinonez and Turner, *Transformation*, 28.
[51] Quinonez and Turner, "From CMSW to LCWR: A Story of Birth and Transformation". 207.
[52] Sister Thomas Aquinas letter to LCWR members, April 24, 1972, CMAS 2/10, UNDA.
[53] Sister Claudia Honsberger letter to Sister Thomas Aquinas, May 18, 1972, CMAS 2/10, UNDA

Many other LCWR members were also unhappy with the actions of the conference's executive committee. Sister Alice Anita Murphy wrote to conference president Sister Thomas Aquinas, saying that she had misused her office by not informing the membership about the Congregation for Religious' concerns. "The imposition of authoritative procedures imposed on us by this thinking is far in excess of any ever directed by [the Congregation for Religious]", she wrote. Sister Alice Anita also complained that before voting by the assembly, there had been no open discussion of changes made to the proposed bylaws by the ad hoc committee, and she questioned how the conference could proceed to put into use new bylaws that had not yet been approved by the Congregation for Religious.[54]

Sister Thomas Aquinas responded that since it had taken the Vatican years to confirm the rules of religious congregations in the past, the conference's national board decided to go ahead and implement the new bylaws at the same time they were presented to the Vatican. Sister Thomas Aquinas tried to justify this action by claiming that this was a common practice by the bishops' conference whenever it wanted something done by any of the congregations at the Vatican or by the pope.[55]

And so the CMSW had transformed itself into the LCWR, and the Vatican was simply informed after the fact that this metamorphosis had taken place. Some US bishops suggested at the November 1971 meeting of their conference that since the women superiors' group had dissolved itself, the bishops should not continue supporting their liaison committee with a group that was defunct. Bishop Floyd Begin asked whether "the mandate of liaison continued, since the Sisters' group to which the committee was accredited no longer exists, but has changed its name, nature, membership and constitution". And Archbishop Paul Leibold said he didn't see how "the liaison committee could have any relationship with a group that no longer exists".[56] But other bishops argued that they should follow the Vatican's lead in reacting to the new conference.

For their part, Vatican officials apparently fell into the trap of prolonged "dialogue" until a few minor compromises were made, and

[54] Sister Alice Anita letter to Sister Thomas Aquinas, May 12, 1972, CMAS 2/11, UNDA.
[55] Sister Thomas Aquinas letter to Sister Alice Anita, May 20, 1972, CMAS 2/11, UNDA.
[56] Minutes of Evening Briefing, November 18, 1971, appended to Report of [NCCB] CMSW Liaison Committee, c. November 14–18, 1971, CLCW 6/21, UNDA.

eventually Congregation for Religious officials realized they could not put the toothpaste back into the tube, as one superior had observed.

Thus, by means of a political coup, activist sisters succeeded in creating a hybridized double identity for the LCWR: one, as the Vatican-approved official conference of major superiors; and the other, as an independent body of leaders of women religious—many of whom were not major superiors—who were determined to decide their own membership, activities, and goals. Surely this success in confrontation with the Vatican energized the change-oriented sisters to proceed with their plans to guide renewal of religious life according to the "Statement on American Religious Life in the Seventies", which had been rejected by the superiors' conference in 1970, but unwittingly affirmed in 1971 with approval of the new bylaws. This trajectory chosen by the leaders of the superiors' conference in 1971 would continue into the twenty-first century.

6

Evolution and Transformation of the Superiors' Conference

Certain actions labeled dissent, disloyalty, disobedience, by one group will be seen as dialogic, faithful, and responsible by the other.[1]

—Sister Lora Ann Quinonez, CDP, LCWR Executive Director

In the years since the LCWR transformed itself in 1971, the organization's philosophy has alternated between ignoring directives from the Vatican, challenging Church authorities in an effort to promote its own agenda, and "dialoguing" endlessly in an effort to delay or deflect corrective action by the Holy See. The result has been a widening chasm between activist sisters who believe it is their destiny to challenge "patriarchal" Church authority and traditional sisters who accept the authority of the hierarchy and the teachings of the Church on religious life. Many of the traditional orders of sisters have withdrawn from membership in the LCWR, and many sisters in orders whose leaders belong to LCWR do not approve of the group's agenda.

The Vatican eventually gave its approval in 1992 to another superiors' conference of women, the Council of Major Superiors of Women Religious (CMSWR), as detailed in the next chapter. This move by the Vatican to recognize an alternate superiors' conference was unprecedented and signaled that the Vatican wanted to encourage women

[1] LCWR memo to members from Sister Lora Ann Quinonez, executive director, December 28, 1979: Report of November 5, 1979, meeting with the Congregation for Religious, CMAS 3/31, UNDA.

religious who espouse loyalty to the Church. It may also have indicated that Vatican authorities had grown weary of dealing with an organization of women who continually ignore or challenge the authority of the Church.

The LCWR is made up of approximately fifteen hundred (as of 2012) sisters who hold leadership positions in their communities. Although the LCWR often claims to speak for all sisters in the United States, in reality the conference is empowered to speak only for its membership. The other thousands of sisters have no input into conference policies and no vote for conference officers.

The LCWR's claim that it speaks for all sisters has resulted in confusion and resentment on the part of non-member sisters who disagree with its actions or those sisters who belong to the group but who are not consulted about some of the organization's more controversial positions and activities. Some controversies have arisen because of actions or decisions of the group's board or one of the group's officers or committees, often resulting in the public perception that these leaders had the approval of the membership, when this was not necessarily the case.

Conference executive directors Sisters Mary Daniel Turner (1972–78) and Lora Ann Quinonez (1978–86) observed that generally the membership of the LCWR was ambivalent about feminism and tended to be more interested in religious life and social-justice issues. And some members regularly cautioned the conference about promoting women's issues. Yet the former executive directors noted that the conference leadership had a far stronger "commitment to name and battle sexism wherever it occurred".[2] Some of the controversies generated by the LCWR actually involved the conference as a whole, while others reflected on the conference, but really were never sanctioned by the membership.

Thus, the road from 1971 to 2012 was a stormy path for the LCWR, within the conference itself, as well as regarding interactions with the Vatican. A brief summary of some conference activities between 1971 and 2012 presented in this chapter demonstrates a certain pattern of behavior over those forty-plus years. It also provides a few examples of those controversies, many of them centered on the women's liberation theme as well as liberation from the teaching authority of the

---

[2] Quinonez and Turner, *Transformation*, 101–2.

Church. Additionally, highlights of LCWR assemblies illustrate why the CDF noted in its 2012 doctrinal assessment that "addresses given during LCWR annual Assemblies manifest problematic statements and serious theological, even doctrinal errors."

Liberation Themes Predominate

In 1972, Sister Francis Borgia Rothluebber was chosen vice president (and thus president-elect for 1973) of the LCWR. Sister Rothluebber had been engaged in an ongoing dispute with the Vatican over renewal changes in her order, so her election was widely read as a message to the Vatican that American sisters stood in solidarity behind her. At the 1972 conference assembly, canon lawyer Clara Henning (the first woman to receive a canon law degree from the Catholic University of America) proposed a single sisterhood of all Catholic women to struggle for women's liberation, in a talk subtitled "Religious Communities as Providential Gift for the Liberation of Women". She also suggested bringing class-action suits against the Church in both civil and ecclesiastical courts and staging an economic boycott against parish churches.[3]

Archbishop Helder Camara of Brazil, an outspoken proponent of liberation theology, addressed the 1973 annual assembly. His address, as well as the presentations of outgoing conference president Sister Margaret Brennan and incoming president Sister Rothluebber, was based on liberation themes.[4]

In the mid-1970s, the conference's Ecclesial Role of Women Committee produced a monograph on the Equal Rights Amendment and the ordination of women, as well as a "consciousness-raising" kit, *Focus on Women*, which was a "collection of booklets for group reflections on sex-role stereotyping, symbol and myth as vehicles of sexism, women and God, and the economic status of women".[5]

In 1974, the conference published *Widening the Dialogue*, a critique of Pope Paul VI's *Evangelica Testificatio*. According to former conference executive directors Sisters Mary Daniel Turner and Lora Ann

---

[3] *National Catholic Reporter*, September 29, 1972.

[4] Gene Burns, *The Frontiers of Catholicism: The Politics of Ideology in a Liberal World* (Berkeley and Los Angeles: University of California Press, 1992), 261.

[5] Quinonez and Turner, *Transformation*, 99.

Quinonez, the tenor of the book was that *Evangelica Testificatio* was just the first word in what should be an ongoing dialogue about religious life rather than an authoritative Church statement about the issues.[6] Also in 1974, a resolution approved by the conference's annual assembly stated that "all ministries in the church be open to women", which was understood to mean ordination of women as priests, according to the *National Catholic Reporter*.[7]

When the first Women's Ordination Conference was being organized in 1975, LCWR president Sister Francine Zeller appointed Dominican Sister Nadine Foley, who was a member of the LCWR Ecclesial Role of Women Committee, as a liaison person to the group organizing the ordination group. The LCWR subsequently received a letter from the Congregation for Religious, directing the conference to dissociate itself from the Women's Ordination Conference. Then–executive director Sister Mary Daniel Turner wrote later that Sister Francine took the issue up with the LCWR executive committee and with their support refused to dissociate from the women's ordination group.[8] In fact, Sister Nadine went on to become coordinator of the organizing task force for the ordination conference. Also during the 1970s, the national board of the conference voted to join the National Organization for Women boycott of convention sites in states that had not ratified the Equal Rights Amendment.[9]

A Contemporary Theology Project launched in 1976 resulted in some controversial conference publications that carried a heavy women's liberation theme, emphasized individualism, and attempted to justify some of the renewal efforts that had been questioned by the Vatican. The first publication, *Steps in the Journey* (1979), offered a history of the project and contained data gathered at various workshops and gatherings on topics such as authority and obedience, social justice, and mutuality and culture. *Starting Points: Six Essays Based on the Experience of U.S. Women Religious*, published in 1980, carried essays reflecting on the "lived experience" of women religious since 1965. The introduction to *Starting Points* explained that "women religious are increasingly willing to trust their experience as a locus of

[6] Ibid., 57.
[7] *National Catholic Reporter*, September 13, 1974.
[8] Quinonez and Turner, *Transformation*, 100.
[9] Ibid., 101.

God's revelation and, therefore, as a valid base for making judgments and choices." [10]

Claiming Our Truth, published in 1988, the third publication of the Contemporary Theology Project, was a collection of papers discussing the questions: "What is the world?", "Who do we say God is?", and "Who do we say we are?" Included in this book were the essays "Women's Center: Incarnational Spirituality", "A World Church and Christian Feminism", and "What's at Stake: Women Religious Naming Ourselves Women". Sister Nadine Foley, editor, observed in the introduction that for women religious, "there is an evident convergence around their sense of identity, particularly their claiming themselves as women and grappling with God images and symbols to fit their emerging self-awareness." [11] Sisters Mary Daniel Turner and Lora Ann Quinonez noted that in the two latter publications, the sisters were reluctant to suggest that there was only one valid theology of religious life. [12]

Disagreements with Church Authorities

In 1977, the LCWR drew a rebuke from the USCCB Committee for Pro-Life Activities. The LCWR had published a booklet entitled *Choose Life* in response to the bishops' Pastoral Plan for Pro-Life Activities. Monsignor James McHugh, director of the bishops' pro-life committee, sent a letter to all the bishops, warning them that the booklet was "ambiguous in regard to the moral prohibition of abortion" and too preoccupied with broadening the context of concern for the quality of life. He further charged that the booklet's public-policy position on abortion was counterproductive to the policies of the bishops. [13]

Sister Mary Daniel Turner, LCWR executive director, then wrote all members, directing them to ask their bishops for "precise concerns" about the *Choose Life* document, and she provided them with material to give to the local media if the press had carried the National Catholic News Service story about Monsignor McHugh's objections.

---

[10] Quinonez, *Starting Points*, ii.
[11] Nadine Foley, OP, ed., *Claiming Our Truth* (Washington: LCWR, 1988), 2.
[12] Quinonez and Turner, *Transformation*, 60.
[13] Msgr. James McHugh letter to bishops, *Origins*, November 3, 1977, 315–17.

The documentation accompanying Sister Mary Daniel's letter suggested, "There is evidence that McHugh's analysis and critique violates principles of logic ... employs accusatory language ... adopts subjective and argumentative style and denies the obvious." [14]

At the 1977 annual assembly, conference president Sister Joan Chittister tried to justify the movement of sisters from their traditional apostolates into individual ministries, explaining: "The old vision of religious life says that the purpose of religious life is to be a labor force to do institutional work. There is a new vision rising that says the purpose of religious life is to be a leaven in society." [15]

In 1979, the conference came under heavy criticism from many fronts because of the actions of its president, Mercy Sister Theresa Kane. As conference president, she had been selected to represent women religious when Pope John Paul II visited the United States. Sister Theresa was to greet the pope when he spoke to five thousand nuns gathered at the National Shrine of the Immaculate Conception in Washington, DC, on October 7. However, in the context of her greeting, Sister Theresa also plugged women's ordination when she said, in part, "The church in its struggle to be faithful to its call for reverence and dignity for all persons must respond by providing the possibility of women as persons being included in all ministries of the church." [16]

Sister Theresa's remarks were considered by many to be in particularly poor taste since the pope had just days before reiterated the Church's official position that ordination was reserved to men only, and the CDF had reconfirmed that teaching in 1976 with the document *Inter Insigniores* (*On the Question of Admission of Women to the Ministerial Priesthood*). Many sisters thought that as LCWR president and representative of all American sisters at the papal event, Sister Theresa should have kept her personal opinions to herself. One sister wrote in the *National Catholic Reporter*'s letters section that the LCWR president "did not have the right to make the impression that she spoke for the majority of sisters in the United States. As representing the LCWR, neither did she have the right to voice her personal views." [17]

[14] Sister Mary Daniel Turner letter to LCWR members, with enclosed documentation, November 11, 1977, CMAS 2/21, UNDA.

[15] *National Catholic Register*, September 25, 1977.

[16] *National Catholic Reporter*, October 19, 1979.

[17] *National Catholic Reporter*, November 9, 1979.

In four months, the conference office received five thousand letters reflecting a variety of opinions about the president's action.

Sister Theresa subsequently wrote all conference members, confirming that the officers were "conscious that directions taken by LCWR might be a cause of discomfort for some of our members", and she asked those who were considering terminating their memberships to "dialogue" with board members, officers, or the executive director before making a decision about leaving the conference.[18]

One month after Sister Theresa's "greeting" of the pope, LCWR leaders attended a regularly scheduled meeting at the Congregation for Religious, a meeting that apparently was quite strained, according to a memo to members by executive director Sister Lora Ann Quinonez. The memo stated that there were "clear differences of understanding and belief between the LCWR representatives and several SCRIS [Congregation for Religious] members". It cited areas of disagreement, including the very nature of the Church, authority and obedience: "There is no question that we are coming from diametrically different concepts ... certain actions labeled dissent, disloyalty, disobedience, by one group will be seen as dialogic, faithful, and responsible by the other."[19]

Continuing Clashes with the Vatican

In 1982, the LCWR held a joint annual assembly with the Conference of Major Superiors of Men. For the assembly's liturgy, five sisters had been asked to be extraordinary eucharistic ministers, but the celebrant, Archbishop Pio Laghi, apostolic delegate, would not allow the sisters to distribute Communion since there were plenty of priests available.[20] His decision was fully consistent with Church regulations on extraordinary eucharistic ministers, but apparently the assigned sisters were not informed until they went forward to get the chalices and were turned away. The episode was interpreted as clerical insensitivity

[18] Sister Theresa Kane letter to LCWR members, February 18, 1980, CLCW 36/24, UNDA.

[19] LCWR memo to members from Sister Lora Ann Quinonez, executive director, December 28, 1979: Report of November 5, 1979, meeting with the Congregation for Religious. CMAS 3/31, UNDA.

[20] National Catholic Reporter, August 27, 1982.

toward women. Sister Mary Daniel Turner described the incident as "a massive psychological jolt to the membership" that caused reactions "ranging from deep anger and pain to bewilderment, fear, denial, and a sense of urgency that action be taken in response. That experience brought home publicly the exclusion of women from realities which are deeply formative in our lives, and ... brought us face to face with our great vulnerabilities."[21]

At the 1984 LCWR annual assembly, the conference agreed to create panels of canon lawyers, theologians, and administrators to help sisters "experiencing difficulties with ecclesiastical authorities". In addition to the LCWR, other religious had also come under Vatican scrutiny. For example, Mercy Sister Agnes Mary Mansour recently had been required to choose between her religious life and her professional life as a Michigan state official who oversaw government funding of abortion, and she chose her job. Additionally, the work of the Quinn Commission to examine religious life in the United States (detailed in chapter 13) was in full swing, and just a few days before the assembly convened, the Vatican had intervened in a matter involving the leadership of the European province of the School Sisters of Saint Francis. Regarding the creation of the panels of canon lawyers, newly elected president Margaret Cafferty, a Sister of the Presentation of the Blessed Virgin Mary, explained: "We live in a time now of dialogue and clarification about how United States sisters live out the life-style and commitments we believe the spirit calls us to. While other segments of the world church may question what they see, we claim the validity of our lived experience, and offer our critics a record of fidelity."[22]

In 1985, the conference invited Mercy Sister Margaret Farley to be a featured speaker at its annual assembly. Sister Margaret was one of the religious who had signed the *New York Times* 1984 statement that claimed there was more than one legitimate Catholic position on abortion (treated in chapter 14). She had not yet resolved her position with the Vatican, and the US bishops and the Vatican asked the conference to withdraw its invitation to Sister Margaret; but the LCWR officers refused to do so. Consequently, Archbishops John Quinn and

---

[21] Turner, cited by Margaret Cafferty, PBVM, LCWR *1986 Conference Report*, 10.
[22] *National Catholic Reporter*, September 7, 1984.

Pio Laghi, apostolic delegate, who had been scheduled to speak at the assembly, canceled their appearances at the meeting. (On June 4, 2012, the CDF, with the approval of Pope Benedict XVI, issued a notification on Sister Margaret's 2006 book *Just Love*. The CDF notification said that the book "is not in conformity with the teaching of the church" and "cannot be used as a valid expression of Catholic teaching, either in counseling and formation, or in ecumenical and inter-religious dialogue".[23])

Transforming Religious Life and Redefining "Violence"

At the 1989 LCWR joint assembly with the Conference of Major Superiors of Men, several "Transformative Elements for Religious Life in the Future" were developed. These ten elements then were published in a brochure and discussed by various regions of the conference over the next few years. In 1995, the brochure on transformative elements was reprinted and continued to be circulated.[24] The brochure explained that five of the elements had not received wide "affirmation" of the religious attending the 1989 assembly, but the conference leadership nevertheless promoted all ten and did so for years thereafter. (The LCWR 2010–2011 Annual Report listed the elements as one of the topics continuing to be discussed by the national board.) The brochure also explained that "over the intervening years, the conferences' various regions and religious institutes have found reflection and work on these elements helpful in their endeavors to move religious life into the future." Among the more startling concepts in the pamphlet was number 8, which articulates a unique new definition of religious life:

> In 2010 religious communities will be characterized by inclusivity and intentionality. These communities may include persons of different ages, genders, cultures, races and sexual orientation. They may include persons who are lay or cleric, married or single, as well as vowed and / or unvowed members. They will have a core group and persons with temporary and permanent commitments.

[23] Nancy Frazier O'Brien. "Vatican Warns Against Errors in Mercy Nun's 2006 Book on Sexual Ethics", Catholic News Service, June 4, 2012.

[24] The author received one of these brochures as part of a press kit for one of the LCWR assemblies.

These communities will be ecumenical, possibly interfaith; faith sharing will be constitutive of the quality of life in this context of expanded membership. Such inclusivity will necessitate a new understanding of membership and a language to accompany it.

Religious life still includes religious congregations of permanently vowed members.

Virtually every modern study of religious life has concluded that this "vision" of religious communities is so inclusive that it would lead to conditions that have no boundaries, and thus neutralize the impact of religious orders and cause them to lose their identity as a group.[25] However, the leaders of the LCWR have persisted in "birthing" new forms of religious life and directing their energies toward the liberation of women and the oppressed rather than toward adherence to the things that are central to the very meaning of religious life, such as prayer and fidelity to the Church.

Among the six goals and objectives the LCWR designated for the years 1989 through 1994 were "to develop structures of solidarity with women in order to work for the liberation of women through the transformation of social and ecclesial structures and relationships" and "to effect action for justice leading to systemic change locally and globally in order to bring about harmony among people in communion with the earth".[26]

On February 8, 1993, the LCWR national board issued the statement "Concerning the Rights of Gay and Lesbian Persons", which charged that "recent Church documents invoke religious principles to justify discrimination against homosexual persons." This statement no doubt was referring to a 1992 background paper from the CDF intended for bishops but leaked to the press and misinterpreted. Also ongoing at the time was a Vatican-commissioned evaluation of the public statements and activities of Salvatorian Father Robert Nugent and School Sister of Notre Dame Jeannine Gramick, cofounders of New Ways Ministry, an outreach to homosexual persons that had been banned in some dioceses because of its flawed moral theology.

In her presentation at the 1993 LCWR national assembly on August 16, Sister of Charity Mary Ann Donovan told the sisters: "Women

---

[25] See the work of Wittberg, Ebaugh, Finke, Starke, Nygren, and Ukeritis.
[26] LCWR *1989 Conference Report*, "Goals and Objectives 1989–94", 11.

find their efforts to live the varying forms of religious life complicated both by the view of women proper to a given society and by the conservative nature of ecclesiastical law and custom." [27] At that same meeting, Sister of Mercy Janet Ruffing critiqued current studies on religious life—including the comprehensive FORUS study—and observed:

> The constraints imposed by church and society upon women regarding ministries, leadership, and relationship to the world are essentially sexist. Apostolic life for women has never meant the same autonomy, freedom, flexibility, or acceptance as it has for monastic, mendicant, or apostolic men; nor does it yet.
>
> As long as the church refuses to resolve the question of women's full participation in leadership in the church, I do not think we will be able to separate the distinctiveness of apostolic religious life for women from ordained ministry. I think a significant but probably small percentage of our members have always been called to ordained ministry. [28]

On May 22, 1994, Pope John Paul II issued his apostolic letter *Ordinatio Sacerdotalis*, in which he confirmed that the Church's teaching that priestly ordination is reserved to men alone is part of the deposit of faith. At the August annual assembly that year, LCWR members decided to embark on a "Benchmarks" project "to evaluate the efforts of the church to make leadership roles more available to women".

In 1995, the LCWR women's liberation theme was extended another five years: "We will work for the liberation of all oppressed people, especially women, through the transformation of social, economic, and ecclesial structures and relationships." [29] Two months later, on October 28, the Congregation for the Doctrine of the Faith issued *Responsum ad Dubium*, which reaffirmed that the teaching in *Ordinatio Sacerdotalis* is to be held as part of the deposit of faith.

The results of the "Benchmarks" study were published by LCWR in 1996 in *Creating a Home: Benchmarks for Church Leadership Roles for Women*. In the introduction, LCWR executive director Sister

[27] Mary Ann Donovan, SC, "A Historical Perspective on Women's Religious Life", talk to LCWR 1993 assembly.

[28] Janet Ruffing, RSM, "Enkindling the Embers: The Challenge of Current Research on Religious Life", at LCWR 1993 assembly.

[29] LCWR *Update* (October 1995).

Margaret Cafferty noted that the two recent documents reserving ordination to men had affirmed the dignity of women, condemned discrimination against women, and called for women's full inclusion in the life of the Church. But, she noted, "against the backdrop of such teaching stands the experience of women that the practice of the church falls short of her pronouncements. . . . Women find that the doors to many offices and ministries, particularly those invested with authority, remain barred. . . . The growing gap between pronouncement and practice alienates many women and threatens the credibility of the church." [30]

The theme for the 1996 LCWR annual assembly in Atlanta was nonviolence, reflecting the conference's continuing priority of placing sociopolitical issues ahead of spiritual issues or the very pressing structural issues confronting institutes of women religious. In planning for the assembly, the conference office revealed an expanded definition of violence when it announced that "current and former LCWR members will reflect on their leadership during a time when their institute or its members were victims of violence. The four panelists will reflect on physical violence suffered by members as well as the violence that results from conflicts with ecclesiastical authorities, social institutions, and the media." [31]

Workshops in 1996 covered issues such as the global relationships in the platform from the 1995 Beijing women's conference, relationships with the media, relationships affected by gender and sexual orientation, and relationships with the earth.

The LCWR Reacts to the Gramick-Nugent Notification

On May 31, 1999, Pope John Paul II approved a notification of penalties for Sister Jeannine Gramick and Father Robert Nugent, who had founded and directed New Ways Ministry, an outreach to homosexual persons. After complaints about their work, the Holy See had established a commission in 1988 to evaluate their statements and activities to determine whether they were faithful to the Church's teachings on homosexuality. The commission found serious deficiencies in

[30] Cafferty in *Creating a Home: Benchmarks for Church Leadership Roles for Women*, ed. Jeanean D. Merkel (Silver Spring, Maryland: Leadership Conference of Women Religious, 1996), 3.
[31] LCWR *Update* (December 1995).

their writings and pastoral activities. The CDF engaged in exchanges with the two religious and their superiors over a two-year period and asked Sister Jeannine and Father Nugent to formulate a public declaration expressing their interior assent to Church teaching on homosexuality. When their response was not sufficient, the CDF permanently prohibited them from any pastoral work with homosexuals. Father Nugent accepted the discipline, but Sister Jeannine refused, saying she felt called by God to ministry with homosexuals.

A July 14 press release from the LCWR said the conference was "deeply saddened" by the notification and added, "We believe that the CDF decision adds to the anguish that many of our sisters experience who minister to those at the margins of our Church and society."

The Gramick-Nugent case thus became a major issue discussed at the LCWR August 1999 assembly. A September 8 letter from the LCWR presidency (a triumvirate of past president, current president, and president-elect) to members explained:

> We also faced the violence many have experienced in the wake of the recent notification by the Congregation for the Doctrine of the Faith regarding the ministry of Jeannine Gramick, SSND, and Robert Nugent, SDS. Acknowledging the pain and misunderstanding caused by this action, the Assembly discussed how this situation cannot be seen in isolation but as an instance of how ecclesiastical authority—when exercised in certain ways—causes suffering and division among many within the U.S. church community. There was a call not to be silent but to engage our brother bishops in conversations regarding this concern. By a near unanimous vote, LCWR members voted to adopt the following special resolution: "After research and reflection, the LCWR presidency and members will initiate conversations with official leaders at all levels of the Roman Catholic Church to address a pattern in the exercise of ecclesiastical authority experienced as a source of suffering and division by many within the Catholic community." The Assembly also adopted a public statement to the homosexual community, their parents and relatives which affirms that the "Church is their home, a place where all are welcome, a place where respect, understanding, compassion and love are the rightful expectations of every person." [32]

[32] A copy of the letter was provided to the author by a sister of an LCWR-affiliated order.

The LCWR leadership then laid out a one-year plan to engage the bishops and the Vatican on the Gramick-Nugent issue. In the January 2000 LCWR newsletter, *Update*, LCWR president Immaculate Heart of Mary Sister Nancy Sylvester said the conference was entering into "conversation with church officials regarding instances where the use of authority has caused suffering to many with the church community". And she was quite direct in noting: "As we attempt to raise up the broader issues of concern, we experience the differing ecclesiologies that are operative."

The LCWR *Conference Report 2000* included a page by past president, Sister of Mercy Camille D'Arienzo, recounting the LCWR presidency's annual visit to the Vatican in May of 2000, when the sisters discussed the Gramick-Nugent matter with the Congregation for Religious:

> As we raised our concerns regarding the implications of the Notification for religious ministering to marginalized people, we found ourselves interpreting cultural differences. Homosexuality is often a subject of conversation in the U.S., but not necessarily in other countries or the Vatican. Similarly, questioning and disagreement are acceptable interactions in our society, but in other settings they may be seen as disloyalty. In spite of the long and sometimes difficult exchange, we believe that another step was taken toward mutual understanding and appreciation.

Sister Camille continued: "There are times when we question the significance of supporting a structure that is so foreign to our commitment to right relationships, to our desire for an inclusive Church."

Dissent as Love and Loyalty

In the July 2000 LCWR newsletter, *Update*, LCWR president Sister Nancy Sylvester also reported on that visit with the Vatican, saying the sisters "cited the ministerial context of women and men religious in the United States" and "highlighted the complexity of these pastoral situations which require creativity, compassion, and difficult judgment calls. We stressed the need to interpret official church teaching through the lens of culture." Sister Nancy added, "We discussed the role of dissent in our culture as a sign of love and loyalty rather than disrespect."

Sister Nancy addressed the Gramick-Nugent notification in her speech at the LCWR August 2000 annual assembly. She explained that she and other women religious "have come to trust our experience and to claim it as a legitimate authority in our lives". The choice to be with "marginalized" people often places "us in pastoral situations that involve sensitive moral issues related to sexuality or woman's role in moral decision-making", Sister Nancy said. Some Vatican officials "do not validate our experience as authentic religious life", she continued, but see consecrated life "as a more static life form". That static form, she said, is the pursuit of holiness through the three vows and a commitment to "a corporate and institutional apostolate under the guidance of the hierarchy and in support of the Magisterium". While this form fits the worldview of a patriarchal culture, she said, "we dare to say that we beg to differ with it."

Differing with this concept of religious life, she noted, has caused "tension and conflict" with the Vatican. While such conflict is unfortunate, sisters want to participate in the decisions that affect them and believe in a person's "right to speak one's own truth", she said. "We believe in the power to change unjust structures and laws" and "respect loyal dissent".

Sisters are "often disappointed, frustrated, angered, and deeply saddened by official responses [from the Vatican] that seem authoritarian, punitive, disrespectful of our legitimate authority as elected leaders, and disrespectful of our capacity to be moral agents", Sister Nancy explained. She then spoke of "setbacks and casualties" sustained from dealing with Church officials and offered a list of "casualties", which included Immaculate Heart of Mary Sisters of Los Angeles, School Sisters of Saint Francis, Sister Agnes Mary Mansour, the sister signers of the 1984 *New York Times* abortion statement, theologians and scholars who had been silenced by the Church, and Sister Jeannine Gramick.

Sister Nancy said that in her meeting with Vatican officials in May 2000 to discuss the Gramick-Nugent notification, it was clear that the LCWR and the Vatican had differing ecclesiologies. Vatican officials expected members and superiors of religious to give "unequivocal support to the directives of the Holy See". They expected religious superiors to assist the members of their communities in understanding and implementing these directives. Thus, Vatican officials "expressed anger" about the letters written by men and women religious objecting to the Gramick-Nugent notification[33]

In the LCWR *Conference Report 2000*, Sister Nancy elaborated more on the LCWR difficulties with the Vatican and revealed resentment that the religious orders living a traditional lifestyle were getting more recognition. Yet she continued to insist that LCWR was on the right path:

> We face new crossroads. Among and within religious congregations there is growing awareness of our diversity. We wrestle with identity questions in the midst of an official church which doesn't understand the journey of our last forty years. This is compounded as we experience traditional forms of religious reemerging and receiving the recognition and pride among some in the church that once was ours. I believe we must claim that who we have become is an authentic expression of the call to religious life and our commitment to live the Gospel....
>
> We claim our ministry to those at the margins and our work for justice are expressions of the Gospel and new forms of evangelization. We acknowledge that solidarity with those who suffer oppression reveals new understandings and new ways that God is acting in our world. We free ourselves to offer such insights to our brother bishops and invite them to see anew some of the official teachings of our church.

Doctrinal Problems Discussed with the LCWR

The year 2001 was significant for the LCWR, but that fact was not known publicly until 2009, when the Congregation for the Doctrine of the Faith revealed that it was initiating a doctrinal assessment of the organization. In May 2001 the CDF discussed doctrinal problems with the leadership of the LCWR. Though the exact nature of these problems was not made public, LCWR officials often hinted that difficulties with the Vatican had arisen at this meeting. They did not, however, correct these problems, and eight years later the CDF announced it was making a more detailed assessment. (See full report on this in chapter 17.)

In the LCWR 2001 Annual Report, Mary Mollisson, a Sister of Saint Agnes and LCWR president, alluded to the doctrinal difficulties that surfaced at the May meeting with Vatican officials and reiterated

---

[33] Nancy Sylvester, IHM, "Risk the Sacred Journey" presidential address given to 2000 LCWR assembly, August 8.

the long-held conference strategy of maintaining dialogue with Church authorities to keep the issues open.

> In keeping with our desire for right relationships among church officials and members of the Conference, the Presidency continues a dialogue with Bishops and Vatican officials. We approach this dialogue with a sense of urgency and with a passion to stay in conversations that will decrease the tension between doctrinal adherence and the pastoral needs of marginalized people. We also continue to express our desire for women to be involved in more decision-making within church structures. The risk of this part of our journey is being misunderstood and being perceived as unfaithful to the Magisterium of the church.

Sister Mary went on to characterize Church officials at that meeting as not comprehending the sisters' message: "Definite efforts were made to bridge the cultural understanding of a 'dialogic process' as we met with church officials. Understanding of authority, obedience, communal discernment, and the prophetic nature of religious need further conversations. This journey into nuances of language and the necessity of simultaneous translation is complex and fraught with the risk of misinterpretations."

That same year, 2001, was designated as a "Year of Contemplation" by the LCWR, which invited others to join the sisters in prayer and fasting to heal "brokenness" in the world and in the Church, again citing the "tension" between doctrine and pastoral care. The LCWR 2001 "Call to Contemplation" stated: "We recognize the Church as the family of God, embracing differences and setting the Spirit free. Yet we experience division, mistrust and increasing polarization within the Church community in the tension between doctrinal adherence and pastoral care. Women and men who are marginalized do not find a home in the Church. Is this the church Jesus calls us to be? *We feel disheartened and powerless*" (italics in original).

Citing "the violence engendered by individualistic use of power in nation and Church", the members of the LCWR national board signed letters of support to those who "made Eucharist possible" at a New Ways Ministry Symposium in Louisville, March 8–10, 2002.[34] Archbishop Tarcisio Bertone, secretary of the Congregation for the Doctrine

[34] LCWR *Annual Report 2002*, 2.

of the Faith, had directed Louisville Archbishop Thomas Kelly, a Dominican, not to allow Mass to be celebrated at the New Ways Ministry conference because the organization did not promote the authentic teachings of the Church. Archbishop Kelly suggested that conference attendees attend Mass at the cathedral instead.[35]

Subsequently, New Ways Ministry organizers claimed that permission was not needed for the Mass, and they asked retired Bishop Leroy Matthiesen of Amarillo, Texas, to celebrate it at the conference. Bishop Matthiesen claimed that since he himself was not told by the Vatican or the archbishop not to celebrate the Mass, it was acceptable for him to do so.[36]

A February 20 letter from the LCWR national board to Bishop Matthiesen noted: "Your willingness to speak at the symposium and your conviction to preside at Eucharist model for us what leadership is called to in difficult situations. You give us hope that thoughtful and loving acts will bring about a Church that invites all to the table." A similar letter was sent to Frank DeBernardo and other staff of New Ways Ministry.[37] The CDF 2012 doctrinal assessment of the LCWR specifically cited LCWR letters about New Ways Ministry conferences as an example of "corporate dissent".

The theme for the August 2002 LCWR national assembly was descriptive of the group's relationship with the Vatican: "Leadership in Dynamic Tension". In her address, LCWR president Kathleen Pruitt, a Sister of Saint Joseph of Peace, talked about the need for "change, reform, renewal, and healing" in the world, among themselves, the nation, "and particularly in our church".[38]

The ecological future of the planet was the theme of the LCWR 2003 assembly, with Brian Swimme, an evolutionary cosmologist, as one of the keynoters. Presentations at the assembly included "permaculture", "ecology's invitation to authentic humanness", "contemplation of the cosmos", and "the call of the Earth Charter". At that

[35] *National Catholic Reporter*, March 15, 2002.

[36] *National Catholic Reporter*, March 22, 2002.

[37] Leadership Conference of Women Religious National Board letters to Most Reverend Leroy T. Matthiesen, Archbishop Thomas C. Kelley, OP, and Frank DeBernardo and Staff, New Ways Ministry, February 20, 2002, posted as a Word document on the LCWR website, www.lcwr.org (accessed September 18, 2012).

[38] Kathleen Pruitt, CSJP, "Tensions Held in the Heart of Hope", presidential address to 2002 LCWR assembly, August 18, 2002.

assembly, Benedictine Sister Christine Vladimiroff was elected vice president. In 2001, as prioress of the Benedictine Sisters of Erie, Pennsylvania, she had refused a directive from the Vatican to tell one of her sisters, Joan Chittister, to decline an invitation to give a talk at the Women's Ordination Worldwide conference in Dublin, Ireland.

The "Most Radical Act of Dissent"?

In 2003, Sister of the Blessed Virgin Mary, Mary Ann Zollmann, LCWR president, told that year's assembly that LCWR leaders should maximize their potential to create the change that is inherent in religious life: "We have uncovered within ourselves the power most necessary for the creation, salvation, and resurrection of our church, our world, and our earth. It is the power of relationship, of our sisterhood with all that is. This power is prophetic; it is the most radical act of dissent." [39]

In 2004, the LCWR assembly was held jointly with the Conference of Major Superiors of Men. At that event, Capuchin Father Michael H. Crosby spoke on "Religious: A Prophetic Voice in the Midst of a Violent World". He expanded the definition of violence to include "the sinful, structural and systemic violence that has come to be canonized in a certain understanding of holiness that is increasingly promoted by the highest clerics and their house prophets in our own church". And he noted that many of the religious at the assembly considered some of the teachings of the Magisterium to be "unjust, violent and sinful". He explained: "We have not been public enough in our protest of patriarchy", and he accused the "'official' patriarchal" church of "unjustifiable violence against women, and, I would also say, against gays". [40]

Mercy Sister Theresa Kane, the former LCWR president who had confronted Pope John Paul II in 1979 about excluding women from ordination, was given the LCWR Outstanding Leadership Award at the 2004 assembly. In accepting, Sister Theresa noted:

> We are developing a consciousness to no longer view ourselves as women religious exclusively in service; we know and identify ourselves as women

---

[39] LCWR press release, August 25, 2003, www.lcwr.org/media/august-23-2003-lcwr-assembly (accessed August 25, 2012).

[40] Michael H. Crosby, OFM Cap., "Religious: A Prophetic Voice in the Midst of a Violent World" keynote address at 2004 LCWR-CMSM joint assembly, August 21.

in solidarity with other women. We experience this solidarity as we acknowledge the painful realization that all women in church and in society are colonized, that all women are patronized, that all women are viewed as objects; that all women are conditioned and expected to be complementary.[41]

Also in 2004, the LCWR published *An Invitation to Systems Thinking: An Opportunity to Act for Systemic Change*, a handbook for religious orders. According to the handbook, some sisters, schooled in "a holistic, organic view of the world" and in "process, liberationist and feminist theologies ... believe that the celebration of Eucharist is so bound up with a church structure caught in negative aspects of the Western mind they can no longer participate with a sense of integrity".[42] The views of these sisters, the booklet advises, must be respected. The 2012 CDF doctrinal assessment of the LCWR cited this same booklet as problematic and directed the group to withdraw it from circulation.

At the LCWR 2005 assembly, Sister Margaret Brennan, who had been president in 1972, spoke about the group's history, noting: "The negative response of the Congregation for Religious to the renewal directions of many congregations with regard to the wearing of the habit, new forms of ministry, particularly into areas of peace and justice, and the adoption of a way of life more adapted to these new initiatives appeared to us as promoting a static and stratified view of religious life—one considered apart from the flow of history." Sister Margaret also acknowledged that the LCWR relationship with the Vatican and many of the hierarchy was marked by "struggle, a discountenancing of our experience along with sometimes voiced and sometimes unvoiced disapproval of who we are and who we had become in our desire to serve the church".[43]

The year 2006 marked the fiftieth anniversary of the founding of the women's original superiors' conference, so it was proclaimed a jubilee year by the LCWR. Thus, the summer 2005 edition of the

---

[41] Sister Theresa Kane, *Vita* (publication of the Sisters of Mercy of the Americas), November 2004.

[42] LCWR, "An Invitation to Systems Thinking", https://lcwr.org/resources/systems-thinking-handbook (accessed September 25, 2012).

[43] Sister Margaret Brennan, IHM, "Leadership Conference of Women Religious: Past, Present, Future", *Origins*, September 8, 2005.

LCWR *Occasional Papers* contained several reflections on the history of the conference. Sister Mary Daniel Turner, executive director from 1972 to 1978, wrote about a "shift" in religious life that "evoked disquiet" within the conference and among those in both the clergy and the laity who "viewed this change as unbecoming political activity for religious". She went on to conclude: "Assembly themes, speakers and workshops over the years evidenced how much the conference has been affected by a world-embracing theology", which has met with objections from both inside and outside the group. Indeed, many of these themes, speakers, and workshops would be cited as problematic in the 2012 CDF doctrinal assessment of the LCWR.

Sister Joan Chittister, president of the LCWR in 1976, gave the keynote address at the 2006 assembly and continued to complain about the male hierarchy, telling the sisters: "If we proclaim ourselves to be ecclesial women we must ask if what we mean by that is that we will do what the men of the church tell us to do or that we will do what the people of the church need to have us do."[44]

The presidential address at that 2006 meeting was given by Sister Beatrice Eichten, a Franciscan, who noted: "We religious have shifted from being 'obedient daughters' and a religious work force to being adult educated women with a mature identity who believe we have something to say about our Church, its teaching and its practice. This shift has strained our relationship with the hierarchical church, where we experience the pain of often being invisible, relegated to third class status, and absent at the table of decision." She also stressed that the LCWR was "challenged to keep open the door of dialog with the hierarchical Church".[45]

"Post-Christian" Sisters?

The LCWR 2007 assembly attracted more attention than most other gatherings of the conference because of a keynote address by Dominican Sister Laurie Brink. Her address could be characterized on one hand as honest, for she named what had become obvious to some

---

[44] Chittister, "Remember the Vision; Embracing the Dream" keynote at 2006 LCWR assembly, August 19.

[45] Beatrice Eichten, OSF, "So Much Is in Bud" presidential address at LCWR 2006 assembly, August 20.

people but has not been previously acknowledged by LCWR: Some congregations of women religious, she said, are "no longer ecclesiastical", having "grown beyond the bounds of institutional religion". She continued: "Religious titles, institutional limitations, ecclesiastical authorities no longer fit this congregation, which in most respects is Post-Christian." On the other hand, she did not endorse this model but seemed to find the phenomenon acceptable, saying, "Who's to say that the movement beyond Christ is not, in reality, a movement into the very heart of God?"[46] The CDF 2012 doctrinal assessment of the LCWR considered this address "a rejection of faith" and "a serious source of scandal" that is "incompatible with religious life".

Receiving the LCWR Outstanding Leadership Award at the 2007 assembly was Sister Joan Chittister, who again repeated her complaint that "women leaders have been kept out of leadership in church and state for no good reason for far too long." And she repeated the LCWR goal of transforming religious life: "But we may be failing to realize that we ourselves are now the new small groups of women leaders who must come from one kind of religious life to begin another kind in a new and different world."[47] Members of the assembly then approved a decidedly non-ecclesial resolution calling for members to work for legislation to preserve and renew wetlands and coastlands and to strengthen Louisiana levees.[48]

"On This Holy Mountain" was the theme of the August 2008 joint LCWR-CMSM assembly in Denver. One keynoter was Sister of Saint Joseph Elizabeth Johnson, who complained about "patriarchal values that, by any objective measure, relegate women to second-class status governed by male-dominated structures, law, and ritual". She did go on to urge forgiveness of church authorities, but added that "forgiving does not mean condoning harmful actions, or ceasing to criticize and resist them."[49]

[46] Laurie Brink, OP, "A Marginal Life: Pursuing Holiness in the 21st Century" keynote address at LCWR 2007 assembly, August 2. https://lcwr.org/sites/default/files/calendar/attachments/2007_Keynote_Address_Laurie_Brink-OP.pdf (accessed September 19, 2012).

[47] Chittister, untitled. Link to document found at https://lcwr.org/calendar/lcwr-assembly-2007 (accessed February 9, 2013).

[48] LCWR press release, August 5, 2007.

[49] John L. Allen Jr., "Theologian Elizabeth Johnson: 'Drench Anger with Forgiveness'", *National Catholic Reporter*, August 4, 2008. Note: Sister Elizabeth's 2007 book, *Quest for the Living God: Mapping Frontiers in the Theology of God*, would be cited in 2011 by the U.S.

In the spring of 2008, when the LCWR officers made their annual visit to the Vatican, they were told that the CDF was going to proceed with a doctrinal assessment because the issues addressed in 2001 had not been resolved.[50] The coming assessment was not revealed until April of 2009, but hints of difficulties with the Vatican were heard in the 2008 assembly presidential address by Sister of the Most Precious Blood Mary Whited. She said women religious can "midwife" religious life into the future, recalling the midwives in the Old Testament who defied Pharaoh so they could bring new life and hope to their people. Alluding to the midwives' bravery, she asked:

> What will it take to bring a reconciling perspective to a painfully divided church? This past year our presidency has continued to engage in significant conversations with Vatican officials, U.S. Bishops, and the Council of Major Superiors of Women Religious. We bring our perspectives as women religious, and LCWR, to each of these groups. In talking with the Vatican, hope lies in our willingness and determination to stay in the conversation for the long haul and to not loose [sic] heart.[51]

The 2009 LCWR annual assembly convened in a charged atmosphere, for earlier in the year the CDF doctrinal assessment of the group had been revealed, and the Congregation for Religious announced it was conducting an apostolic visitation of all US women's religious orders. The assembly theme described the current mood: "Women of Spirit: Creating in Chaos". The *National Catholic Reporter* observed that at the assembly, "Many women, in informal conversations, spoke of their determination not to let these Vatican actions get in the way of their ministries and religious life." [52]

Speaking about the "present challenges in our way of life within this Church and world", LCWR president Sister J. Lora Dambroski, a Franciscan, told the assembly: "We claim and often work from the

---

Bishops' Committee on Doctrine for "unacceptable departures from the Catholic theological tradition". The doctrine committee observed, "The author employs standards from outside the faith to criticize and to revise in a radical fashion the conception of God revealed in Scripture and taught by the Magisterium."

[50] Archbishop J. Peter Sartain, "Deepening Communion", *America*, June 18, 2012.

[51] Mary Whited, CPPS, untitled presidential address to LCWR 2008 assembly, August 4.

[52] "Under Fire, Women Religious Leaders Gather in New Orleans", *National Catholic Reporter*, August 12, 2009.

premise that we as women have other ways of living in and working through conflict and chaos ... [ellipsis in original] more relational, respectful, transparent, dialogic, less judgmental and more reflective. The respectful stance is that while holding and relating out of our own truth we are open to the truth of the other." It is difficult to do this, she continued, when sisters are in "someone else's cross hairs" and "under pressure, judgment and public scrutiny".[53] The 2009 assembly also approved a "focus" for particular attention during 2010: the ecclesial role of women religious.

"Creative Fidelity"?

On March 17, 2010, a letter was sent to members of Congress by the lobbying organization Network, which is closely affiliated with the LCWR (see chapter 14). That letter urged Congress to approve the Patient Protection and Affordable Care Act (PPACA), commonly called Obamacare. Franciscan Sister Marlene Weisenbeck signed the letter as LCWR president, along with about sixty other sisters, even though the US bishops had opposed the bill because it funded abortion and failed to provide an adequate conscience clause.

The LCWR 2009–2010 Annual Report noted that "according to feedback from members of the White House staff, members of Congress, Network, and others, this letter had a significant impact on the debate over the bill and helped lead to its passage on March 21." And in spite of the US bishops' opposition to the bill, the report noted that the LCWR had responded to media inquiries with the assurance that the "LCWR stands with the United States Conference of Catholic Bishops and other Catholics in their tireless efforts to promote the sacredness of life and to assure that federal funding is not used for abortions." The statement explained that the LCWR is not in opposition to the bishops regarding their pro-life stance, but it indicated that "the right to health care, for all" was the overriding consideration. The report concluded: "The impact of this action by LCWR and women religious leaders underscores the strength of the moral authority of women religious and the responsibility to exercise that

---

[53] J. Lora Dambroski, OSF, LCWR presidential address to LCWR 2009 assembly, August 14.

authority with great care. As a result, the officers and staff reviewed LCWR's policies and practices to assure that the conference continues to employ its authority with integrity as it works to guarantee the rights and dignity of all persons."

The August 2010 LCWR assembly's theme was "Hope in the Midst of Darkness". In his keynote address, theologian Richard Gaillardetz, then of the University of Toledo, told the sisters that some tensions were normal in ecclesial life, "however, in our current situation, it is very difficult to avoid the impression that we are now veering dangerously close to an instance of ecclesial dysfunction". Religious give "public testimony to the obligations and responsibilities of all Christians", he said. "That means that the way you respond to the ecclesial tensions you are experiencing right now will be a witness to all Christians, instructing all of us in how to most fruitfully and productively respond to the inevitable ecclesial tensions that we undergo."

Gaillardetz said that the disagreement between the US bishops and women religious over the health-reform bill "was limited to different interpretations of exceedingly technical policy jargon". The resulting tensions, he said, were "a direct result of the failure to recognize the diversity of roles that bishops, theologians, politicians, health care practitioners and women religious played in discerning the appropriate application of God's word". The bishops were right to proclaim the moral values in health care reform, he continued, and they exercised their legitimate authority in making a judgment about the contents of the bill. But, he added, the bishops erred "in claiming an exclusive right and responsibility to make such prudential judgments". And he concluded that it was not the bishops, but "the LCWR, women religious communities and the Catholic Health Association that were most faithful to the teaching of the [Second Vatican] Council regarding their proper participation in the church's mission in the world".[54]

An August 16, 2010, LCWR press release reported that "in her address to the assembly, LCWR president Marlene Weisenbeck, a Sister

---

[54] Richard Galliardetz, "Contemporary Religious Life: Creative Fidelity to the Vision of Vatican II", keynote address to 2010 LCWR assembly, transcribed by the author from a CD authorized by the LCWR and sold by Gem Tapes.

of the Third Order of Saint Francis of Perpetual Adoration, urged the body to claim its role in the church. She said, 'We do not have to mimic our founders to find the answer about how to articulate our ecclesial role. The Gospel will show us what to do, how we must act with the attitude of Jesus who emphasized an inclusive love of all in right relationships. We take our power from the Word of God.' "

The LCWR's difficulties with the Vatican became a sort of badge of honor for the organization, for other progressive Catholic entities rushed to offer their support and sympathy for the organization. In 2010, *Pax Christi* gave the LCWR its annual award, and the National Federation of Priests' Councils presented its Mandatum Award. The University of San Francisco (USF) invited Dominican Sister Mary Hughes, LCWR president, to be a speaker at its fall commencement and to accept an honorary doctoral degree to laud the LCWR members for their contributions to the country and to the Church. The *National Catholic Reporter* characterized the USF honor as "yet another visible contrary endorsement of the work of the women and one more signal to the Vatican that U.S. Catholics are not at all pleased with the Vatican moves".[55]

The 2011 annual assembly explored "Mystery Unfolding: Religious Life for the World" and repeated the theme of women Religious transforming religious life and the Church. Theologian and Benedictine Sister Maricarmen Bracamontes told the assembly, "Once we realize that cultural models are human creations and therefore, can be changed and adapted, we become more creative and dynamic in our search for transforming alternatives: other worlds become possible, other ways of being church become possible, other forms of religious life become possible." [56]

Dominican Sister Barbara Reid told the assembly that "as we find the forms and structures of religious life realigning with groups merging, dissolving, forming new alliances with other religious, lay people and with institutions that share similar values, we should not be surprised; we are in concert with the creative rhythms of our universe." She added that "the re-forming occurring in our day is a

[55] Thomas Fox, "Women Religious Honored by University of San Francisco", *National Catholic Reporter*, December 18, 2010.
[56] LCWR News Release, August 16, 2011.

sign of life and vitality, of being in harmony with the dynamics of the cosmos."[57]

The assembly ended with the presentation of the LCWR's highest honor, its Outstanding Leadership Award, to Daughter of Charity Sister Carol Keehan. As president and CEO of the Catholic Health Association (CHA), she had helped lead the successful passage of Obamacare.

When President Obama signed the bill into law on March 23, 2010, Sister Carol was photographed at his side, given one of the pens the president used to sign the bill, and praised by some lawmakers for having secured the necessary votes to win the day. In a May 21 statement, the three bishops who were most involved in the health-reform topic at that time—Cardinal Daniel DiNardo of Galveston-Houston, Bishop William Murphy of Rockville Centre, New York, and Bishop John Wester of Salt Lake City—reaffirmed the US bishops' position and made clear that it is the role of bishops, not the task of individuals or groups, to make moral judgments and provide guidance to Catholics. They specifically named the CHA and concluded that the organization's "fundamental" disagreement with the bishops had "resulted in confusion and a wound to Catholic unity".[58]

The winter 2011 LCWR *Occasional Papers* contained an interview with Father Charles Curran, then a professor of Human Values at Southern Methodist University. He had famously led the dissent against *Humanae Vitae* in 1968 (see chapter 9) when he was a theology professor at the Catholic University of America and subsequently lost his teaching position there.

When questioned about issues facing the nation, the church, and religious congregations, Father Curran said the "primary" reason Catholics leave the Church is "the church's position on moral issues—divorce, sexuality, homosexuality". He continued: "I fear that the unwillingness of the church leadership to deal with these tensions on a much deeper level is going to cause more people to give up on the church because they see no change going on there." Regarding women religious, Father Curran observed: "The leadership of communities of women religious has been a model and template for the rest of the

[57] Ibid.
[58] USCCB press release, May 21, 2010.

church. Women religious leaders have lived out that tension between the prophetic and the dialogical."

The 2012 LCWR annual assembly will be discussed in chapter 17 on the doctrinal assessment by CDF because that topic dominated that meeting.

Looking at this history, it is clear that the transformation of the LCWR had a wide impact on the Catholic Church in the United States and even, in the case of health care, on American society. The next chapter details the division of the LCWR that occurred because of the direction its leaders took.

7

Traditional Sisters Assert Themselves

Both CMSM [Conference of Major Superiors of Men] and [the] Leadership Conference of Women Religious are on record as seeing clearly that at least in the countries of the western democracies, the pattern of religious life that has prevailed for several centuries has, for all practical purposes, served its purpose and is passing away.[1]

— Sister Elizabeth Johnson, CSJ

The LCWR believed that the definition of religious life should come from sisters' own "lived experience" rather than from the Vatican, and this conviction led those sisters down the pathway described in the last two chapters. But as renewal efforts continued after the Second Vatican Council, there were many other sisters—and superiors—who were concerned about the direction renewal was taking in communities that drastically altered not only their lifestyles and the mission of their institutes, but also the entire concept of religious life. In many cases, their concerns centered on a tendency by the change-oriented sisters to redefine religious life in light of the American experience and to apply American-style democracy to their relationships with each other and with the Magisterium. This polarization between the change-oriented and traditional sisters caused a conflict in the superiors' conference that simmered for twenty-two years before an alternate superiors' conference for traditional sisters was recognized by the Vatican in 1992.

[1] Elizabeth A. Johnson, CSJ, "And Their Eyes Were Opened", address presented to CMSM-LCWR joint assembly, August 24, 1995.

The growing divide was mentioned in an April 11, 1970, article in *America* magazine by Father John C. Haughey, who observed that two positions on religious life were beginning to emerge among sisters: one that accepted the essential elements of religious life as traditionally defined by the Church and articulated by the Magisterium and another that wanted a new definition of religious life to come from the sisters themselves; Father Haughey came down solidly on the side of the sisters who wanted to create their own definition. He noted that a new phenomenon was occurring in the American Catholic Church: Women religious were beginning to join together in national organizations. "The phenomenon says something about the turbulence within contemporary Roman Catholicism", he wrote. "It says even more about the Americanization of religious life and is an interesting testimony to the new assertiveness of modern woman." [2]

The polarization over the definition of religious life was seen at the 1970 annual assembly of the CMSW, particularly when some superiors attempted to have the assembly endorse the statement on religious life that had been formulated by an informal group of women and men religious just prior to the conference assembly. As discussed in the last chapter, that statement contended that American religious need to function under a democratic system and therefore could not continue to accept automatically directives coming from the Vatican. The statement also put the Vatican on notice that American religious considered themselves free to determine their own patterns of life, to explore a variety of ministries, and to engage in secular occupations. The statement concluded that American religious would listen to Church authorities but would make their own decisions about following directives from the Vatican.

The statement did not pass the 1970 assembly, but the officers of the men's and women's conferences of major superiors sent it to members of the Bishops' Liaison Committee as a "springboard to the meaningful discussion they anticipated having" with the committee.[3] The statement had shared the agenda at the 1970 assembly with some other controversial matters, including an address by Father Haughey, who encouraged sisters to ignore directives from the Vatican that were not

[2] Haughey, "U.S. Sisters Organize", *America*, April 11, 1970, 388–89.
[3] *Searching*, no. 3 (December 1970), CLCW 1/25, UNDA.

communicated directly to them and about which they were not consulted.

Consortium Perfectae Caritatis

These events of the 1970 assembly were just too much for some major superiors who had been concerned for some time that the CMSW was headed in the wrong direction, that is, away from Church authority. According to the recollections of Sister Mary Elise Krantz,[4] some of these superiors, who had not been acquainted before, shared their concerns with one another during coffee breaks at the meeting. Among those sisters were Sister Alice Anita Murphy of Chestnut Hill, Pennsylvania; Sister Mary Claudia Honsberger of Immaculata, Pennsylvania; Sister of Saint Joseph Marie Assumpta McKinley of Watertown, New York; and Franciscan Sister Sixtina Reul of Alton, Illinois. During the days of the assembly, these women discussed forming an organization dedicated to studying the documents of Vatican II regarding religious life. Their discussions resulted in the Consortium Perfectae Caritatis, an organization that paved the way for a new conference of major superiors to represent thousands of traditional American sisters.

The first formal meeting of the group took place at Sister Mary Elise's motherhouse in Chardon, Ohio, on December 2, 1970. Attending that meeting was Cardinal Egidio Vagnozzi, president of the Prefecture for Economic Affairs of the Holy See and former apostolic delegate to the United States, as well as two bishops, several priests, and about sixty sisters from throughout the country. About thirty other bishops sent their greetings.[5] One proposed title for the organization was "North American Association of Religious Women", but chosen instead was the name that refers to the Vatican II document on religious life, Perfectae Caritatis.

At the group's first general assembly, from February 28 to March 2, 1971, in Washington, DC, Bishop Fulton J. Sheen spoke, along with apostolic delegate Archbishop Luigi Raimondi. At that assembly, the essentials of religious life—as the sisters interpreted them to be defined

---

[4] Mary Elise Krantz, SND, personal interview with author, May 13–14, 1995.

[5] Consortium Perfectae Caritatis, informational reprint on the history and purpose of the organization, c. 1979, CMAS 3/28, UNDA.

in Vatican II documents—were adopted as the guiding principles of the consortium. These essentials included: 1) pursuit of holiness through the vows; 2) a "clear and unequivocal position in support of the Holy See and the right she has to interpret the norms of religious life for the universal Church and the local Churches"; 3) belief in a permanent ecclesial commitment to a corporate and institutional apostolate under the guidance of the hierarchy; 4) willingness to respond to the pope and the Congregation for Religious; 5) "acceptance of life in a Eucharistic Community under legitimately elected superiors"; 6) wearing of a religious habit; 7) life in community with communal and liturgical prayer; 8) concern to foster vocations.

The main activity of the consortium was sponsoring semiannual assemblies that were designed to be educational in nature, which any sister, not just superiors, could attend. Among the speakers at those assemblies were prominent members of the hierarchy, such as Cardinals John Carberry, Jean Danielou, John Krol, William Baum, James Hickey, and Archbishop Fulton Sheen. The consortium also published an educational newsletter, which included documentary material from the Congregation for Religious. Funding was obtained by conference fees and donations from sympathetic clergy and hierarchy as well as lay individuals. The Knights of Columbus also was a generous donor.

Originally the consortium was made up of major superiors who endorsed the group's essentials of religious life. The consortium never was a membership organization, but it invited any religious who shared its philosophy to attend its meetings and subscribe to its mailings. While the consortium was intended to be an educational enterprise to enable sisters to accomplish the renewal mandated by Vatican II, it took on an additional role of trying to help sisters address excesses and abuses that they encountered in their communities. Indeed, consortium records indicate that many religious found support and comfort in the organization at a time when renewal in their congregations seemed to be moving far beyond that envisioned by Vatican II.

The consortium meetings usually drew between one hundred and two hundred sisters, but the organization was not effective in attracting more. One difficulty was that many sisters could not obtain permission from their superiors to attend consortium meetings, because their superiors either did not understand what the consortium was about or did not agree with its philosophy. Other sisters have indicated that they did not attend consortium meetings because they felt they should have received a specific invitation from the organization.

The consortium probably also did not attract large numbers because it projected an image of being much more conservative than the record indicates it actually was. Rather than trying to return religious life to a preconciliar mold—as its critics charged—the consortium records indicate that it heavily promoted the teachings of the Second Vatican Council, even publishing a book—*Religious Life: A Mystery in Christ*—that collected pertinent documents on religious life from Vatican II, the popes, and the Congregation for Religious. And consortium records contain letters from men and women religious and hierarchy who attended consortium assemblies for the first time and were pleasantly surprised that the organization was not the ultraconservative group that they had perceived it to be. But the consortium sisters seem to have made several key mistakes that saddled their organization with the conservative image, an image they were never successful in overcoming.

The first mistake was the name of the organization. In choosing a Latin title, the sisters seemed to be setting themselves apart from the updating called for by Vatican II. People unfamiliar with the Council document on religious life, *Perfectae Caritatis*, translated into English as "perfect charity", perceived a holier-than-thou image when the title of the organization was translated as the Association of Perfect Charity. The consortium further projected a reactionary image quite out of step with the legitimate women's movement with its male coordinator, Father James Viall, a friend of Sister Mary Elise. Further, a hefty majority of the speakers at the consortium assemblies were men, giving fuel to the argument that the group believed women had nothing significant to say about important issues in the Church and religious life. Some members of the consortium board had addressed the problem of a women's organization having a male leader, and some suggested that a committee should have more input into which speakers would address the consortium assemblies, since speakers usually were chosen by Father Viall. But consortium leaders apparently felt a great loyalty to Father Viall, who had been supportive of the organization from its inception and who had numerous contacts in the Church through his position as president of the Confraternity of Catholic Clergy.

The organization of the consortium itself also proved to be a weakness. Since it was a loosely defined group with a purpose of education, there was not much formal structure and no official membership. In the early days of the consortium, there was not even a board of directors. Eventually, an administrative board—usually numbering about fourteen—was formed from interested sisters, and four of those board members functioned as president, vice president, secretary, and treasurer. One sister became executive director.

Some sisters attending the consortium assemblies found it distressing that there appeared to be no specific leaders in charge of the group. Others who were more familiar with the structure of the consortium suggested that leaders be changed more frequently, as the board had retained many of the same members throughout the years. Additionally, because the consortium was the only organization of women religious during the early 1970s that vigorously endorsed official Church positions and supported the hierarchy and the Vatican, it attracted some sisters who were still very resistant to the post-conciliar changes, thus enforcing the image of conservatism, which was strengthened when a few conservative bishops and priests publicly aligned themselves with the organization.

Because of its outspoken loyalty to the Magisterium, the consortium had the backing of many prominent members of the hierarchy, both in this country and in Rome. In 1980, fifty US bishops signed a petition that the pope declare the consortium a pontifical forum.[6] (Consortium records indicate that the organization repeatedly asked the Vatican for recognition, not as a major superiors' conference, as its critics charged, but rather to gain pontifical approval and legitimacy that would help attract more sisters to its meetings and mailing list.) In 1972, the consortium received Vatican approval of sorts in the form of a *decretum laudis*—a decree of praise—from the Congregation for Religious.[7] In 1973, Bishop James J. Hogan, chairman of the Bishops' Liaison Committee with the LCWR, observed that a growing number of bishops saw the consortium as representing a valid point of view, and those bishops were looking for a means of rapprochement with the group.[8]

Still, many US bishops steered clear of endorsing the consortium because the LCWR clearly viewed it as a threat, and most bishops did

---

[6] Minutes of CPC administrative council meeting, April 13, 1980, CMAS 3/31, UNDA.

[7] Mary Elise Krantz, SND, "The Essential Elements for Women Religious: Testimony on Behalf of the Consortium Perfectae Caritatis", *Origins*, October 3, 1985, 252.

[8] Bishop James J. Hogan letter to Sister Mary Daniel Turner, SND, June 4, 1973, CMAS 2/11, UNDA.

not want to come down on one side or the other. Bishop William Connare of Greensburg, Pennsylvania, wrote the consortium in 1976, stating that many bishops supported the group but did not say so openly because they did not want to contribute to the worrisome division between American sisters.

He observed: "Unfortunately the leadership of the LCWR has lost its bearings. I know many bishops feel that way. Privately we discuss the situation, but seem hesitant to criticize openly. Maybe the time has come for the latter approach." [9] Bishop Floyd Begin of Oakland, California, who had worked on the staff of the Congregation for Religious, observed in 1977 that many bishops were confused and uninformed about the LCWR and the consortium. He suggested that bishops had been cautious about endorsing the consortium because they wanted to "preserve the wealth of potential service contained in LCWR".[10] Indeed, bishops agonized privately over what would become of the schools and hospitals in their dioceses if they antagonized the orders affiliated with the LCWR by publicly supporting the consortium.

The consortium and the LCWR were, in fact, two dichotomous groups that bumped heads frequently. The LCWR feared that the consortium was trying to cozy up to the Vatican in an effort to replace the conference as the Vatican-approved organization of American women superiors. The consortium perceived that the conference had lost its loyalty to the Church and was leading sisters away from the model of religious life prescribed by Church documents and canon law. In a seeming contradiction, some sisters maintained membership in both groups simultaneously. The Congregation for Religious advised consortium members who were major superiors to continue their membership in the LCWR, even if they did not approve of the direction the conference was taking. Apparently those Church authorities hoped that the consortium sisters would bring a moderating influence to the LCWR. Eventually, however, most of the consortium members left the LCWR, thus delineating the differences between the two groups even more dramatically.

[9] Bishop William Connare letter to Sister Rose Eileen Masterman, July 12, 1976, CMAS 2/23, UNDA.
[10] Bishop Floyd Begin letter to Sister Patricia Marie Mulpeters, PBVM, February 25, 1977, CMAS 3/15, UNDA.

Dialogue between the Sisters' Groups

The Congregation for Religious, and eventually the pope, urged the two groups to resolve their differences, and dialogues for this purpose eventually led to the creation of an alternate conference of women's superiors in the United States, but in a manner probably none of the parties would have anticipated.

The first of these formal dialogues occurred on March 15, 1972.[11] The consortium presented four rights that it wanted the LCWR to affirm: 1) to bear as a religious community one's historic witness; 2) to have a voice in the picking of speakers and being spared Gregory Baum's reflections on premarital sex (Father Baum had spoken at the LCWR 1971 assembly); 3) to get Hans Küng straight, instead of being filtered through Father McBrien (Father Richard McBrien also had addressed the 1971 assembly); 4) to have one's positive positions accepted as such, rather than being labeled negative.

It became clear during the discussion that the LCWR representatives favored a continuing dialogue with the Vatican about regulations on religious life. The consortium representatives suggested that dialogue was fine until the Vatican spoke definitively on a subject, and then dialogue should cease. However, conference president Sister Thomas Aquinas said that since the Vatican curia had not yet caught up to Vatican II, sisters were merely being helpful by questioning certain issues. LCWR representatives also pointed out that the official Church had made incorrect statements before, as in the case of Galileo.

Then the consortium grilled Sister Thomas Aquinas on her decision not to pass along to members of the LCWR a 1971 letter from the Congregation for Religious that commented on the pope's evaluation of renewal. Sister Thomas Aquinas explained that, in her capacity as president, she had to decide which actions would do more harm than good, and she had decided that passing that information along to conference members would "do more to diminish the image of the

---

[11] Representing the LCWR were members of its executive committee: Sisters Thomas Aquinas (Elizabeth) Carroll, Angelita Myerscough, Joan deLourdes Leonard, Francis Borgia Rothluebber, and Margaret Brennan. Also attending was the conference executive director, Immaculate Heart of Mary Sister Ann Virginia Bowling. Representing the Consortium board were Sisters Mary Elise Krantz, Alice Anita Murphy, Mary Claudia Honsberger, Dominican Sister Marie William MacGregor, Little Sister of the Poor Gertrude Elizabeth McGovern, and Sister of Notre Dame Mary Nathan Hess.

Congregation for Religious among many sisters than it would enhance it. . . . I feel that very, very often I am placed in a position of trying to uphold the Congregation for Religious against its own acts. And this is a terrible position to be in." [12]

So went the dialogue; instead of coming to agreement on any issues, the two parties had merely succeeded in elaborating on their differences.

The two groups met again in November of 1974, this time in Rome, in the presence of officials from the Congregation for Religious. [13] Cardinal Arturo Tabera, prefect of the congregation, led the meeting, assisted by his undersecretary, Franciscan Father Basil Heiser, an American.

Proceedings of that meeting indicate that Cardinal Tabera was very concerned over the polarization between the two groups of sisters. The LCWR sisters contended that there were acceptable, diverse ways of renewing religious institutes. The consortium sisters countered that they were obliged to accept the authority of the Church and the official interpretation of documents. And Cardinal Tabera observed that in response to the Vatican II call for renewal, there had been some "immobility" as well as "progressivism which went beyond" what was required by the Church. He cited problems with religious institutes whose renewal was based not on Church doctrine, but on "ideology not proper to the Church, on authors who speak and write as independent and autonomous authority, without the due regard which the magisterium rightfully merits". He stressed that religious must not lose their identity or betray the fundamental values of their life by embracing secularization.

The LCWR representatives admitted that there had been abuses in the renewal process, but they contended that those missteps were largely a matter of the past. Cardinal Tabera stressed that the principal responsibility of a national conference of religious was "to follow the norms

[12] CPC record of meeting between CPC administrative board and LCWR executive committee, March 15, 1972, CMAS 2/29, UNDA.

[13] Representing the LCWR were Sister Francine Zeller, conference president; Sister of Charity Barbara Thomas, vice president; Sister Mary Daniel Turner, executive director; and Sister Margaret Brennan, conference president, 1972–1973. The consortium representatives were Sisters Mary Elise, Mary Claudia, Marie William, and Holy Cross Sister Rose Eileen Masterman.

of the documents of the Magisterium for the promotion of religious life". He observed that the LCWR had made mistakes in some of its assembly speakers and some of its publications, but he said those could be remedied. The consortium sisters reported that many of the documents of Vatican II had not been disseminated to American women religious, and they asked the congregation to issue a specific document on religious life (which actually happened in 1983, with *Essential Elements*). About the only issue agreed on by the two groups of sisters was that the consortium did not cause the polarization that existed among women religious, as that division was already present when the consortium was founded.[14]

The Congregation for Religious requested that the dialogue between the LCWR and the consortium continue, so in 1975, Archbishop Mayer, secretary of the congregation, asked Archbishop James J. Byrne of Dubuque to preside at another meeting between the two groups. (Archbishop Byrne was head of the US Bishops' Liaison Committee with the LCWR.) However, the LCWR executive committee was "disconcerted and saddened" that Archbishop Byrne had been asked to mediate the dialogue, as it was the executive committee's contention that Cardinal Tabera had wanted the sisters to continue their dialogue alone. So, the conference executive committee wrote Cardinal Tabera of "our concern about the necessity of a third party presiding at any sharing between LCWR / CPC".[15]

After Archbishop Mayer convinced the LCWR sisters that Archbishop Byrne was to act as a representative of the Congregation for Religious,[16] a meeting eventually took place in Chicago on September 3, 1975. The same sisters who had participated in the 1974 meeting in Rome again represented their organizations, and the differences between the two groups of sisters continued to be obvious. The LCWR sisters suggested that since canon law was being revised, it was acceptable to act in anticipation of the new code. The consortium sisters stressed the importance of following the official documents of the Church that already existed. But again, the only area of agreement

---

[14] Proceedings of combined meeting of Congregation for Religious, LCWR and CPC, November 12–14, 1974, CMAS 3/4, UNDA.

[15] Sister Francine Zeller letter to Sister Mary Elise, March 11, 1975, CMAS 3/7, UNDA.

[16] Archbishop Augustine Mayer letter to Sister Mary Daniel Turner, April 4, 1975, CMAS 3/4, UNDA.

that surfaced was the acknowledgment that the two groups held very different theologies of religious life.[17]

Even though these dialogues had not resulted in any meeting of the minds, they did serve a useful purpose of at least highlighting the enormous gap between the two groups of sisters: LCWR leaders had made it clear they could not accept the premise of the consortium that the conference was leading sisters along a false renewal path; and the consortium sisters were unwilling to consider any renewal ideas that did not follow the pronouncements of Church authorities to the letter.

During the next few years, the two organizations of sisters treated one another with civility, usually inviting a representative of the other group to their annual meetings, but they did not arrive at any consensus.

In 1974, the LCWR published a book titled *Widening the Dialogue*, a collection of essays criticizing the apostolic exhortation *Evangelica Testificatio* and defending the renewal practices undertaken by the more change-oriented religious institutes. The book claimed that *Evangelica Testificatio* was not a conclusive document and that its tone was "not one of finality but of ambivalence". Further, the book claimed that *Evangelica Testificatio* "interprets religious life in a traditional frame and in traditional language, both of which point religious life to the past". Hence, the book's authors concluded, it was necessary to dialogue with the papal document.[18]

In early 1976, the consortium published the booklet *"Widening the Dialogue" . . . ?*, which critiqued the LCWR's 1974 book. "Does one 'dialogue' with a document?", the consortium publication asked, and it disputed, point by point, the LCWR's version of Pope Paul VI's exhortation. The booklet also claimed that "errors, several of which are basic to the understanding of the Church", were being promulgated by the LCWR book and seminars based on it.[19]

New Organizations Emerge

Clearly, no progress was being made in bridging the gap between the two groups of sisters. In the meantime, a third party entered the picture.

[17] Unofficial transcript of September 3, 1975, meeting with Archbishop Byrne and representatives of the CPC and LCWR, O'Hare Airport Hotel, CMAS 3/4, UNDA.

[18] LCWR, *Widening the Dialogue* (Silver Springs, Maryland: LCWR, 1974), 245–46.

[19] Consortium Perfectae Caritatis, *"Widening the Dialogue" . . . ?* (Huntington, Ind.: Our Sunday Visitor, Inc., 1975), 1.

The Institute on Religious Life was founded in Chicago in 1974 by a coalition of hierarchy, clergy, religious, and laity, including Cardinal John Carberry of Saint Louis, Bishop James J. Hogan of Altoona-Johnstown, and Sister Mary Claudia Honsberger, who also was a member of the consortium. According to information published by the institute, its purpose is to gather bishops, priests, religious, and laity "to work together to find solutions confronting religious communities", to "promote authentic religious life as taught by Vatican II", and to encourage vocations. The institute sponsors regional and national meetings, as well as various educational programs. It also publishes related literature and maintains a catalogue of relevant publications. Membership is open to religious communities as well as to individual religious and laity.

Initially there was some tension between the institute and the consortium, including some hard feelings when both organizations scheduled their 1977 annual meetings at the same time, thus forcing some sisters who held membership in both organizations to choose between the two. But eventually those tensions diminished, partly through the efforts of Sister Mary Claudia Honsberger, who as a member of both groups convinced her colleagues that the two groups were organized for two distinct purposes and were complementary rather than competitive.

Other women religious, however, did not look so kindly on the Institute on Religious Life. The January 1978 newsletter of NCAN carried a long harangue about the institute's 1977 conference in Saint Louis, titled "Whatever Happened to Religious Life?" The NCAN newsletter said that the title of the conference was insulting to thousands of religious men and women and that the conference would "not diminish the undeniable reality which is twentieth century religious life, not over-the-shoulder nostalgia." The newsletter also observed that the conference speakers looked like "Who's Who in Right Wing America" (speakers included Phyllis Schlafly; Congressman Henry Hyde; Virgil C. Dechant, supreme knight of the Knights of Columbus; Geraldine Frawley of *Twin Circle*; and Dale Francis of *Our Sunday Visitor*).[20]

The LCWR was not happy with the Institute on Religious Life either. Minutes from their 1979 annual assembly indicate their growing concern over the institute's activities, especially its new office in

[20] *NCAN News* (January 1978), CLCW 27/8, UNDA.

the Vatican, which communicated directly with the Congregation for Religious. Additional concern was raised about financial contributions "from conservative lay persons in the church, and the endorsement of some of the Bishops". The minutes indicate that LCWR leaders had already discussed the institute with apostolic delegate Archbishop Jean Jadot, Archbishop John Quinn, and the Bishops' Liaison Committee with Religious.[21]

The LCWR was further dismayed when in 1983 the pope appointed Archbishop John Quinn to lead the study of religious life in the United States. The pope also authorized the Congregation for Religious to issue *Essential Elements*, a document summarizing Church teaching on religious life. Some LCWR members railed against the pope's study at their 1983 assembly, calling it an effort to get American sisters "back in line".[22] Just two months after the LCWR assembly, the November 1983 newsletter of the Institute on Religious Life carried an "Open Letter to U.S. Bishops". The open letter referred to "discordant voices" that had publicly questioned the right of the pope to direct religious in the United States, an obvious reference to the disparaging remarks at the LCWR assembly and to those made at the recent meeting of the Conference of Major Superiors of Men. The institute letter went on to welcome the study of religious life and to thank the pope for *Essential Elements*. The institute's open letter contained the signatures of superiors from 126 religious institutes, as well as those of several laity.[23]

The Institute on Religious Life was not deterred by the opposition of its detractors. Its board of directors attracted several prominent members of the hierarchy, including Cardinals William Baum, Anthony Bevilacqua, John Carberry, James Hickey, John Krol, and John O'Connor, and its annual meetings regularly drew hundreds of religious and laity.

The institute also played a major role in the erection of a second conference of women's superiors in the United States. At the institute's national meeting in 1986, a special session was set aside for major superiors to discuss the possibility of forming an association of women's superiors within the institute. Dominican Sister Assumpta Long, who had served on the consortium board, chaired a committee to study the

---

[21] Minutes of LCWR 1979 assembly, August 28, 1979, CMAS 3/31, UNDA.
[22] Quinonez and Turner, *Transformation*, 87.
[23] Institute on Religious Life newsletter, *Religious Life* (November 1983).

possibility. One year later, the Forum of Major Superiors was established as a part of the Institute on Religious Life at the 1987 national meeting. Sister Assumpta was elected first president of the forum and was succeeded by Little Sister of the Poor Mary Bernard Nettle in 1989. The forum was designed to promote communication and cooperation between the superiors and was open to any women major superiors, even those not affiliated with the Institute on Religious Life.

By 1988, most women superiors who belonged to the Consortium Perfectae Caritatis also held membership in the Institute's Forum of Major Superiors.[24] A few of these sisters maintained membership in the LCWR as well, but most of them had severed ties with the conference over ideological differences.

Meanwhile, Pope John Paul II was becoming increasingly concerned about the state of religious life in the United States, particularly about the polarization between sisters. The work of the Quinn Commission (see chapter 13) did little to calm those concerns, and in early March 1989, thirty-five US bishops met with the pope and Vatican officials to discuss the topic.

In the March 9 session of the meeting, Cardinal Jean Jerome Hamer, prefect of the Congregation for Religious, told the bishops that they were responsible not only for the apostolic work done by religious in their dioceses, but also for overseeing the observance of their vows, their "fraternal life in community"; the witness they "bear to God before the people of God"; and their "fidelity to their distinct charism". Cardinal Hamer explained that the pope was not giving the bishops new powers over religious but rather was highlighting the authority they already had. "This pastoral service of religious life must be not only pursued, but intensified", he said.[25]

A Significant Intervention by Cardinal James Hickey

Cardinal James Hickey of Washington also spoke at that meeting, and his remarks would turn out to be more significant than most people

---

[24] Minutes of the October 9, 1988, CPC administrative board meeting, CCPC 2/04, UNDA.

[25] Cardinal Jean Jerome Hamer, OP, "The Pastoral Responsibility of Bishops to Religious Life", *Origins*, March 23, 1989, 691–92.

realized at the time. Cardinal Hickey noted the deep divisions among religious in the United States, even religious living in the same institute. And he mentioned the many sisters who had no formal communication link with the Vatican because they did not support the views of the LCWR and therefore did not hold membership in the superiors' conference.

The cardinal spoke about a "crisis which many religious congregations in the United States are facing" because of an overall membership decline and a rising average age. He said that "within the same religious institute divergent views have arisen on many seminal issues which previously bound members closely together." These issues included living in community, the value of various religious practices, and the authority of the ordinary Magisterium. "In some cases the very meaning of vowed religious life and its relationship to the church, both local and universal, remain points of disagreement and even division among members of the same institute", he said. Cardinal Hickey also observed that an emphasis on justice issues and social needs had "profoundly affected" the way religious view themselves and their ministries, with the result that political activism often overshadowed the "transcendent nature of religious life".

Cardinal Hickey identified two basic orientations toward religious life in the United States. The first model describes the change-oriented institutes discussed in this book. He said this model stresses mission and ministry and seems to characterize the majority of religious institutes in this country. These religious embrace "the importance of being in the midst of the world in order to address its needs", he said, and so "the external structures of religious life are de-emphasized." In some cases, these religious "describe the fundamental purpose of religious life as 'community for mission'". Cardinal Hickey listed the following characteristics of some of these religious institutes: living in small communities or alone, choosing one's own ministry, engaging in works not associated with the Church, turning away from corporate commitments in order to work on social-justice issues, and becoming more politically active. "Many religious are convinced they are developing new forms of religious life while at the same time living in a manner consonant with membership in an approved religious institute", he said.

Cardinal Hickey said that the second, traditional model focuses on "consecration through the vows as a value in itself and a basis for community apostolate". He said these institutes emphasize "the centrality of common life, common prayer, the religious habit and community-based ministries". Such institutes, he said, "look to the magisterium and their own traditions to determine future directions". Cardinal Hickey enumerated five duties of bishops regarding religious life: 1) sharing the teaching of the Church on religious life; 2) spending time with religious to develop mutual understanding; 3) strengthening communication between religious and the Holy See; 4) holding up to the young the highest esteem for religious life; and 5) assisting religious with pressing problems, such as recruitment, adequate wage compensation, and retirement funding.

Regarding his third point, about communication between the Vatican and religious, Cardinal Hickey said that the Conference of Major Superiors of Men and the LCWR were the only official channels between the Holy See and religious in the United States. But, he said, "a significant number of religious relate to the Consortium Perfectae Caritatis or the Institute on Religious Life. I see a need for us as bishops to foster discussion at the local and the universal level among religious holding divergent points of view. We should also remember that many religious women not represented by the LCWR desire some representation with the Holy See." [26]

The Pope Acts

On March 29, a little over two weeks after the Vatican meeting, Pope John Paul II addressed a letter to US bishops in which he asked them to continue their "special pastoral service" to religious begun in 1983 when he appointed the Quinn Commission. He said that the bishops had done the listening and dialoguing he had asked for, but that the teaching of "a sound theological exposition of religious life" must be ongoing, not temporary. In the letter, the pope expressed his concern about the division between sisters and stressed that all superiors had the right to belong to the LCWR and all members of the conference had the right to make their concerns heard. "The conference must find realistic and equitable ways to express the concerns of all women

---

[26] Cardinal James Hickey, "The Pastoral Responsibility of Bishops Regarding Religious Life in the United States", *Origins*, March 23, 1989, 692–93.

religious", he urged, and he directed bishops to find "effective ways to remove the causes of their division". He also exhorted the women to "speak to one another about the issues which divide them." The pope acknowledged that other organizations had been founded to promote religious life and said that, while such associations of the faithful were distinct from superiors' conferences, there was a legitimate place in the Church for them.[27]

A month later, in an unprecedented move, Pope John Paul II gave a clear indication that he had heard the pleas of the traditional sisters. The pope appointed Cardinal Hickey to a three-year term as official liaison to the Vatican for sisters who were not affiliated with the LCWR. In a May 2 letter making the appointment, the pope also asked Cardinal Hickey to act as a facilitator of communication between the LCWR and the sisters who were not affiliated with it.[28] Thus, Cardinal Hickey attempted to bring the sisters together.

The cardinal arranged for a series of dialogue sessions between the LCWR, the Consortium Perfectae Caritatis, and sisters representing both the Forum of Major Superiors from the Institute on Religious Life and the institute itself. The first session took place in October 1989 and was followed by sessions in April and September 1990.

The transcript of the September 1990 meeting revealed seemingly irreconcilable differences. The consortium sisters wanted to discuss "absolute truths that would transcend ... any age, any period of time, any period of history", as well as "the relationship between the living tradition ... and the hierarchy, or the teaching office of the Church."[29] But Sister Doris Gottemoeller of the LCWR responded, "I can't think of anything that's infallibly taught, nor anything in Scripture, about religious life. The Church has given us a great deal of latitude in terms of the way in which we live out the calling that we received, that our founders have received and that we, in concert with them, follow, and the Church sort of blesses it in retrospect, the Church doesn't originate it."[30]

---

[27] Pope John Paul II letter to U.S. bishops, "Religious Life in the United States", *Origins*, April 13, 1989, 749.

[28] *National Catholic Register*, May 28, 1989.

[29] "Transcribed Text of the Meeting of the Consortium and the LCWR Dialogue Teams September 8, 1990, Silver Spring, Maryland". A copy was given to the author by Sister Mary Elise.

[30] Ibid., 30.

When it came time to plan future dialogues, the LCWR president indicated that her organization had little patience for continuing conversations with either the consortium or the Institute on Religious Life. She said that her conference would be willing to continue "official communication" with the Forum of Major Superiors, since it was an entity made up only of superiors and thus was comparable to the conference. The LCWR suggested that if the consortium and the institute wished to continue dialogue with the LCWR, the conference would send a representative to such a meeting, but that such a dialogue should probably bring in other organizations of sisters, such as the NARW. Finally, Sister Doris suggested that if women superiors wished to continue dialoguing with the LCWR, they should simply join the conference. The meeting ended with the groups agreeing to give further thought to when or whether future dialogues would take place.

After the meeting, consortium president Sister Vincent Marie Finnegan, a Carmelite, had her secretary transcribe the audiotapes of the meeting into a ninety-four-page text. These transcripts then were sent out to all parties for approval. The LCWR representatives refused to approve the text as the official record of the meeting and instead proposed a six-page summary as the official record. The consortium representatives thought that the conference's six-page summary did not adequately represent the deep theological divisions that had become evident at the meeting, so they eventually signed the conference minutes under protest and added comments of their own.[31] The complete ninety-four-page transcript of the meeting was nevertheless given to Cardinal Hickey, who presented it at a meeting of the USCCB and eventually took it to Rome. Apparently, the transcript helped set the stage for Vatican approval of a new conference of women's superiors.

New Conference of Major Superiors Is Approved

In April 1991, the consortium administrative board met to discuss the previous September's dialogue meeting and to plan future strategy. It was suggested at the meeting that the Vatican had ordered dialogue

[31] As reported in minutes of annual meeting of the CPC administrative board, April 24, 1992, CCPC 2/08, UNDA.

between the groups of sisters in order to get in writing their clear differences. Holy Cross Sister Mary Gerald Hartney observed that the LCWR did make a valid point about the various groups—the consortium, the forum, and the Institute on Religious Life—being so disunited and diverse. The sisters also discussed their concern that the emerging new communities of sisters who were basing their constitutions on Vatican II teachings about religious life had nowhere else to go if they did not feel comfortable with the direction of the LCWR. The consortium was not a leadership group, and the Forum of Major Superiors really was not an independent body, but a part of the Institute on Religious Life. The idea eventually emerged that the best course of action would be to create a new entity, and the consortium board agreed to approach the Forum of Major Superiors about this possibility.[32]

The consortium and forum officers met on September 5, 1991, to discuss uniting the two groups. But during discussion of a possible merger, it became clear that it would be more helpful to women religious all over the country to form one distinct new organization composed only of major superiors that would seek approval from the Vatican.[33] Consultation with canon lawyers verified that there was nothing in canon law to prevent the approval of more than one conference of superiors in a country, though this had never before happened. The two groups of sisters decided to proceed by having the consortium board meet with the board of the Institute on Religious Life.

The eventual conclusion reached at a December 14, 1991, meeting of the officers of the consortium, the forum, and the institute was that a new council of major superiors of women religious should be formed and should seek Vatican approval. Cardinal Hickey was present at the meeting as papal liaison and was supportive of the idea.

Forming the new conference of women's superiors with Cardinal Hickey's help had to be done quickly, because the cardinal's three-year papal appointment as Vatican liaison was due to expire in five months. A steering committee was formed to draft a mission statement and statutes for the new organization. Serving on that committee were Sisters Vincent Marie Finnegan, chairwoman; Mary Bernard Nettle; M.

---

[32] Minutes of CPC administrative board meeting, April 5, 1991, CCPC 2/08, UNDA.
[33] Minutes of Consortium Perfectae Caritatis administrative board, October 13, 1991, CCPC 2/08, UNDA.

de Chantal Saint Julien, a Sister of the Holy Family; and Franciscan Sister Leticia Rodriguez. Assisting the committee were Bishop John J. Myers of Peoria; Bishop John Sheets, a Jesuit and auxiliary bishop of Fort Wayne–South Bend, Indiana; and an unnamed canon lawyer.[34]

In just three days, the steering committee wrote an initial draft for a mission statement, which began: "There is a need for religious not aligned with LCWR to have a permanent organization or structure by which their needs could be represented to the Holy See and through which the Holy See could communicate its concerns, directives and encouragement."[35] Then the sisters finished the statutes and sought support for them from religious institutes and ecclesial authorities across the country.

In January 1992, Cardinal Hickey presented the proposal for the new conference to Pope John Paul II and Cardinal Eduardo Martinez Somalo, prefect of the Congregation for Religious. A month later, Cardinal Hickey told the Forum of Major Superiors that the pope and Cardinal Somalo had been in favor of their proposal, but approval was not yet official. Then on February 19 Archbishop Agostino Cacciavillan, apostolic delegate to the United States, met with representatives of the LCWR and the CMSM and informed them that a new Vatican-approved Council of Major Superiors of Women Religious was coming into existence.

The LCWR Is Not Happy

After hearing the news, the stunned president of the LCWR requested a meeting with the Congregation for Religious. On April 10, Cardinal Somalo, the prefect, and members of his staff met in Rome with the LCWR president, Dominican Sister Donna Markham, and conference executive director Sister Janet Roesener. Accompanying the sisters for moral support—and indicating the tacit support of their conferences—were Christian Brother Paul Hennessy, president of the CMSM, and Monsignor Robert Lynch, general secretary of the USCCB. Sister Donna reported after the meeting that Cardinal Somalo had

[34] Minutes of annual meeting of the CPC administrative board, April 24, 1992, CCPC 2/08, UNDA.

[35] "The Formation of an Association of Major Superiors of Women Religious", Mission Statement, initial draft, December 17, 1991, CCPC 6/66, UNDA.

assured her that the new council would not be perceived as equal to the LCWR nor would it be considered a parallel or alternative national conference.[36] According to Brother Paul's recollection of the meeting, the Americans "all expressed concern that the canonical approval of a small group of religious as parallel to a conference could be hurtful and divisive." He said that the congregation listened to their delegation "very attentively and with great courtesy" and assured them "that a parallel group would not be established." Brother Paul added, "I informed the gathering that in my years of interaction with LCWR, they had reached out over and over, with little success, to those women who had formed their own unofficial union."[37]

However, at the very moment the American contingent sat in the meeting with the Congregation for Religious, pleading the case of the LCWR, a bombshell was exploding in other parts of the Vatican. A new book, *The Transformation of American Catholic Sisters*, had just been released, and it told the story of the LCWR from the perspective of two former executive directors, Sisters Mary Daniel Turner (1972–1978) and Lora Ann Quinonez (1978–1986). The two authors spared no details in characterizing the transformation of the superior's conference from an entity created by and loyal to the Vatican into an independent organization of sisters determined to conduct their business the American democratic way. The book also detailed the conference's ongoing conflict with the Vatican over the nature of religious life and its often-stormy relations with ecclesiastical authority.[38] Supporters of the new traditional superiors' conference made sure that plenty of copies of the book were made available in Rome. The book could not have been published at a worse time for the LCWR or a better time for the fledgling new council, for it confirmed and vividly detailed what the traditional sisters had been saying about the LCWR.

The new Council of Major Superiors of Women Religious was formally established by the Congregation for Religious on June 13, 1992, with tentative approval of its statutes for five years. The approval was made known to the US bishops by Cardinal Hickey in a closed session

---

[36] Jerry Filteau, "Vatican Official Calls LCWR 'The' U.S. Conference", Catholic News Service, July 29, 1992.

[37] Paul K. Hennessy, CFC, letter to "Dear Brother Members of CMSM", June 22, 1992.

[38] Quinonez and Turner, *Transformation*, 161.

of their spring meeting on June 19. Sister Donna Markham, president of the LCWR, also was informed of the decision while she was at the bishops' meeting.[39]

Announcement to the public came in a June 22 press release from the Archdiocese of Washington, which said that the new CMSWR had equal canonical standing with the LCWR and was an alternative to the conference. The press release also stressed that the status of the LCWR remained unchanged, and it noted that, while the two groups of women superiors had equal canonical status, they were not linked organizationally, though the Holy See desired cooperation between them. The June 22 announcement also brought the news that Cardinal Hickey had been reappointed to serve as papal liaison to sisters not affiliated with the LCWR.

After the new council was created, the Consortium Perfectae Caritatis and the Forum of Major Superiors were dissolved by their own memberships, and the assets of the consortium were transferred to the council. Sister Vincent Marie Finnegan acted as spokeswoman for the new organization.

Some eighty-four superiors, representing about ten thousand professed sisters and another nine hundred in formation, applied for membership in the new council.[40] The new council represented only about 10 percent of women religious at that time, but it represented a significantly higher percentage of the women who were then in formation, and that trend has continued into the second decade of the twenty-first century.

The statutes of the new council included membership criteria based, as Sister Mary Elise had suggested, on the essential elements of religious life defined by Pope John Paul II. Consequently, membership in the new council was open to major superiors and vicars of institutes that live in community, follow the teaching of the Magisterium, share common prayer, practice community-based ministries, adhere to the authority of a superior, and wear religious garb. Potential members were required to apply for membership in the organization and then be approved by the council's board.[41]

[39] Hennessy, June 22 letter.

[40] Congregation for Institutes of Consecrated Life and Societies of Apostolic Life, "Decree Recognizing New Council of Major Superiors of Women Religious", *Origins*, July 23, 1992, 161.

[41] Ibid., 159.

Needless to say, the LCWR was not happy with approval of the new group, nor was the CMSM. Adding to their discomfort was the fact that there had been some misunderstanding about the canonical standing of the new council. A joint statement issued by the two conferences on June 22 observed that both conferences, as well as the International Union of Superiors General had "directly expressed" to the Congregation for Religious "their opposition to the plans to take this action". And the statement contended that at the April 10 meeting in Rome, the Congregation for Religious "affirmed LCWR as the official conference for women religious leaders in the United States and assured the representatives that any new group would not be parallel to or a substitute for LCWR". The joint statement declared, "LCWR and CMSM are concerned that the establishment of this separate council will open old wounds within congregations and between congregations. Such an action is contrary to a primary function of leadership—to promote unity and understanding."

Brother Paul Hennessy, president of the CMSM, expressed his dismay in a letter to his members, saying that approval of the new conference was "offensive" and "not unifying". The CMSM president also reported that he would write Cardinal Somalo "to express my regret and disappointment that despite my trip to Rome and all our communications, we were not included in a notification about the establishment of the new council. We clearly indicated to him our belief that this is not [a] 'women's issue' but a religious life issue, and we had to learn of the establishment through hearsay and through the press." [42]

Sister Donna Markham, president of the LCWR, wrote Cardinal Somalo, complaining about the language used to describe the new council, being particularly disturbed that the new group was depicted as being an alternative to the LCWR. She told Catholic News Service that Cardinal Somalo had responded in July that each conference had its own distinct purpose and that superiors could belong to either or both organizations.[43] A further clarification came in August from a spokesman for Cardinal Hickey. Monsignor William Lori said that the new council had the same "juridical nature" as the LCWR, and it

[42] Hennessy, June 22 letter.
[43] Filteau, "Vatican Official Calls LCWR 'The' U.S. Conference".

was an official association of major superiors in the United States that had been "erected canonically by the Holy See". Monsignor Lori said the chief differences between the new council and the LCWR were in their specific purposes and their membership.[44]

USCCB president Archbishop Daniel Pilarczyk extended good wishes to the new council, but he indicated that its approval was a big surprise and tried to smooth over matters by adding, "I wish to assure the members of the LCWR that their valuable contribution and witness in the life of the church in the United States continues to be greatly appreciated by the bishops of our conference."[45] Archbishop Quinn seemed similarly surprised and perplexed by the move, saying, "In faith and obedience to the church I accept this decision and pray that the new council will be effective for the church." Archbishop Quinn also hastened to praise the LCWR and its members, saying that the conference still was approved by the Vatican and that "the constitutions of the individual congregations belonging to the LCWR have also been approved by the Holy See, giving authenticity to the way of life lived in accord with those constitutions."[46] (Note: Most, but not all constitutions of communities affiliated with the LCWR had been approved by the Vatican at that time.)

Message from the Vatican?

Why did the Vatican approve the new council?

Some Vatican watchers speculated that the "special pastoral service" the pope had asked of US bishops, to proclaim anew "the church's teaching on consecrated life", had not been very effectively rendered to, or accepted by, a good many women religious. Further, the LCWR had made a habit of "dialoguing" about directives from the Vatican rather than implementing them, and the Vatican may simply have run out of patience with these debates. Since so few sisters still staffed Catholic institutions in the United States, the prospect that religious

[44] Filteau, "New Nuns' Council Called a Real Alternative to LCWR", Catholic News Service, August 11, 1992.

[45] Archbishop Daniel Pilarczyk statement in "Decree Recognizing New Council of Major Superiors of Women Religious", Origins, July 23, 1992, 159.

[46] Archbishop John Quinn statement in "Decree Recognizing New Council of Major Superiors of Women Religious", ibid.

orders might withdraw from service if Church authorities approved another superiors' conference had disappeared. Another factor certainly must have been the delivery to Rome of the text of the September 1990 sisters' dialogue, which should have made very clear to Vatican officials the deep theological and philosophical differences dividing the groups of sisters.

Additionally, it was becoming clear that the orders that maintain a traditional religious lifestyle—living in community, praying regularly and together, wearing religious garb, working in Catholic Church institutions, espousing fidelity to the pope—attract most of the new vocations. As a result, they have a lower median age than the change-orientated communities. Approval of the new council may have reflected the Vatican's recognition that future growth of religious life in the United States appears to be taking the direction pursued by the new council members.

Also, the communities affiliated with the new Council of Major Superiors of Women Religious clearly are more inclined to make a corporate commitment to staff Catholic institutions within dioceses—something orders with an open placement policy cannot effectively do. A 2012 survey showed that sisters in institutes affiliated with CMSWR live or serve in 129 US dioceses, as well as 54 locations outside the country.[47]

The Vatican apparently was well pleased with the council's performance during its first three years in existence, for in late 1995 it gave final approval to the council's statutes, two years before its probationary period ended. In spite of all the hard feelings, the LCWR and the CMSWR have managed to interact gracefully since the new council was approved, and representatives of each group usually attend the annual meeting of the other group.

---

[47] CMSWR 2012 statistics provided to the author Oct. 10, 2012, by Sister Regina Marie Gorman, OCD, chairwoman of the CMSWR board of directors.

PART II

HOW DID ALL OF THIS HAPPEN?

8

The Many Faces of Indoctrination

How did all this ever happen to us? . . . All this did not just *happen*. We did it to ourselves.[1]

— Sister Elizabeth McDonough, OP

The largest project in the history of the Conference of Major Religious Superiors of Women's Institutes—renamed the LCWR—was a twenty-five-year study directed by Sister Marie Augusta Neal, a sociologist. The second stage of that project, a 1967 survey sent to almost every active sister in the United States, proved to be a major tool for shaping renewal in American convents and developing the revolutionary new concepts of religious life embraced by many modern sisters. Consequently, the change-oriented leaders lauded the survey as a renewal project that exceeded their wildest expectations, while the survey's detractors have called it a biased instrument with political motives that accomplished the most comprehensive indoctrination of American nuns ever.

One sister who completed the survey observed that if sisters weren't already dissatisfied with religious life before they answered the questions, they certainly had reasons to be afterward. Plenty of questions promoted dissatisfaction, such as those about the value of the vows, the authority of superiors, some doctrinal teachings of the Church, and the very significance of religious life. Sisters have told the author that they remember completing the survey and being confused by the

[1] McDonough, "Beyond the Liberal Model: Quo Vadis?" *Review for Religious* (January / February 1992): 173.

statements and questions, many of which really had no one answer. One sister recalled skipping over questions that she felt would indicate disloyalty to the Church. Although some sisters told the author they threw the questionnaire away after they saw its content, most sisters dutifully completed the survey in obedience to their superiors.

Sociologist Sister Patricia Wittberg has observed, "For many, simply completing the survey was a consciousness-raising experience. By asking whether a sister had read a particular modern theologian's writings, for example, or whether she had attended 'meetings of people other than her fellow community members', the survey legitimated such activities for many respondents who would not otherwise have thought of doing so on their own." [2]

In analyzing the effect of the Sisters' Survey, former LCWR executive directors Sisters Mary Daniel Turner and Lora Ann Quinonez said that it "proved catalytic far beyond what its creators dreamed". And they proudly reported that the survey results were used as a basis for proposals to renew the lives of sisters and help them understand what was involved "in living into a new image, in fact a new paradigm, of religious life". [3] Sister Thomas Aquinas (Elizabeth) Carroll (a member of the Sisters' Survey Committee and LCWR president in 1971) wrote later that the survey, along with Vatican II, "served to unleash new concepts of what religious life could and should be, and contributed immensely to the creativity and ferment of special chapters all over the country". [4]

What these commentators did not say was that the Sisters' Survey was more than a questionnaire. It was an educational tool (some would say a propaganda tool) used to introduce into every American convent a concept of renewal that had been conceived by an elite group of sisters—one that differed vastly from the instructions for renewal set forth in the Vatican II documents. This vision of religious life would be adopted by most orders of women in the United States.

Whatever one's opinion of the 1967 Sisters' Survey, it unquestionably stands out as the most extensive effort ever to find out what American Catholic nuns thought about a myriad of issues. Nearly 140,000

---

[2] Patricia Wittberg, SC, *The Rise and Fall of Catholic Religious Orders* (Albany: State University of New York Press, 1994), 215.

[3] Quinonez and Turner, *Transformation*, 43–44, 49.

[4] Elizabeth Carroll, RSM, "Reaping the Fruits of Redemption", in *Midwives*, 64.

sisters took hours to wade through the 649 questions in the twenty-three-page survey, which was given to every sister in almost every religious institute, with the exception of contemplative institutes. The survey originally was to have been limited to a sampling of sisters, but eventually grew into a much broader project that touched almost every American woman religious.

The Changing Sister

The beginnings of the Sisters' Survey can be traced back to the summer of 1964, when ten sisters, ten priests, and forty lay Catholics got together for a week at Grailville, Ohio, to study preliminary drafts of documents coming out of the Second Vatican Council. The drafts had been translated and distributed by a lay organization, so they were not the official or final Council documents.[5] Among the sisters attending that meeting were Sisters Mary Luke Tobin, then president of the CMSW; Mary Daniel Turner, a conference board member and chair of the conference's Sister Formation Committee; Sister of Notre Dame de Namur Margaret Claydon, president of Trinity College, Washington, DC; Sister of Charity of the Blessed Virgin Mary, Ann Ida Gannon, president of Mundelein College, Chicago; Sister of Loretto Jacqueline Grennan, president of Webster College, Saint Louis; Holy Cross Sister Charles Borromeo (Mary Ellen) Muckenhirn, chair of the Theology Department at Saint Mary's College, Notre Dame, Indiana, and editor of the "Sisters' Forum" for the *National Catholic Reporter*; and Sister Marie Augusta Neal, sociologist at Emmanuel College, Boston.[6] (Jacqueline Grennan and Mary Ellen Muckenhirn shortly thereafter left religious life.)

The sisters at that Grailville meeting decided to publish a book about the impact of the coming renewal on sisters. *The Changing Sister*, edited by Sister Charles Borromeo, was published in June 1965, several months before the Council document on religious life, *Perfectae Caritatis*, was published, and more than a year before the publication of the blueprint for implementing reform, *Ecclesiae Sanctae*. So, rather than reflecting the final version of the Council documents, *The Changing Sister*

[5] Neal, *From Nuns to Sisters*, 55–56.
[6] Ibid.

drew heavily on the writings of several progressive theologians: Jesuit Father Pierre Teilhard de Chardin, Dominican Father Edward Schillebeeckx, Dominican Father Yves Congar, Jesuit Father Karl Rahner, and Redemptorist Father Bernard Haring.

Nine sisters contributed a chapter to the book: Mary Daniel Turner, Marie Augusta Neal, Charles Borromeo (Mary Ellen) Muckenhirn, Holy Cross Sister Elena Malits, Sister of Saint Joseph M. Aloysius Schaldenbrand, Loretto Sister Jane Marie Richardson, Immaculate Heart of Mary Sister M. Corita Kent, Franciscan Sister Angelica Seng, and Benedictine Sister Jane-Marie Luecke.

After the book was published, and before the 1965 annual assembly of the superiors' conference, the executive committee of the conference appointed a committee of five superiors to conduct research they determined to be necessary for the adaptation and renewal of religious life. Sister Mary Daniel Turner was named chair of that Research Committee on Religious Life. Other superiors appointed to the committee were Sisters Angelita Myerscough (conference president, 1970–1971), Thomas Aquinas (Elizabeth) Carroll (conference president, 1971–1972), Humiliata (Anita) Caspary, and Sister of Saint Joseph Isabel Concannon. Sister Mary Luke Tobin (conference president, 1964–1967) was named an ex officio member.[7] The research committee then selected the nine sister-authors of *The Changing Sister* to be consultants to their committee. These nine sisters also were invited to speak at the August 1965 annual assembly of the CMSW, where conference president Sister Mary Luke announced that the research committee had been formed.

The research committee subsequently proposed the idea of conducting a national survey of sisters, ostensibly to determine the readiness of the sisters of the United States for renewal and to decide what direction the planning should take. However, some critics of the Sisters' Survey suggest that the survey actually was designed to determine where the majority of sisters stood on a myriad of issues so that a strategy could be implemented to dissuade the sisters from their convictions. Other critics charge that the survey was intended as an indoctrination tool to prepare sisters for the agenda that some of the sister-leaders wished to pursue.

---

[7] *Proceedings of the LCWR Annual Assembly, 1965,* 194.

There is some evidence to support both charges in the minutes of the meeting of the Research and Study Project on Religious Life that took place in Mequon, Wisconsin, on September 25, 1965. The minutes make it clear that the idea for the research committee and the survey originated within the leadership of the conference's Sister Formation Committee, chaired by Sister Mary Daniel Turner (who was one of the contributors to *The Changing Sister*). The minutes mention the "necessity of permissiveness in regard to experimentation" and suggest that the Sisters' Survey must "strive to get at 'attitudes'" and be "educative in purpose".[8]

It is important to note that all of these events occurred before the publication of the Council decree on the proper renewal of religious life, *Perfectae Caritatis*, which was issued on October 28, 1965. *Ecclesiae Sanctae*, the blueprint for implementing *Perfectae Caritatis*, was not issued until August 1966, so the sisters were not working from the final version of these official Council documents. (*Lumen Gentium*, which contained a section about consecrated life in terms of the universal call to holiness had been issued in November 1964, so that document was available.)

Stage one of the research project was to survey the superiors of the women's religious institutes about personnel, resources and projected ten-year plans. That first stage took place during the summer of 1966, in the form of a questionnaire sent to more than four hundred superiors.

Originally the research committee had planned for stage two to be a random sample survey of several hundred sisters to determine how they felt about change and to get their ideas about what changes they would like make. But, after seeing the results of the survey of leaders, the board of the superiors' conference decided in early 1967 to survey the entire population of sisters whose leaders belonged to the conference. In sociological circles, it is considered highly unusual to survey an entire population simply to ascertain where the population stands on particular issues; such data can be obtained with a very low margin of error by surveying a small but statistically significant percentage of a population. This fact gives credence to the argument of survey critics that the survey was intended as an indoctrination tool as well as a

---

[8] Minutes of the meeting of the Research and Study Project on Religious Life, September 25, 1965, CLCW 86/05, UNDA.

tool for comparing orders with each other. In any event, in the spring of 1967, the national Sisters' Survey was sent to 157,000 sisters. An impressive 88 percent—139,691—completed and returned it.[9]

Once the survey got into circulation, controversy arose over its content, which seemed to mirror the theology of the sisters who created the survey, rather than that presented in the Council documents. Sister Marie Augusta insisted repeatedly that the survey questions were based on Vatican II documents, but there is more similarity between the questions and *The Changing Sister* than between the questions and *Perfectae Caritatis* and *Lumen Gentium*.

The essays in *The Changing Sister* frequently carried a revolutionary theme and a heavy new emphasis on the sociological aspects of religious life rather than the spiritual ones. The writers in *The Changing Sister* also deviated from the long-standing principle that the traditional, primary value of religious men and women is who they *are*—consecrated persons who witness to the transcendent—and instead placed nearly the entire emphasis on what religious *do*. And they introduced a new primary mission for religious—social justice, which they claimed had superiority over the traditional apostolates, even though these have consistently encompassed the works of mercy.

Sister Marie Augusta expounded on this new value of consecrated persons in a paper presented at the June 1966 Institute on Religious Life in the Modern World: "Finally, social justice and charity are the keys for determining the adequacy of a congregation's work. Social justice refers to a condition existing in a society where the rules are such that abiding by them allows the greatest possible freedom for each man to develop his human potential. Many modern communities are far from this ideal.... This is the ideal of the Christian community and the goal of religious life." [10]

These new values were reflected quite recognizably in the Sisters' Survey, as we can see by comparing the following statements from *The Changing Sister* with subsequent statements from the Sisters' Survey, with which sisters were to indicate their level of agreement or disagreement.

---

[9] Marie Augusta Neal, SND, "Part I. The Relation between Religious Belief and Structural Change in Religious Orders: Developing an Effective Measuring Instrument", *Review of Religious Research* (Fall 1970): 5–6.

[10] Neal, "The Value of Religious Community", in *Vows but No Walls*, ed. Eugene E. Grollmes, SJ (Saint Louis: B. Herder Book Co., 1967), 170.

In *The Changing Sister*, Sister Marie Augusta asserted that "the old structure [of religious communities] is no longer relevant to new needs." [11]

Sisters' Survey:

91. Every religious community in the spirit of the council must adjust to the changed conditions of the times. This means that no community can continue in the traditional form and be working with the mind of the church.

99. I feel that communities of the future should consist of small groups of sisters living a shared life by doing different kinds of work.

155. Any organizational structure becomes a deadening weight in time and needs to be revitalized.

In *The Changing Sister*, Sister Charles Borromeo wrote that religious communities of women had been "deforming young persons" for many years and were "rigid and dead forms of a culture bypassed decades ago in the ordinary world".[12] She also introduced some ideas about the vows that would become popular with avant-garde reformers: obedience defined as openness to the Spirit, and one's work being one's prayer.

Sisters' Survey:

69. The traditional way of presenting chastity in religious life has allowed for the development of isolation and false mysticism among sisters.

79. One of the main characteristics of the new poverty will be openness and liberality of mind, heart, and goods.

90. The vow of obedience is a promise to listen to the community as it speaks through many voices.

In *The Changing Sister*, Sister M. Aloysius Schaldenbrand suggested that "human law, rightly understood, is simply an attempt to express what is due to the person; as an attempt that is never completely successful, moreover, it is always open to completion and correction by due process. Nor does divine law subordinate the person to legal prescription." [13]

[11] Neal, "Sociology and Community Change", *The Changing Sister*, ed. M. Charles Borromeo Muckenhirn, CSC (Notre Dame: Fides Publishers, Inc., 1965), 17.

[12] M. Charles Borromeo, CSC, "Introduction", *The Changing Sister*, 79–80.

[13] M. Aloysius Schaldenbrand, SSJ, "Personal Fulfillment and Apostolic Effectiveness", *The Changing Sister*, 169.

Sisters' Survey:

> 643. The only purpose of the vows of poverty, chastity, and obedience is to create a community wherein people can effectively channel their human energy to the most immediate realization of the gospel.
>
> 644. All authentic law is by its very nature flexible and can be changed by the community in which it is operative.

In *The Changing Sister*, Sister Jane Marie Richardson proclaimed that "Sisters today have the enviable and glorious possibility of standing in the forefront of the Church's renewal. Indeed, their vocation to be human, to be Christian, to be religious demands that they do so.... Unless sisters are living in the Church of today, they are not living in the Church at all." [14]

Sisters' Survey:

> 134. When I think of social reform, I think of things I believe in so deeply I could dedicate all my efforts to them.
>
> 143. Every great step in world history has been accomplished through the inspiration of reformers and creative men.

In *The Changing Sister*, Sister M. Corita Kent, an Immaculate Heart College art professor (who later left religious life as well as the Catholic Church), wrote, "And if our business is to put the always new truth into new wineskins, we need to know the very latest about wineskin making. This means we should be listening to the most experimental (or *avant garde* or whatever) music, seeing the newest plays and films, reading the latest poems and novels." [15]

In questions 246–51 of the Sisters' Survey, participants were asked to indicate whether they had seen, or had any interest in seeing, certain films and television programs. Among those listed were *Nights of Cabiria*, *Wild Strawberries*, *La Dolce Vita*, *Who's Afraid of Virginia Woolf?*, *David and Lisa*, *Batman*, *The Man from U.N.C.L.E.*, *Bonanza*, and films by Alfred Hitchcock.

In *The Changing Sister*, Sister M. Angelica Seng wrote that a sister must be in dialogue with her own times by working in inner cities,

---

[14] Jane Marie Richardson, SL, "The Influence of Scripture and Liturgy", *The Changing Sister*, 206.

[15] M. Corita Kent, IHM, "Art and Beauty in the Life of the Sister", *The Changing Sister*, 226–28.

visiting homes, participating in protests, joining civic causes, challenging priests for more authority in parishes, and getting more involved in parish groups. She wrote, "If the structure, organization and atmosphere of religious institutes do not permit and encourage freedom and initiative in the sisters, then the structure must be changed in view of the needs of our time ... The purpose of the structure of religious communities must be to free the person to respond to the needs of the time." [16]

Sisters' Survey:

44. Since Christ speaks to us through the events of our times, sisters cannot be apostolically effective in the modern world unless they understand and respond to social and political conditions.

49. I think that sisters who feel called to do so ought to be witnessing to Christ on the picket line and speaking out on controversial issues, as well as performing with professional competence among their lay peers in science labs, at conferences, and on the speaker's platform.

Questions 376–87 asked sisters to indicate if their orders worked, or planned to work, with drug addicts and alcoholics, racial minorities, war protesters, "mixed communities groups working to reorganize the city in an integrated fashion", "people experimenting with new ways of living in community, i.e., mixed groups of religious and lay members", "groups of people seeking dialogue with communists" and "groups in protest against affluence".

In *The Changing Sister*, Sister Jane-Marie Luecke declared that "an apostolate in the secular life outside our institutions is also essential if we are to be true to our renewed image." [17]

Sisters' Survey:

495. Do you think all sisters should be allowed to wear contemporary dress at all times?

532. Do you think sisters should be involved in planning and participating in local community events of a civic, artistic, and / or cultural nature?

534. Do you think some sisters in the United States should work in public schools as faculty or staff members?

535. Do you think some sisters in the United States should get involved in civic protest movements?

---

[16] M. Angelica Seng, OSF, "The Sister in the New City", *The Changing Sister*, 260.
[17] Jane-Marie Leucke, OSB, "The Sister in Secular Life", *The Changing Sister*, 294.

536. Do you think sisters should be active in the public sector of society?

In *The Changing Sister*, Sister Mary Daniel Turner urged that sisters must be open "to new programs for Christian formation, new techniques for the apostolate, new research and experimentation for implementing the *aggiornamento*. Committed she must be to liturgical reform, to a kerygmatic religious formation of our people, to ecumenical objectives, to social justice and inner-city renewal." [18]

Sisters' Survey:

504. Do you feel your religious order is sufficiently engaged in work for the poor?

513. Would you stand up for a sister's right in conscience to speak, write, march, demonstrate, picket, etc. when this conflicts with a higher superior's or a bishop's wishes?

524. Would you want to see forms of hospital administration tried which would be different from the characteristic religious community ownership now most common?

525. Would you like to see basic changes in the parochial school system?

The Vatican Is Surprised

The content of the Sister's Survey was apparently unknown to the Vatican until some sisters sent their concerns about it to the Holy See. Shortly after the survey was circulated, Father Bernard Ransing, who was the Congregation for Religious adviser to the CMSW, sent a letter to conference secretary, Sister Rose Emmanuella Brennan. Father Ransing wrote that he was gathering information informally to try to fend off "an inquiry" by the Vatican about the survey. He asked for immediate information as to who was on the survey committee and who formulated the questions. He reminded the conference secretary that responsibility for renewal was to be with each individual institute, and he indicated the Vatican's concern that the autonomy of each institute would not be preserved if survey results were publicized or used to compare one institute with another.[19]

---

[18] Mary Daniel Turner, SND, "The American Sister Today", *The Changing Sister*, 319.

[19] Father Bernard Ransing letter to Sister Emmanuella, April 23, 1967, CLCW 1/12, UNDA.

Subsequent to this letter, the conference leaders seemed concerned about keeping the project secret, and some superiors ordered that the booklets be collected and burned. On May 2, Sister Marie Augusta wrote to superiors, calling in all extra survey booklets, and warning that "use of the instrument by those not understanding its purposes could be serious for unwanted publicity prior to analysis and use for chapters."[20]

That same day, Sister Marie Augusta wrote Sister Mary Luke that Cardinal Egidio Vagnozzi, prefect of the Congregation for Religious, had asked for a copy of the survey. Sister Marie Augusta told Sister Mary Luke that she thought the cardinal's request as well as Father Ransing's inquiry "have been responses to letters from sisters for whom the questionnaire was a problem".[21]

Sister Mary Luke wrote back to Sister Marie Augusta, "I suppose it is inevitable that we are being investigated for our questionnaire. I think it is just as well that we do not have any Bishops, even including Archbishop Dearden, at our meeting [the August 1967 annual assembly at which the survey results would be discussed]. I am hoping one will not be 'appointed' by the Holy See as last year."[22]

Father Ransing again wrote the sisters, saying that the Congregation for Religious would be quite unhappy if the survey results were made public. He also pointed out that objections could be made to the way many of the questions were stated, and he observed there was no one answer to some of the questions. He indicated again that interpretation of the survey should be left to the communities themselves.[23]

Evaluation: Fascism and Anomie

Interpretation of the survey was not left to the communities themselves, however. Computer printouts that compared the scores of each individual community with national totals were made available to superiors,[24] although there was an effort to keep the information within

[20] Neal letter to mothers superior, May 2, 1967, CLCW 86/02, UNDA.
[21] Neal letter to Sister Mary Luke, May 2, 1967, CLCW 86/02, UNDA.
[22] Sister Mary Luke letter to Sister Marie Augusta, May 10, 1967, CLCW 86/02, UNDA.
[23] Father Bernard Ransing letter to Sister Emmanuella, June 4, 1967, CLCW 1/12, UNDA.
[24] Kolmer, *Religious Women*, 42.

the conference. Sister Mary Daniel Turner, chair of the conference's Research Committee on Religious Life that conducted the survey, told the 1967 annual assembly: "The major concern about the survey made during the past two years is the confidentiality of the national totals. National totals and scores are the trust of the Conference. Each member of the CMSW is responsible for guaranteeing that this trust will be respected." [25]

In addition to giving each institute data on how its scores compared with the national totals, a complex interpretation of the scores was provided by Sister Marie Augusta, who had developed complicated, elaborate scales for evaluating the responses of the sisters. At the 1967 annual CMSW assembly, superiors were given a partial interpretation of survey results, which was subsequently published in the assembly proceedings. In her report to the assembly, Sister Marie Augusta explained that responses to certain groups of questions could identify sisters who had characteristics of "over-submissiveness to legitimate authority along with an aggression against defenseless people, a tendency to superstition, synicism [sic], fascination with power, over-curiosity about sex, and a resistance to looking at one's own inner motivation, plus a pseudo-toughness and a high stress on conventional norms". These folks, Sister Marie Augusta contended, "have a proneness for fascism that is an easy acceptance of arbitrary strong command".[26] A sister was lumped in with the fascists by Sister Marie Augusta's scale if she had agreed with survey statements such as these:

> 145. What youth needs most is strict discipline, rugged determination, and the will to work and fight for family and country.
> 160. Science has its place, but there are many important things that must always be beyond human understanding.
> 166. If people would talk less and work more, everybody would be better off.
> 169. The best teacher or boss is the one who tells us just exactly what is to be done and how to go about it.

Regarding her political pessimism scale, Sister Marie Augusta explained that the political pessimism of sisters was "quite high" because the following items were accepted by more than 50 percent of them:

[25] *Proceedings of the Annual Assembly, 1967*, 193.
[26] Ibid., 23.

176. In the past 25 years, this country has moved dangerously close to Socialism.

177. The state of morals in this country is pretty bad, and getting worse.

179. The American Communists are a great danger to this country at the present time.

180. The United States is losing power in the world and this disturbs me a great deal.

She concluded, "The scores suggest a naiveté about the social order that is perhaps a bit high for teaching personnel and indicates a need for more competent teaching of the social sciences in the training programs of novitiates in general." [27]

Another of Sister Marie Augusta's scales was the Anomie Scale. She defined *anomie* as "an experience of meaninglessness among those who, lacking an enthusiasm for and not understanding or appreciating the new ways, cannot turn to these new ways with spontaneity when their conforming to the old ways has lost its rewards. With no new vision, and a clouding of the old, life loses its zest." [28] Anomie was identified by affirmative responses to items such as these:

118. With everything so uncertain these days it almost seems as though anything could happen.

121. What is lacking in the world today is the old kind of friendship that lasted for a life time.

130. I often feel that many things our parents stood for are just going to ruin before our very eyes.

133. The trouble with the world today is that most people really don't believe in anything.

Sister Marie Augusta also interpreted her pre–Vatican II and post–Vatican II scales for the 1967 assembly. "A high post-Vatican score can be interpreted to mean that the sisters are oriented to the thinking of Vatican II. A low score on this scale indicate the opposite." Sisters were considered to be "post–Vatican II" if they responded affirmatively to statements such as these:[29]

[27] Ibid., 24–25.
[28] Ibid., 23–24.
[29] Ibid., 22–23.

6. I regard the word of God as speaking always and in diverse ways through events, other persons, and my own conscience, as well as through the Bible and the Church's magisterium.

14. I prefer to think of Jesus as our Mediator with the Father, rather than as the Second Person of the Blessed Trinity.

64. If a sister shuns involvement with persons I think she betrays the purpose of her vow of chastity.

76. The drama of renewal will consist largely in laying aside power, ownership, and esteem.

94. Holiness consists in utter self-sacrificing involvement in human needs.

100. It seems to me that sisters should be especially interested in establishing centers where people could come together to experience Christian community through worship, discussion, and the joy of shared activity.

According to a further explanation by Sister Marie Augusta in a memo to the Congregation for Religious, the "post–Vatican II" sisters "expect changes in their style of life, in the orientation of apostolic works, liturgical participation, congregation government. They are eager to participate in the transformation of the world, the taking on of service to the poor in new forms and new places. They are unusually sensitive to the current problems facing the Third World. They want to stay to renew with the Church. At the same time they are much more critical of current conditions in the church and in their community responses to current exigencies." And the "post–Vatican II" sisters "are better read theologically, read more, are better informed politically and socially, and are more willing to extend their life of service beyond the conventional." [30]

Sisters were considered to be "pre–Vatican II" if they responded affirmatively to these statements: [31]

5. The mystery of the Trinity is so profound and so central I feel I should humbly accept it as given and not seek to plumb its depths.

12. I sometimes wish I had been alive at the time of Christ rather than now so that I could have really known Him.

33. I like to attend as many Masses as possible each day.

[30] Neal, "Memo for Congregation for Religious on Sisters' Survey, June, 1969", CLCW 10/15, UNDA.

[31] *Proceedings of the Annual Assembly, 1967*, 22–23.

72. As long as a sister is personally poor, I think it is good for the community to be financially secure.

95. I feel that the parochial school is still the most effective means for educating Catholics.

97. Personal sanctification comes first, then duties of the apostolate.

312. Christians should look first to the salvation of their souls; then they should be concerned with helping others.

319. The best contribution sisters can make to world problems is to pray about them.

322. I think of heaven as the state in which my soul will rest in blissful possession of the Beatific Vision.

324. What my daily work consists of matters little, since I see it as a way to gain merit for heaven.

The survey creators judged a sister to be "pre–Vatican II" if she preferred reading the work of traditional theologians such as Fulton J. Sheen, John Henry Newman, and Thomas à Kempis rather than that by modern ones such as Daniel Berrigan, Yves Congar, Hans Küng, Charles A. Curran, Gregory Baum, Gabriel Moran, and Edward Schillebeeckx. And communities were judged to be "nonexperimental" if they did not make available the works of the so-called "post–Vatican II" theologians.[32]

Sister Marie Augusta explained in her memo to the Congregation for Religious that pre–Vatican II sisters "are upset by the changes, do not want to evaluate the current effectiveness of their modes of service, are more concerned with saving their own souls than in helping in the renewal of the world, prefer a life apart, see the changes as detrimental to a spiritual life, do not want changes in life styles, are satisfied with current service to the poor and the witness their life gives to poverty, and are quite satisfied with a slower pace of change". And she declared that a pre–Vatican II orientation in a Church that had moved into a post–Vatican II era showed disrespect for spiritual things as well as "a tendency to define the holy in terms of the old, the traditional"; such a mindset was "even harmful to the degree that what is held on to is harmful". Sister Marie Augusta also suggested that these "pre–Vatican II" sisters were responsible for much of the friction about renewal in congregations and that these sisters gave

---

[32] Neal, "Part II. The Relation between Religious Belief and Structural Change in Religious Orders: Some Evidence", *Review of Religious Research* (Spring 1971): 158–59.

"witness to the irrelevancy of religious life". She wrote that the only way to stem departures from religious life was to "give evidence of genuine support for sincere efforts to realize the gospel in modern ways. Without this support the efforts are going to be turned to manifestations of frustration, anomie, and indifference." [33]

In 1968, Sister Marie Augusta told a workshop sponsored by the Canon Law Society of America that the reading recommendations made by religious superiors were a key factor in understanding the philosophy of a particular religious community. She reported that of the 410 superiors questioned in a preliminary survey before the Sisters' Survey, 222 had recommended a "mixed" reading list to their sisters. Only 55 out of the 410 superiors recommended readings that "if digested would have allowed the sisters to develop a real awareness of what was going on in the world and what was happening in the Church". Thus, she concluded, "The Sisters' Survey confirmed our hypotheses that one of the most critical variables separating religious communities able to respond creatively to change from those involved with problems of ambivalence and confusion is the reading and viewing preferences of the sisters." And the enlightened sisters who read contemporary theologians, Sister Marie Augusta contended, "were better able to realize that the Church was passing through a period of radical transition and could rejoice in and celebrate the process." Her conclusion, naturally, was that "the Survey indicates and suggests strongly a reform of reading and of viewing habits." [34]

Here again, even though the vast majority of superiors were steering a middle course in approaching the "new theology", and 355 out of 410 superiors were not enthused about all the theologians touted by the survey committee, the powers that be in the CMSW were telling superiors that if they were going to get with the renewal program, they had to reject pre–Vatican II thinkers entirely and get their sisters immersed in the works of other theologians, some of whom were considered to be quite controversial at that time and some who later would be cited by the Vatican for theological speculation or error.

---

[33] Neal, "Memo for Congregation for Religious on Sisters' Survey, June, 1969", CLCW 10/15, UNDA.

[34] Neal, "Renewal through Community and Experimentation", in *Proceedings of the Canon Law Society of America: 1968*, 151–52.

Sociologist Gene Burns observed that "the Sisters' Survey was one of many activities within CMSW that increased commitment to a feminist, antihierarchial worldview." The leaders who conducted and interpreted the survey were "articulating a radical view of religious life." [35]

The Survey Is Pushed Again

The conference leadership was pushing the agenda of the Sisters' Survey committee so hard that the survey was the main topic again at the 1968 assembly, even though many superiors had asked that the assembly return to more spiritual matters. And the results of the Sisters' Survey were used by the survey committee to push for revising the conference statutes, supposedly to give more power to the membership in the conference, because the survey results indicated that sisters wanted to play a more active role in decision making. [36] (As chapter 6 detailed, the revised conference bylaws actually gave more power to the executive committee, not to the general membership.)

The Sisters' Survey results apparently were used in a variety of ways. Sister Claudia Zeller, CMSW executive secretary, wrote Sister Marie Augusta, suggesting that the survey results be used to identify sisters with expertise who might serve on CMSW committees since the CMSW had opened up committee membership to non-superiors. [37] Unfortunately—or perhaps fortunately for the sisters—the individual survey responses were anonymous, and so individuals could not be identified, even though the conference secretariat apparently hoped to locate politically correct sisters through the survey.

Nevertheless, the indoctrination of sisters apparently was somewhat successful, for the Sisters' Survey was used in a good number of renewal chapters. Many of its proposals, along with the ideas of some of the "post–Vatican II" theologians, were incorporated into chapter decrees, even though many of those ideas and proposals clearly were contrary to documents coming out of the Second Vatican Council, not to mention

[35] Burns, *The Frontiers of Catholicism*, 147.
[36] According to the report of the Research Committee on Religious Life given by Sister Mary Daniel Turner, *Proceedings of the Annual Assembly, 1967*, 193–94.
[37] Sister Mary Claudia letter to Sister Marie Augusta, October 17, 1969, CLCW 158/19, UNDA.

contrary to canon law and the intrinsic rights of members of those institutes.

The autumn 1968 issue of the *Sister Formation Bulletin*, published by the Sister Formation Committee of the CMSW, gives some indication of the impact of the Sisters' Survey on chapters and constitutions. A report from a Sister Formation Conference workshop at Woodstock, Maryland, in the summer of 1968, contained the following recommendations regarding the survey:

> 5. Each congregation should know its CMSW Sisters' Survey profile and develop its formation and renewal programs accordingly.
>
> 6. In view of the question of authoritarianism raised by this Survey and keeping in mind the thrust of conciliar theology, each congregation should create governmental structures to incorporate: (a) genuine decentralization of authority, (b) actual adherence to the principle of subsidiarity, (c) room for personal freedom and responsibility.

While the suggestions in number 6 sound quite reasonable, even necessary, in actuality sisters used these very terms to justify the total deconstruction of their institutes, where authority was all but abolished, the concept of subsidiarity was distorted to mean democracy, and personal responsibility decayed into individualism.

Critics of the Survey

Dominican Sister Elizabeth McDonough, a canon lawyer, has argued that the Sisters' Survey had a destructive effect upon American religious.

> Critics of [Sister] Neal's work point to survey questions formulated in qualitative language, to information reported in questionable categories, and to Neal's apparently subjective interpretations expressed in her follow-up memos as being especially problematic. The surveys engendered ever more controversy as findings originally proposed as an information base on resources for renewal began to function instead as LCWR's single central source for pursing social-justice agendas, for questioning ecclesiastical authority, and for picking up the pace of renewal. Indeed, the quarter-century survey project that coincided with the postconciliar constitutional revision in women's institutes may arguably be the single most significant factor that can account for the systematic

and progressive deconstruction evident among so many institutes of women religious today.[38]

Sister Elizabeth also has suggested that:

In addition to problems with the instrument, interpretation, agenda, etc., the "Sisters' Survey" study may have fallen into two aberrations that are common with such surveys, namely of: (1) becoming the basic decision maker for renewal and of (2) being confused with renewal itself. That is to say, either the survey itself was the decision maker about what happened next or those responsible for the survey made the decisions about what happened next.... The systematic and progressive deconstruction of conventual religious life for women in America may have been a consciously programmed occurrence or it may have been orchestrated by persons relatively unaware of fundamentals in the theology, history, evolution and structure of religious life.[39]

In an April 4, 1990, retrospective lecture at Saint Michael's College in Colchester, Vermont, Sister Marie Augusta expounded on her ideas about ecclesiastical authority and what she had ordained to be the new mission of the Church—social justice. This lecture, "The Church, Women and Society", was characterized by Sister Marie Augusta as a "challenge to patriarchy", and her remarks offered many insights into the person who constructed and interpreted the Sisters' Survey.

Sister Marie Augusta said that the pastoral patterns of the Church in first-world countries "are now dysfunctional for its new mission to bring the Good News to the poor, that is, to the newly migrating peoples of the world". She contended that the Church was having difficulty implementing this new mission to migrating people because it is hierarchical and patriarchal. "The solution of the social problems associated with its mission today, however, calls for a democratic structure modeled on a community of peers rather than on the ancient traditional structure of an extended family ruled by a patriarch", she said. This lack of democracy in the Church, she added, leads its members to reject the sacraments: "A tradition that does not speak to the experience of the people, or which provides power over others to the advantage of some at the expense of exploiting the remainder of

[38] McDonough, "Beyond the Liberal Model", 179.
[39] McDonough, "Juridical Deconstruction of Religious Institutes", *Studia Canonica* 26 (1992): 336–37.

the population, engenders alienation and anomie in the society and disbelief in the sacraments of the Church." [40]

Indeed, Sister Marie Augusta's stated goal of democratizing the Catholic Church and liberating women is quite evident throughout the Sisters' Survey. She obviously found many supporters of like mind in the leadership of the CMSW, for this revolutionary philosophy was promulgated to almost every Catholic sister through the Sisters' Survey. This philosophy was then used as the ideal by many communities of women Religious in rewriting their constitutions to prepare for post–Vatican II renewal, and it permeated the women superiors' conference thereafter.

Surely, communities of women Religious are still experiencing the consequences of that 1964 Grailville meeting, where a small group of people formulated this new ecclesiology and philosophy of religious life and packaged it as a legitimate interpretation of how the Second Vatican Council wanted religious to adapt to the modern age, even before the final version of the official Council documents on religious life were released. Every major study of religious life done since the early 1990s has found that religious communities that embraced the philosophy of democracy and liberation set forth in the Sisters' Survey have experienced diminishing membership, loss of corporate identity, fracturing of community, and an uncertain future.

Yet, in spite of these facts, the LCWR continued to praise the impact of the Sisters' Survey on women Religious for decades. In her 1995 conference report, LCWR executive director Sister Margaret Cafferty wrote that "the Sisters' Survey, undertaken at the request of LCWR, played a decisive role in readying United States religious institutes for renewal and thus helped to shape the United States church that emerged from Vatican Council II." And she continued, "The learnings from the study helped guide religious institutes through the first difficult years of renewal, providing valuable insights for each participating institute about its own strengths and weaknesses. The study also led the conference to change its name and revise its organizational structure, in keeping with the values of renewal." But apparently the survey didn't sufficiently liberate women, for Sister Margaret also observed,

---

[40] Neal, "The Church, Women and Society", lecture delivered April 4, 1990 (Colchester, Vt.: Saint Michael's College, 1990).

"While teaching the essential equality of all, the church continues to alienate women."[41]

Lay "Change Agents"

Certainly, sisters, priests, and theologians were not solely responsible for the indoctrination of religious during the turbulent time of renewal. Laypeople also got in on the act. Religious institutes began to consult laypeople for help in writing new constitutions and formulating chapter decrees. Unfortunately, some of these lay consultants helped not to renew but to unravel the orders that turned to them for advice.

One of the laymen who worked frequently with religious during the 1960s and 1970s was psychologist William Coulson. With a doctorate in philosophy from the University of Notre Dame and another in counseling psychology from the University of California, Coulson for many years was an associate of Carl R. Rogers and Abraham H. Maslow at the Western Behavioral Sciences Institute in La Jolla, California.

Coulson and his colleagues became famous for popularizing the encounter group, a form of group psychotherapy also known as sensitivity training. Members of an encounter group reveal to each other, without being subjected to any moral judgment, their inmost thoughts, beliefs, feelings and desires. Coulson later recanted his association with this method of therapy and for many years wrote and spoke about his regret for the influence he had on many American sisters.

In an interview with the author,[42] Coulson recalled that literally dozens of religious orders requested encounter groups in order to prepare them for renewal efforts. "We were change agents", Coulson said. "Our job was to be, as Rogers later wrote, revolutionaries."

As the "resident Catholic" at the institute, Coulson led most of the encounter groups consisting of nuns. Among these were the Immaculate Heart of Mary Sisters of Los Angeles, the Dominicans of San Raphael, Sisters of Providence of Seattle, Mercy Sisters of Burlingame, and Madames of the Sacred Heart of San Francisco and San Diego. Coulson blames the workshops for the demise of the Los Angeles

---

[41] LCWR *1995 Conference Report*, "Transforming Leadership for the New Millennium," 4–5.

[42] Telephone interview with author, March 13, 1995.

IHMs and for the movement among many orders to close schools and other Catholic institutions staffed by nuns.

The pilot program with the IHMs in 1966 went "so swimmingly", Coulson said, that the order invited him to do encounter groups with every participant in their chapter the following summer. Organizations often invited him back, he added, "but in no case more concertedly" than the IHMs.

In the encounter groups sisters were not allowed "happy talk or holy talk", Coulson said, even if they came into the session sensing no real dissatisfaction in their lives. Instead, the participants were pushed "to be real". In those days "being real" in a psychological exercise meant being miserable. If the sisters were not miserable, Coulson added, he would find ways to make them confess that they were.

By the early 1970s, Coulson's institute in La Jolla was offering summer training for facilitators of Rogerian human-potential workshops, another name for encounter groups. "We trained many thousands from more than thirty-five countries", he said, with Catholic religious representing the largest single vocation group that attended the program. Hundreds of Catholic religious women and men were prepared to lead workshops in their home communities.

"We thought what we were doing was immanently human", Coulson explained. "It turned out to be all too human, because one of the things we could achieve was that we freed everybody from local doctrine. They were no longer constrained by rules because we persuaded them to make their own rules for themselves."

But making one's own rules is not compatible with community life, or even with the Catholic faith, Coulson realized later, and it wasn't long before values-free therapy groups were causing conflicts within religious orders.

"Jesuits of the Northwest Province stopped their young men from coming to La Jolla because they saw that they had become just exactly what Rogers said they should become: quiet revolutionaries, subversives", Coulson said.

"It is not the case that we didn't believe in institutions", Coulson continued. "We believed only in our own. So, it was stupid for the Church to allow this to happen because it was inviting the enemy in. We were the Trojan horse."

Other sorts of consultants were also being brought into religious communities, for example, organizational-development specialists pushing democratic models of decision-making and gurus of fashionable self-help practices, such as intensive journaling and the enneagram, a system that defines nine personality types.[43] (A 2003 Vatican document *Jesus Christ, the Bearer of the Water of Life: A Christian Reflection on the "New Age"* warned about the ways the enneagram, when used as a method of spiritual direction, can introduce "an ambiguity in the doctrine and the life of the Christian faith".)[44]

"Everybody likes to play psychiatrist," Coulson explained, "and the best way to play psychiatrist is not to bother going to medical school and residency, but rather to go to a weekend workshop. . . . Nuns and priests who do psychologically oriented workshops and give questionnaires on things like how do you feel about this or that—they are amateurs, rank amateur psychiatrists. And you're getting exactly the kind of damage that you would predict."

The sad result of all the presumably therapeutic getting in touch, opening up, and scrapping the rules has been the breakdown of religious life, Coulson realized. "We persuaded a whole raft of Catholic communities to try openness, and the predictable thing happened: They fell apart."

It was politically correct in the 1960s to say that pre–Vatican II religious communities were overly structured and authoritarian, Coulson explained, but "the human spirit calls for containment. No life is possible except under authority."

Yet now, he observed, we have some Catholic leaders and organizations that seem dedicated to seeding the whole American church with their failed experiments. "It's really irrational," he said, "the net effect of what I call TMP—Too Much Psychology." He added that some religious persist in the folly of formlessness for the sake of revenge. Rather than admitting they have made mistakes in their own communities, they seek to spread their misery to others.

---

[43] For a detailed description, analysis and personal experience of the enneagram, see Mitch Pacwa, SJ, *Catholics and the New Age* (Ann Arbor: Servant Publications, 1992).

[44] Pontifical Council for Culture and Pontifical Council for Interreligious Dialogue, "Jesus Christ, the Bearer of the Water of Life—A Christian Reflection on the New Age", February 3, 2003, http://www.vatican.va/roman_curia/pontifical_councils/interelg/documents/rc_pc_interelg_doc_20030203_new-age_en.html.

But young men and women with religious vocations are not attracted to the structureless life that has evolved in many religious communities, Coulson concluded. Thus more traditional forms of religious life are making a comeback. "It would make no sense to say religious life is dying", he said. "What's dying is the American experiment with the '60s. And let it go, I say. There is no call for keeping the '60s alive; it's over."

Enneagrams, Goddesses, and Other Aquarian Oddities

Many programs born of the "Age of Aquarius" continued to be promoted by and for religious even after the 1960s and 1970s. Rather than deepening an understanding of Catholic theology and spirituality, many of these programs promoted New Age ideas and practices that did little to orient a sister toward Christ and his Church. Rather, they offered "ecofeminist" and "earth-honoring" theology, the "new cosmology", transpersonal psychology, Zen meditation, and self-awareness exercises such as the enneagram discussed previously. Still, religious orders encouraged their members to attend these programs by paying the enrollment fees or even financially sponsoring the events.

These New Age programs became less popular in the twenty-first century, but some, such as the "Earth Spirit Rising" conference, persisted. The 2007 conference in Cincinnati featured as one of its speakers the self-proclaimed witch Starhawk, who was thusly described in promotional materials: "She is the author or coauthor of ten books, including *The Spiral Dance: A Rebirth of the Ancient Religion of the Great Goddess*, long considered the essential text for the Neo-Pagan movement." [45] Among the cosponsors for the conference were twelve orders of Catholic sisters.

Many women religious have been introduced to the practice of Reiki—a Japanese healing technique in which the practitioner places her hands on the patient's body to facilitate the flow of "universal life energy". The US Bishops' Committee on Doctrine issued *Guidelines for Evaluating Reiki as an Alternative Therapy* in 2009. Catholics who put their trust in Reiki would be "operating in the realm of superstition", the document said, and "superstition corrupts one's worship of

[45] Earth Spirit Rising webpage, www.co-intelligence.org/newsletter/EarthspiritRising07. html (accessed September 18, 2012).

God by turning one's religious feeling and practice in a false direction." The document concluded that "since Reiki therapy is not compatible with either Christian teaching or scientific evidence, it would be inappropriate for Catholic institutions, such as Catholic health care facilities and retreat centers, or persons representing the Church, such as Catholic chaplains, to promote or to provide support for Reiki therapy." [46]

The sisters' new emphasis on ecology, an offshoot of their focus on social justice, was discussed by Father Albert DiIanni, a theologian and former vicar general of the Society of Mary, in his book, *Religious Life as Adventure*. While religious have historically and rightly cared for the poor, explained Father DiIanni, their primary duty is to love God. He argued that a new theology of religious life has replaced the traditional one that considered striving for personal holiness primary and ministering to one's neighbor secondary. Father DiIanni wrote:

> Some peace and justice workers, in a way similar to [Karl] Marx, have lost sight of the deep meaning of Christianity as well as confidence in the Resurrection. Partly due to a lack of faith in other worldly and eschatological realities, they have found it necessary to find a totally earthly locus for their passion. . . . They continue to use God-language and to quote the Scriptures, but on their lips such language often seems a mythic overlay, a symbolic vehicle for motivating people to become engaged in the more important task of social, economic, and ecological reform.
>
> They speak frequently of the need to "build up the kingdom" and insist that "salvation must begin on earth" but have only lip-service for the eschatological aspects of the Kingdom and salvation. They are more at home with social action and politics than with piety, with prayer of petition, with praise of the Lord. They espouse most of the liberal or radical social causes of the day, criticizing neo-conservatism as escapism and remain quite silent on moral issues such as abortion. They tend to shy away from the "mere sacramental ministry" and at times translate liturgy into a political statement.[47]

[46] USCCB Committee on Doctrine, "Guidelines for Evaluating Reiki as an Alternative Therapy", *Origins*, April 16, 2009.

[47] Albert DiIanni, SM, *Religious Life as Adventure* (Staten Island, NY: Alba House, 1994), 72–73.

This philosophy described by Father DiIanni is in part a legacy of the Sisters' Survey, which ordained social justice as the primary mission of religious life. Reforming religious into agents of social and political change was carried forward through various educational efforts, including the influential Sister Formation Conference, which is discussed in the next chapter.

9

The Reeducation of Sister Lucy

It is difficult to overemphasize the seminal importance of Sister Formation in the changing of American nuns. For many the SFC initiated a conceptual shift in theology and spirituality ... and grounded still other, more radical, conceptual shifts.[1]

— Sister Mary Daniel Turner, SNDdeN,
and Sister Lora Ann Quinonez, CDP

Like the CMSW, the Sister Formation Conference had a noble beginning and was instrumental in promoting needed reforms among women religious. But, like the conference of superiors, the Sister Formation Conference evolved beyond its original purpose, which was to promote better education for nuns before they were sent out into their apostolates. After the Second Vatican Council, the Sister Formation Conference began adding questionable theologies and experimental concepts of religious life to their programs. Thus, the group eventually contributed to the de-Christianization of sisters and the deconstruction of women's religious institutes in the United States.

Educating Sister Lucy

Holy Cross Sister Madeleva Wolff, who was president of Saint Mary's College at Notre Dame, Indiana, from 1934 to 1961, was one of the pioneers of the Sister Formation Conference. Sister Madeleva had

[1] Quinonez and Turner, *Transformation*, 11.

recognized the educational problems of sisters for many years. Not only were young sisters being placed in professional positions before they were adequately prepared, but the orders were having a hard time coming up with money to educate the growing number of sisters. Sister Madeleva also saw the need to train female teachers of theology, but neither sisters nor laywomen were admitted to graduate theology programs at that time.[2]

Sister Madeleva took matters into her own hands and established the School of Sacred Theology at Saint Mary's College in 1943. The graduate school of theology offered a master's degree or doctorate to sisters and laywomen and became a model for Regina Mundi, a pontifical institute for sisters that opened in Rome in 1953. The Saint Mary's School of Sacred Theology operated for twenty-four years, educating theology teachers—mostly sisters—for high schools, colleges, and formation programs within congregations of women. The school was closed in 1967 for financial reasons and because Catholic universities finally were opening up graduate theology programs to women.[3]

Also during the 1940s, Sister Madeleva and several other concerned parties repeatedly asked the National Catholic Educational Association (NCEA) to establish a section for teacher preparation, which it did in 1948. The following year, at the NCEA annual meeting, Sister Madeleva presented a paper, later published as "The Education of Sister Lucy", which turned out to have a major impact on sister training.

Sister Madeleva suggested in her paper that young sisters who were going to be teachers should receive their baccalaureate and teacher certification prior to final profession of vows and being assigned to full-time teaching. She acknowledged the problems in trying to attain this ideal—the expense involved in educating a sister before she made a decision to stay in the community and take her final vows, and the growing pressure for sisters to staff parochial schools—but she insisted that "if we cannot afford to prepare our young sisters for the work of our communities, we should not accept them at all. We should direct them to communities that will prepare them."[4] Sister Madeleva's paper

[2] Maria Assunta Werner, CSC, *Madeleva* (Notre Dame: Congregation of the Sisters of the Holy Cross, 1993), 158.

[3] Mary Immaculate Creek, CSC, *A Panorama: 1844–1977, Saint Mary's College Notre Dame, Indiana* (Notre Dame: Saint Mary's College, 1977), 94–100.

[4] *Sister Formation Bulletin* 18, no. 4 (Summer 1972): 4.

proved to be a major impetus for establishing the Sister Formation Conference as a committee within the NCEA.[5]

Initially, the Sister Formation Conference was founded to promote the education and professional certification of sisters before they were assigned as teachers, nurses, and social workers. This original purpose was a tremendous benefit to the sisters who then started to receive adequate preparation for their work assignments, and it also gave a needed boost to the reputation of Catholic institutions where the sisters worked. During the 1950s, approximately 150 religious institutes established degree programs for their sisters, variously called juniorates or motherhouse colleges. National sister formation programs open to sisters from any religious institute were offered at various sites during the summer months.

Religious institutes that already operated four-year women's colleges often welcomed sisters from other congregations, but Sister Formation leaders tended to prefer that in these colleges the sisters be separated from lay students. Thus, some specific religious formation colleges were born. Seattle University opened a College of Sister Formation in 1958 that had equal status with other Seattle University colleges. The university provided faculty and facilities until Providence Heights College was finished in 1960 and staffed by Sisters of Charity of Providence.[6]

Another formation college, Marillac College in Saint Louis, run by the Daughters of Charity, had originally been founded in 1937 as an extension program of DePaul University. In 1955, Marillac Junior College became part of Saint Louis University. In 1957, it became an independent four-year liberal arts college exclusively for sisters. In the 1959–1960 academic year, the thirty-four faculty members represented fifteen religious communities. Daughter of Charity Sister Bertrande Meyers, president of Marillac, had been one of the promoters of sister education for years and served on the National Sister Formation Committee. By 1963, Marillac enrolled 350 students from twenty-five religious congregations. Daughters of Charity made up about two-thirds of the student body in 1963 and took their novidate year between the freshman and sophomore years of study, thus composing a five-year program. Student sisters from other orders usually entered Marillac in the sophomore year and lived off campus in their

[5] Creek, *Panorama*, 94–100.
[6] *Sister Formation Bulletin* (Autumn 1958): 13.

own housing under the supervision of their own orders to preserve their distinctive spirituality.[7] (Canon law required that the novitiate year be spent in one's own religious institution.) By 1966, there were sisters from thirty-five orders at Marillac, outnumbering the Daughters of Charity by more than two to one.

Dissent at Catholic Universities

Not all sisters attended sister formation schools or colleges, and beginning in the 1950s, it became increasingly common for sisters to attend various Catholic universities, particularly for graduate degrees. Some of these sisters went full time, but many studied only during the summer months, and it was quite common to see more religious than laity on the campuses of some Catholic universities during the summer session. In general, superiors felt comfortable sending their young religious off to study at Catholic institutions in the company of religious from other institutes. However, this feeling of comfort began to dissipate during the turbulent 1960s, when many sisters were radicalized by their professors and fellow students at Catholic colleges and universities. Some superiors observed that some of their sisters even lost their faith when they were sent off to Catholic universities to study. The situation was viewed so seriously by some superiors that they started to enroll their young sisters in state colleges and universities, where they received little to no theology training, but at least the sisters weren't exposed to some of the Catholic theologians who, in the 1960s, began to attack the Magisterium, loosely interpret Vatican II documents, and dissent from Church teaching.

The most publicized example of theological dissent during the 1960s was an unprecedented statement of opposition to Pope Paul's encyclical *Humanae Vitae*. The statement was composed by Father Charles Curran, a theology professor at Catholic University, and eventually signed by more than six hundred leading theologians, philosophers, and canon lawyers.[8] A list of the signatories was published in the *National Catholic Reporter* on August 14, 1968, and among them was (former) Jesuit Father Daniel Maguire, along with nine priest faculty members

[7] Edward Wakin, "West Point for Nuns", *The Sign* (March 1963): 45–46.
[8] *National Catholic Reporter*, August 14, 1968.

from Catholic University. Father Bernard Haring and Benedictine Father Godfrey Diekmann, both of whom would go on to teach at Catholic University in the 1970s, also signed. Priest signers from the University of Notre Dame included Benedictine Father Aidan Kavanaugh. Father Richard McBrien, who was at Gregorian University in Rome when he signed the statement, went on to become chairman of the Theology Department at Notre Dame.

Other prominent signers were (former) Father Bernard Cooke, chairman of the Theology Department at Marquette University; Father Peter Riga of La Salle College; Christian Brother Paul K. Hennessy of Iona College, New Rochelle, New York; and Christian Brother Gabriel Moran, from Manhattan College. Among the fourteen priests from Fordham University whose names were on the statement was Jesuit Father Christopher Mooney, chairman of the Theology Department. Also included were the names of five priests from each of the faculties of Loyola University in Chicago, Saint Mary's Seminary and University in Baltimore, and Woodstock College in Maryland.[9] (Note that many of these men had been or would be featured speakers at the national assemblies of the CMSW / LCWR.) Priests, religious, and lay faculty from numerous other Catholic colleges and universities also signed the statement of dissent.

This reaction to *Humanae Vitae* gives some indication of the attitude toward Church teaching and authority taking root in Catholic universities during the 1960s and 1970s. And these very schools were being charged with the higher education of sisters during the same years that women religious were given the task of rewriting their constitutions.

From Professional to Spiritual Formation

The Sister Formation Conference was affected by the rebellious trend in Catholic academia. In addition to the specialized sister formation colleges such as Marillac and Providence Heights, many ad hoc programs eventually were offered under the umbrella of the conference, and these increasingly reflected the spirit of the age. As the 1960s progressed, the scope of sister formation programs expanded beyond strictly professional preparation and started to include spirituality and

[9] Ibid., 8.

theology, causing considerable controversy among religious superiors and other Church leaders.

Canon law directed that spiritual formation of religious was to be under the supervision of their own superiors, who were familiar with the spirit and charism of their own institutes. (This stipulation eventually led the Congregation for Religious to insist that the Sister Formation Conference be placed under the control of the CMSW in 1964.) Some superiors, therefore, asserted that spiritual formation programs should be kept within their own congregations, and they bumped heads with Sister Formation Conference leaders who believed that small programs were academically inferior and financially impossible. (Historian Philip Gleason has noted that by 1960, ninety-three of these smaller colleges had fewer than fifty-five students, and only three of those were accredited.)[10] Consequently, some superiors refused to get involved in the Sister Formation Conference because they saw it as a danger to religious life. Others embraced it enthusiastically.

In addition to the canonical issues, the content of some sister formation programs worried some superiors and Church officials. Certainly, many sister formation courses presented orthodox teaching from some of the finest theologians and professors of the time. But others seemed increasingly designed to reeducate Sister Lucy in the latest theological, sociological, psychological—and eventually New Age—fads.

Likewise, the *Sister Formation Bulletin*, published by the Sister Formation Conference, contained some excellent articles. But the *SF Bulletin* consistently presented the most contemporary theological thought, much of which was controversial and speculative at that time. While this level of theological inquiry might be stimulating and appropriate for theologians or graduate students, it was not appropriate for sisters with little or no training in theology. As a result, some of the *Bulletin* articles were not critically assessed by the sisters who read them, causing much confusion and misinterpretation.

The *SF Bulletin*, which was widely read by nuns and reached a peak circulation of eleven thousand, often published the first English translation of the writings of controversial European theologians. Appearing regularly was the work of Fathers Karl Rahner, Bernard Haring,

---

[10] Philip Gleason, *Contending with Modernity* (New York: Oxford University Press, 1995), 234.

and Edward Schillebeeckx. A *Time* magazine education writer observed in 1964 that the sister formation courses and *Bulletin* "sometimes offer more *avante-garde* theology than most seminaries for priests allow".[11] Franciscan Sister Angelyn Dries observed that "during the 1950's and '60's, many authors who were excerpted in the *Bulletin* were influential among American progressive groups".[12]

Unfortunately, many sisters reading the *Bulletin* simply did not have the training necessary to distinguish between groundbreaking theological inquiry, outright theological speculation, and the actual dogmas of the Church. Decades after the Vatican Council had closed, trained theologians with doctoral degrees still struggle to sort out and understand some of the authors whose work appeared in the *Bulletin* regularly.

Significantly, many of the sisters who took sister formation courses and followed the *Bulletin* closely were the very women who were in leadership positions in their congregations and were responsible for the training of younger sisters. In some convents, the *Bulletin* was the designated reading material during meals. So, every sister in those communities came into contact with controversial theology, and this during an era when there was so much speculation about what was happening or would happen at the Second Vatican Council.

The *SF Bulletin* also was a showcase for the writing of American sisters, some of whom were beginning to reflect the women's liberation agenda and to question the meaning of the vows, the importance of community, and the role of authority, as evidenced in the previous chapters of this book.

For example, in the autumn 1966 *SF Bulletin*, Sister Formation executive secretary, Sister of Charity Rose Dominic Gabisch, observed after a trip to Europe that "the religious women of Germany seem to be eager to stop making minor adaptations; they would prefer a radical use of contemporary theology to acquire an entirely new view of religious life."[13]

In the same issue, Sister Rose Dominic summarized a September 1966 colloquium on "World Apostolate of Women Religious" at the Catholic University of Louvain, in Belgium, reporting that the entire

[11] *Time*, July 17, 1964, 43.
[12] Angelyn Dries, OSF, "Living in Ambiguity: A Paradigm Shift Experienced by the Sister Formation Movement", *Catholic Historical Review* (July 1993): 485.
[13] *Sister Formation Bulletin* (Autumn 1966): 9.

conference adopted the conclusions of the English-speaking group: that if obstacles to religious fulfillment are to be removed, "extensive—and in some cases, revolutionary—experimentation will be essential.... This response will entail immediate and extensive experimentation in various forms of the 'community without walls'." [14] This kind of reform was far more radical than that actually mandated by the Second Vatican Council, which never suggested religious orders undertake revolutionary experimentation or community life without walls. Nevertheless, this interpretation of renewal was set forth in the *Bulletin* as normative.

In a lengthy article in the Summer 1967 *SF Bulletin*, Sister of the Holy Names of Jesus and Mary, Mary Audrey (Lillanna) Kopp, discussed "The Renewed Nuns: Collegial Christians". In the article, Sister Mary Audrey wrote that the modes of authority in religious life were dysfunctional and even heretical, and she wrote of "our split-level convent, about to nail up a sign reading, 'Condemned for human occupancy'". [15] Congregation of the Mission Father James W. Richardson wrote a letter of concern to the *Bulletin* editor, Sister of Notre Dame de Namur Joan Bland, about that article, noting that Sister Mary Audrey was quite correct in calling for abandoning authoritarianism in religious life but had been "excessive in excluding jurisdictional power from the Church" and in saying obedience is simply a response to a group decision summed up and expressed by an elected spokesperson. [16]

However, Sister Formation leaders didn't seem to share Father Richardson's concern. Sister Rose Emmanuella Brennan, executive secretary of the conference of major superiors, who was a former Sister Formation regional chairwoman, wrote Sister Mary Audrey, telling her the article was "excellent" and suggesting it become a major theme for Sister Formation discussions during the coming year. Sister Rose Emmanuella dismissed Father Richardson's comments by saying he was just showing interest in the sisters. [17] (Apparently even this support was not strong enough and change was not fast enough for Sister Mary Audrey, for she left her order in 1969 and founded a noncanonical

---

[14] Ibid.

[15] *Sister Formation Bulletin* (Summer 1967): 13.

[16] Father James W. Richardson letter to Sister Joan Bland, September 11, 1967, CLCW 34/25, UNDA.

[17] Sister Emmanuella letter to Sister Mary Audrey, September 18, 1967, CMSW 34/25, UNDA.

organization called Sisters for Christian Community. That same year, she also cofounded the National Coalition of American Nuns (NCAN) with School Sister of Notre Dame Margaret Ellen Traxler. NCAN is profiled in chapter 14.)

Another influential leader of Sister Formation, Sister Ritamary Bradley of the Congregation of the Humility of Mary, edited the *Sister Formation Bulletin* from its inception in 1954 until 1964. She was largely responsible for determining its content. She observed in the summer 1964 *Bulletin* that "not everyone agreed with all that was going into print in the *Bulletin* recently." She went on to suggest that one of the roles of the publication was to "stimulate leadership in assuring that the clarified notions of 'liberty of conscience' and 'religious liberty' be used without admixture of unworthy ends and without cowardice". She also called for a "negative" role for future publications of the *Bulletin*: "that of keeping the literature about Sisters from regressing into being 'spiritual' in an isolated sense; that of preventing the intellectual formation of Sisters from being only 'theological,' thereby thwarting the properly human development in which the rest is rooted".[18]

Sister Ritamary eventually left her congregation and joined Lillanna Kopp in the noncanonical Sisters for Christian Community and also became a leader of NCAN.

Psychology, Politics, and Many Opinions

Just as some of the *Sister Formation Bulletin* offerings were quite solid, many of the Sister Formation programs and courses were theologically and philosophically strong. But, like some of the offerings in the *Bulletin*, some of the Sister Formation programs and courses eventually proved to be unorthodox.

With a grant from the Ford Foundation, a group of fifteen sister educators met at Everett, Washington, in 1956 to devise what came to be known as the Everett Curriculum. This curriculum stressed "the study of psychology, sociology, political science and current events, subjects usually not part of normal school training".[19] One sister who

---

[18] *Sister Formation Bulletin* (Summer 1964): 35.
[19] Mary L. Schneider, OSF, "American Sisters and the Roots of Change: 1950s", *U.S. Catholic Historian* (Winter 1988): 65.

had experience with the Everett Curriculum has noted that it was valuable to have courses in the social sciences but that the program did not provide for adequate theological and spiritual education. So the training of the sisters swung from one extreme of being too spiritually oriented and inadequately professional to the other extreme of emphasis on the professional to the detriment of the spiritual.

Starting in 1958, a series of summer workshops for Sister Formation personnel convened at Marquette University. There, superiors and directresses of formation learned about how to apply the Everett Curriculum to individual formation programs of religious communities.[20] But, after the first year, when more than one hundred sisters from thirty-seven religious communities attended, the emphasis on professional training changed. According to historian Marjorie Noterman Beane: "Discussion of what was important and changing in sister education allowed the emphasis of the Marquette Workshops to change dramatically in the next years.... Perhaps only someone who attended all SFC-sponsored conferences and workshops could see how all the activities led to one goal—that of better understanding the changing face of religious life and thus the need to change formation programs."[21]

Thus, the Sister Formation Conference was evolving past its original goal of establishing better professional preparation for sisters and instead getting directly involved in structuring the spiritual formation of sisters. Moreover, by entering into this area of spiritual formation that had traditionally been handled strictly within individual religious institutes, the Sister Formation Conference intruded on the autonomy of individual religious institutes. In effect, Sister Formation leaders began to exert an inordinate influence on the very structure of individual congregations while receiving very little guidance or oversight from the official Church. And this was occurring at the very time that religious institutes were engaged in rewriting their constitutions.

For example, the changing nature of religious life was a topic open to wide interpretations in the late 1950s and early 1960s, and the Marquette workshop participants apparently were exposed to a myriad of opinions, depending on who was teaching in the program. Several of

---

[20] Marjorie Noterman Beane, *From Framework to Freedom* (Lanham: University Press of America, Inc., 1993), 84.

[21] Ibid., 85–86.

the sisters teaching in the Marquette workshops held a radical view of religious life that was based on humanistic psychology and leftist politics, and clearly they wanted those concepts to be injected into the professional and spiritual formation of sisters. Sister Ritamary Bradley regularly taught in the Marquette summer workshops, as did Sister of Saint Joseph Annette Walter, Sister Formation executive secretary for several years and a frequent lecturer on psychology. Sister Annette remained a member of her order until her death, but she also held membership in the noncanonical Sisters for Christian Community, even though "one cannot simultaneously hold membership in a canonical religious institute and in a non-canonical group", according to the Vatican Congregation for Religious.[22] Sister Annette also went on to become a leader in NCAN.

Other sisters who taught in the Marquette Sister Formation programs would go on to challenge openly Church teaching and authority. Two of these teachers were Sister Thomas Aquinas (Elizabeth) Carroll and Sister Humiliata (Anita) Caspary. Sister Thomas Aquinas had been on the Sister Formation executive committee and would go on to become president of the conference of major superiors at their stormy 1971 assembly, when the group changed its name to the LCWR. Sister Thomas Aquinas eventually joined the staff of the Center of Concern, where for many years she led efforts to promote ordination of women and passage of the Equal Rights Amendment. Sister Humiliata (Anita) Caspary had been a Sister Formation regional chairwoman. In 1970, Anita Caspary led more than three hundred members of her Immaculate Heart of Mary order in asking for dispensation from their vows because Cardinal James McIntyre of Los Angeles and the Vatican's Congregation for Religious did not approve of changes the sisters made in their constitution and lifestyle (described in chapter 12).

The Sister Formation Conference also heavily promoted other programs such as the Eleventh Annual Institute on Religious and Sacerdotal Vocations at Fordham University in the summer of 1961. The spring 1961 *Bulletin* urged mistresses of novices, postulants, and juniors, as well as superiors, to attend the program, whose featured speakers

[22] Archbishop Augustine Mayer, OSB, letter to Most Reverend Aloyisius Wycislo, April 9, 1981, CCPC 1/33, UNDA.

were Sister Annette Walter, Father Charles Curran, and Father Daniel Berrigan.[23]

The Leadership Network

At the insistence of the Vatican Congregation for Religious, the Sister Formation Conference became a committee of the major superiors in 1964. But under the major superiors, Sister Formation would move even further away from its original purpose, since the superiors' organization itself was in a process of evolution; indeed, some would say, revolution. The Sister Formation Conference would also prove to have been an effective training ground for sister-administrators who would move into leadership roles in the transformed major superiors' organization. The leadership of both sisters' organizations had evolved from the busy mother superiors and novice directresses of the 1950s, who had little time for conference work, to highly educated professional administrators of the 1960s and 1970s, who had decreasing responsibilities in their own congregations and plenty of experience in marketing, networking, and politics. These modern leaders also were skilled in identifying and grooming like-minded successors, and many of the same sisters simply rotated into different leadership positions in the two organizations.

These women also frequently helped determine the reading material offered to sisters during the years of renewal, thus significantly shaping the information available to sisters. For example, in 1964, the advisory board of *Sponsa Regis*, a monthly spiritual magazine for sisters (later named *Sisters Today*), included several sisters who were leaders in Sister Formation or the major superiors' conference, or both.

Also in the 1960s, during the renewal years, the *National Catholic Reporter* published a "Sisters Forum", which was planned and written by many of these sister-leaders and edited by Sister Charles Borromeo (Mary Ellen) Muckenhirn. Before she left religious life, Muckenhirn also edited *The Changing Sister*, which became the basis for the controversial 1967 Sisters' Survey. Under the major superiors of women, the Sister Formation Committee went on to endorse controversial programs, such as the 1967 Collegial Weekend at Barat College, Lake

---

[23] *Sister Formation Bulletin* (Spring 1961): 12.

Forest, Illinois, promoted in the winter 1967 issue of the *Sister Formation Bulletin*. At these weekends, sisters could hear, among other speakers, Father Charles Curran talk about "The New Morality". (The following summer, Father Curran would lead the dissent from *Humanae Vitae*.)

At another 1967 Barat Collegial Weekend, sisters were invited to join priests, brothers, and laypeople for a program on "The Cosmic Christ of Saint Paul and the Omega Point of Teilhard de Chardin". A workshop at Marquette University cited in the winter 1966 *Bulletin* was "designed to serve the National Sister Formation Committee's purpose of providing philosophical insights into the social science and practical demonstrations of social projects". Included in that program, which promised investigation of "the new knowledge of person and society", was the "study of Teilhard de Chardin." [24]

These programs were recommended by the Sister Formation Conference even though the work of Father de Chardin was still under a *monitum*, or warning, from the Vatican Congregation of the Holy Office because of confusion it might cause. [25] Earlier, Cardinal Egidia Vagnozzi, apostolic delegate to the United States, had warned against placing Teilhard de Chardin's works in seminary libraries. [26]

Also advertised in the autumn 1966 issue of the *Bulletin* were Traveling Workshops under the sponsorship of the National Catholic Conference for Interracial Justice. Among the traveling faculty were Sisters Mary Audrey (Lillanna) Kopp and Mary Peter (Margaret Ellen) Traxler, whose intention went beyond race relations as the following passage written by Sister Mary Audrey shows:

> From city-to-city, state-to-state, and coast-to-coast our race relations team traveled with a double agenda. We prayed that we might somehow make a small gain toward bettering race relations. We'll really never know. But that our gatherings made an impact on American Sister Renewal, we have no doubt. During them, American sisters envisioned together wholly new religious life models for the Twenty-first Century, and they are working still to make them a reality. Our mutural [sic]

[24] *Sister Formation Bulletin* (Winter 1966): 24.

[25] Matthew Bunson, ed., *Our Sunday Visitor's Encyclopedia of Catholic History* (Huntington, Ind.: Our Sunday Visitor Publishing Division, Our Sunday Visitor, Inc., 1995), 814.

[26] Cardinal Egidia Vagnozzi letter to Bishop Karl Alter, September 11, 1961, CLCW 1/9, UNDA.

concern for genuine change in sisterhoods was so intense, it lighted a prairie fire of determination, a grassroots revolution among sisters.[27]

Sister Mary Peter acknowledged that she and Sister Mary Audrey successfully recruited eleven hundred sisters for their NCAN while they were doing the traveling workshops. "All you had to do was mention the coalition [NCAN] and they signed up. You didn't even have to ask them", Sister Mary Peter related.[28] These workshops, which also functioned as a recruiting front for NCAN, were promoted in the *Bulletin* by the Sister Formation Conference, a committee of the major superiors' conference.

"Highly Recommended Resource Material"

The Sister Formation Conference regained its autonomy in 1970, while the CMSW was being transformed into the LCWR.[29] It is unclear why the Vatican's Congregation for Religious allowed this dissociation to happen, since the Congregation for Religious had originally insisted that the Sister Formation Conference be placed under the major superiors of women. The action apparently was a fait accompli about which the Vatican was not consulted, just like the move to dissolve the original structure of the women superiors' conference; the Vatican was simply informed after the action had taken place.

With its new autonomy, the Sister Formation Conference was even less inhibited. By 1974 the conference was calling for the ordination of women.[30] In 1975 the conference was promoting a Futureshop on Formation at the Mercy Generalate in Bethesda, Maryland. The September 1975 issue of *In-formation*—the publication that replaced the *Bulletin*—listed "highly recommended resource material" for the Futureshop, including *Lifestyle*, described as "a reflection / action workbook for those seeking greater freedom in their style of living and dying". On the Futureshop program were the films *Meditation: Yoga and Other Spiritual Trips*; *Universities: Tearing Down the Ivy*; and *Multiple Man*.

[27] Lillanna Audrey Kopp, "Don't Fence Me In", *Midwives*, 211.

[28] *National Catholic Reporter*, August 13, 1969.

[29] Report of the CMSW Ad Hoc Committee on the Agenda, December 17, 1970, CLCW 34/28, UNDA.

[30] SFC statement of October 1974, in *In-formation* (November 1974), CLCW 35/02, UNDA.

Speakers included Sister Nadine Foley, who was a leader in the women's ordination movement. (Sister Nadine would become president of the LCWR in 1988.) Participants in Futureshop then returned to their communities to conduct "mini-Futureshops".[31]

A Futureshop report predicted trends for the 1980s: "Personal self-development and aspiration of members of an organization will take gradual priority over organizational conveniences, order, efficiency, and expenditures for profit" and "Increasing demand for participation is replacing the old authoritarianism or executive power. A growth in anti-authoritarianism will continue, resulting in greater alienation from outmoded institutions."[32] The later prediction was quite accurate, for women religious did become increasingly focused on individualism and alienated from their institutions, outmoded or not.

By 1978 *In-formation* was promoting enneagram workshops and presenting the "Sufi System of nine personality types in the context of prayer and discernment", which was described as "a useful tool for getting in touch with ego fixations". Also being pushed was a program at Mundelein College in Chicago described as an "Institute in Creation Centered Spirituality for Those Who Believe Holiness Is Holness". Books recommended by the newsletter included *Jesus and Freedom* and *Christian Education for Liberation and Other Upsetting Ideas*.[33]

During the mid-1970s, the Sister Formation Conference continued to undergo a complete transformation from its original purpose, reflecting a growing feminist agenda and urging support for left-wing groups. In 1976 the group became a member of the National Catholic Coalition for the Equal Rights Amendment, and its newsletter contained a progress report on Priests for Equality, a group of priests organized by Jesuit Father William Callahan to support women's ordination.[34]

In 1976 the Sister Formation Conference changed its name to Religious Formation Conference (RFC), a change that accommodated new categories of membership, including men. The twenty-first-century RFC's website describes its mission as supporting and serving "the ministry of initial and life-long formation in religious congregations

---

[31] *In-formation* (September 1975), CLCW 35/02, UNDA.
[32] Mimeographed report concerning a "Brainstorming Session on October 2, 1975", from Futureshop, CLCW 35/03, UNDA.
[33] *In-formation* (Lent-Easter, 1978), CLCW 34/34, UNDA.
[34] *In-formation* (May 1976), CLCW 35/02, UNDA.

of men and women".[35] However, the new organization never became as influential as the original Sister Formation Conference.

It is indeed ironic that the organization that did so much good in promoting the necessary education of sisters also fostered questionable theologies that eventually undermined the religious institutes they intended to help. Significantly, the educational efforts of the Sister Formation Conference were made at the same time that institutes of women religious were engaged in rewriting their constitutions and setting a course for renewal as directed by the Second Vatican Council. The sisters who were taught sloppy, speculative, or downright erroneous courses often carried this misinformation back to their congregations, where it was disseminated as truth and caused great confusion.

[35] See www.relforcon.org.

10

Radical Reformers Gain Control

Every element, every assumption, every custom, every jot and tittle of the rule, no matter how longstanding and sacrosanct, became refreshingly suspect, tiringly suspect. Here was a social scouring of immense proportions, one of the most total in social history, perhaps.[1]

— Sister Joan Chittister, OSB

Many sisters who did not favor deviation from the essential elements of religious life did attempt to steer their orders along the pathway defined by Council and Vatican documents. These same sisters, in the face of criticism for being old-fashioned and reactionary, resisted the radical changes being introduced in their communities. How then did uncalled for and sweeping changes get approved in so many orders? How did radical reformers get elected to positions of authority when so many congregations were not overwhelmingly in favor of "birthing new forms of religious life"?

Skilled Organizers and Vulnerable Institutions

The answers to these questions seem to follow the same patterns. As we have seen, religious institutes of women were badly in need of updating and reforming by the time Vatican II called for renewal. Since many orders were in this weakened condition, they were vulnerable to takeover by activists determined to modernize their communities.

---

[1] Chittister, *The Fire in These Ashes* (Kansas City: Sheed & Ward, 1995), 34.

The problem was not with modernization—that was a necessity long overdue. The problem was that the renewal desired and promoted by some religious was not what the Council Fathers and the Magisterium had envisioned and subsequently mandated. Some religious turned the call for reform into a crusade to liberate sisters from male oppression and to forward some specific sociopolitical agenda at the expense of the spiritual aspects of religious life. Not surprisingly, the cultural upheaval of the 1960s was the setting and the impetus for this revolution.

Often the sisters who were being groomed for leadership roles were sent to institutions for higher education or continuing formation, which frequently brought these sisters into contact with questionable theologies and revolutionary views on religious life. Many of these sisters also learned community organization and political action tactics and applied these to promote their agenda. They made swift progress among women who were primarily teachers, nurses, and social workers with little political acumen. Furthermore, the average sister was too trusting that superiors would always make the right decisions and that all institute members would respect those decisions. Thus, the activists, who often were the most educated sisters in their orders, were able to push through the changes they wanted.

Sister Maureen Fiedler, who transferred to the Sisters of Loretto from the Sisters of Mercy because she "wanted to be part of a women's community challenging the church from within ecclesial structures",[2] wrote about the importance of political savvy when it came to effecting change in religious institutes: "The spring and summer of 1968 introduced me to an important skill: political organizing. Those of us who wanted fundamental change in community structures held late night meetings in basements, developed phone networks to keep allies informed, and learned the importance of setting agendas, preparing proposals in advance, and determining who would speak most effectively for our point of view."[3]

Obviously the average sister who was preoccupied with her job and prayer life did not have time for such political maneuvering, nor did she develop the skills to recognize or counteract it in her community.

[2] Maureen Fiedler, SL, "Riding the City Bus From Pittsburgh", in *Midwives*, 47.
[3] Ibid., 42–43.

Liberation theology was also influencing American sisters in the 1960s. Developed in Latin America from an attempt to marry Christianity and Marxism, liberation theology emphasizes the Christian commitment to the poor and criticizes "sinful social structures" that oppress the poor. Many orders of women had generously responded to Pope John XXIII's 1961 request for American religious to send missionaries to Latin America. When some of these American sisters rotated back home to their congregations, they brought with them an experience with—and belief in—liberation theology. Their emphasis on liberating the poor and downtrodden readily flowed into the emerging tide of feminism and the desire of some women religious to free themselves from what they saw as male oppression in the Church.

Sister Janet Ruffing has explained that "feminist theology is liberation theology done from the perspective of women's experiences." [4] But a 1984–1986 study of liberation theology by the Vatican's Congregation for the Doctrine of the Faith expressed serious reservations about the theology's Marxist elements and its narrow understanding of the term *liberation*.

The liberation theme also dovetailed with a growing philosophy among some religious, both men and women, that social justice—not spirituality—should be the foundation of religious life, a philosophy that has endured into the twenty-first century. This emphasis on liberation and social justice, almost to the exclusion of spirituality, was contained in the Sisters' Survey and is reflected in many constitutions and decrees written during the 1960s and 1970s. Sister Marie Augusta Neal, creator of the Sisters' Survey, observed in 1990 that "the work of the sisters on their constitutions focused . . . on the implementation of the new agenda calling for a critical social analysis of existing political, economic and social systems . . . even the structures of the church itself." [5] A preoccupation with the poor also explains why many congregations withdrew their sisters from Catholic schools in which many of the students tended to come from the middle class or the wealthy.

Unfortunately, some sisters did not grasp the Vatican II message that renewal included figuring out ways to address pressing social issues

[4] Janet K. Ruffing, RSM, "Leadership a New Way: If Christ Is Growing in Us", in *The Church and Consecrated Life*, David L. Fleming, SJ, and Elizabeth McDonough, OP, eds. (Saint Louis: Review for Religious, 1996), 199.

[5] Neal, *From Nuns to Sisters*, 47.

while at the same time preserving the heritage, nature, and work of their institutes. Certainly some orders maintained this balance, but too many sisters felt they had to discard their traditions and apostolates in order to become modern religious attuned to the needs of the world. What many of them did not realize was that they already were attending to the needs of the world through their work in education, health care, catechesis, and social and pastoral services but perhaps needed to expand those services to assist underserved people.

Election Maneuvering

The transformation of many orders often occurred while the majority of their sisters were hundreds of miles away from their motherhouses, doing the jobs they were assigned to do. Also many sisters lacked copies of Church documents pertaining to religious life and relied on their superiors to keep them informed of the changes occurring in their orders. Sisters tended not to question this practice, because they had always trusted their superiors; it did not occur to them to seek out and read the original documents for themselves, which would not have been an easy task in pre-Internet days. Most sisters simply did not realize anything was amiss until it was too late to do anything about the situation.

One sister who had been a Catholic school teacher and principal for several years in a state away from her motherhouse didn't notice what had happened in her congregation until she received an assignment that brought her back to the motherhouse. Only after she returned did she realize that the leadership in her order had been taken over by gender feminists who resisted direction from the Vatican while pursuing a model of religious life quite foreign to the majority of sisters in the order.

Sisters began to see maneuvering in election processes for chapter delegates and for officers of their congregations. Chapters are general meetings of a religious order usually held about every three to five years for the purpose of electing leaders and determining important business of the community, such as constitutional changes. Delegates to the chapter are elected by sisters in the community, but the selection process for delegates differs from congregation to congregation. Canon law provides that all vowed members of a religious institute have "active voice"—the right to participate in governance by voting. Professed members also have "passive voice"—the right to run for election to office. Chapter delegates usually elect officers of the institute. All elections are supposed to be secret, according to canon law, but some sisters from various institutes have reported elections by telephone and by numbered ballots that would reveal who was casting the vote.

Direct election of superiors had not been the past practice of most religious institutes before Vatican II, but generally sisters felt they had adequate input in choosing superiors and making their wishes known to the chapter, and these rights are guaranteed by canon law. Generally, too, sisters felt they could elect delegates to the chapter who would be aware of the common good of the community and thus represent the nature, spirit, and character of the institute at the chapter meetings.

This changed in many communities when leadership teams came into existence after Vatican II. Often that team—or a committee appointed by the leadership team—acts as a nominating committee, determines the election process, and runs the election, as well as plans and conducts the chapter. The result in some orders is that the same leaders simply play musical chairs year after year in the various leadership positions, with very little chance for new players to be admitted to the game. (Indeed, leadership teams themselves are canonically questionable, as canon law directs that personal authority resides in a superior; some constitutions of women religious, however, empower a superior to act only in concert with her council or leadership team.)

In many congregations that have a large proportion of elderly, the vote of the elderly sisters is diluted considerably when voting is done by age blocs, for blocs of elderly usually have more numbers in them than blocks of younger sisters. Some of these blocs may be determined by years in the community, and some may be determined by place of residence.

For example, a general chapter of the Sisters of Loretto in 1969 set up voting blocs of sisters according to their years in religious life in this way: 50 and over, 45–49, 40–44, 35–39, 30–34, 25–29, 20–24, 15–19, 10–14, and less than 10 years.[6] Obviously, the age blocs that have the largest numbers have less representation than those blocs with

---

[6] Helen Sanders, SL, *More Than a Renewal* (Nerinx, Ky.: Sisters of Loretto, 1982), 325.

small numbers. This may have been a fairly even distribution in 1969, when this particular model was used, but as the median age of sisters has risen into the 70s in most orders, the elderly have less representation when voting is done this way.

Determining voting blocs by living units, as some orders do, still dilutes the vote of the elderly, as they tend to live in retirement communities of twenty or more sisters. When voting by living units, a large community of elderly might have the same representation as a smaller unit of younger sisters (which may be a combination of several small households).

Defending this practice, a sister of Saint Joseph who was a member of her provincial leadership team told the author that the elderly have a shorter future in the community than do the younger members, so it is appropriate for the younger sisters who will be around for many more years to have a greater voice. Thus, some religious institutes believe it is logical to dilute the voting power of the retired members, and this explains how some of the constitutional changes in religious institutes were effected, even though many of the elderly sisters did not endorse those changes.

Another issue is group dynamics. Once the chapter meeting convenes, a group psychology is at work in which delegates are pressured to come around to support the politically correct viewpoint or to go along with what is suggested so as not to be "divisive". Often the sisters who are skilled in group dynamics are able to manipulate those who are less sophisticated.

Another difficulty at the chapters is that delegates often feel intimidated by their more vocal colleagues. Holy Cross Sister Rose Eileen Masterman wrote of her order's 1973 chapter that "certain minority groups in Chapter can manage to turn the thinking of many other sincere capitulants [delegates]." [7] Admittedly, there were some immovable sisters who wanted no changes at all, not even those mandated by the Vatican. But even sisters who were eager to follow the Vatican's directives often found themselves being derided by others for being too "conservative" or resistant to change or behind the times or, in Marxist terms, indoctrinated by the oppressors.

---

[7] Rose Eileen Masterman, CSC, letter to Rev. Barnabas Mary Ahern, CP, March 12, 1974, CMAS 2/23, UNDA.

With few exceptions, most religious institutes of women had trained their sisters (before Vatican II) to be docile and unquestionably obedient, so when a superior suggested changes that the sisters might not have agreed with, they were not inclined to vote against the superior's wishes; nor were they inclined even to question what the superior was suggesting. Sisters in general trusted their superiors implicitly. Indeed, one sister recalled that when certain changes that went far beyond those called for by the Vatican II were being promoted in her own congregation, a well-liked former superior exploited her leadership position by making the rounds to each of the elderly sisters, lobbying for the changes. Because the elderly sisters trusted this superior and wanted to please her, many of them went along with her wishes without really understanding, analyzing, or agreeing with the proposed changes.

The late Father Thomas Dubay, who observed the chapter meetings of several religious orders as well as his own, told the author about a certain "psychology of large meetings" in chapters. He reported that this psychology results in individuals wanting to be seen as upbeat, politically correct, and with the times; as a result, they are reluctant to vote no, especially when proposed changes are cloaked in pleasant terms.

A Dominican sister told the author that she had observed this psychology at one of her order's chapter meetings. Everyone present at the chapter meeting—including nondelegates and laypersons who were not members of the institute and did not have the right to vote—was given a color-coded card to indicate "pro" or "con" on matters considered by the chapter. A straw vote, in which everyone present was invited to hold up her card, indicating her opinion on the issues, was taken. Then the meeting was adjourned for a coffee break—and for lobbying efforts. After the break, the delegates cast the actual vote by holding up the appropriate card. While on the surface this process seems to be a congenial exercise in consensus building, in actual practice it was an effort to pressure delegates to vote for the majority position of those casting the straw vote, even though some of those people did not have voting rights and did not even belong to the order.

Sister (Thomas Aquinas) Elizabeth Carroll, former superior of the Sisters of Mercy of Pittsburgh (and member of the Sisters' Survey Committee and 1972 president of the LCWR), wrote that her order's special renewal chapter "completely altered almost all the accidentals of our life together", and "in the end, we had almost total unanimity from the delegates on the final decision. Unfortunately less than ten percent of the congregation immediately shared in this excitement, struggle and agreement."[8] When fewer than 10 percent of the sisters in a religious institute are happy with the chapter decisions of an order, how well is the common good of a congregation represented? How well did the delegates represent the sisters who had elected them?

Additionally, some of the exercises which allegedly prepare members of an institute for an upcoming chapter are quite questionable. Some of those preparation sessions, as well as some of the processes orchestrated by facilitators during chapter meetings, have become highly sophisticated psychological exercises that suggest the possibility of thought reform and manipulation rather than the guarantee by canon law that all members of the institute must have free input into the chapter. In fact, "facilitating" chapter meetings has become a burgeoning industry, particularly for former sisters who have experience doing this and have built careers by selling their expertise. These "consultants" are in high demand, and some are quite skilled at seeing to it that chapters arrive at conclusions preordained by the people who have hired them.[9]

In *Review for Religious*, Jesuit Father David Coughlan, a consultant on organizational development, discussed a model of conducting an assembly or a chapter of a religious institute that conjures up images of cult-like intimidation. Father Coughlan spoke of "targeting" individuals and the need to arouse "guilt" or "anxiety" in delegates in order to accomplish goals.[10]

Invalid Chapter Meetings?

Canon law designates that only professed members of a religious institute have the right to participate in governance of the institute. They formerly did this by voting for chapter delegates and by making suggestions to the chapter. Now some religious institutes have adopted

---

[8] Elizabeth Carroll, RSM, "Reaping the Fruits of Redemption", in *Midwives*, 63.

[9] See, for example, Ted Dunn, "Election and Communal Discernment: Goals, Myths, and Gifts", *Review for Religious* (July/August/September, 2004).

[10] David Coughlan, SJ, "Towards Jerusalem: The Process of an Assembly", *Review for Religious* (November/December 1994): 923–24.

what they call "total participation", which means every sister supposedly participates in the chapter and chooses her degree of participation.
While total participation sounds quite democratic on paper, degree of
participation may range from praying for the success of the chapter to
serving on planning committees to acting as a chapter delegate. The
canonical problem with this model is that the chapter delegates are thus
self-appointed, and sisters unable to serve as delegate thus have no voice.

As canonist Sister Elizabeth McDonough explained in her Canonical Counsel column, this total-participation model tends to minimize
or even eliminate the possibility of "active" participation by members
who happen to be elderly or ill or stationed at a distance or unable to
serve on committees and attend numerous meetings:

> This, in turn, results in arbitrary curtailment or elimination of the acquired
> right of these members to participate in the governance of their insti-
> tute in a juridic manner. Since those who are elderly or ill currently
> often comprise a large portion of the membership of religious insti-
> tutes, a significant number of religious in institutes and provinces are
> actually subtly disenfranchised by these supposedly 'full' participation
> methods of conducting chapters.

Sister Elizabeth added that each religious has the canonical right to
submit specific proposals to the chapter. However, some religious institutes establish procedures in which a steering committee attempts to
bring sisters to a consensus before the meeting, and the chapter simply rubber-stamps the previously formed consensus. Sister Elizabeth
cautioned that such practices "cannot validly or legally be enacted and
implemented if these procedures totally eliminate the possibility of an
individual religious actually submitting matters to the chapters".[11]

Jesuit Father Richard A. Hill, a canon lawyer, has expressed similar
concerns about the freedom and validity of the consensus-style election that has been used in some women's institutes. Father Hill wrote
that sometimes chapter committees consider themselves empowered
to create election procedures. This is not valid, Father Hill wrote, for
"the election procedures most recently approved by a general chapter
are to be followed." Of course, chapter decisions are subject to canon
law, and he warned that any process that inhibits the rights of individual

---

[11] McDonough, "Participation in Governance", *Review for Religious* (October 1991): 775–80.

religious to participate in governance renders an election invalid, and invalidly elected superiors cannot act validly on any subsequent matters of the religious institute. While presenting slates of candidates to a chapter is licit, Father Hill wrote, "it is never allowed that the members of the chapter are obligated to limit their votes to these pre-selected members of the community." [12] Yet Medical Mission Sister Catherine M. Harmer, a consultant and facilitator for religious chapters, observed that "so many chapters now use consensus that actual voting is not common anymore." [13]

Who Belongs to a Religious Order?

Another canonical problem turning up at chapter meetings is so-called associate members or comembers—laypeople who want to be closely associated with the spirituality and work of the institute—participating in chapter meetings or serving on committees that impact the governance of an institute. However, canon law precludes anyone other than a vowed member from participating directly in the governance of an institute. Yet, Sisters of Mercy associate Karen Schwarz observed:

> Many co-members live or affiliate with sisters in congregational living groups.... Some co-members serve on congregational committees, many work in congregational ministries and sit on boards of congregationally sponsored institutions, and most attend and participate in congregational meetings. Many participate in congregational discernment....
> ... These new forms, however, are not without their problems.... Many fear that the associates / co-members will be gone tomorrow, after having made unwise decisions about already short congregational assets and taking private congregational information with them. [14]

Also of concern is the use of congregation funds for individual projects of comembers or associates that, however worthwhile, are totally unrelated to religious life, such as building houses for Habitat for

[12] Richard Hill, SJ, "Election by Consensus—Part II", *Review for Religious* (July / August, 1987): 620–24.

[13] Catherine Harmer, "Chapters Present and Future", *Review for Religious* (January / February 1994): 124.

[14] Karen Schwarz, "Alternative Membership in Religious Congregations", *Review for Religious* (July / August 1991): 561.

Humanity. Some sisters have alleged that congregational funds have been transferred to lay comembers in anticipation of the possibility that some members of the congregation may eventually decide to form noncanonical communities and thus will already have a funding base in place that would not have to be approved by the Vatican. Another problem these sisters have reported is the employment of lay comembers or associates by a congregation whose own sisters could fill these positions with less expenditure of congregational funds.

In addition to allowing lay associate members some voice in congregational governance, some women's institutes have placed associates or comembers in leadership roles. Canon law requires that only a vowed religious may be a superior, but that canon is often circumvented by using other titles, such as coordinator.

The outgoing president of the LCWR told the conference's annual assembly in 1995, "We seem to be clear that associates participate with vowed members in spirituality and mission. Tensions arise, however, when some of us believe that associates should participate in our internal forum, having equal access with vowed members to decision making about our lives together without having the same accountability to live the consequences." [15]

While the connection of associates to a religious institute may have some benefits for all involved, the associate category nevertheless carries with it the possibility of blurring the distinction between religious life and secular life. Pope John Paul II referred to this concern in his 1996 apostolic exhortation *Vita Consecrata*, in which he wrote that integrating lay associates into a religious institute "should always be done in such a way that the identity of the institute in its internal life is not harmed" (56). Still, religious institutes of women that are in decline seem to believe their associate programs will ensure survival of the order, even though the order is no longer able to attract vowed members. This attitude betrays a basic misunderstanding of the nature of religious life, for associate members can never be considered actual members of a religious institute.

Father David F. O'Connor, a canon lawyer and a priest of the Missionary Servants of the Most Holy Trinity, wrote that "lay volunteers,

---

[15] Andree Fries, CPPS, "Transformative Leadership—Key to Viability", presidential address to 1995 joint CMSM / LCWR assembly, August 26, 1995.

associates or affiliates are not members of the institute. It is misleading to apply that term to them. They have none of the rights or obligations of members in the institute.... It seems best not to speak of them as members but only as volunteers, associates, affiliates, or some similar term." [16] Religious institutes of women seem oblivious to this fact, however, for Vincentian Father David Nygren, a psychologist, found in a 1988 survey of 740 leaders of religious institutes that 70 percent of the female leaders were "adapting their membership to include full or partial membership by laity".[17]

The Bitter Fruit of Renewal Chapters

Certainly, through their renewal chapters and various experiments, some religious institutes managed to effect a version of renewal fully in compliance with the Vatican II documents and other pertinent legislation. But too many institutes exceeded the limits of valid experimentation and brought confusion and chaos when they discarded many of their practices and traditions and even the basic purposes of their institutes.

Jesuit Father Thomas J. Casey, a sociologist, observed the following just five years after the close of Vatican II:

> Old structures have been abolished and little social support remains to underlay the religious life. Religious communities increasingly resemble boarding houses rather than communities.... Change is one thing, but change that proceeds at an unreasonable pace or that substitutes nothing reasonable for what it has destroyed can hardly be considered progress....
>
> ... So far more adeptness has been shown in destroying all forms and structures, in abolishing traditional symbols and expressions, than in creating new and viable ones. One therefore legitimately suspects that fundamental values in the religious life are under attack.[18]

Canonist Father David O'Connor wrote that religious were not adequately prepared for the renewal period:

[16] David O'Connor, ST, "Lay Associate Programs: Some Canonical and Practical Considerations", *Review for Religious* (March / April 1985): 262.

[17] A 1988 study by David Nygren, CM, cited in "Executive Summary of Study on the Future of Religious Orders in the United States", *Origins*, September 24, 1992, 261.

[18] Thomas Casey, SJ, "The Democratization of Religious Life", *Cross and Crown* (September 1970): 298–99.

They lacked, frequently, a sense of history—an understanding of what had gone before. Their theological acumen was often too minimal or outrightly deficient. Psychologically, they were forced out of a rigid and tightly-controlled lifestyle into a new-found freedom that appeared, at times, to overwhelm many of them in a variety of ways. Some of their brothers and sisters escaped from the confusion and instability of the times and sought dispensations. Change in the church became a way of life. It took place while the west, especially North America, was going through its own cultural and social revolution. It soured many on institutions, structures, authority, law and order.[19]

Thus, with so much turmoil and uncertainty, the stage was set for deconstruction of religious orders, treated in the next chapter.

---

[19] David O'Connor, *Witness and Service* (New York: Paulist Press, 1990), 46.

11

Deconstruction of Ministry, Community, and Prayer

Making religion a career logically calls for a 'religious form of life,' i.e., one in which the principal structures and practices give witness to what transcends the world.[1]

—Sister Mary Anne Huddleston, IHM

The souring of many sisters on "institutions, structures, authority, law and order" described at the end of the last chapter profoundly affected the lives of women religious even more than their male counterparts, because, with the exception of brothers, the men had the identity of the priesthood to sustain and anchor them. Many women religious suffered a significant identity crisis, which affected every aspect of their lives.

Apostolic religious institutes are supposed to undertake specific apostolates in the name of the Church. As Father O'Connor has written, "The exercise of the apostolate by religious is never entirely a private and personal ministry. It is always, in some sense, a public and corporate one." Further, apostolic work done in the name of the Church is to be guided by legitimate Church authority: "Religious are always to be subject to their own superiors and to the local bishop in the exercise of all forms of the external apostolate."[2] (Canon 674 states:

---

[1] Mary Anne Huddleston, IHM, *Sisters Today* (January 1993): 46.
[2] O'Connor, "The Public and Witness Dimension of Religious Life", *Review for Religious* (September / October 1987): 669–70.

"Apostolic action, to be exercised in the name and by the mandate of the Church, is to be carried out in its communion.")

The Breakdown of Ministry

Traditionally, the apostolates of religious orders were performed within the framework of Catholic institutions. Many sisters were school teachers; some worked in health care, social services, or in parish and diocesan programs. However, under the influence of the feminist movement and some of the other social movements of the 1960s, some sisters began to believe that they were simply preaching to the choir by teaching Catholic children in Catholic schools or by being confined behind the walls of Catholic institutions. Possibly because they received little feedback for their efforts, many sisters failed to realize that their apostolic works already were a powerful influence in eliminating ignorance, poverty, abuse and prejudice.

Nevertheless, many sisters felt their time would be better spent working with adults or children who were not enrolled in Catholic schools. Some of these sisters even felt that to be true evangelizers they were called to work among the nonbelieving poor and afflicted.

Certainly the ministry of women religious needed to be better adapted to the needs of the times and sisters needed to be better informed about the forgotten members of society. The problem was, some sisters seemed to be convinced they had to deconstruct their religious institutes in order to serve the poor, and some thought that their institutes could not serve both Catholics and non-Catholics at the same time. Others thought that their energies were better spent on ministries they identified themselves, rather than on a corporate ministry adopted by the institute.

Sister Joan Chittister, who was president of the LCWR from 1976 to 1977, explained this new philosophy of religious life in this way:

> For all practical purposes, the task that most [religious] communities came to this country to do had—with the ascension of John F. Kennedy to the presidency of the United States—been completed. Through the school system, the faith had been preserved in a strange land; Catholics had been inserted into a Protestant culture; the church had a tightly organized catechetical base and major institutional system. But whole new pockets of poor and oppressed people have arisen in this society

and women Religious are attempting to start all over again with the same bias toward the poor of this generation.[3]

Somehow, Sister Joan rationalized that the poor could be helped only by the deconstruction of the traditional forms of religious life. She went on to explain that in order for religious to serve the poor, they "have to put a lot of things down: so-called religious garb, institutionalism, withdrawal, a common apostolate in favor of corporate commitments to global issues of peace, poverty, hunger, minority concerns, human rights and the equality of women."

But women religious can very effectively serve the oppressed within the structure of their institute, as Mother Teresa's Missionaries of Charity have demonstrated. Additionally, sociologists have observed that organizations are usually better able to perform their services from a strong corporate base.[4]

Sister Joan's philosophy has been echoed by other women who answered the legitimate call of Vatican II to make religious life less authoritarian, but rather than implementing reasonable reforms, they threw off all semblance of authority and eventually discarded most of the traditions of their institutes, even the reasonable ones, including the apostolate that the institute had always performed. Gone with the structure and traditions was the specific end or purpose of the institute, even though Vatican II decrees stressed that the purpose of the institute must be preserved. Additionally, Canon 612 states, "In order that a religious house be converted to apostolic works different from those for which it was established the consent of the diocesan bishop is required."

Self-selecting Ministries

One sister in a teaching order told the author that in the late 1960s and early 1970s her community adopted a policy of "open placement". Previously, sisters had received their September teaching assignments as late as August and often had little time to prepare themselves to travel to assigned duties about which they had no input whatsoever. Nor did they always have sufficient notice to familiarize

[3] Chittister, "No Time for Tying Cats", in *Midwives*, 17.
[4] See Wittberg, "Outward Orientation in Declining Organizations", in *Claiming Our Truth*.

themselves with new textbooks or prepare themselves for classes they may not ever have taught before. So the new open placement policy was welcomed by the sisters. With the new policy, assignments were agreed upon in advance in consultation between the sister and her superiors.

The sister in question said that the new policy worked quite well, and the sisters enjoyed and appreciated having some input regarding which assignments they felt competent to undertake, while still adhering to their vows of obedience. However, before long, this scenario of consultation soon deteriorated into sisters' "doing their own thing" without consulting superiors. Since the mission of the congregation was education, some sisters undertook work that they rationalized was educational, such as selling encyclopedias, assisting political campaigns, and working in travel agencies. And superiors did not stand in their way. This sister observed, "We have a saying in our congregation to describe our so-called 'freedom.' It is said that if a sister decides that going to hell might be fulfilling for her, the leadership will pay her way, generously, and never check on her again!"

The author's college English professor, Sister of Saint Joseph Marcella Marie Holloway, voiced her concern about such excesses and abuses in a September 1970 article in *Liguorian* magazine. She wrote of her admiration for a sister colleague who stayed to teach because she felt obligated to do so after her community supported her education to obtain graduate degrees. But she also wrote about other teaching sisters who were searching endlessly for other careers, and living off the working sisters in the community while they conducted this search. "For us who remain [in teaching], it is often difficult to reconcile a Sister's release for study, for training in a specific area, and then her coming home to announce after six years that 'teaching is not her thing' and so another release period of training for another kind of work, *ad infinitum.*"

Indeed, Catholic sisters are the most educated group of women in the United States, probably even in the world. But how much of that education is now obtained to serve the needs of the Church or of society or of the sisters' religious institutes? And while the professional interests of sisters may change over time, just as the needs of society change, are there some jobs that are not suitable for religious, who through their public vows and membership in canonical religious institute are representatives of the Catholic Church?

Today, sisters are engaged in diverse and secular occupations, and this raises the question of how such diversity can reflect a corporate apostolate that serves the Church. Here is Sister Margaret Ellen (Mary Peter) Traxler (a founder of the NCAN): "In 1965, when I began work in another province of my community and worked at an independent agency, our community directory showed that I was only one of several Notre Dame Sisters working thus. Now, 20 years later, our community directory shows hundreds of our sisters working apart from the formal institutions of convent and church." [5]

Ironically, along with this trend for sisters to self-select their jobs, there also was a devaluing of "domestic" work done by sisters. Even though some sisters preferred to be the "homemakers" for the order, supervising the kitchen and laundry and attending to all of the other details necessary for operating an institution, this kind of service was no longer acceptable to some women religious. Instead, laypeople were hired for domestic tasks, and young women who were not academically suited for, or personally interested in, higher degrees were turned away as potential members of many orders.

The trend of sisters' self-selecting their jobs also impacted those sisters who wished to continue doing the traditional work of their institutes, for often a religious institute had to withdraw its other sisters from a school or hospital or social-service institution since in allowing a few to leave it could not guarantee that enough sisters would make themselves available to staff the positions. Complex financial and demographic factors—some of which were linked to a shortage of sisters—also forced the closing of many Catholic institutions where sisters traditionally worked. Thus, even sisters who wished to remain in their original apostolates often found themselves without a place to work because their institute had withdrawn from or sold the institution traditionally staffed by that order.

In his 2011 book *When the Sisters Said Farewell: The Transition of Leadership in Catholic Elementary Schools*, Father Michael Caruso wrote about the agony of sisters who were forced to leave schools they loved

---

[5] Margaret Ellen Traxler, SSND, "Gread [sic] Tide of Returning", in *Midwives*, 136.

and had served for years. He also noted the devastating effect their withdrawal had on parishes and parish families.

> Those sisters who were the last members of their communities to serve in elementary schools exited the schools either under the open-placement policy or at the direction of the community's leadership according to protocols that were adopted. It would be difficult to calculate which scenario of departure would be more difficult for these individual sisters. Each model presented difficulties for the sisters on the front line.[6]

Sisters—many of whom were middle-aged or approaching retirement—often found themselves in the entirely new position—that of being unemployed, a phenomenon never before experienced by nuns. Mercy Sister Georgine M. Scarpino, a research consultant and former employment director for the Job Training Partnership Act Program, reported in 1988 that unemployment among sisters exceeded the national unemployment rate.[7] This is indeed an ironic situation when most administrators of Catholic institutions would be delighted to have a sister on staff, but there is a problem of matching positions with the qualifications—and desires —of available sisters. It is a fact, too, that unlike unemployed laypersons, an unemployed sister usually can maintain a roof over her head and food on her table through the support of her community. So sisters often do not feel the same financial pressures as laypersons to take jobs that may not fit their ideal of what "the spirit" is calling them to do.

One other difficulty encountered when choosing individual ministries is income-tax status. When religious were engaged in the work of their institutes in Church-related positions, they were exempt from income tax. However, when religious moved into jobs with secular entities, they no longer automatically enjoyed that tax-exempt status, even when assigned to those jobs by their orders. The federal government has tended to apply the tax laws much more strictly in the last several years, and many court rulings on the taxability of clergy and religious have occurred. Furthermore, tax lawyers warn that as more and more members of a religious institute choose secular

---

[6] Caruso, *When the Sisters Said Farewell*, 61.

[7] Georgine Scarpino, RSM, "The Unemployed Sister: Challenges and Opportunity," *Review for Religious* (May / June 1988): 399.

occupations, the tax-exempt status of the institute itself is placed in jeopardy. One potential outcome of having a large number of members employed outside Catholic institutions is that the religious institute could be interpreted as being in the "business" of loaning employees. If this determination is made by the government and upheld in court, the institute could be taxed on the profits of that "business".

Perhaps the most significant and ominous result of the trend for sisters to determine their own work is that their religious institutes lost their corporate identity when they opted for this occupational diversity.

Religious Orders Lose Their Identity

According to the largest study ever done of American religious, the loss of corporate identity had a huge impact on the ability of religious institutes to sustain the loyalty of their members and to attract new vocations. Sister of Saint Joseph Miriam Ukeritis and Vincentian Father David Nygren, both psychologists, spent three years gathering and analyzing data from 10,000 men and women Religious from 816 congregations that had a total of 121,000 members. In September of 1992 they released the results of that study, called *Future of Religious Orders in the United States* (FORUS). Regarding corporate identity, they concluded that orders that do not have a clearly defined mission do not attract new members. And an emphasis on individual ministry has "eclipsed the symbolism of and statement previously made by corporate commitments" (IV-4).

This individualism also impacted the relationship of the religious to her institute and to the Catholic Church, the study found: "Many religious have migrated to the periphery of their congregation, often living lives that reflect significant ministerial contributions but which have little to do with their congregations or religious life" (IV-1). Thus, "the loss of conviction about the vows, lack of clarity about the role of religious, reactance [sic] to authority, lack of corporate mission and ministry, and disillusionment with leadership pose significant threats to the future of religious life" (III-A). The FORUS study found that orders that appeared to be rebounding or stabilizing had carefully reinstated monastic practices and a sense of clarity regarding their life and work (IV-4).

That trend continued into the twenty-first century, for the 2009 study, *Recent Vocations to Religious Life*, confirmed that the orders most successful in attracting new vocations have a distinct spirituality, community life, and communal prayer life. The study was conducted by the respected Center for Applied Research in the Apostolate (CARA) for the National Religious Vocation Conference.

Sociologists Rodney Stark and Roger Finke also found in their studies that "the data clearly support the thesis that to the degree that religious orders provide intense communal life, they will be more successful in recruiting new members."[8]

Community Life Disintegrates

As open placement and diverse individual apostolates became widespread in some religious institutes, community life was inevitably affected. When religious shared a community apostolate, they lived with other members of their community in large or small groups. Living in community, they shared a common life, meals together, the daily Eucharist, common prayer, and ongoing relationships with each other. Sisters living apart from their community were rare exceptions, and a concerted effort was made to keep those sisters in frequent contact with their order.

However, when sisters within congregations began to choose diverse ministries, daily schedules varied considerably, and it became more common for sisters to live closer to their work. Indeed, many sisters took jobs in locations where their religious institute did not even have a presence, so they began to live alone, with sisters of other religious institutes or with laypeople.

Some sisters moved away from their communities even when their institute maintained a convent in the same city because they did not want to continue living a common life. Sister Sandra Schneiders calls this phenomenon "psychological-spiritual".

As religious become more aware of the uniqueness of personality and of the different needs an individual has at various stages of human growth and spiritual development, they are less hesitant to recognize that lifestyle is an important factor in mental and spiritual health.... Increasing

---

[8] Rodney Stark and Roger Finke, *Acts of Faith: Explaining the Human Side of Religion* (Berkeley: University of California Press, 2000), 189.

numbers of religious have good personal and spiritual reasons for choosing lifestyles other than the traditional one, at least at certain periods of their lives, and they will increasingly insist that those choices be honoured.[9]

Prior to Vatican II, most religious institutes did not pay much attention to the psychological or social needs of members, and sisters who were burned-out or unable to cope with the demands of common life were usually sent off on retreat for a week or just told to pray about their difficulties. But there is a great deal of middle ground between ignoring the psychological and social needs of a sister and giving sisters complete carte blanche to select their own style of life. Religious institutes can exercise sensitivity toward the changing needs of their members while still expecting those members to adhere to certain standards of the institute. This penchant displayed by some religious to "do their own thing" surely has alienated some laypersons who also grow weary of their families from time to time but who remain faithful to their duties. Also, few laypersons can afford individual residences for all the members of their family.

Sisters often have little choice about where they live, however, for many communities have sold most of their property for a variety of legitimate reasons: They needed the money; their numbers had dwindled and they didn't need the space; or the old buildings were too expensive to maintain. But some other philosophies also motivated sisters to sell off their property, some of them based on a strange interpretation of religious life.

For example, Sister Dorothy Vidulich indicated that owning property somehow inhibited the sisters' ability to pursue their ministry. She wrote that her congregation, the Sisters of Saint Joseph of Peace, was committed to work for justice locally and globally, so, "sensitive to the need to divest ourselves of excess property, we sold our motherhouse with its acres of land."[10]

Noting this trend in their book *Catholic Higher Education*, Melanie Morey and Jesuit Father John Piderit wrote that women religious came to define their purpose as the work of justice, not traditional ministries

---

[9] Sandra M. Schneiders, "Formation for New Forms of Religious Community Life", *The Way Supplement* (Summer 1988): 64.

[10] Vidulich, "Finding a Founder," *Midwives*, 166.

and saw their own property as an obstacle to their mission. "Over time, the legacy of justice became so culturally pervasive and intense in religious congregations of women that all institutions became suspect. Institutions were contrary to their missions because they 'institutionalized injustice'".[11]

Sister Doris Gottemoeller (president of the LCWR, 1993–94) felt that the only acceptable reason for keeping institutions was to serve the poor: "If sponsorship of institutions is to continue to be a way to realize the mission of religious life, it must be because we are able to enlist them as powerful instruments on the side of the poor, to alter the oppressive structures in society which perpetuate poverty."[12]

Selling or Gifting Religious Properties

Some of this "alienation of property", as it is referred to in canon law, was done without the necessary permissions of higher Church authority. Current canon law requires that property owned by church entities, including religious institutes, cannot be sold without Vatican approval if the property is valued over a certain amount. (That amount was five million dollars in 2012, but was unrealistically lower in the 1960s and 1970s, when many Church institutions were sold or converted to secular entities.) The reason behind requiring these permissions is to safeguard Church property, much of which has been acquired by religious institutes operating as official representatives of the Church. Furthermore, these properties often were acquired through the donations of the faithful who expect religious institutions to operate in service to the Church. Vatican approval to alienate property usually is given only with the concurrence of the local bishop.

In the 1960s and 1970s, a number of the institutions owned by religious orders were converted to secular entities in order to obtain additional funding. However, many of the religious orders that reorganized their corporate apostolates, giving up corporate control of their institutions to lay-dominated boards, relied on a controversial interpretation of canon law set forth by Monsignor John J. McGrath, a professor of

[11] Melanie M. Morey and John Piderit, SJ, *Catholic Higher Education* (New York: Oxford University Press, 2006), 258. Also see chapter 9, "Cultural Collapse and Religious Congregations of Women".

[12] Doris Gottemoeller, RSM, in *Starting Points*, 27.

canon law at Catholic University who became president of Saint Mary's College in Notre Dame, Indiana, in 1968.

In his 1968 book, *Catholic Institutions in the United States: Canonical and Civil Law Status*, which was published by Catholic University, Monsignor McGrath contended that schools and hospitals that were separately incorporated from the religious institutes that owned them were not subject to canon law. That interpretation, however, was determined to be faulty:

> The McGrath thesis was relied upon by ecclesiastical entities such as religious orders which operated universities, colleges, and hospitals to secularize them in order to obtain government funding. Such secularization threatened the Catholic character of these institutions and the canonical safeguarding of millions of dollars of church property. The Holy See, through the Congregation for Catholic Education and the Congregation for Religious and Secular Institutes, protested that the McGrath thesis was never considered valid and had never been accepted.[13]

Indeed, some properties owned by women's religious orders were disposed of or secularized under the "McGrath thesis" without ecclesial approval.

Disposing of motherhouses, convents, schools, hospitals, and other institutions was, in some cases, obviously the only prudent course a religious institute could take, especially given the dire financial straits of some orders. But there are sisters who contend that their orders sold off property in a subversive effort to cut all ties with past traditions of the order and in a heavy-handed way to force sisters into small living units and away from like-minded individuals who might unify to protest the actions of the leadership. (And some laypeople whose families contributed to acquiring or building those properties interpret these sales as a betrayal of their investment in the future of the Church.)

One unique transfer of property to a secular entity occurred in Madison, Wisconsin, in 2006 and was reminiscent of the transfer of the IHM properties in Los Angeles by Anita Caspary. Benedictine Sisters from Iowa had established their monastery in Madison in 1953. Their girls' high school closed in 1966, and the sisters continued to offer retreats, interfaith dialogue, and prayer at their monastery.

---

[13] John E. Lynch, CSP, "Laying Down the (Canon) Law at Catholic University", *The Jurist*, 50, (1990): 40.

The order was small and aging, and the two remaining active sisters eventually set up a secular corporation. Subsequently, they asked for dispensation from their vows as Catholic sisters. They kept the former monastery and grounds since the title had already been transferred to the civil Benedictine Women corporation.[14]

The women eventually had the former monastery building demolished and replaced it with an eco-friendly eight-million-dollar building. According to their website, they offer an "ecumenical" worship service. "Each Sunday, we gather for worship as a community. Through scripture readings, prayer and sharing the Bread of Life around a common table, we respond to Jesus' invitation, 'Do this in memory of me.' ... Our Assembly shares concern for social justice and peace; we embrace works of charity and care for the earth."[15]

Divestiture of property also meant that sometimes sisters could not find a convent of their own congregation to live in, even if they wanted to live in community, which many of the sisters did desire. Even today, some middle-aged or younger sisters accept jobs in their orders' retirement centers because that is the only vestige of community life left in their congregations. Unfortunately, some sisters are forced to live alone because the sisters in their community live in small, self-selected groups, and no one has selected them. It is indeed ironic that some sisters are not welcome in communities of their own institute, especially when some of the leaders who forced this lifestyle on their communities were the very ones to complain that the all-male Church hierarchy oppressed women by being exclusive.

As Sister Joan Chittister explained: "Now we live in self-selected groups where interests and schedules and needs match and we come together as a large group at the priory time and again throughout the year for liturgy, for community projects, for celebration, for discussion, for education, for retreat, for chapter concerns, for parties."[16] And Sister Sandra Schneiders defined community as "the psycho-socio-spiritual unity of minds and hearts in Christ". She

[14] Robert McClory, "Ecumenical Monastery in Wisconsin Charts a New Way", *National Catholic Reporter*, August 17, 2007.

[15] See http://benedictinewomen.org/communities/sunday-assembly/ (accessed September 4, 2012).

[16] Chittister, "No Time for Tying Cats", *Midwives*, 8.

continued that "there are religious who, in terms of lifestyle, live singly, but who are living fully in community because of the intensity of their felt belonging and participation in the life of the congregation." [17]

Certainly, these are not the definitions of community life according to canon law. Canon 665 states: "Observing a common life, religious are to live in their own religious house and not be absent from it without the permission of their superior." The teaching of the Church on this matter is further explained in the 1994 letter from the Congregation for Religious, *Fraternal Life in Community*. The letter stressed that community life—physically living together in common—is essential to the identity of religious. The document cited a "culture of individualism" that weakened the ideal of life in common and commitment to community projects. In a true fraternal community, it stated, each member contributes to sharing, understanding and mutual help, and supporting other members of the community on a day-to-day basis: "Religious community is the place where the daily and patient passage from 'me' to 'us' takes place, from my commitment to a commitment entrusted to the community, from seeking 'my things' to seeking 'the things of Christ.'" And, the document concluded, each institute must have a common mission, with its members conducting works proper to that institute. But "should there be institutes in which, unfortunately, the majority of members no longer live in community, such institutes would no longer be able to be considered true religious institutes" (4, 39, 65). Many religious communities of women in the United States, however, have ignored these clear directives.

New Ways to Pray

Along with the disintegration of community life came the deterioration of prayer life for many sisters. Certainly some of the renewal efforts in prayer life were valuable and enriched the spiritual lives of the sisters. Some communities designed community prayer to be less rote recitation and more meaningful, with appropriate connections to liturgy and Scripture. There was a new emphasis on personal prayer.

---

[17] Schneiders, "Formation for New Forms of Religious Community Life", 68.

Unfortunately, some communities offered so much flexibility to their members that sisters began to feel no obligation to continue communal prayer of any kind, and some even absented themselves from the daily Mass. Then, as living arrangements and jobs became more diverse, community prayer went by the wayside, and some sisters even eschewed personal prayer, claiming that their work was their prayer.

While some sisters no doubt are very conscientious about prayer, many have had difficulty sustaining their prayer life without community support. Some sisters have told the author that they are much more inclined to pray if a particular time for personal and communal prayer is set aside each day and observed by the whole community

Many communities make no provision at all for personal or group prayer. One sister of Saint Joseph who lives alone observed that her community provides no guidelines to its members regarding prayer. Nor does the order provide for regularly scheduled spiritual events for the members who live away from community. She did say, however, that many of the sisters who live alone do arrange to get together occasionally for prayer groups, aerobics, or potluck dinners.

As for the Mass, some sisters refuse to attend Mass because they resent the all-male priesthood. In a 1991 address to the LCWR, Benedictine Sister Mary Collins, a longtime theology professor at Catholic University, observed:

> In my judgment as a student of liturgical performance, the crux of the troubled relationship American women religious have with the Roman Catholic Church is clear. It is centered in contemporary Catholic eucharistic praxis. . . .
>
> . . . As we pass through this decade of the 1990s, matters related to women and the eucharist promise only to become more publicly conflicted. . . .
>
> . . . Who among you sees as insignificant the alienation of the sisters who chose to remain members of your communities but who no longer participate in any eucharistic liturgy? 'I am no longer part of the institutional church,' they say. And they identify eucharistic liturgy as part of the system of power and privilege they reject.[18]

---

[18] Mary Collins, OSB, "Is the Eucharist Still a Source of Meaning for Women?", in Paul J. Philibert, OP, ed., *Living in the Meantime* (New York: Paulist Press, 1994), 186, 189.

Sister Ann Patrick Ware has noted that "there are increasing numbers of women religious who quietly celebrate the eucharist or participate in such a celebration out of the public eye. There are many
who have prepared themselves theologically for ordination. There are
Sisters who refuse to take part in Catholic rites as inherently sexist in
nature." [19] And Mary Jo Leddy, a former Canadian sister of Our Lady
of Sion, has observed that the sacraments of reconciliation and the
Eucharist "have never seemed more problematic, especially to female
religious. Women are realizing how much these liberating sacraments
have also served to reinforce a patriarchal structure in the church. This
experience has moved some women to develop their own rituals of
cleansing and celebration." [20]

In 2004 the LCWR published *An Invitation to Systems Thinking: An
Opportunity to Act for Systemic Change*, a handbook for religious orders.
The booklet mentioned sisters who "believe that the celebration of
Eucharist is so bound up with a church structure caught in negative
aspects of the Western mind they can no longer participate with a
sense of integrity".[21] In her 2007 keynote address to the annual assembly of the LCWR, Sister Laurie Brink noted that some sisters no
longer receive the sacraments because they are "angry" about "the
ecclesial deafness that refuses to hear the call of the Spirit summoning
not only celibate males, but married men and women to serve at the
Table of the Lord".[22]

However, in *Vita Consecrata* Pope John Paul II wrote, "By its very
nature the Eucharist is at the center of the consecrated life, both for
individuals and for communities. It is the daily viaticum and source of
the spiritual life for the individual and for the institute" (95). And the
Congregation for Religious document *Fraternal Life in Community* stressed
that prayer in common has always been considered the foundation of
all community life. Therefore, it said, all religious "must remain strongly
convinced that community is built up starting from the liturgy, especially from celebration of the Eucharist and the other sacraments" (14).

---

[19] Ann Patrick Ware, SL, "Dissent, a New Phenomenon among Catholic Women", in
A Leaf from the Great Tree, 89.

[20] Mary Jo Leddy, *Reweaving Religious Life* (Mystic, Conn.: Twenty-Third Publications,
1990), 97.

[21] LCWR, *An Invitation to Systems Thinking*, 16.

[22] Brink, "A Marginal Life: Pursuing Holiness in the 21st Century".

The document noted that "religious community is regulated by a rhythmic horarium to give determined times to prayer and especially so that one can learn to give time to God (*vacare Deo*)" (13).

Prayer of the Faithful?

Even in orders where community prayer has been maintained, the public prayer of the Church often is changed. In some cases inclusive language has been imposed upon the *Roman Missal* and the *Lectionary*, resulting in the elimination of male pronouns that refer to the First and Second Persons of the Trinity and creating strange new gender-neutral doxologies such as "the Creator, the Redeemer, and the Sanctifier". Such modifications are in violation of Church liturgical law.

The documents of Vatican II as well as the Code of Canon Law encourage religious to pray all or part of the Liturgy of the Hours, also known as the Divine Office, and many religious orders require daily prayer of the Divine Office in their constitutions. Since the Liturgy of the Hours is part of the public prayer of the Church, there is only one version approved by the Church for use in the United States: *Christian Prayer: The Liturgy of the Hours*. Many orders of sisters, however, have introduced feminist versions of the Liturgy of the Hours. Some orders have written their own versions, but the most widely used alternate breviaries were published by the Discalced Carmelite Nuns of Indianapolis. At first the nuns created the alternate text for their own use, but they received so many requests for it that they began publishing alternate breviaries such as *Companion to the Breviary* in 1985, *Woman's Prayer Companion* in 1994, and *People's Companion to the Breviary* in 1997. Because of advancing age and dwindling numbers, in 2008 the Indianapolis Carmelite nuns moved their remaining members to Oldenburg, Indiana, to live on the campus of the Franciscan Sisters there. Their alternate breviaries, however, remain in print and sometimes are sold in secular and religious bookstores alongside the official version.

Reinterpreting the Vows

Fraternal Life in Community observed that one of the fruits of renewal was that religious communities became less formalistic and less authoritarian. However, this reaction against rigid structures had a downside too, for some religious and some institutes did not adjust well to new concepts of freedom and personal responsibility. The Congregation for Religious observed in *Fraternal Life*:

> As a result, a certain number of communities have been led to live with no one in charge, while other communities make all decisions collegially. All of this brings with it the danger, not merely hypothetical, of a complete breakdown of community life; it tends to give priority to individual paths and simultaneously to blur the function of authority—a function which is both necessary for the growth of fraternal life in community and for the spiritual journey of the consecrated person. (48)

Even though canon law requires that religious live in a house of their institute under the authority of a legitimate superior, some religious communities actually do function as if no one were in charge. Often in a religious house there is a person called a coordinator, but in effect the coordinator is merely a communications person who passes along information. Sister Marie Augusta Neal reported that in 1982, 75 percent of women's religious institutes already had some or all living units without a local superior.[23]

An earlier LCWR survey reported in 1977 that "the role of authority is seen as a service role exercised within the community rather than from above" and that "there is a more mature acceptance of obedience as a positive orientation of one's life to the will of the father and as a commitment to engage with others in a search for the expression of that will." Tensions reported by the survey that were a result of these changes in the practice of authority included: less articulate members allowing themselves to be manipulated by the more vocal; confusion about locus of authority; polarization between liberal and conservative members; measures of accountability being somewhat undeveloped; authority sometimes eroding, especially at the local level, allowing the group to drift; fewer persons willing to accept leadership; and individualism that caused tension.[24]

Many of these problems also were cited in the FORUS study some fifteen years later. In fact, the FORUS study contended that authority in religious life was "the most pressing question" (IV-3) for religious

---

[23] Neal, *Catholic Sisters in Transition* (Wilmington, Md.: Michael Glazier, 1984), 54.
[24] "Patterns in Authority and Obedience", LCWR, May 15, 1978, 7, 12.

to solve and that the effectiveness of leaders was inhibited by a lack of respect for authority, both local and Church-wide. The study also found that there is little structure to consensual decision making by religious (III-B) and that the concept of a personal call to individual ministry has a higher priority for many religious than does the mission of their congregation.

With this struggle over the concept of authority, vows have taken on new meanings quite foreign to the way they have been tradition-ally understood. The vow of obedience, for example, is now often interpreted as the practice of the community "discerning" what should be done and the "superior" ratifying the decision. Frequently, obedi-ence is defined as responding to "the spirit", but the problem with this concept is that each individual is thus in control of what "the spirit" directs. The result for some religious, according to the FORUS study, is that "the dynamics of individualism and 'inner authority' have come to dominate over any notion of vocation that entails either obe-dience or even discernment of the will of God in the context of a congregational commitment" (V-1).

Likewise, poverty is interpreted diversely and in some cases seems to have little connection to the tradition of foregoing private owner-ship of property and living a lifestyle based on spiritual values rather than material goods. The new definitions of poverty range from mak-ing oneself available to other people, to engaging in open dialogue, to working for redistribution of wealth, to stewarding the earth's resources, to divesting religious institutes of their buildings and property. Sister Sandra Schneiders offered an unusual generic definition: "Religious poverty is an evangelically inspired and structured relationship to mate-rial creation which involves owning well, using well, and suffering well for the purpose of transforming human existence, our own included." [25]

The FORUS study found that while most religious congregations proclaim a mission to serve the poor, "a significant number of reli-gious feel no personal commitment" to this mission, and "the impulse to generosity among some religious is being eclipsed by self-preoccupation, psychological decompensation, stark individualism and a lessening of the willingness to sacrifice" (IV-1).

[25] Schneiders, *New Wineskins*, 190.

Sister Mary Anne Huddleston wrote that potential members of religious institutes have been put off not only by the wide range of occupations that sisters pursue, but also by the diverse lifestyles of sisters that sometimes give little witness to poverty: "While some members reside in huge motherhouse complexes, some (few these days) live in small groups in well-worn parish convents. While some live individually and simply in studio apartments, others live in twos or alone in more comfortable houses, apartments, or condominia complete with the state-of-the-art audio-visual systems, and canine or feline pets." [26]

Similarly, some laypeople are put off by sisters who wear expensive fashions accessorized by jewelry. And while laypeople understand that sisters need transportation, those who struggle to balance the family budget are often puzzled by sisters who seem to have the latest-model cars and electronic devices and can afford to take multiple trips every year.

Breaking the Habit

Of all the aspects of religious life for women, the issue of the habit has caused some of the most heated debates. While many sisters dismiss the habit simply as a minor detail regarding what clothing one chooses to wear, controversy over the habit touches on far deeper issues.

The habit identifies a woman as a vowed member of a particular religious institute that is empowered to exercise its apostolate in the name of the Church. The habit also serves as a visible sign of poverty. The Vatican's insistence on the habit and the subsequent refusal by some sisters to wear it is not just a dispute about clothing—it is a dispute about authority. Sociologist Gene Burns has noted that the controversy over the habit was "somewhat symbolic in the minds of both sisters and the SCR [Congregation for Religious] of the ultimate locus of authority over renewal".[27] In spite of the fact that the Vatican has been equally insistent that male religious and clergy wear a habit or other clerical garments, some feminists claim that patriarchal structures in the Church require the habit in order to keep women in their place, as subordinate to men. Thus, the refusal of some sisters to wear

---

[26] Mary Anne Huddleston, IHM, "Almost on Empty: Religious Life as Many Seekers See It", *Sisters Today* (January 1993): 43.

[27] Burns, *The Frontiers of Catholicism*, 143.

a habit is their declaration of independence from patriarchal authority, as explained by author Marcelle Bernstein in *The Nuns*:

> The churchmen who want their daughters in religion to be veiled and robed insist they do so to protect them, to preserve their modesty and chastity as much as to make them a sign of God in the world. But it is surely significant that in other societies where women are so treated, covered up and hidden from sight, it is not done out of any kind of respect but because they are scarcely seen as people in their own right. They are the property of men, and in a masculine society they are second-class citizens. No wonder the overwhelming reaction of nuns who have abandoned the habit has been that for the first time they feel they have achieved liberty.[28]

The issue of religious dress takes on added dimensions of importance because the style of habit—or lack of habit—frequently reflects a religious person's (or order's) attitude about accepting the authority of the Church. For example, some nuns still wear long, voluminous habits and elaborate veils that have not been changed since before the Second Vatican Council. Habits that have not been modified in any way raise the question of whether an order has heeded the Church's call for renewal. On the other hand, sisters who wear no form of religious garb appear to be unaware of or defiant of the Church's requirement that they dress in a way that distinguishes them as belonging to a religious order.

The Church is very clear in declaring the necessity of a religious habit. The directive is found in canon law, the writings of several popes, and numerous other documents emanating from the Vatican. Canon lawyer Sister Elizabeth McDonough observed that "no sound interpretations of conciliar and postconciliar legal texts even suggest that wholesale abandonment of simple, identifiable garb for religious was (or is) intended."[29]

In early 1972, Cardinal John Krol, president of the USCCB, received a letter on this matter from Archbishop Luigi Raimondi, apostolic delegate to the United States, which Cardinal Krol in turn sent to all US bishops. The letter called attention to the fact that religious men and women "in ever-increasing numbers, are abandoning the religious

---

[28] Marcelle Bernstein, *The Nuns* (Philadelphia: Lippincott, 1976), 265–66.
[29] McDonough, "Juridical Deconstruction of Religious Institutes", 325.

habit and also any distinctive external sign." The Raimondi letter contained a letter from Cardinal Antoniutti, prefect of the Congregation for Religious, which stated:

> The religious habit has been considered by the Second Vatican Council as a sign of consecration for those who have embraced in a public way the state of perfection of the evangelical counsels.... Religious institutes, in their general chapters, may, and in some cases, ought to, modify the traditional habit in accord with practical requirements and the needs of hygiene, but they may not abolish it altogether or leave it to the judgment of individual sisters.

The Antoniutti letter also stated that secular clothes could be permitted by competent superiors when the habit would constitute an impediment or obstacle for sisters doing certain necessary activities, but even then the dress should be in some way different from every day secular clothes.[30]

Cardinal Antoniutti elaborated on this point in a February 5, 1972, response to an inquiry by Bishop Leo A. Pursley of Fort Wayne–South Bend:

> In regard to the Religious Habit, as you are aware, various Institutes have taken liberties far beyond what was ever intended by the Council. And if they say that Rome has approved their wearing of contemporary secular dress, they should be challenged to show proof of this.... Never has any positive approval been given to laying aside the Religious Habit. Neither has such a provision been passed over in silence, unless, in some rare case, through an oversight. Nor does 'silence give consent' as some have contended, who presume that because they have heard nothing from this Sacred Congregation, their Interim Constitutions are approved....
>
> ... We would ask you to continue your insistence on the habit, Your Excellency. As you know, it is not only your right but your duty, in keeping with the Motu Proprio "Ecclesiae Sanctae."[31]

In spite of these clear directives, some sisters insisted that the topic is still open to debate. Sister Thomas Aquinas (Elizabeth) Carroll, president of the LCWR from 1971 to 1972 and general director of the

---

[30] Cardinal Antoniutti letter, quoted in *National Catholic Reporter*, February 18, 1972, 5.

[31] Cardinal Antoniutti letter to Bishop Leo Pursley, February 5, 1972, CCPC 5/47, UNDA.

Sisters of Mercy of Pittsburgh, wrote the members of her order on February 21, 1972, that Archbishop Raimondi's letter was "not a legal document and was not promulgated to the religious congregations". She told her sisters to put to rest any conscience problems they might have with the letter; she was continuing to authorize the sisters to wear either "modified habit, recognizable symbol, or purely secular clothes conformable to the 'poverty, simplicity and modesty proper to the religious state'". She called for an end to "mutual condemnations" regarding clothing and said it would be "impertinent to establish any form of clothing as an essential of a life dedicated to the following of Christ." Instead, she said, that the sisters' diversity of dress should be used as means of personal development and growth in charity.[32]

The habit was such an emotional topic among sisters that most bishops simply avoided the issue. Clearly some bishops feared that if they insisted sisters wear the habit, the sisters would simply depart from their dioceses, leaving many Catholic institutions unstaffed at a time when demand for the services of Catholic institutions was at an all-time high. Indeed, Bishop Vincent Waters, of Raleigh, North Carolina, saw many sisters leave his diocese when he insisted that they wear a recognizable habit.

Bishop Leo A. Pursley, of Fort Wayne–South Bend, was the only other bishop to take a firm stand publicly during the turbulent 1960s and 1970s, though many bishops no doubt agonized over the situation privately. Bishop Pursley wrote Cardinal John Wright: "Apparently I am the only anti–Women's Liberation member of the U.S. Hierarchy to join Bishop Waters in his one-man crusade. It is likely that Sisters leaving this Diocese will be promptly signed up by another [diocese], like free agents in pro football. This is collegiality? Why not stand together behind our own votes at Vatican II?"[33]

Abandonment of the habit may have been encouraged by some bishops. In a January 27, 1976, letter to all pontifical nuncios and delegates, Cardinal Sebastiano Baggio, prefect of the Sacred Congregation for Bishops, wrote that Church norms regarding the dress of priests and religious

---

[32] Sister M. Thomas Aquinas letter to "My dear sisters", February 21, 1972, CCPC 5/41, UNDA.

[33] Bishop Leo Pursley letter to Cardinal John Wright, February 8, 1972, CCPC 5/47, UNDA.

have been largely neglected and even attacked, under evasive doctrinal and pastoral motives, with serious and harmful effects, among which are the embarrassment and confusion of the faithful. But what constitutes the motive of my present letter is the painful evidence that such self-will has not rarely had its source in the bishops themselves and has been encouraged by their example, if not directly by their formal expression, as in the cases of communities of women impelled by some bishops to abandon the religious habit.[34]

Subsequently, Archbishop Jean Jadot, apostolic delegate to the United States, wrote Cardinal Joseph Bernardin, then president of the USCCB, about the duty of bishops to require that priests and religious in their dioceses wear proper attire. He stated that "in some cases the arbitrary rejection of appropriate attire for priests and religious can be traced to bishops who have tolerated abuses or who have not given the proper example by their own choice of clothing. It has even been reported that some bishops have directly advised religious communities of women in their dioceses to abandon the religious habit."[35]

Confusion and defiance with respect to the habit continued, however. A Washington, DC, priest reported in 1979 that when he showed some sisters a copy of *Origins* in which the pope was quoted as saying that religious should wear some kind of habit, the sisters responded with "the Holy Father was misquoted and never said this" or "their Mother General had written to them saying that this particular wish on his part did not apply to them, going so far as to say that this particular reference was countermanded later on by another statement saying that he [the pope] did not mean what he said."[36]

In May of 1983, the Congregation for Religious had a confrontational meeting in Rome with leaders of the LCWR over the habit issue. A July 29 *National Catholic Reporter* article said that the Congregation for Religious had accused American women superiors of deviating from Vatican II directives, canon law, and statements of the pope regarding religious garb. The LCWR contingent, headed by its president

[34] Cardinal Sebastiano Baggio letter to pontifical nuncios and delegates, January 27, 1976, *Review for Religious* (January 1979): 54.

[35] Archbishop Jean Jadot letter to Most Reverend Joseph L. Bernardin, February 28, 1976, CCPC 5/37, UNDA.

[36] Rev. Msgr. William J. Awalt letter to Sister Rose Eileen Masterman, CSC, September 19, 1979, CMAS 3/30, UNDA.

Helen Flaherty, of the Sisters of Charity, responded that requiring distinctive religious garb would cause polarization in orders, loss of membership, and "a weakening of the authority and credibility of the institutional church". Further, the LCWR delegation insisted that an "evolution" had taken place and that their sisters no longer considered rules about habit to be "binding in conscience".

The article reported that the Church officials reminded the LCWR leaders that their authority came from the Church and not from their own orders and that the revised constitutions of some US religious orders confused "the process of decision-making with the definition of the vow of obedience". An unnamed source was quoted in the article as saying that "the real issue behind the religious garb focus ... was Vatican control over essential aspects of American religious life."

Catherine Pinkerton, of the Sisters of Saint Joseph of Cleveland, president-elect of the LCWR, was quoted in the article as saying that "the Vatican representatives understandably were presenting a traditional theology of religious life, while the Americans were open to a variety of theologies."

With their leaders making such statements, women religious were confused and misinformed on the habit issue. Several sisters told the author that they sincerely felt they were following the directives of Vatican II and being obedient to the pope and their orders when they switched to lay clothing. Others tell of the trauma of being forced by superiors to give up the habits and rosaries they had been wearing for decades, allegedly because Vatican II had mandated it. Thus many sisters were very surprised when they finally read *Perfectae Caritatis* or *Evangelica Testificatio* or *Ecclesiae Sanctae* or heard one of the pope's statements on the habit.

Vatican officials no doubt have contributed, perhaps unknowingly, to confusion over the requirement of religious garb, for the Vatican has approved constitutions for some religious orders that include very vague statements on the dress of the institute's members, statements that are open to wide interpretation. For example, this statement on religious garb is from a constitution approved by the Vatican for a large congregation of American sisters: "Our dress ... simple and modest and appropriate to women consecrated to the service of the Lord, identifies us as religious in the Church. It is worn with the symbol of the Congregation or some other religious symbol." As one sister reported, this "other religious symbol" in her order was a butterfly pin. Many sisters confirm that constitutions are often written in these general terms so that, while the Vatican might give the sisters the benefit of the doubt about such vague language, the sisters can then interpret the constitution in the broadest possible way.

While the habit might not be the most important issue facing religious orders, it is not to be underestimated as a powerful sign of a life consecrated to God. The 2009 CARA study on *Recent Vocations to Religious Life* found, for example, that "having a religious habit was an important factor for a significant number of new members" of religious orders. (13)

What Did the Bishops Think about the Transformations?

During the 1970s, when constitutions and rule books were being rewritten, there was some effort by the US bishops to address some of the problems in religious orders, but it seems that the bishops' concerns were not passed along to sisters by their leadership.

In 1971, Bishop James Hogan, chairman of the USCCB Liaison Committee with the CMSW, wrote all bishops to ask if they had any issues they wanted to be brought to the attention of American sisters. Then, at the April 25, 1971, meeting of his liaison committee with representatives of the women superiors' conference, Bishop Hogan presented each of the nuns in attendance the remarks of the fifty-five bishops who had responded to his letter. These remarks included the following:

- The bishops were concerned over "confusion, tension, anxiety and disunity in some congregations", which had a negative impact on vocations and caused sisters to depart because the congregations had changed so much.
- "Many bishops are persuaded that, in good faith, misinterpretation of Vatican II's documents crept in" even though Vatican II documents are very clear on the essentials of religious life.
- Bishops could not respond to the conference's request that they support the chapter decrees of religious institutes when such decrees "were deemed to be at variance with the mind of the Church".

- Bishops were concerned that the writings of some sisters reflected "a negative attitude toward and inordinate criticism of the Holy See".
- The bishops had difficulty justifying requests for larger salaries, apartments, cars, and clothing, given the sisters' vow of poverty.
- The bishops were "not happy with growth of extra-community residences", which resulted in fragmentation and resentment on the part of some laity.
- Bishops were unhappy with congregations opening new houses and undertaking new apostolic works without consulting the local bishop.
- Bishops were concerned that some congregations belittled and criticized the important work of the teaching sister.[37]

Sister Angelita Myerscough, president of the superiors' conference, responded to Bishop Hogan, "In order to facilitate further dialogue and to widen the input from CMSW a bit more, we are circulating the pages among the members of our National Board (about twenty members)."[38] The concerns of the bishops, however, apparently went only as far as the twenty-member national board and were not passed along to the members of the superiors' conference. Sister Angelita in fact directed the national board not to distribute the bishops' comments in their regions. She observed in a letter to the members of the conference's national board and liaison committee with bishops that

> in no sense was this compilation [of bishops' comments] prepared for wide distribution or publication, but simply as an instrument for dialogue among our CMSW committee members and the Bishops' Liaison Committee. Hence we are limited in its distribution at the time, and I would ask you not to send it out in the regions. If the Bishops were to prepare something for that kind of circulation, I am sure they would want to put it into a somewhat different form.[39]

[37] Minutes of the Meeting of the Bishops' Liaison Committee and CMSW Committee for Liaison with the Bishops, April 25, 1971, and attached copy of the "Points submitted by various bishops for the consideration of the CMSW. Presented to the representatives of the CMSW by the NCCB Liaison Committee, April 25, 1971 in Detroit." CLCW 6/18, UNDA.

[38] Myerscough, ASC, letter to Most Reverend James J. Hogan, April 28, 1971, CLCW 6/18, UNDA.

[39] Myerscough, ASC, letter to members of the National Board and CMSW Committee for Liaison with the Bishops, April 28, 1971, CLCW 6/18, UNDA.

Bishop Hogan, however, had intended for the bishops' comments to be passed along to all the members of the conference. After the September 1971 annual assembly of the CMSW, which Bishop Hogan attended, he made a report to the USCCB. In it he observed: "It does not appear that the relative concerns of some 55 bishops submitted to the Sisters in Detroit last April [at the Liaison Committee meeting] evoked subsequent discussion." [40]

In 1973, Bishop Hogan wrote conference executive director Sister Mary Daniel Turner about replies to another questionnaire he had sent to bishops. He wrote that "the following points continue to be elements of concern." Among these were the following:

- Free placement in which sisters were permitted to find their own work lessened stability and made it impossible for the community to maintain a commitment to a specific work in a diocese or parish.
- Regarding the sisters' leaving Catholic schools, the bishops said they didn't minimize the sisters' intense concern for the poor and oppressed, but they wondered how Christian leaders could be trained for the social apostolate if the sisters left the Catholic schools.
- "In the light of some experimentation regarding life style and government, have some communities *defacto* [sic] moved into the status of Secular Institutes?"
- Bishops were not always informed about who was performing what apostolate in their dioceses.
- Bishops "continue to express their solidarity with Vatican II and the Holy Father in asking for some significant external sign manifesting Religious commitment." [41]

Bishop Hogan wrote that he hoped these concerns could be discussed at the LCWR's annual assembly in August and at the bishops' annual meeting in November. However, the author found no evidence that the entire membership of the superiors' conference were ever informed that some bishops had raised these concerns, for the leaders of the conference were intent on pursing the course of renewal

[40] "Report of [NCCB] CMSW Liaison Committee," c. November 14–18, 1971, CLCW 6/21, UNDA.

[41] Bishop James J. Hogan letter to Sister Mary Daniel Turner, SNDdeN, June 4, 1973, CMAS 2/11, UNDA.

they had defined for themselves. Failing to pass along pertinent information to members was not unprecedented for LCWR leaders, as noted previously in this book.

Over the years, the Congregation for Religious and the pope have regularly set out clear directives to guide religious orders regarding their role in the Church, such as *Fraternal Life in Community* and the pope's apostolic exhortation *Vita Consecrata*, both discussed previously. Additionally, on June 14, 2002, the Congregation for Religious released *Starting Afresh from Christ: A Renewed Commitment to Consecrated Life in the Third Millennium*. In that document, religious men and women were praised, but problems in orders also were cited, such as a decrease in members, "taking on of middle-class values and of a consumer mentality", "the risk of obscuring Gospel originality and of weakening spiritual motivations", and the "prevalence of personal projects over community endeavors" (12).

Later that same year, the Congregation for Catholic Education issued *Consecrated Persons and Their Mission in Schools: Reflections and Guidelines*. That document stated: "It thus becomes clear that consecrated persons in schools, in communion with the bishops, carry out an ecclesial mission that is vitally important inasmuch as while they educate they are also evangelizing." (6)

Nevertheless, as noted earlier, the number of teaching sisters dropped by one hundred thousand between 1965 and 2012. The following chapter presents two examples of self-styled renewal of women's religious institutes—both teaching orders—that had tragic results for both the sisters in those institutes and for the Church in general.

12

Two Communities versus the Hierarchy

We set out to push back the boundaries of religious life.[1]

— Anita Caspary, former superior,
Immaculate Heart of Mary Sisters, Los Angeles, California

The chaos experienced by many religious orders during the renewal years can be understood more easily by looking at two specific examples: the Sisters of the Immaculate Heart of Mary (IHM) of Los Angeles and the School Sisters of Saint Francis of Milwaukee. These religious institutes made headlines in the 1960s and early 1970s because of their self-styled approaches to renewal and subsequent clashes with Church authorities over their renewal decisions. Other religious institutes of women watched these communities closely, and the ultimate disposition of these conflicts with the Vatican affected them as well. In turn, the Catholic institutions traditionally staffed by sisters were also impacted dramatically.

The IHMs and Cardinal McIntyre

The conflict between the IHM Sisters and Cardinal James McIntyre, archbishop of Los Angeles, during the late 1960s was widely reported by the press and caused much consternation among women religious. The major difficulty with the whole situation was that few people knew all the facts, and much misinformation was circulated. The prevailing

[1] *Newsweek*, February 16, 1970, 34.

piece of misinformation—carried by periodicals such as *Time* and *Newsweek*—was that the IHM Sisters were dutifully complying with the directives of Vatican II to renew their order but were being obstructed by Cardinal McIntyre. *Newsweek* described the cardinal as "an old guard standard-bearer of the Roman Catholic hierarchy" who would not allow the sisters to modernize in accordance with Council's call for renewal. Backing him up was Congregation for Religious prefect Cardinal Ildebrando Antoniutti, described by *Newsweek* as "the aging misogynist who jealously guards Catholicism's monastic traditions".[2]

In 1970 IHM superior Anita Caspary, formerly Sister Humiliata, led approximately three hundred of the IHM Sisters out of the order into a lay organization called the Immaculate Heart Community, leaving behind about sixty IHM Sisters who wanted to retain their canonical status as a religious institute in the Catholic Church. The exodus was a traumatic situation for all involved, but it was hardly the fault of an intransigent hierarchy determined to preserve the pre–Vatican II model of religious life, as the secular press and much of the Catholic press reported.

So, what really happened?

Like many other religious institutes, the IHM Sisters went far beyond the reforms requested by Vatican II and subsequent Church documents. Heavily influenced by the women's liberation movement and the popular psychology of the 1960s, the institute had declared virtually all of its past traditions and practices to be optional, including common prayer, community life, the religious habit, the corporate apostolate of education, and the shared Eucharist. When Cardinal McIntyre told the order that these innovations did not adhere to the renewal called for by the Church, the sisters appealed to the Vatican, which came down on the side of Cardinal McIntyre. The sisters skillfully solicited support from sympathetic American religious and laity and some members of the women superiors' conference, claiming that Cardinal McIntyre and the Vatican were trying to prevent them from following the mandates of the Second Vatican Council.

Support for the sisters was plentiful, including sympathy from sectors of the secular and Catholic press, which depicted the IHM Sisters as obedient daughters of the Church who were being prevented from

---

[2] *Newsweek*, September 8, 1969, 80.

renewing their order by a misogynist hierarchy. But the Vatican and Cardinal McIntyre did not back down from the position that the essentials of religious life could not be changed. Subsequently, 80 percent of the sisters chose to leave the order rather than accede to the Magisterium. Thus, the IHM Sisters of Los Angeles became a cause célèbre during the very time most other religious institutes were rewriting their constitutions.

The IHM Chapter Decrees

The October 1967 IHM chapter decrees provide solid evidence of how much the sisters were influenced by the women's liberation movement. One can also detect in the decrees a heavy emphasis on individualism that was described in chapter 8 by psychologist William Coulson, who had provided workshops to the sisters. Here is an excerpt from the prologue to the IHM 1967 chapter decrees:

> Women, perhaps especially dedicated women, insist on the latitude to serve, to work, to decide according to their own lights. Our community's history ... speaks of our readiness to abandon dying forms in order to pursue living reality. It expresses, also, our willingness to seek human validity rather than some spurious supernaturalism.
>
> Women around the world, young and old, are playing decisive roles in public life, changing their world, developing new life styles. What is significant about this new power for women is not that it will always be for the good, nor that it will always edify, but that there can be no reversing of it now. Women who want to serve and who are capable of service have already given evidence that they can no longer uncritically accept the judgment of others as to where and how that service ought to be extended. American religious women want to be in the mainstream of this new, potentially fruitful, and inevitable bid for self-determination by women.[3]

The chapter decrees followed the same pattern as the prologue, including these declarations: "Every humanizing work would seem to be a proper apostolate for us." "Participation in the temporal order calls for a new style of communal existence—one which will not rigidly

---

[3] Sarah Bentley Doely, ed., "Prologue to IHM Chapter Decrees", *Women's Liberation and the Church* (New York: Association Press, 1970), 71.

separate us by customs, cloister, or clothing from those we serve."
And "our religious obedience consists not in passive submission but in
cooperative interaction with other members of the community." Community was defined to have "no fixed pattern or structure nor even a
permanent involvement in one type or manner of work".[4]

Anita Caspary wrote in her 2002 memoir, *Witness to Integrity: The
Crisis of the Immaculate Heart Community of California*, that the sisters
were particularly influenced by two retreat masters: Dominican Father
Noel Mailloux and Holy Spirit Father Adrian Van Kaam, both psychologists. "Van Kaam's hope that the 'present split between Church
and culture'—his way of describing the unfortunate dichotomy between
the sacred and the secular—might eventually be overcome by an enlightened humanity became for the IHMs an important underlying philosophy in the formulation of their 1967 decrees", Caspary wrote. She
also identified as influential speakers Father Gregory Baum and Maryknoll Father Eugene Kennedy, both of whom would later leave the
priesthood and become featured speakers at conferences of the Church-
reform group Call to Action.[5]

News reports indicated the chapter decrees gave IHM Sisters the
freedom to choose the type of work they wanted to do and removed
the requirement of having a local superior at each convent. Convents
also were given wide discretion in government and community prayer
schedules. And individual sisters were free to choose their own style
of clothing, whether a religious habit or secular clothing.

Cardinal McIntyre subsequently told the sisters that the Vatican II
documents and other Church legislation required them to wear some
kind of religious garb, to have daily prayer in common, and to continue the work of their institute, which was education. The Congregation for Religious backed up Cardinal McIntyre, issuing a letter on
February 21, 1968, explaining that the purpose of an institute must be
kept intact, and it cited the purpose of the IHMs from their own
constitution as follows: "The specific end is to labor for the salvation
of souls through the work of Catholic education." The Congregation
for Religious letter also stated that every community of IHM Sisters

[4] The 1967 Chapter Decrees of Immaculate Heart of Mary Sisters of Los Angeles, CLCW
34/07, UNDA.
[5] Anita Caspary. *Witness to Integrity: The Crisis of the Immaculate Heart Community of
California* (Collegeville: The Liturgical Press, 2003), 51.

should meet daily for some kind of common prayer, at the very least by attending Mass together. And the letter reaffirmed the authority of the local bishop over the works of the apostolate of a religious institute. Additionally, the letter confirmed that lay clothing for religious was not permitted under *Perfectae Caritatis*, canon law, or *Ecclesiae Sanctae*.[6]

Everything in the congregation's letter was in accordance with the renewal called for by the Second Vatican Council. However, the press painted a picture of sisters trying to follow what the Council had decreed who were being forced back into a pre–Vatican II mold by a conservative hierarchy. And many religious from other orders, as well as many laypeople unfamiliar with Church documents, accepted this scenario.

Anita Caspary admitted that the main issue that caused the controversy with Cardinal McIntyre was the issue of the sisters' lifestyle, as she wrote in her memoir: "Religious life of the past, we felt certain, had to develop into new forms." [7] As Sister Dorothy Vidulich observed, Anita Caspary and her followers "had rejected a life pattern of community that had to conform to a *Code of Canon Law* issued by male clerics of another culture".[8] According to his biographer, Cardinal McIntyre gave the sisters the choice of observing canon law and obeying the Magisterium or withdrawing from archdiocesan schools.[9] Needless to say, this decision would have a tremendous impact on Catholic schools in southern California, for in 1967 the IHM Sisters had 197 teachers in twenty-eight grade schools and eight high schools throughout the Archdiocese of Los Angeles.[10]

Naturally this situation was being watched closely by Catholics all over the country. Bishops whose parochial schools were overflowing with baby boom children worried about what they would do if they lost their teaching sisters. Catholic parents also worried about the nuns leaving their schools. And other religious institutes watched with fascination for clues about how the IHM renewal would affect them and

---

[6] *National Catholic Reporter*, March 27, 1968.

[7] Caspary, *Witness*, 103.

[8] Sister Dorothy Vidulich, *National Catholic Reporter*, June 30, 1995.

[9] Francis Weber, *His Eminence of Los Angeles: James Francis Cardinal McIntyre* (Mission Hills, California: Saint Francis Historical Society, 1997).

[10] *National Catholic Reporter*, November 15, 1967.

the direction of their communities. In reality, many other orders of women were considering or had already passed chapter decrees similar to those of the IHMs, but few bishops had raised any protest over them. Apparently some US bishops themselves were not familiar with Church documents on religious life. Some were confused about the bishop's role relative to religious in his diocese, and some even quietly applauded the sisters' resistance to the Vatican. Probably most bishops feared a mass exodus of sisters from Catholic schools, hospitals, and social-service agencies if they interfered with the renewal efforts.

Support for the Sisters

Even though she had been asked by the apostolic delegate not to discuss the matter publicly, Sister Anita Caspary took to the lecture circuit.[11] Consequently, all Catholic eyes were on Los Angeles, and the media had a field day with the situation, which dragged on into 1970. Headlines such as the following appeared in both the Catholic and secular press: "McIntyre to Oust 200 Updating Nuns",[12] "13 Jesuits Praise L.A. Nuns' Renewal",[13] "Vatican Rules against IHM Nuns on Changes Opposed by McIntyre",[14] "3,000 Sisters Support IHMs",[15] "Immaculate Heart Sisters—Hemlines and Humbug",[16] and "Battling for "Nuns' Rights".[17] A sympathetic editorial in *Ave Maria* concluded, "It is unfortunate that this controversy has clouded the announcement of the Immaculate Heart Sisters' response to the spirit of the Council."[18] A *Commonweal* editorial opined: "Our first impulse, and undoubtedly the impulse of many, is to counsel the IHMs to stop playing diplomatic games with their Cardinal and Rome, and just walk out. But there is reason to be hesitant about this impulse. Rome should be given the chance to open itself to reason and protest." The editors

[11] Weber, *His Eminence*, 424.
[12] *National Catholic Reporter*, November 15, 1967.
[13] *National Catholic Reporter*, January 31, 1968.
[14] *National Catholic Reporter*, March 13, 1968.
[15] *National Catholic Reporter*, March 27, 1968.
[16] *Commonweal*, April 5, 1968, 63–64.
[17] *Newsweek*, September 8, 1969, 80.
[18] "An Open Letter to Sister Anita", on editorial page and signed by thirteen faculty members from Alma College, Jesuit Seminary, Los Gatos, California, *Ave Maria*, February 3, 1968, 4.

then called for a letter-writing crusade to protest the treatment of the IHM Sisters.[19]

America editors called on US bishops to intervene with the Vatican on behalf of the IHM Sisters to allow completion of their renewal program and thus win "a degree of flexibility" with the Congregation for Religious. The *America* editorial did admit that a "literal interpretation" of the Church documents on religious life backed up the position of the Congregation for Religious; but the *America* editor also declared that "a more liberal, more empirical approach to the subject provides the Immaculate Heart Sisters with a strong case as well."[20]

Behind the scenes, sisters who supported the IHM vision of renewal were hard at work to garner support for them, knowing that the outcome of the IHM case would impact renewal in their own communities.

The IHM Community Splits

In late April 1968, the Congregation for Religious appointed a four-member visitation team, made up of three American bishops and a priest, to look into the IHM controversy. That team reported that there already was a split within the IHM over the chapter decrees. The team directed that the IHM Sisters should decide between the two groups—Sister Anita Caspary and those who supported the controversial 1967 chapter decrees or sisters who wanted to follow the original IHM constitutions, under the direction of Sister Eileen MacDonald. (More than one hundred IHM Sisters chose neither option and left their order during this time of turmoil.) The Congregation for Religious team issued a decree that Sister Anita's group would be "given a reasonable time, taking account of the points already made known to them, to experiment, to reflect and to come to definitive decisions concerning their rule of life to be submitted to the Holy See".[21]

As 1969 passed, it became clear that neither the Congregation for Religious nor the IHM Sisters aligned with Sister Anita Caspary would back down. In August 1969, Sister Margaret Ellen Traxler and Sister

[19] A. V. Krebs, Jr., "Hemlines and Humbug", *Commonweal*, April 5, 1968, 60, 63.
[20] "The IHMs and the Bishops", unsigned editorial, *America*, October 25, 1969, 349–50.
[21] *National Catholic Reporter*, June 19, 1968.

Mary Audrey Kopp founded the National Coalition of American Nuns (NCAN) "to protest the interference by men in the internal affairs of the sisters", an obvious reference to the IHM situation.[22] And in September, the annual assembly of the CMSW debated a resolution to support Sister Anita's group in its dispute with the hierarchy, as described in chapter 4. That resolution failed by one vote, even though Sisters Angelita Myerscough and Thomas Aquinas Carroll (both members of the Sisters' Survey Committee) lobbied hard to get the assembly to approve the resolution. After the assembly, some conference members tried to keep the issue alive, and Sister Rosalie Murphy, a member of the 1970 conference executive committee, sent a letter to conference members soliciting signatures of superiors for a petition to the Congregation for Religious.[23]

In February of 1970, 315 IHM Sisters announced that they would seek dispensation from their vows and establish the Immaculate Heart Community, an independent nondenominational organization of laity under the leadership of Anita Caspary. The organization went on to admit men as well as women, both single and married, "with a mission to create community, to work as advocates for the marginalized, for social and economic justice and peace, and for the integrity of creation".[24] Predictably, many press accounts reported that the sisters were forced out of their order by Church authorities, even though the decision was made by the women themselves not to accept Church authority regarding their renewal decisions. (Clearly, this was not an easy decision for many of the sisters who left the canonical group, but some sisters followed Anita Caspary out of a sense of loyalty and because they had been convinced that their chapter decrees were valid.) Caspary would later write: "It was not a single cardinal who forced us to abandon canonical status in the Catholic Church. It was a vast ecclesiastical system that for centuries has used every ploy to keep women beholden to its curiously antiquated rules and regulations."[25]

Caspary's group had quietly transferred title of the IHM properties to secular corporations prior to announcing the decision to leave the

[22] *Newsweek*, September 8, 1969, 80–81.

[23] Sister Rosalie Murphy letter to CMSW members, September 26, 1969, CLCW 34/07, UNDA.

[24] See https://www.immaculateheartcommunity.org (accessed June 30, 2012).

[25] Caspary, *Witness*, 51.

canonical order. Cardinal Timothy Manning, Cardinal McIntyre's successor who had just become archbishop of Los Angeles the month before the sisters' departure, was advised that, while that maneuver was "plainly erroneous" under canon law, it would be difficult to challenge in civil courts and would cause unnecessary scandal if the property ownership issue were legally contested.[26] Later financial settlements deeded Immaculate Heart College, Immaculate Heart of Mary High School, Queen of the Valley Hospital, and the retreat center La Casa de Maria to Anita Caspary's lay group.[27] (The college closed in 1980 due to financial issues and declining enrollment. The hospital became part of Saint Joseph Health System.) When Caspary died on October 5, 2011, her obituary in the *New York Times* reported that the Immaculate Heart Community had 160 members.[28]

The sixty IHM Sisters who chose to retain their canonical status were awarded the esteem of the Church but lost the IHM properties. They eventually received a cash settlement that amounted to $300,000, or one-sixth of the IHM's overall holdings. The canonical sisters continued to teach in the archdiocesan schools, and Cardinal Manning helped them purchase Villa San Giuseppe for their motherhouse.[29] In 1976, the sisters established an additional community in Wichita, Kansas. That community became autonomous in 1979 as the Immaculate Heart of Mary Sisters of Wichita, and its sisters continue to teach in primary and secondary schools.

"An Entirely New Manner of Religious Life"

While the IHM controversy was brewing in California, a similar situation was developing in the Midwest in a far larger community, the School Sisters of Saint Francis, who numbered about 2,800. Sister Francis Borgia Rothluebber was elected superior general of the School Sisters in 1966. That same year, the School Sisters' chapter meeting produced "Response in Faith", to be the experimental rule of the community, replacing the order's 1964 constitution.

---

[26] Francis Weber, *Magnificat: The Life and Times of Timothy Cardinal Manning* (Mission Hills, California: Saint Francis Historical Society, 1999), 373.

[27] *National Catholic Reporter*, April 9, 1971.

[28] Anita Caspary obituary, *New York Times*, October 18, 2011.

[29] Weber, *Magnificat*, 364.

Some of the changes instituted in the 1966 decrees were quite radical for that time, especially considering that sisters had previously lived in a tightly controlled atmosphere that offered little opportunity for personal decision making or responsibility. Thus sisters were ill prepared for the task of reforming their institute. As Sister Francis Borgia told the 1969 meeting of the Canon Law Society of America, the sisters' 1966 chapter decrees had included the following innovations: sisters moved from convents to self-selected small-group living situations; local superiors were removed from even large-group settings; time spent in community became optional; prayer took on a free form; the order's traditional mission of Catholic education became optional; open placement (sisters choosing their own jobs) became common; and the formation program for new members became quite unstructured.[30]

In short, the School Sisters of Saint Francis were on the same road to renewal that had been taken by the IHM Sisters in Los Angeles. However, the outcome of their story is quite different from that of the IHMs. This ill-conceived brand of renewal also had disastrous consequences for the institute, but the School Sisters encountered no resistance to their changes from Milwaukee Archbishop William E. Cousins. To the contrary, the School Sisters apparently had strong allies in influential positions, both in the hierarchy and in the men's and women's superiors' conferences, for an effort by the Congregation for Religious to correct the aberrations in the sisters' renewal evaporated. And Sister Francis Borgia went on to be elected vice president of the LCWR in 1972, becoming president of the conference in 1973, a not-so-subtle indication that leaders of many other institutes of women applauded the example of the School Sisters of Saint Francis.

In her October 1969 presentation at the annual convention of the Canon Law Society of America, Sister Francis Borgia made it clear that her community was forging a new definition of religious life. She explained that "within the forms and structures of the old, an entirely new manner of religious life is developing."

Sister Francis Borgia defined religious life from a humanistic viewpoint, saying it is "based on a respect for person." She also reduced the concept of authority to a pragmatic level: "The primary authority

---

[30] *Proceedings of the Thirty-First Annual Convention 1969*, Canon Law Society of America, 1970, 123–26.

in religious life is fellowship authority. All authority is concerned with deepening the quality of life." Sister Francis Borgia was correct when she contended that "a new texture, a whole new manner of living has come into being." But she neglected to mention that this new manner of living did not conform to her institute's charism and apostolate or to the needs of the sisters, let alone to the Church teachings on religious life. Sister Francis Borgia had addressed the issue of Church legislation about religious life when, in her speech, she dismissed the requirement that every religious institute maintain its nature and end. She related: "A canonist asked recently whether we were abiding by our primary and secondary purposes. Such a separation no longer seems valid." [31]

According to a former member of the School Sisters of Saint Francis interviewed by the author, Sister Francis Borgia was not alone in pushing for this unmitigated new style of life, for a group within the School Sisters was promoting experimentation even broader than Sister Francis Borgia was advocating. In fact, this former sister felt that Sister Francis Borgia succeeded in getting elected in 1966 because she was more moderate than others in the community who were promoting a much more radical feminist agenda.

Many School Sisters of Saint Francis were unhappy with the ensuing style of renewal in their congregation, and some contacted the Vatican about their concerns. Thus, in 1969 the Vatican ordered an apostolic visitation to the community to investigate reported abuses, naming Franciscan Father Benjamin Roebel of Cincinnati as apostolic visitator.

The Vatican Reacts

On August 17, Cardinal Antoniutti, prefect of the Congregation for Religious, wrote Sister Francis Borgia with the Vatican's response to the apostolic visitation of the School Sisters of Saint Francis. He wrote that the Congregation for Religious was pleased with many elements of the sisters' renewal, including pioneering efforts in race relations and a concern for the poor. However, Cardinal Antoniutti cited "uncontrolled experimentation ... allegedly in the name of the Renewal" that was not based on the documents of Vatican II or the teachings of

[31] Ibid.

the Church. He cited in particular "an exaggerated cult of freedom", "a tendency to nullify authority on all levels", and "considerable 'secularism'". Regarding the mission of the School Sisters to teach, Cardinal Antoniutti wrote: "The special end of your Congregation seems to have been relegated to a subordinate place and to have given way to a wide-open apostolate, which is no longer a matter of corporate commitment to the Church, or even to the Community, as Religious Life should be, but of personal commitment to whatever type of activity appeals to the individual."

Cardinal Antoniutti noted "a large number" of School Sisters wanted to live a true religious life but were subjected to pressures and even threats to give up their ideals. He ended by suggesting that if some sisters could not embrace the religious state as defined by the Church, they were free to pursue their goals and new lifestyle as lay persons: "We would raise no objection to their following their convictions, but not inside the Religious State. It is altogether unjust to remain in this [religious] State, harming it from within for those who wish to preserve it and live it. If experimentation in another life-style is to be carried on it should be developed separately and on its own, not to the detriment of a State recognized and esteemed by the Church." [32]

As with the situation involving the IHM Sisters, a great deal of activity ensued to gather support for the School Sisters of Saint Francis, especially among religious who wanted to test the Vatican's limits in their push for unlimited experimentation. An informal meeting of selected members of the conferences of major superiors of women and of men—and others of like mind, including Anita Caspary—took place September 3–5 in Saint Louis just prior to the 1970 annual assembly of the CMSW (which was discussed in chapter 5). Some sisters believed that this informal meeting was called specifically to garner support for Sister Francis Borgia, especially since Anita Caspary had failed to persuade the Congregation for Religious to allow unlimited experimentation for the Los Angeles IHM Sisters. That informal 1970 meeting issued the famous "Statement" or "Manifesto" on religious life, and at least one section of the statement seemed to relate to Cardinal Antoniutti's August 17 letter to Sister Francis Borgia. That part

---

[32] Cardinal Antoniutti letter to Sister Francis Borgia, August 17, 1970. CMAS 2/9,UNDA.

of the statement read: "Therefore we deem it destructive if a religious congregation is required to ask a brother or sister to depart, or the congregation itself is asked to abandon its public ecclesial character for the reason that a particular style of life is deemed *a priori*, incompatible with religious life."

The *National Catholic Reporter* published Cardinal Antoniutti's letter and quoted Sister Francis Borgia as saying that there had been some "mistakes and some excessive applications" in their renewal; but, she continued, "I happen to believe what we're doing is authentic religious life. We'll try to communicate this to Rome." [33]

The School Sisters continued along the renewal path they had set in 1966, but not without efforts by a group of sisters to prompt the Vatican to intervene in what they considered to be the order's destructive path. A former member of the order told the author that several School Sisters confronted Sister Francis Borgia in late 1971 about the fact that she had not shared with the community a document she had received from the Vatican about the conclusions of the apostolic visitation. Receiving no satisfaction from Sister Francis Borgia on the issue, five of the School Sisters flew to the Vatican to meet with the Congregation for Religious about the situation. The sisters were received graciously by the congregation, which gave a sympathetic ear to their concerns. But still nothing official transpired.

On October 22, 1972, seven School Sisters calling themselves the Representative Group sent a letter to all School Sisters of Saint Francis, with copies to several bishops and the Congregation for Religious. In the letter, the sisters stated that the order was experiencing "two opposing ecclesiologies", with one recognizing the Holy See as "divinely authorized to pass decisive judgment" on how religious vows were lived out, and the other admitting "at most" a consultative or advisory role for the Holy See. The letter stated that a number of sisters in their institute wanted to maintain their corporate apostolate of teaching, as well as community life and prayer. These sisters cited the solution offered at the end of Cardinal Antoniutti's letter and suggested that "secularizing communities" conduct private polls as to whether sisters wished to live religious life as defined by the Church or whether they would prefer a form of lay apostolate that would also

[33] *National Catholic Reporter*, September 25, 1970.

be of service to the Church. The group suggested, "This would have a double effect of giving them [the lay group] ecclesiastical recognition and hopefully an opportunity of serving the Church as an organization of dedicated lay people; and it would free those thousands of sisters in the United States who are willing and ready to be religious according to the vowed commitment they made as the Church understands Religious Life to be in our age as in any age." The sisters ended their letter by asking the Holy See to resolve the problem.[34]

Again, Catholics watched the situation with great interest to see what precedent would be set. Many people speculated that the School Sisters would split into two groups—noncanonical and canonical—as did the IHM Sisters. Bishops, priests, and parents were fearful that action by the Vatican would result in a sudden loss of School Sisters from Catholic schools that already were experiencing teacher shortages, much like the IHM experience in California, but on a far larger scale. And sisters who wanted to support the Church's official version of religious life were painfully aware that in the IHM case, the sisters who decided to remain canonical and under the direction of the Congregation for Religious, came away from the deal stripped of their order's institutions.

Apparently the School Sisters had strong allies in influential positions, for the Vatican made no further public move to alter the course of the sisters' renewal. Additionally, Sister Francis Borgia possessed considerable personal popularity, for she had been elected president of the LCWR for 1973. Thus, Vatican officials had reason to fear that she would be viewed as a martyr if she were reprimanded or if her decisions were countermanded by Church authorities. Given the outcome of the Los Angeles IHM experience, the Vatican also probably feared a mass exodus of sisters to noncanonical status, which would have had a great impact on Church institutions, since the School Sisters numbered well over two thousand members at that time. But predictably, the Vatican's decision not to interfere in the direction being taken by the School Sisters gave a green light to other sisters who had been contemplating a similar pattern of change in their own institutes.

[34] Letter to Task Force of the General Legislative Assembly, and to each member of the Congregation of the School Sisters of Saint Francis, from the Representative Group, October 22, 1972, CCPC 7/44, UNDA.

Eventually, in 1981, five sisters who continued to be unhappy with the direction of renewal in their order left the School Sisters and reestablished themselves in Davenport, Iowa, as a new religious order, the Franciscan Sisters of Christ the Divine Teacher, with Sister Bernadette Counihan as superior. Other sisters who were unhappy with the form of renewal in their order either left or opted to stay with the School Sisters to work for changes from within.

The School Sisters of Saint Francis lost 1,000 members from 1965 to 1995; they numbered 956 in 2012, with only 564 in the United States. As did Anita Caspary, Sister Francis Borgia Rothluebber left religious life. In 1995, she asked for and was granted dispensation from her vows as a religious after writing a controversial book, *Nobody Owns Me*.

While these are two very specific examples of the chaos of renewal, they are quite representative of the experience of not all, but certainly many, women religious in a variety of orders in this country, as verified by the dozens of sisters who contacted the author after the first edition of this book was released.

Poorly conceived renewal programs were imposed on sisters who were not well prepared for massive change. And when that change did come, it was not introduced at a reasonable, incremental pace so that the sisters could assess the experiments and gradually assimilate the positive elements into their constitutions, as Vatican II had directed. Rather, sisters who had been accustomed to having every detail of their lives spelled out for them abruptly found themselves in a "free-form" community. After these sweeping changes, sisters suddenly were expected to make decisions that had always been predetermined for them: where they would work and live; what work they would perform; with whom they would live; what they would wear; when and how they would pray. The sisters also found that the distinct spirituality of their orders was almost erased, and ties with the institutional Church were weakened considerably.

In the case of the IHMs and the School Sisters of Saint Francis, media-savvy, charismatic leaders promoted an extreme version of renewal in the name of the Church. They succeeded in convincing a good many people that they were in the vanguard of religious eager to respond to the call of Vatican II but were being impeded unfairly by aging Vatican chauvinists who wanted to keep women in a subordinate role.

The results of this radical approach to renewal have been devastating for many communities of women religious. Ironically, some of the sisters who pushed most vehemently for extreme change in their orders departed from their communities, leaving their legacy of turmoil to the sisters who remained. And what has been the result? Abandonment of apostolates, polarization within communities, confusion of the faithful, a significant increase in departures from religious life, and a dramatic decline in vocations.

13

The Quinn Commission Examines
Religious Life

Because religious are public persons in the Church, their own
obligation—as men and women who follow the obedient Christ—is to
reflect accurately and clearly the teaching of the Church.[1]

— Pope John Paul II

As the numbers of men and women religious in the United States rapidly declined because of death, departure, and the dearth of new vocations, the Vatican became alarmed. As we have seen, in 1983 Pope John
Paul II asked the US bishops to study American religious life and to
determine the reasons for its decline. The pope also asked the Congregation for Religious to summarize the Church's teachings on religious
life in a document that the bishops could use as a reference in their study.

Both the document and the study met with considerable resistance
from many religious, particularly from some openly hostile sisters who
accused the pope of trying to return religious orders to a pre–Vatican II
authoritarian model. Most organizations of sisters, such as the National
Assembly of Religious Women (NARW), also opposed the study. As it
progressed and bishops held meetings around the country to hear what
religious had to say, sisters who were engaged in rewriting the definition
of religious life seized the opportunity to educate the hierarchy about
the "new paradigms" they had created through their "lived experience".

[1] John Paul II letter to bishops of the United States, February 22, 1989, *Origins*, April
13, 1989, 745–48.

During this time, however, some change-orientated sisters became angry with the Vatican for chastising the American sisters who signed a 1984 abortion-rights statement in the *New York Times*. They became further inflamed when the Vatican insisted that Sister Agnes Mary Mansour could not remain a religious while directing a state government office that disbursed funds for abortions. By the time the study came to an end, some sisters were making it abundantly clear that they believed the Vatican and the bishops had nothing of value to say to them.

When all was said and done, the 1983–1985 study accomplished little more than emphasizing the polarization that had occurred in religious institutes and the Church's inability to deal with the crisis in religious life. The commission of bishops conducting the study nevertheless concluded that religious life was in generally good shape with the exception of a few minor problems. Perhaps concerned about airing dirty laundry in public or alienating their diocesan workforces, the bishops seemed reluctant to ask hard questions or to make specific demands on religious, even though part of the pope's charge was that bishops instruct errant sisters about the essentials of religious life. In the end, the bishops seemed to accept the recommendation of one of their number that they simply do nothing until the turn of the century, hoping that the whole mess somehow would work itself out. Here is that story.

Pope John Paul II Creates the Quinn Commission

On Easter Sunday 1983, Pope John Paul II wrote the bishops of the United States about his concern over "the marked decline in recent years in the numbers of young people seeking to enter religious life, particularly in the case of institutes of apostolic life". The pope asked the bishops to conduct a study to determine the reasons for the declining numbers of religious because it placed an undue burden on those sisters who try "to continue manifold services without adequate numbers", thus resulting in "a consequent risk to their health and spiritual vitality".

Pope John Paul also asked the bishops to "render special pastoral service to the religious of your dioceses and your country" by "proclaiming anew to all the people of God the church's teaching on consecrated life". The pope observed that the teachings on consecrated life were set out in *Lumen Gentium*, *Perfectae Caritatis*, and *Evangelica Testificatio*, in his addresses and those of his predecessor Paul VI, as well as in the new Code of Canon Law. And he summarized what he called "basic elements" of religious life, including public vows, stable community life, fidelity to charisms and sound traditions, corporate apostolate, personal and liturgical prayer, public witness, and government by religious authority. The pope observed that fidelity to these elements "guarantees the strength of religious life and grounds our hope for its future growth".

The pope appointed Archbishop John Quinn of San Francisco to head a commission to oversee a study of religious life by the bishops. Also appointed as members of the commission were Archbishop Thomas Kelly of Louisville, a Dominican, and Bishop Raymond Lessard of Savannah. The pope asked that the bishops consult with a number of religious to profit from their insights. He added that the commission would work in union with the Congregation for Religious and follow a document that the congregation was making available to all the bishops.[2]

The pope's April 3 letter was not released to the general public until June 22, when it was accompanied by the "document of guidelines" for the bishops, to which the pope had referred in his letter. This document was titled *Essential Elements in Church Teaching on Religious Life*. The document, prepared by the Congregation for Religious, noted that superiors, chapters, and bishops had asked the congregation "for directives as they assess the recent past and look toward the future". The pope's letter observed that the renewal of religious life had had mixed results:

> These institutes have been dealing with sudden shifts in their own internal situations; rising median age, fewer vocations, diminishing numbers, pluriformity of lifestyle and works, and frequently insecurity regarding identity. The result has been an understandably mixed experience with many positive aspects and some which raise important questions.
>
> Now, with the ending of the period of special experimentation mandated by *Ecclesiae Sanctae II*, many religious institutes dedicated to the works of the apostolate are reviewing their experience.

The *Essential Elements* document, then, was to be used as a guide for evaluating the renewal experience. The document broke no new ground but drew frequently and heavily on Vatican II documents and several

[2] John Paul II letter to bishops of the United States, Easter, 1983, *Origins*, July 7, 1983, 133.

papal exhortations and addresses, as well as the new Code of Canon Law, which had been released on January 25, 1983, and would go into effect the following November. The renewal efforts of many religious institutes in the United States did not conform to Church teaching for a variety of reasons that have been discussed in this book, and the establishment of the Quinn Commission by the Holy Father and the subsequent issuance of *Essential Elements* angered and concerned many religious. Some considered the appointment of the Quinn Commission to be an undeserved inquisition by patriarchal authority. Others felt that American religious were being singled out by the Vatican for undue criticism, since religious in other countries were not receiving the same attention. And some religious tried to discredit the *Essential Elements* document, saying it did not have proper authority because it was not signed by the pope. Others resented the fact that the document was prepared without any consultation with the religious of this country.

The Agnes Mary Mansour Affair

The timing of the commission also was viewed with alarm, particularly by some sisters, because just one month before it was announced, Sister Agnes Mary Mansour had requested dispensation from her vows after months of negotiations with the Vatican about her political appointment as director of social services for the State of Michigan. Archbishop Edmund Szoka of Detroit had directed Sister Agnes Mary to take a clear stand against Medicaid payments for abortion or else resign the state position, as he felt the situation presented scandal and confusion.[3] When Sister Agnes Mary did not do so, Archbishop Szoka told her provincial leadership team on February 23, 1983, that she did not have his permission to remain in the position and must resign. (At that time, canon law required that a religious needed the permission of the local bishop to hold political office. The new Code of Canon Law has a generic prohibition against religious' holding any public office.)

On March 4, 1983, Archbishop Szoka met again with the provincial leadership team, which acknowledged that Sister Agnes Mary needed

[3] The timeline for the following events and the quotations were taken from "Chronology of Events in the Matter of Agnes Mary Mansour", by Bishop Anthony Bevilacqua. *Origins*, September 1, 1983.

the archbishop's permission to retain the position but that they had not asked her to step down, contending that the archbishop's directive did not have to be followed if "a greater good was involved." In her state confirmation hearing on March 8, Sister Agnes Mary testified that she was opposed to abortion but could tolerate Medicaid funding for it through the Michigan Department of Social Services. On March 10, Archbishop Szoka contacted the Vatican, reporting that "Catholic people are confused, disturbed and dismayed by the spectacle of a Catholic nun being in the position of director of a department which pays for abortions and refusing to state her opposition to such payments."

The apostolic delegate, Archbishop Pio Laghi, instructed Sister Theresa Kane, president of the Sisters of Mercy of the Union, to require Sister Agnes Mary to submit her resignation as director of social services. On April 11, Sister Theresa Kane requested a formal reconsideration of the decision reached by the Congregation for Religious. The congregation then appointed Bishop Anthony Bevilacqua (who was chair of the bishops' Canonical Affairs Committee) as the Vatican's ad hoc delegate for the Mansour case. The congregation issued a letter on April 16, reporting that the pope had directed Bishop Bevilacqua "to approach Sister Agnes Mary Mansour directly and to require, in the name of the Holy See and by virtue of her vow of obedience, that she immediately resign as director" of the Department of Social Services.

On May 9, 1983, Bishop Bevilacqua met with Sister Agnes Mary and explained to her that if she refused to resign from her state job, the canonical process of imposed secularization would be initiated. At that May 9 meeting, Sister Agnes Mary requested dispensation from her vows rather than resign her state job or have the canonical process of secularization be initiated.

Sister Agnes Mary and the Mercy leaders contended that the process had been unfair and that insufficient dialogue had taken place. Thus the Agnes Mary Mansour case became a rallying point for sisters who felt that the Vatican was unfairly wielding patriarchal power over a nun who was sincerely committed to helping poor women. She was even referred to as a martyr.

Few sisters seemed to recognize that the Mansour case also was a power struggle between the hierarchy and the leaders of the Mercy Sisters, who at the provincial and national levels had refused to comply with the directives of the local bishop and the Holy See. In a press release, Network (a political lobbying group composed mainly of sisters whose sponsorship of the "Nuns on the Bus" tour in 2012 is treated in chapter 17) revealed the extent to which individualism had been enshrined in some religious communities. The press release expressed Network's support of Sister Agnes Mary Mansour because of "the individual's right to act on the dictates of conscience in pursuit of the public good". The press release cited "authoritarian exercise of administrative power on the part of Vatican officials and their representatives" and affirmed "the right to individual and corporate dissent within ecclesial as well as political structures".[4]

The NARW and the NCAN issued a joint press release on the Mansour case contending that the "Roman Congregation for Religious in their fear of losing 'authority' has ignored the principle of freedom of conscience." The press release asked that women protest on Pentecost Sunday 1983 "as a visible witness to the arrogant use of power in a male dominated church".[5]

Thus, joining in a small protest outside Saint Matthew Cathedral in Washington, DC, were Sister Theresa Kane, Sister Dorothy Vidulich, and Ruth McDonough Fitzpatrick (executive director of the Women's Ordination Conference and a representative of the NARW). Dominican Sister Donna Quinn, president of NCAN, protested outside the Holy Name Cathedral in Chicago. Sister Donna was later quoted in the September 1983 issue of *Ms.* magazine: "The Pope's order of obedience without consulting the administrative team, without due process, tramples on who we are as women religious in the United States." And *Ms.* Writer Mary Kay Blakely, described in the article's credit line as a "recovering Catholic", added her own opinion: "Will the Pope know, now, that a slowly smoldering brushfire is moving toward the Vatican? I hope so. If he thought, though, that forcing out Sister Mansour solved the 'little sister' problem in America, then Mansour is right: the Pope doesn't understand the American people, and he doesn't understand the American nun."

It was in the middle of this volatile situation that Archbishop Quinn began the work of his commission.

[4] Network press release, May 15, 1983, CARW 4/47, UNDA.
[5] Joint NARW and NCAN press release, May 13, 1983, CARW 4/47, UNDA.

Educating the Bishops

Archbishop Quinn appointed a committee of religious to assist his commission. Some religious questioned the committee's makeup, suggesting that its members represented only the left wing of the Catholic Church in the United States. Some were concerned that heavy representation from the two superiors' conferences would result in study conclusions based on the opinions of the conference leaders, who sought no input from the thousands of men and women religious who disagreed with them.

Appointed to the committee were the following: School Sister of Notre Dame Clare Fitzgerald (past president of the LCWR, 1980–1981); Sister of Saint Joseph Bette Moslander (past president of the LCWR, 1981–1982); Daughter of Charity Sister Teresa Piro; Providence Sister Alexa Suelzer; Franciscan Father Alan McCoy (past president of the Conference of Major Superiors of Men); and Xaverian Brother Thomas More Page (former executive director of the Conference of Major Superiors of Men).

In order to discuss the work of the commission as soon as possible with religious, Archbishop Kelly attended the annual assembly of the Conference of Major Superiors of Men on August 8, 1983, and Archbishop Quinn met with the women superiors at their assembly on August 16. News reports of those two meetings indicate that neither the study nor the pope's document was well received by some of the major superiors, even though the bishop members of the commission had hastened to reassure them about the intent of the study. Concerns raised by the male superiors included the fear that the commission represented "Roman interventionism" and had been "set up as a watchdog agency to deal with religious who stray from Church norms". But other male superiors indicated support for the commission, with one observing that a stricter definition of religious life could help end confusion among the laity about the role of religious.[6]

In a panel discussion at the meeting of male superiors, Bishop Kelly, a Dominican, said many bishops had not involved themselves in the changes occurring in religious life because they did not think they had the understanding and authority to evaluate those changes. "If

[6] "LCWR, CMSM Air Concerns about Papal Commission", *Hospital Progress* (September 1983): 20–21.

there is anything that's going to come out of this study and the mandate that is given to the bishops," Bishop Kelly said, "it is precisely that they will come to understand religious life, be able to articulate it and, as the mandate is on them, to preach the values of religious life to the churches they serve."[7]

Former women's conference directors Sisters Mary Daniel Turner and Lora Ann Quinonez described the meeting of their group with Archbishop Quinn in their book *The Transformation of American Catholic Sisters*. They wrote that "one member after another voiced her dismay at Pope John Paul II's mandate for a review of religious life in the United States." Further:

> From microphones scattered throughout the hall, voice after voice placed ministry, the work for justice and peace, and deep involvement in the mission of the church in the world at the core of religious identity. Repudiating the characterization of religious life in *Essential Elements* as alien to the experience of American sisters, they held up the truth of their own experience.... Their words held a consistent message: no one, not even church officials, and nothing, not even ecclesiastical pronouncements, will divert them from that quest. They trust themselves and they trust their journey. Their destination they are willing to discover in the process.[8]

At a news conference after the meeting, Archbishop Quinn said he had "sensed real anxiety on the part of the sisters about whether the Vatican's directives will be interpreted 'blindly or with flexibility'". Sister Helen Flaherty, president of the LCWR, was blunter than the archbishop at the news conference, saying, for example, that most major superiors did not agree with the Vatican's analysis of the decline in vocations. "We see the decline as a positive part of the trend toward greater participation by the laity in the ministry of the Church", Sister Helen said. "It's not a numbers game."[9]

Members of the NARW, meeting immediately after the women superiors, were equally unrestrained in their assessment of the Vatican's interference. The assembly's national coordinator, Dominican Sister

---

[7] Archbishop Thomas Kelly, OP, quoted in "Margin Notes", *Origins*, September 8, 1983, 220.

[8] Quinonez and Turner, *Transformation*, 62–63, 86–87.

[9] "LCWR, CMSM Air Concerns about Papal Commission", 20.

Marjorie Tuite, said that "what we are seeing today is an escalating pattern of oppression against women religious by the Vatican. It amounts to a witch hunt." Assembly board member Sister of Charity Barbara Aires observed that sisters needed to rally together to protect their renewal efforts: "We sweated, suffered and died in our congregations. We're past that. We won't go through that upheaval again!" [10]

Sister Margaret Ellen Traxler of NCAN also reacted angrily to the Quinn Commission and *Essential Elements*. "I observe that in the United States Rome is cutting itself off", she said. "When the pope speaks, he's speaking from another world. . . . The feeling of the American Sisters is that nobody is going to turn us around." [11]

Sister Margaret Ellen and several other sisters produced a book of essays to instruct the Quinn Commission about their version of religious life and what renewal meant to them. The collection, much of which was written by active members of NCAN, was funded by an anonymous donor, as well as the Sisters of Loretto and the Sisters of the Mercy of the Union, and published as *Midwives of the Future*.

In November of 1983, Sister Bette Moslander addressed the fall meeting of the USCCB. A past president of the LCWR, she was one of the six religious on the advisory committee for the Quinn Commission. Sister Bette discussed the hopes and concerns of women religious regarding the study, indicating that the sisters intended to be on the speaking end of the dialogue, not on the listening end.

According to Sister Bette, American sisters hoped that (1) the bishops would allow sisters to share with them as they would with brothers and friends, (2) through such sharing sisters "might dispel some of the confusion and negative judgments that have accompanied the changes of the past 20 years", and (3) through the process "the whole church in the United States will be enriched by a deeper understanding as the people of God in this country and in this time".

The concerns of the women religious expressed by Sister Bette were these:

1. "We are concerned lest this study promote division and polarization within our religious communities and among the various

---

[10] *National Catholic Reporter*, September 26, 1983.
[11] *National Catholic Register*, October 9, 1983.

religious congregations. . . . The heavy imposition of a narrow and fundamentalist interpretation of the 'Essential Elements' document or a simplistic application of the document to all religious communities without respect for the unique charisms or diverse experiences of the communities may fragment religious communities and bring immense pain and suffering."

2. "We are concerned lest the study become preoccupied with in-house self-examination and divert us from the very grave needs of our people and of the world."

3. "Last, we are concerned lest women in our country look upon this study as another painful example of the inability of the clerical church to receive and honor the experience of women as full members of the church." [12]

At that same November 1983 meeting of the bishops, Archbishop Quinn observed that with the study the pope was asking the bishops to render pastoral service to religious, which was not to be construed as interfering in the internal business of the religious institutes. "By reason of the apostolic structure of the Church, bishops have a responsibility for religious life in their churches", he said, and he stressed that "*Essential Elements* is a compilation from conciliar and other magisterial documents and from the new *Code of Canon Law*" and that these sources should be consulted in interpreting the document. He told the bishops they were not asked to condemn, but rather "to invite those relatively few among the larger number of faithful religious who may be living in conflict with the Church's norms or teaching, to walk together with us anew the journey of conversion".[13]

In spite of Archbishop Quinn's public optimism, some US bishops apparently had misgivings about the pope's intentions and about *Essential Elements*. Some of those concerns were mentioned by Archbishop Quinn in a report: "While the attitude of the bishops was basically positive, there were certain fears and apprehensions which are shared also by religious." Some bishops expressed the fear that the pope's mandate would imply the right of bishops to interfere in the internal

---

[12] Bette Moslander, CSJ, address to USCCB fall meeting, *Origins*, December 1, 1983, 430–31.

[13] Archbishop John Quinn address to USCCB fall meeting, *Review for Religious* (March / April 1984): 161–69.

affairs of religious institutes. Others feared that the pope wanted religious life to revert to a pre–Vatican II model, and some thought that the pope intended to "monasticise" all forms of religious life.

Explaining the bishops' concerns, Archbishop Quinn observed that "most of the bishops are not well acquainted with *Perfectae Caritatis*, *Evangelica Testificatio*, or *Mutuae Relationes* [a 1978 document from the Congregations for Religious and for Bishops that gave doctrinal background and practical norms for cooperation between religious and the hierarchy], or other such documents of the Magisterium pertaining to religious life." He also noted that "most bishops have little understanding of religious life and still less understanding of what has taken place in religious life since the Council. Thus in this matter there is a wide gap in understanding between religious and bishops. . . . On the other hand many religious do not understand the problems and outlook of the bishops."

Archbishop Quinn concluded that most religious loved the Church and wanted to cooperate with the bishops. He wrote that there were "some individual religious and some groups of religious who give cause for concern. But I think it would be a mistake to make them the focus of our efforts at this time." He advocated, rather, that the moderate religious be strengthened and encouraged in order to lessen the influence of "the extreme left and the extreme right". The "radical" religious were losing some of their influence, Archbishop Quinn wrote, and direct confrontation "with the left runs the risk of restoring them to a position of greater importance than they merit".[14]

By the spring of 1984, the Quinn Commission had been at work for almost a year, and religious were continuing to let the Vatican and the US bishops know that they did not take kindly to their study of religious life. A March 19, 1984, article in *Newsweek* quoted Archbishop Rembert Weakland of Milwaukee, a Benedictine: "The Vatican's Congregation for Religious and the American sisters are at total odds." The same article quoted Servants of Mary Sister Sean Fox, described by *Newsweek* as a divorce lawyer in Oak Park, Illinois: "The American bishops, she believes, are 'walking a tightrope' between Rome and the

---

[14] "Report of Archbishop John R. Quinn, Pontifical Delegate, on the Meeting of the Bishops of the United States and Related Matters Concerning Religious Life in the United States", December 21, 1983, CLCW 85/9, UNDA.

sisters. They'll want to tread lightly, she adds, 'because they might lose their work force.' " The article concluded that "many American sisters now say they will refuse all Vatican efforts to revive traditional convent life. Sister Lora Ann Quinonez, executive director of the Leadership Conference of Women Religious, believes the church should recognize that sisters in apostolic orders 'are called to ministry, not community'."

It is interesting to note that the executive director of the superiors' conference perceived community and ministry as being mutually exclusive, whereas the classical understanding of religious life is that community supports and enables ministry.

Hostile Elites, Silent Rank and File

The bishops forged ahead, and during 1984 many of them initiated in their dioceses "listening sessions", in which invited religious would discuss their experiences. The bishops then would make an interim report about these sessions to Archbishop Quinn before the bishops met again in November of 1984.

In some—or perhaps many—dioceses, there appears to have been little effort to engage rank and file religious in the process. On the other hand, a number of high-profile religious gathered during the summer of 1984 to speak at two formal programs about the meaning and implications of the Quinn Commission, and some of them were openly hostile.

The first program was a conference at Boston College, June 20–22, 1984, featuring a number of speakers, including Sister Margaret Brennan, who had been president of the LCWR (1972–1973); Jesuit Fathers James Hennessy and John Padberg; Franciscan Father Richard Rohr; and Claretian Father John Lozano. Sister Marie Augusta Neal, creator of the Sisters' Survey, sounded her familiar theme when she told the conference that "peace, poverty and human rights are the central concerns of the committed Christian" and religious institutes had been "endeavoring to be obedient to this mandate to participate in the righting of the wrongs of injustice".[15]

Archbishop John Whealon of Hartford, however, told the same gathering that, as one of the few remaining US bishops who had attended

[15] Robert J. Daly, SJ, et al., eds., *Religious Life in the American Church* (New York: Paulist Press, 1984), 152–53.

the Second Vatican Council, he could confirm that the developments in religious life being discussed at the meeting were "not in the least foreseen" by the Council Fathers. Rather, he said, those developments resulted from sociological trends in society rather than from Vatican II. Archbishop Whealon also observed that the presentations at the meeting "did not express the viewpoints of all United States religious". More than half of the leaders of religious institutes in his diocese, he said, had told him that their views and experiences matched the official teaching of the Church. The voice of those satisfied religious, he added, was not being heard at the gathering.

After the meeting, Archbishop Whealon expressed his chagrin that the conference was not a "constructive, positive, happy meeting ... because so much of the conference was given to criticism (indeed 'resentment' was one verb used)" of the Congregation for Religious and *Essential Elements*. "Major applause here", he added, "was given to anti-document protests." [16]

The second program was a lecture series at the University of San Francisco during the summer of 1984. Among the speakers was Sister Helen Flaherty, a past president of the LCWR (1982–1983), who stressed the American emphasis on democracy, even in ecclesial matters: "There is strong reason to believe that the church of the future is the church rising from below, not imposed from the top. ... Modeling participative and corporate authority will have a particularly powerful, prophetic impact on this country because, as we know, high value is placed on rights, due process and individual freedom." [17]

On September 10, 1984, two months before the US bishops' fall meeting, the administrative board of the Consortium Perfectae Caritatis sent Archbishop Quinn and the other bishops a letter of their concerns. The consortium was a group of traditional sisters who had banded together in 1971 because they believed that the LCWR was moving away from the definition of religious life approved by the Holy See (see chapter 7). In their letter, the consortium stated that (1) *Essential Elements* had not been communicated to "a great number of individual religious in the United States", (2) "several general chapters have been held since the publication of the *Essential Elements* without

---

[16] Ibid., 173–74.
[17] Ibid., 300.

any reference whatsoever to the existence of this document", (3) the pope would not receive a report from the commission that would clearly indicate "the seriousness of the condition of religious life in the United States" because "the voice of many in leadership positions will not communicate the lived reality of the large number of religious who are prevented from living out their vowed commitment to the Holy Father as their highest superior", and (4) the present state of religious life fails to inspire vocations.

The Consortium sisters also asked the bishops several questions in their letter, including the following:

- Would religious "continue to be prevented from community prayer life, corporate apostolate, authentic community living, personal and corporate poverty, and identifiable public witness through religious apparel" because of the absence of an authority structure required by the Church?
- Would the "Holy Father hear the voices of the many religious who are suffering because their leaders will not follow the guidelines for authentic renewal mandated by our Holy Father? And what will be done to help them in their powerlessness?"

The sisters further asked the bishops to do the following: (1) investigate the dioceses where *Essential Elements* has not been circulated, (2) follow this study with a survey to ascertain the commitment of each religious to living out *Essential Elements*, and (3) establish and extend canonical approval to a new conference of major superiors of women religious, to which members who implemented *Essential Elements* could belong.[18] (This last suggestion became a reality eight years later, as detailed in chapter 7.)

The New York Times *Statement*

On October 7, 1984, the Sunday designated by the US bishops as Respect Life Sunday, a thirty-thousand-dollar display ad appeared in the *New York Times* headlined "A Diversity of Opinion Regarding

[18] The administrative board of Consortium Perfectae Caritatis letter to Most Reverend John R. Quinn and the National Conference of Catholic Bishops, September 10, 1984, CCPC 2/14, UNDA.

Abortion Exists among Committed Catholics". The full-page ad was sponsored by Catholics for a Free Choice and included a "Catholic Statement on Pluralism and Abortion". The statement began: "Continued confusion and polarization within the Catholic community on the subject of abortion prompt us to issue this statement. Statements of recent popes and of the Catholic hierarchy have condemned the direct termination of prenatal life as morally wrong in all instances. There is the mistaken belief in American society that this is the only legitimate Catholic position. In fact, a diversity of opinions regarding abortion exists among committed Catholics." [19] The statement was signed by approximately one hundred people, and among them were twenty-six women religious,[20] two religious brothers, one religious priest, and one diocesan priest.

In late November, the Vatican sent letters to the orders of the religious who signed the statement, directing the signatories to retract publicly their support of the statement or face expulsion from their institutes. Most signatories and their orders initially refused to comply, but eventually agreements allegedly were reached between the Vatican and all the religious involved except for Sisters of Notre Dame de Namur Barbara Ferraro and Patricia Hussey, who eventually resigned from their order four years later.[21] Several of the sisters who had signed the statement later denied that they had retracted their support and maintained that their superiors had finessed a settlement with the Vatican.[22]

---

[19] New York Times, October 7, 1984, E-7.

[20] The following women religious were named on the October 7, 1984, New York Times Catholic statement on pluralism and abortion: Loretto Sisters Mary Ann Cunningham, Mary Louise Denny, Maureen Fiedler, Pat Kenoyer, Ann Patrick Ware, and Virginia Williams; Sisters of Notre Dame de Namur Barbara Ferraro and Patricia Hussey; School Sisters of Notre Dame Jeannine Gramick and Margaret Ellen Traxler; Dominican Sisters Kathleen Hebbeler, Donna Quinn, Ellen Shanahan, and Marjorie Tuite; Sisters of Charity Roseann Mazzeo, Margaret Nulty, Margaret A. O'Neill, and Marilyn Thie; Sister of Saint Joseph Judith Vaughan; Mercy Sister Margaret A. Farley; Ann Carr, a Sister of Charity of the Blessed Virgin Mary; Religious Sister of Charity Mary J. Byles; Maryknoll Sister Rose Dominic Trapasso; and Kathryn Bissell and Caridad Inda, Sisters of the Humility of Mary.

[21] See Barbara Ferraro and Patricia Hussey, No Turning Back (New York: Ivy Books, 1992).

[22] See, for example, Frances Kissling, "Women's Freedom and Reproductive Rights: The Core Fear of Patriarchy", in Encyclopedia of Women and Religion in North America, ed. Rosemary Skinner Kelly, Rosemary Radford Ruether, and Marie Cantion, (Bloomington, Ind.: University of Indiana Press, 2006); "Nuns Deny They Back Church's Abortion Policy", Los Angeles Times, July 24, 1986; and "Nun Doesn't Have to Retract Abortion Stand", Los Angeles Times, April 1, 1986.

When the November 1984 meeting of the US bishops convened, again there was ongoing turmoil surrounding sisters, and the polarization among women religious was even more obvious, given the fallout from the *New York Times* affair. At the meeting, Archbishop Quinn reported that 70 percent of the diocesan bishops had made interim reports on the listening sessions. He gave a summary of those reports, which discussed some of the strengths and weaknesses discovered in the past twenty years of renewal.

Strengths included an effort to return to the spirit and charism of the founder; a deepening of the life of prayer; greater integration of the community, spiritual, and apostolic dimension of religious life; a growing sense of solidarity with the church; greater maturity of candidates entering religious life; appreciation of the feminine; and more mature understanding of the vow of obedience. Weaknesses, which he said almost all bishops agreed on, included a decline in numbers entering religious life; a loss in membership; the necessity of leaving traditional works and institutions; tensions across generations; a rejection and hostility toward religious by some bishops, priests, and laypeople because of changes in religious life; and growing financial problems. Bishops also found that some congregations had lost their identity, and hence numbers, by abandoning uniform religious garb and community life. A sense of the cross had been lost through an overemphasis on the individual and on the women's movement. Finally, authority was not properly recognized and respected either within various religious communities or in the Church at large.

Archbishop Quinn told the bishops that their study of religious life was just in the initial stages. After all the data had been collected and collated, it would be submitted to experts in theology, Church history, psychology, and cultural anthropology for "reflection and reaction". He reported on his visit to Rome the previous month (October 1984), during which the commission members discussed their progress with the Congregation for Religious. He said that the congregation affirmed that *Essential Elements* should be interpreted in light of its source documents and that "it is not the intent of the document to monasticise religious life." Archbishop Quinn proposed that the bishops set aside time at their next meeting, in June of 1985, to develop a common understanding of the five points that generated the most interest at the listening sessions: (1) community life, (2) religious obedience, (3) structures of authority, (4) public witness and religious identity, and (5) consecration and mission. He recommended that bishops invite religious to dialogue about those major themes by answering three questions:

1. How do the religious understand these issues and how do they feel they are fulfilling the expectations of the Church in living these points?
2. How do the bishops understand these issues? How do they see religious in actual fact fulfilling the expectations of the Church in their dioceses?
3. Where there are differences in understanding, how can these be resolved in a peaceful, non-threatening and loving way that will build up the Body of Christ and promote religious life?[23]

A "Don't Ask, Don't Tell" Policy?

Apparently a number of bishops distributed these three questions to some or all religious in their dioceses. But the questions were criticized by some sisters as unbalanced, in that they did not solicit their opinions about what abuses and excesses had occurred in their institutes, nor did the questions invite religious to address their concerns about polarization in their communities and what they considered to be rejection of Church authority and teachings. The questions also did not offer the opportunity to address in a significant manner the five main points of interest that Archbishop Quinn said had come out of the listening sessions.

At any rate, many bishops seem to have made a diligent effort to respond to Archbishop Quinn's plan. But the listening sessions, dialogues, and openness of bishops and religious varied from diocese to diocese, resulting in a very uneven experience. Many religious were not invited to any such meetings at all; in fact, some religious didn't even know such listening sessions were going on. Some diocesan meetings were conducted by religious themselves at the direction of the local bishop. Often these religious had a predetermined agenda that did not coincide with the points the bishops wanted to be addressed.

---

[23] Archbishop John Quinn report to USCCB Fall 1984 meeting, *Origins*, November 29, 1984, 392–93.

Some religious even looked upon the meetings as their opportunity to instruct the bishops and the Vatican about religious life. These people often did not even consider the possibility that they had made any mistakes in renewal or had anything to learn from *Essential Elements*.

Some meetings were dominated by the most vocal leaders and offered little opportunity for input from rank and file religious. One sister reported that speakers from the LCWR dominated the statewide meeting she attended. She said she was disappointed because religious had been invited to discuss *Essential Elements* but instead were led in a discussion about the "injustices and sufferings" they had endured during the past ten years.

Marist Father Thomas Dubay, a theologian who often gave retreats to religious orders, told the author that some religious were asked to reflect only on the positive results of renewal and were instructed not to mention any negative ones. He provided the author with a copy of a letter he wrote Archbishop Quinn at the time, which stated:

> Another source of disillusionment with the current study of religious life is the questionnaire and the diocesan meetings. One of the former which I received told us expressly not to mention negative developments in our institutes but to report what we have found to be favorable happenings since Vatican II. This is an almost incredible rigging of results, and it can give only a rosy picture to the Holy See. The evidence I have indicates that religious across the country have experienced in diocesan meetings a similar slanting.

Father Dubay had indicated earlier in his letter that as a retreat master on the road for many years, he had met and counseled thousands of religious and usually received about seventy-five letters a month from sisters and brothers all over the country. He wrote that most of the religious he heard from were "on the middle and left of the opinion spectrum", so it was not the "far right" who were lodging complaints with him. His letter to Archbishop Quinn continued:

> The study consequently is not representative of all of us. We could not without impoliteness express our real views, and thus despite the meetings, thousands of us remain unheard and unrepresented in any effective way. Rome, therefore, will receive an optimistic report that (a) most American religious are quite happy with what has happened in their congregations; (b) we have no grave problems, for we mentioned

none—indeed we were told not to mention them (c) contrary reports to Rome are consequently unfounded, reactionary, and thus to be disregarded.

The questionnaire likewise did not raise the Holy Father's chief concern: Why the great drop in religious vocations? Could it be that secularized congregations are embarrassed at how poorly they are doing, while those who gladly accept Vatican II and canon law are attracting goodly numbers, sometimes very large numbers? For this statement I can offer specific documentation should you wish it. Young men and women are voting with their feet. And it is clear where they are going and where the future of religious life lies.[24]

Archbishop Whealon offered his perspective on the study process in a 1984 letter to Pope John Paul II. (Each bishop was directed to write a letter to the pope, expressing the results of his diocesan sessions and indicating his conclusions about the condition of religious life in his diocese.) He reported that he had visited with either the provincial or council or community of the ten religious institutes that had provincial houses in the Archdiocese of Hartford. Of those ten, Archbishop Whealon wrote, seven institutes—four of women and three of men— perceived that the ten essentials of religious life named by the pope described the way they were living. Most of those seven communities had already had their constitutions approved by the Vatican.

The three remaining communities—all women's institutes— "experienced renewal in a different way", according to Archbishop Whealon. They had "experienced the reduction of centralized and local authority in favor of a more collegial approach and openness to difference in the individual apostolates; a willingness to permit smaller groups to live apart from the larger community and the replacement of religious garb with simple secular dress". In all three communities, the archbishop noted, a minority had retained their religious garb. He then shared six conclusions with the pope:

(1) We have today in the U.S.A. two sharply different approaches to religious life. The one approach follows the ten essentials; the other approach follows some of the ten essentials but has adopted a noticeably more democratic approach to authority, work, living arrangements and religious garb. (2) These two approaches are irreconcilable. There

[24] Thomas Dubay, SM, letter to Archbishop John Quinn, August 18, 1984.

is a painful division between the two groups and a more painful division within a community in which the leadership and most younger members have followed a progressive approach to renewal while most of the older members have remained conservative. (3) Some, not all, conservative communities are growing. The more progressive—our largest communities of women—are showing no growth. (4) Because of these two different approaches to religious life there is widespread confusion about the identity of religious life. (5) The progressive group include many of our best, brightest, most dedicated religious. Their life style and works of religion are to the credit of their community and Church. That they are not growing in numbers is cause for lamentation. (6) The progressive group is confirmed that its approach to renewal will be judged as not valid and they will loose [sic] their status as religious in the Church. One answer to this is that they have already effectively converted the community to the status of a secular institute.

The archbishop then suggested two possibilities for dealing with what he called the "extraordinarily complex" situation:

(1) Following the Gamaliel principle, do nothing. In fifteen years—a brief time in the life of the Church—the picture will be much more clear. At the end of the century a decision can be made.
(2) Designate the religious following the ten essentials, including individuals in progressive communities, as religious of strict observance and designate the others by a different terminology. The conservatives in progressive communities should be given special consideration.

Archbishop Whealon wrote that in the long run, there probably would be little difference in the two courses of action he recommended. But he added that his second suggestion—to designate the two types of religious by different titles—would help identify the religious in the Church and would encourage religious vocations.[25]

Consultants Consider the Problem

In October of 1986, the Quinn Commission presented its 152-page final report to the Vatican. That report was given in summary form to

[25] Archbishop John Whealon letter to Pope John Paul II, read by Archbishop Whealon in presentation to October 13, 1984, meeting of the Consortium Perfectae Caritatis, entitled "Religious Life as Unchanging", CCPC 2/16, UNDA.

the US bishops at their November 1986 meeting and subsequently published in *Origins*. The process for arriving at the final report had continued past the gathering of data at the listening sessions. That data was given to forty people, identified by Archbishop Quinn as experts in a variety of fields. The experts then met and wrote a core report. That core report was given to seventeen bishops, who were asked to react to the report and to get the reaction of priests, religious, and laity in their dioceses.

Some insight into the opinion of the approximately forty consultants who worked with the Quinn Commission may be found in the book *The Crisis in Religious Vocations*, which contains sixteen of the thirty-four essays written by the consultants. Those essays accompanied the Quinn Commission report to the Vatican. The consultants had been given data from the Center for Applied Research in the Apostolate at Georgetown University, published as *Religious Life in the United States: The Experience of Men's Communities*. Significantly, the book serving as a source on sisters was *Catholic Sisters in Transition: From the 1960s to the 1980s* by Sister Marie Augusta Neal, creator of the Sisters' Survey. Based on these sources, as well as their own expertise, the consultants were asked to answer two questions: "Why did religious leave their congregations?" and "Why are young people not entering in greater numbers?"

Here is a very brief synopsis of what some of these experts concluded. It is apparent in some of their comments that the Sister Agnes Mary Mansour case and the controversy over the *New York Times* abortion-rights statement had an appreciable impact on many religious. Some of the consultants seemed to think that American religious had more reason to instruct the Vatican than to learn anything from the Vatican.

Jesuit Father John Padberg, director of the Institute of Jesuit Sources in Saint Louis and president of the International Conference of Catholic Theological Institutes, concluded that the lack of vocations was due to: (1) loss of corporate identity, (2) external regulations (imposed by the Vatican), (3) disillusionment with actions of Church officials, (4) disillusionment with outmoded structures and activities of religious communities, (5) alienation caused by some of the present teachings of the Church (e.g., no ordination of women), and (6) concern over how social justice can be practiced in religious life. Father Padberg wrote that recommendations about religious life "will have to be made in the context of what makes up this American people in an American tradition".[26]

Sister Mary Ann Donovan, a professor of historical theology at the Jesuit School of Theology, Berkeley, determined that religious life had become less attractive because of (1) the emerging lay role; (2) the "institutional face of the church" that is "often hardened by clericalism and the accompanying patriarchalism which is destructive of healthy relationships"; (3) "the current situation of women religious in the church", i.e., the process of approving constitutions of congregations, the handling of cases such as the religious who signed the *New York Times* abortion-rights statement, and "the papal intervention in apostolic religious life in the United States". She concluded: "Our task is to enable the laity to assume their rightful role in the church and to be content with our smaller numbers. It is my conviction that a reduction in numbers does not constitute a crisis of vocations, but rather is God's unique gift to the American church today."[27]

Dominican Sister Mary Ewens, associate director of the Cushwa Center for the Study of American Catholicism at the University of Notre Dame linked the decline in vocations with the wrong kind of interference by the hierarchy. She observed:

> The signs of the times need to be studied not only by religious communities, but also by their bishops and members of the curia.…
>
> A closer affiliation with the church and its hierarchy through entrance into religious life will not attract zealous young women if the church is seen to transgress basic human rights, to eschew due process, to violate freedom of conscience, to treat women like second-class citizens, and to summarily dismiss from their communities sisters whose work for the poor and study of the gospel imperative take them into the political arena.[28]

Sister Donna Markham, a psychologist who founded the Dominican Consultation Center in Detroit and who would be elected president of the LCWR in 1991, offered her opinion about how the hierarchy should relate to women religious: "Compassionate

[26] John W. Padberg, SJ, "The Contexts of Comings and Goings", in *The Crisis in Religious Vocations*, ed. Laurie Felknor (New York: Paulist Press, 1989), 26–29.

[27] Mary Ann Donovan, SC, "A More Limited Witness: An Historical Theologian Looks at the Signposts", in *Crisis in Religious Vocations*, 87–90, 97.

[28] Mary Ewens, OP, "The Vocation Decline of Women Religious: Some Historical Perspectives", in *Crisis in Religious Vocations*, 179–80.

understanding, non-judgmental respect, and support of all members [of religious congregations] whose varying ways of giving expression to their religious commitment co-exist within the institution of religious life today are crucial." [29]

Similar advice was offered by Sister of Saint Joseph Rose McDermott, a canon lawyer: "Church authorities should be careful to avoid stifling the variety of gifts and the prophetic utterance of religious in the church." She noted that women religious were "moving away from pre-conciliar structures and norms which never adequately conveyed their gifts and potential to the church. As women take their proper place in society, they cannot be denied it in a church that teaches the fundamental equality of persons and justice in the world." [30]

Religious Life in the United States Is in "Good Condition"

The final report of the Quinn Commission sidestepped the bishops' responsibility to proclaim "anew to all the people of God the church's teaching on consecrated life". It did, however, identify the following reasons for declining vocations in the United States:

1. Cultural factors, such as new attitudes about freedom, authority, sexuality, the role of women, etc.
2. The impact of Vatican II, which called the laity to holiness and stressed the importance of lay ministry and the social dimensions of the gospel
3. Developments in the Church in the United States, including the movement of Catholics into the mainstream of American society, the movement of Catholics to the suburbs, and the rise of the women's movement
4. The expanding economy, which made more vocational options available to women
5. The civil rights movement, which changed the focus of many religious to service to the world by promoting justice and human rights.

[29] Donna J. Markham, OP, "The Decline of Vocations in the United States: Reflections from a Psychological Perspective", in *Crisis in Religious Vocations*, 195.

[30] Rose McDermott, SSJ, "A Canonical Perspective on the Departures from Religious Life", *Crisis in Religious Vocations*, 225–26.

6. Experiences that had an impact on personal vocations, such as an identity crisis resulting from a blurred corporate identity, the removal of structures that one had depended upon, more careful screening by religious orders, and rejection of the requirement of celibacy and permanence.

The report admitted that the role of superiors was an issue of concern and that there needed to be "a correct synthesis of the consultative and collegial approach [to decision making] with a correct understanding of personal authority in religious life". It cited "certain tensions which exist between some religious and the Holy See", as well as "some individuals and some groups which give cause for concern and do not appear to fulfill the ideals of religious life." But the report made no promises or proposals to address those issues and concluded, "Our three years' work leads us to believe that in general religious life in the United States is in good condition."[31]

So, in an effort to steer a middle course and to avoid confrontation with feminist sisters, the Quinn Commission accomplished very little, and Father Dubay's prediction that the commission would whitewash the state of religious life in the United States appeared to have been fulfilled. Additionally, Father Dubay's observation that young people were voting with their feet and joining religious orders that maintain the essentials of religious life has proven to be accurate, given the results of the 2009 study *Recent Vocations to Religious Life*.

Eventually, some twenty-six years after the Quinn Commission was established to study religious life in the United States, the Vatican would take its own action in 2009 by initiating an apostolic visitation of American women religious and a doctrinal assessment of the women's superiors' group, the LCWR, as detailed in chapters 16 and 17.

While the Quinn Commission did initiate some interaction between religious and bishops that would not have occurred otherwise, the work of the commission appears to have reached no important conclusions and had little impact on religious life in the United States. As Sister Margaret Cafferty, executive director of the LCWR, observed in 1993: "For Religious, the greatest benefit of the work of the Quinn

---

[31] Pontifical Commission on Religious Life, "Report to U.S. Bishops on Religious Life and the Decline of Vocations", *Origins*, December 4, 1986, 467–70.

Commission was the dialogue it generated, not the Commission's final report."[32]

It was as if the "Gamaliel principle" recommendation of Archbishop Whealon simply to do nothing was quietly adopted by most bishops and accepted by the Vatican. Furthermore, the issuance of *Essential Elements* seemed to have only further polarized those religious who had sought to follow the teachings of the Magisterium from those who considered such teachings to be without real authority and open to wide interpretation and dialogue. Within religious institutes which have members of both persuasions, life has been very difficult.

A final wrap-up meeting involving the Quinn Commission took place in Rome in early March of 1989 and included Pope John Paul II, Vatican officials, and thirty-five US bishops. At that meeting, there were some subtle hints that the Vatican was not completely pleased with the outcome of the study on religious life. Cardinal Jean Jerome Hamer, a Dominican who was prefect of the Congregation for Religious, reminded the bishops that a bishop is

> responsible not only for the apostolate of men and women religious (regarding their work in schools, hospitals, catechetics, parish assistance, etc.) but also, to a certain extent, for their religious life as such. That is, he must oversee their observance of chastity, poverty and obedience; their fraternal life in community; the witness they must bear to God before the people of God; and their fidelity to their distinct charism, which ought to place its stamp on all religious life.

Cardinal Hamer commended the bishops for their work on the study of religious life, but he reminded them that their attention to religious life should be ongoing as part of their pastoral office. "This pastoral service of religious life must be not only pursued, but intensified", he said. "We must exercise it within the framework of the actual situation of the church in the United States."[33]

Barely three weeks after that Rome meeting, Pope John Paul II wrote all the US bishops. In that letter, he thanked the bishops for their response to his request for the study, and he observed that the

---

[32] *LCWR 1993 Conference Report*, 9.

[33] Cardinal Jean Jerome Hamer, OP, "The Pastoral Responsibility of Bishops Regarding Religious Life in the United States", *Origins*, 691–92.

bishops had "generally been positive about the state of religious life" in their dioceses. But he also pointed out that the Quinn Commission had reported on only two stages of the bishops' work—listening and dialogue. The pope reminded the bishops that he had directed them to perform "special pastoral service", which should not be temporary, and he urged them to meet on a regular basis with the religious in their dioceses. He wrote that religious "must be constantly exhorted" to remain faithful to the Church's mission and teaching. "In your role as bishops you have the responsibility to teach all your people, including men and women religious. Related to that teaching office is the need and obligation to present a sound theological exposition of religious life."

The pope chided "tendencies to excessive self-fulfillment and autonomy in living, working and decision making" and said "serious work must be done on the charisms, community life and vowed life." He added that "the substitution of a management model of authority for a government model" is not the way to correct past abuses of authority. "Management may be useful in producing products, but the purpose of government in religious life is to safeguard the charism and stimulate its growth." He also reminded bishops of the public character of religious life: "Because religious are public persons in the church, their own obligation—as men and women who follow the obedient Christ—is to reflect accurately and clearly the teaching of the church. When necessary, you and their superiors must remind them of this reality." [34]

In June 1998, the pope again brought up the topic of religious life in the United States. During their *ad limina* visits, the pope reminded the bishops from Missouri, Iowa, Nebraska, and Kansas: "You have a duty to safeguard and proclaim the values of religious life in order that they may be faithfully preserved and passed on within the life of your diocesan communities." The pope underlined the importance of community witness:

> An institute's capacity to conduct a common or community apostolate is of vital concern to the life of a particular church. It is not enough that all members of an institute subscribe to the same general values or work "according to the founding spirit, with each one responsible for finding some place of apostolic activity and a residence....

[34] John Paul II letter to US bishops, March 29, 1989, *Origins*, April 13, 1989, 745–48.

...Where institutes are already engaged in community apostolates such as education and health care, they should be encouraged and helped to persevere. Sensitivity to new needs and to the new poor, however necessary and laudable, should not entail neglect of the old poor, those in need of genuine Catholic education, the sick and the elderly.

You should also encourage religious to give explicit attention to the specifically Catholic dimension of their activities. Only on this basis will Catholic schools and centers of higher learning be able to promote a culture imbued with Catholic values and morality; only in this way will Catholic health care facilities ensure that the sick and needy are taken care of "for the sake of Christ" and according to Catholic moral and ethical principles.[35]

In spite of clear instructions from the Holy Father and the Congregation for Religious, the American hierarchy has not been inclined to confront sisters who do not reflect the teaching of the Church or even those who publicly reject that teaching. This reticence is somewhat understandable when one considers the strident nature of some of the most outspoken and hostile sisters and the fact that these sisters know how to use the media to their advantage.

In addition to being media-savvy, activist sisters also are politically astute, and they have created organizations that give the impression that these groups speak for the majority of sisters. Thus, it indeed is difficult to know where the majority of sisters stand on issues. The next chapter examines some of the organizations in which sisters have been influential and analyzes the impact of these groups on the public image of sisters, as well as the influence of these groups on religious life in the United States.

---

[35] John Paul II, "Renewal and Rebirth of the Consecrated Life", given at *ad limina* visit of bishops of Missouri, Nebraska, Iowa, and Kansas June 13, 1998, *Origins*, July 13, 1998, 169.

14

Ideological Transformation of Sisters' Organizations

We had to spill blood, but we didn't disband our communities to do that. We changed our forms of government, lifestyles, prayer forms, corporate commitments.[1]

—Sister Catherine Pinkerton, CSJ,
National Assembly of Women Religious

Many people rarely encounter a Catholic sister unless she is working in a local parish. Thus the image of contemporary women religious often is shaped by media reports about high-profile sisters and the organizations they lead. But this media image can be quite distorted, for the most vocal Catholic sisters and their organizations do not represent the average sister, even if they claim to do so. Rather, these individuals and organizations seem preoccupied with promoting a "justice" agenda heavily influenced by feminist causes and determined to confront ecclesial authorities in order to remake religious life and the Catholic Church.

A notable example of this phenomenon occurred in 2010 when Network, a sisters' political lobbying organization, sent a letter to all members of Congress, asking them to support the Patient Protection and Affordable Care Act. That bill, commonly referred to as Obamacare, was opposed by the US bishops because it funded abortion and did not provide adequate conscience protection to religious individuals

[1] *National Catholic Reporter*, August 29, 1975.

and organizations who object to funding or participating in immoral procedures. The March 17, 2010, letter from Network stated: "As the heads of major Catholic women's religious orders in the United States, we represent 59,000 Catholic Sisters in the United States who respond to needs of people in many ways."[2]

This claim of representation was immediately challenged the next day by the US bishops' director of media relations, Mercy Sister Mary Ann Walsh, who wrote in a press release:

> A recent letter from Network, a social justice lobby of sisters, grossly overstated whom they represent in a letter to Congress that was also released to media.
>
> Network's letter, about health care reform, was signed by a few dozen people, and despite what Network said, they do not come anywhere near representing 59,000 American sisters.
>
> The letter had 55 signatories, some individuals, some groups of three to five persons. One endorser signed twice.
>
> There are 793 religious communities in the United States.
>
> The math is clear. Network is far off the mark.[3]

While Network and other organizations of sisters may grab the head-lines, they do not represent the sizable percentage of women religious who adhere to their vows, are loyal to the Church, and continue to serve the Church and society in a variety of ways. Nevertheless, to understand the complete picture of how the crisis in women's reli-gious communities has developed, it is important to examine some of these groups and the effect they have had on the sisters themselves, the public perception of sisters, and the image of the Church.

Though none of these organizations has had the same influence as the LCWR, these groups nevertheless reflect many of the issues affect-ing sisters during the renewal years and even to the present time. The organizations also gravitated toward a confrontational approach with the Vatican and embraced the principal agenda of women's liberation in the Church and in society.

[2] Network press release, March 17, 2010, www.networklobby.org (accessed March 17, 2010).

[3] USCCB press release, March 18, 2010, http://old.usccb.org/comm/archives/2010/10-048.shtml (accessed September 20, 2012).

The emergence of many of these groups prompted *Time* magazine to comment in 1972 that "U.S. nuns have organized their reform activities in a proliferation of groups that bear a marked similarity to secular Women's Lib federations."[4] Though some of these organizations purported to speak for mainstream sisters, and the media often portrayed these groups as representative of them, none ever achieved the support or sympathy of a significant number of sisters, except for the LCWR, which was discussed in chapters 3, 4, and 5. These groups also frequently shared overlapping memberships, for many activist sisters participated in several of these groups at the same time.

The National Assembly of Women Religious (NAWR)

The NAWR started as a grassroots organization of sisters and later changed its name to the National Assembly of Religious Women (NARW) after it opened its membership to laypeople. The concept of such an organization was born in 1968 at the First International Conference of Councils and Senates of Women Religious. At that meeting in Portland, Maine, four hundred sisters from twenty-three diocesan sisters' councils discussed how the newly formed councils could most effectively function. A subsequent 1969 meeting in Chicago attracted about fifteen hundred sisters. Featured speakers included Brother Gabriel Moran and Sister Margaret Ellen Traxler, founder of NCAN, and a task force was appointed to draw up plans for a national body of American sisters. Then, on April 19, 1970, about thirteen hundred sisters,[5] fewer than half the number that had been expected by the task force,[6] met in Cleveland and voted to form the NAWR. (There were about 161,000 sisters in the country at that time.) The organization was designed to be a counterpart to the newly formed National Federation of Priests' Councils organized by the activist priest Monsignor Jack Egan of Chicago. The ultimate goal of the NAWR was to represent nuns on a national pastoral council affiliated with the USCCB. However, the US bishops never did approve the idea for a national pastoral council.

[4] *Time*, March 20, 1972, 64.
[5] *National Catholic Reporter*, May 1, 1970.
[6] Newsletter, task force / NAWR, March 1970, vol. 1, no. 4, CARW 4/50, UNDA.

Sister Ethne Kennedy of the Society of Helpers, task force chairwoman, became the first coordinator of the NAWR. The rationale for the new organization reflected the quite reasonable desire for sisters to network with one another and to take a more active role in Church affairs:

> Sisters feel a need for corporate identity, a voice to express their stands on issues of concern to the church in the world. Sisters want top-level communications with one another to share research, personnel, facilities, vision. Sisters ask to be inserted into the ecclesial process of decision-making, to participate from the grass roots with bishops, priests, and lay men and women, so that the creative insights of women religious can influence Church thinking and action.[7]

In actual practice, however, the NAWR became more involved in controversial issues than its original purpose had indicated. Some flavor of the organization was evident at the April 1970 meeting in the keynote address by Sister Francis Borgia Rothluebber, president of the School Sisters of Saint Francis, who at that time was engaged in a dispute with the Vatican about questionable renewal practices in her own community. Sister Francis Borgia told the first meeting that the Church and religious had a tendency to be static, and there was "too great a security in the status quo, or in authority, or in rule-keeping, or in any inflexible structures . . . all hostile to the future, to hope, to being present today".[8] Sister Marie Augusta Neal, creator of the Sisters' Survey, also spoke at that meeting. Resolutions passed by the 1970 assembly supported the boycott of grapes picked by migrant labor, new forms of Christian community, and the former IHM Sisters of Los Angeles who left religious life rather than comply with Vatican definitions of renewal.

Membership in the NAWR grew from forty-three sisters' councils and 2,029 individual or associate members in 1970 to seventy-five councils and 4,567 individuals or associates in 1971.[9] Then, in 1972, the organization's leaders discarded its original purpose of facilitating networking between American sisters and instead picked up the power

---

[7] "The National Assembly of Women Religious (NAWR) 1968–1979 History", CARW 10/05, UNDA.

[8] A report on the Cleveland meeting of NAWR, April 17–19, 1970, CARW 4/50, UNDA.

[9] NAWR membership report as of 1980, CARW 10/32, UNDA.

and liberation theme that the LCWR had adopted. The organization's new "vision-goal" became "a ministry of justice by the continuous use of our organized power to effect local and national policy for the liberation of all peoples from oppression, to work actively to promote respect for all human life, and to insure effective participation of people in decisions which affect their lives".[10] This abrupt change in direction apparently impacted membership numbers, for between 1971 and 1972, the organization lost ten councils and 1,600 individual or associate members.[11] Finances also became an issue of concern. In its January 1972 newsletter, the group stated it had a debt of $4,537.

At the 1975 convention in San Francisco, ordination of women jumped into the spotlight. (The Women's Ordination Conference, treated later in this chapter, was founded in 1975.) The *National Catholic Reporter* headlined its article on the convention: "NAWR: Power in Church Sisters' Aim". The article reported that the newly elected president, Sister of Saint Joseph Kathleen Keating, said women should have the same option as men to seek ordination.[12]

The 1976 assembly was so controversial that the organization's membership figures fell dramatically after that event, though even at its peak membership in 1971, the NAWR never attracted more than 3 percent of American sisters. The *National Catholic Reporter* ran a front-page photo and article about the 1976 assembly, which included an "unfinished liturgy" performed by Sister of Mercy Mary Reilly and two laywomen: Anita Caspary (formerly Sister Humiliata, superior of the IHM Sisters of Los Angeles) and Mary Beckman of the Catholic Charities Social Action Office in Brooklyn.[13] *Commonweal* magazine, under the headline "Aborted Liturgy", explained that the three women read the prayers of the Mass proper to the priest until they arrived at the Consecration. "After a pause, a delegate seized the microphone and, referring to women's inability to complete the Eucharistic celebration, said: 'I hope you are all as disturbed by this as I am.' " The *Commonweal* article reported that some sisters present approved of the action, including Sister Maggie Fisher, who observed that the demonstration would lead women to consider the injustice of being excluded

[10] "NAWR 1968–1979 History", CARW 10/06, UNDA.
[11] NAWR membership report as of 1980, CARW 10/32, UNDA.
[12] *National Catholic Reporter*, August 29, 1975.
[13] *National Catholic Reporter*, August 27, 1976.

from ordination. However, another sister present was quoted as saying, "I wouldn't want to be part of an effort to go beyond the boundaries of our authorized liturgy." [14]

More controversy arose in 1977 when the NAWR convention meeting in New Orleans passed an affirmation of Sister of Mercy Elizabeth Candon.[15] Sister Elizabeth was the state secretary for human services in Vermont. When the US Supreme Court ruled that states were not required to make Medicaid payments for abortion, Sister Elizabeth was quoted by Vermont newspapers as saying that although she was personally opposed to abortion, she favored continuing state abortion payments for the poor. Bishop John Marshall of Burlington, Vermont, countered in a letter to Vermont Catholics that Sister Elizabeth's action was "confusing, misleading and scandalous", and he pointed out that "these free-will decisions can place her outside the sacramental life of the Roman Catholic Church and deprive her of her good standing as a member of a religious community in that church." [16]

NAWR officials claimed the affirmation of Sister Elizabeth was not supporting abortion, but rather standing with a sister who had been threatened with excommunication. The resolution said, in part: "Be it resolved that NAWR affirms Sister Elizabeth Candon, secretary of Human Services of the State of Vermont, through a letter of support of her stand regarding the equal access of all women to legal rights." [17] Many people, however, did not interpret this affirmation so innocently. Archbishop Philip Hannan of New Orleans, in whose diocese the meeting took place, called the affirmation "absolutely deplorable, contrary to Catholic doctrine and completely illogical".[18] Several members of the NAWR also took issue with the action, and some questioned the process that resulted in the resolution.

The number of sisters' councils belonging to the NAWR slipped from eighty-two in 1977 to sixty-seven in 1978.[19] Several individual sisters also terminated or did not renew their memberships because

[14] "Aborted Liturgy", in "News & Views", *Commonweal*, September 10, 1976, 578.
[15] "NAWR Approves Support for Candon", in "On File". *Origins*, September 8, 1977, 178.
[16] "Abortion and Catholic Public Officials", *Origins*, August 11, 1977, 136–37.
[17] NAWR affirmation, CARW 10/43, UNDA
[18] "On File", *Origins*, September 8, 1977, 179.
[19] NAWR membership report as of 1980, CARW 10/32, UNDA.

the Candon resolution appeared to give the organization a pro-choice position. For some sisters who were already embarrassed by the "uncompleted Mass", the Candon affirmation was the last straw.

In 1978, the NAWR extended full membership to laywomen, but even this move did not serve to bolster dwindling membership. The individual membership numbers dropped from 2,291 in 1978 to 1,548 in 1979.[20] By 1980, individual membership stood at 1,400, with only twenty-three sisters' councils still belonging.[21] Not only had the NAWR lost its focus as a grassroots organization for the average sister; it also had taken on an agenda that was not supported by most sisters, even the most progressive ones.

The corresponding secretary for the Sisters Council of the Diocese of Grand Island, Nebraska, wrote Sister Kathleen Keating on March 14, 1978, expressing concern about the direction of the organization. "We find it imperative that the National Association make a clear statement concerning its opposition to abortion under any circumstance", she wrote. The letter also expressed opposition "to opening NAWR to lay women, as this is not in conjunction with the original purpose of NAWR". She asked that the agenda of the summer 1978 meeting include reevaluation of the group's goals. "We feel that social justice has received undue emphasis to the exclusion of such Gospel-oriented ministries as evangelization, reaching out to the unchurched, fostering spiritual growth, religious vocations, Catholic education, and healing of the sick."[22] In spite of declining membership and the accompanying loss of funds, NAWR leaders demonstrated no inclination to heed the concerns voiced in the letter.

At the NAWR 1980 annual meeting in Milwaukee, the *National Catholic Reporter* observed that "separate liturgies were held during the conference to accommodate women who will not participate in liturgies presided over by males as long as females are excluded from ordination."[23] Elected president of the board in 1980 was Sister Marjorie Tuite, a founder of the NAWR who had strongly influenced the social justice and feminist direction of the organization.

[20] Ibid.
[21] *Probe* (Summer 1995).
[22] Hope Steffens, OP, letter to Sister Kathleen Keating, March 14, 1978, CARW 10/43, UNDA.
[23] *National Catholic Reporter*, August 29, 1980.

In 1982, the group further distanced itself from its original purpose as a grassroots organization for American sisters when it transposed the last two words in its title to become the National Assembly of Religious Women (NARW). As *Probe*, the organization's newsletter, explained, the name was changed "'to concretize inclusiveness and the bonding of women' and as an indication of unwillingness to participate in the strategy of dividing Catholic women against each other".[24] Sister Catherine Pinkerton, a NAWR founder and leader who went on to become president of the LCWR in 1983 and later a lobbyist for Network, observed later that the name change helped the organization find a more profound level in the women's movement and "enriched us all by being the vehicle for uniting women of various cultures, races, ethnicities and differing faith dimensions, and developing as a result processes and programs which focus on inclusivity and equality".[25] By 1983, one-third of the organization's membership were laywomen.

The 1984 annual conference in August attracted 225 participants, one-quarter of whom were laywomen, according to an August 26, 1984, article in the *National Catholic Register*. The *Register* reported that at the meeting Sister Theresa Kane, former president of the LCWR, "called for feminist liturgies, 'new rituals of Eucharist,' where women can remember each other's stories of pain and oppression". While Sister Theresa advocated nonviolence, NARW board member Ada Maria Isasi-Diaz disagreed, saying, "I want to be aggressive about taking power. This talk of non-violence is problematic." Another board member, Maureen Reiff, declared that "the institution [Catholic Church] is dying and the Vatican is making desperate moves in its throes of death."

Later in 1984, many members of the NARW including its president, Sister Marjorie Tuite, signed the October 7 statement in the *New York Times* "A Diversity of Opinion Regarding Abortion Exists among Committed Catholics", as detailed in chapter 13. The Vatican had instructed religious institutes to demand a retraction from their members who had signed the statement and to begin the dismissal procedure against those who refused to retract. Some sisters still were in a state of "dialogue" over the incident when a subsequent "Declaration of Solidarity" statement appeared in the *New York Times* on

[24] *Probe*, Summer 1995.
[25] Ibid., 3.

March 2, 1986. This statement invited sympathizers to write the Vatican Congregation for Religious to protest disciplinary actions against religious who had signed the 1984 statement, and it, too, bore the names of NARW members. The 1986 declaration also called on US bishops to "protect and defend the right of Catholic religious, scholars and activists to speak out on controversial issues of public policy freely, fully and without reprisal".

In lieu of a national conference in 1986, the organization sponsored an interfaith women's conference in Chicago: "Women of Faith: Same Journey, Different Paths". In 1992, the NARW national conference attracted about five hundred women, including fifty teenagers, to Spokane, Washington. "This conference was to be a counter-conference to the Columbus celebration", according to Sister of Mercy Maureen O'Sullivan writing in *Probe*. She observed that "all the conference's ritual garments, the Great Hoop and the Dream Catcher were made in nearby forest ceremonies." [26] The 1993 conference was not held so that the NARW could give "support and solidarity to the Women-Church / Convergence Conference".[27]

The NARW was one of about twenty-five feminist organizations making up the Women-Church Convergence. *New York Times* religion writer Peter Steinfels has described Women-Church as originally "a movement founded by Roman Catholic feminists as an outgrowth of their blocked efforts to get the church to ordain women as priests". And he observed "the movement's drift toward a kind of free-style Unitarianism, a creedless faith in an undefined divinity expressed in a profusion of rituals as well as in politically liberal good works".[28]

By 1994, NARW leaders were sending out signals that the organization was nearing its end. It had become a very different entity from the group envisioned by the four hundred sisters who met in Maine in 1968 to create a national organization for the ordinary nun. In January of 1995, the board sent out nearly fifteen hundred letters to former members seeking input about the future of the organization. The winter 1995 issue of *Probe* announced that elections to the board had been suspended, and it suggested the possibility that the organization

---

[26] *Probe*, Summer 1995.
[27] Ibid.
[28] *New York Times*, May 1, 1993, 10.

should be disbanded. But the newsletter still promoted a national conference for the upcoming July to celebrate the twenty-fifth anniversary of NAWR / NARW and included a registration blank for the event.

Also in that issue of *Probe* was a new mission statement written at the February 1995 board meeting: "The National Assembly of Religious Women (NARW) is diverse women of faith, creatively networking across barriers of race, gender, class and sexual orientation. NARW, rooted in the catholic tradition, provides critique and analysis of social issues, education and organizing for action. NARW is committed to mutuality, diversity and making connections between prophetic vision and systemic change."

The summer 1995 and final issue of *Probe* brought the news that the NARW was being dissolved by its national coordinating team. The organization was about $20,000 in debt and unable to attract substantial membership, support, or even enthusiasm for the twenty-fifth anniversary celebration. The national coordinating team attributed the demise of the organization to several factors, including decline in funding by religious communities and the proliferation of other grassroots organizations with a similar or related focus that competed for funds and members.

National Coalition of American Nuns

The stated primary purpose of the National Coalition of American Nuns (NCAN) is "women's liberation".[29] NCAN was started in Chicago by Sister Margaret Ellen (Mary Peter) Traxler and Sister Mary Audrey (Lillanna) Kopp. Both Lillanna Kopp and Sister Margaret Ellen were staff members of the National Catholic Conference for Interracial Justice in Chicago during the 1960s, and it was out of that organization that they developed NCAN in 1969.

Sister Margaret Ellen told the *National Catholic Reporter* that it was easy to attract sisters to her organization, for "the first concern of these sisters is obviously that they don't want their communities interfered with on the part of bishops, or the bishops for religious, or Rome." Among the examples of hierarchical interference she cited were the dispute between Cardinal James McIntyre and the IHM Sisters of Los Angeles and the apostolic visitation of the School Sisters of

---

[29] *If Anyone Can, NCAN* (Chicago: NCAN, 1989), ii.

Saint Francis in Milwaukee. The article also quoted *Trans-Sister*, the newsletter representing the coalition at that time, as saying that the NCAN organization would help nuns defend themselves "against those who would interfere with the internal and / or renewal [they] alone must and can evolve in [their] communities".[30]

Also in 1969, Sister Mary Audrey Kopp left her religious order and resumed her baptismal name of Lillanna. She went on to found the noncanonical group Sisters for Christian Community in 1970.[31] Kopp had been influential in the Sister Formation Conference, and she and some other former conference leaders eventually became directors of NCAN, including Sister Annette Walter and former Sister Ritamary Bradley.

Like the NAWR, NCAN was not successful in attracting a significant number of American sisters—at the most, 2 percent of all sisters, according to NCAN's own estimates. But NCAN members tended to be politically savvy, organizationally astute, very aggressive, and extremely vocal. They knew how to get press coverage for their activities and their positions, even though only a handful of nuns were involved.

Throughout its entire history, NCAN has been led by sisters who espouse a very radical agenda that is contrary to Catholic Church teaching on several issues. Key leaders throughout those years have been Sisters Jeannine Gramick and Donna Quinn. Sister Jeannine had been banned from work in homosexual ministry by the Vatican in 1999 because of doctrinal errors. She refused to accept the discipline and transferred from the School Sisters of Notre Dame in 2001 and joined the Sisters of Loretto, where she continued to speak on homosexual issues, claiming that she did not have to follow the Vatican discipline imposed by her former order. Over a five-year period, the Congregation for Religious sent letters to the Loretto leadership explaining that the discipline pertained, no matter where Sister Jeannine belonged. In 2006, the Loretto leadership informed its members that Sister Jeannine was taking a one-year sabbatical from public engagements regarding homosexuality. She resumed her public involvement with homosexual issues, however, apparently without ecclesial censure. She went on to give

---

[30] *National Catholic Reporter*, August 13, 1969.

[31] The so-called Sisters for Christian Community often is officially listed on diocesan websites as being among the "women Religious" serving in a particular diocese, even though it is not recognized as a religious institute by the Vatican.

public speeches supporting efforts to pass "same-sex marriage" laws in various states.[32] The February 14, 2012, *Washington Post* published a letter Sister Jeannine cosigned with Frank DeBernardo, executive director of New Ways Ministry, titled "A Catholic Case for Same-sex Marriage". At that time, the states of Maryland and Washington were considering "same-sex marriage" legislation. In that Valentine's Day letter, Sister Jeannine and DeBernardo wrote: "As Catholics who are involved in lesbian and gay ministry and outreach, we are aware that many people, some of them Catholics, believe that Catholics cannot faithfully disobey the public policies of the church's hierarchy. But this is not the case. The Catholic Church is not a democracy, but neither is it a dictatorship."

Sister Jeannine and DeBernardo even went on to suggest that the US bishops were attempting to impose Church law on civil society: "And still others realize that their own lives would be very different if the bishops had the power to make church law into state law—say by banning artificial contraception or making it impossible to remarry after a divorce." [33]

Dominican Sister Donna Quinn had a similar activist background of dissenting against Church teachings. A photo of her wearing a "Nuns for Choice" T-shirt illustrated an April 21, 2004, *Chicago Tribune* article about Sister Donna joining others "to demonstrate support for women's reproductive freedom in the March for Women's Lives", an annual event in Washington, DC, intended to counter the annual pro-life March for Life. Sister Donna told the *Tribune*, "This is one issue for women that is so basic. We have to be in control of our mind, spirit and body."

One of NCAN's first organized activities was to launch an all-out drive for women's ordination, and it hosted the first three organizational meetings of the Women's Ordination Conference in 1970. In 1971, the organization set 1976 as a cut-off year for granting full priesthood for women and declared that if this did not happen, NCAN would call upon "the universal sisterhood of women" to boycott church

---

[32] See various entries on New Ways Ministry Bondings 2.0 Blog, http://newwaysministry blog.wordpress.com. Also see various videos of Sister Jeannine Gramick posted on YouTube.

[33] Jeannine Gramick and Francis DeBernardo, "A Catholic Case for Same-sex Marriage", *Washington Post*, February 14, 2012, http://articles.washingtonpost.com/2012-02-14/local/35445773_1_marriage-equality-catholics-civil-unions (accessed February 6, 2013).

collections by placing only straws in the collection baskets as a symbol that "we will no longer pay for the straws for the bricks Pharaoh mandates."[34]

In 1973, NCAN criticized canon law, calling it "rule without the consent of the governed". The organization also contested "the non-authority of the (non) Sacred Congregation for (against) Religious".[35] The 1976 NCAN medal of honor was awarded to Anita Caspary, the former superior of the IHM Sisters of Los Angeles who led the majority of her order into noncanonical status rather than accede to the norms for renewal set forth by the Vatican.[36]

In 1977, NCAN called for the decriminalization of prostitution so that prostitutes could receive retirement benefits and health insurance, and it reaffirmed commitment to passage of the Equal Rights Amendment (ERA). In 1978, NCAN endorsed the statement of the Catholic Coalition for Gay Civil Rights, and it protested "sexist language" in the liturgy. In 1979, the group voiced support for Bella Abzug, a lawyer and politician who championed abortion rights and the ERA.[37]

NCAN went on record opposing the Hatch Amendment in 1982, thus taking a position contrary to the USCCB, which had endorsed the bill. The Hatch Amendment would have given states the right to determine whether abortion would be legal and was eventually defeated in the US Senate. That same year, four NCAN members—Sisters Ann Patrick Ware, Margaret Ellen Traxler, and Donna Quinn, as well as Deborah Barrett, a member of Sisters for Christian Community—went on the *Phil Donahue Show* to expound on their position on "the right to choose".

Reflecting on negative responses to NCAN's position on abortion, Sister Ann Patrick later wrote in the September 1983 issue of *Ms.* magazine: "The virulence of those in opposition to women having choice over their pregnancies cannot be overestimated. None of the constraints of civil discourse seems to apply when this subject is discussed. In fact, one may make the case that a certain 'holy fanaticism'

---

[34] *NCAN News*, undated, c. 1975, CLCW 27/8, UNDA.

[35] NCAN reprint, "A Backward Glance: Twelve Years in Remembering", insert in December 1981 *NCAN News*, CARW 39/40, UNDA.

[36] NCAN Newsletter, February 1, 1976, CLCW 27/8, UNDA.

[37] *If Anyone Can*, NCAN, 29–40.

takes over and makes them even more intolerant and dangerous. Charity, the end-all and be-all of the Christian faith, in these hearts is dead for all except fetuses."

In 1984, seven NCAN board members signed the controversial abortion-rights statement in the *New York Times*: Sisters Margaret Ellen Traxler, Ann Patrick Ware, Donna Quinn (past president), Maureen Fiedler, and Jeannine Gramick; Elisabeth Schussler Fiorenza (then a lay theology professor at the University of Notre Dame); and Frances Kissling, director of Catholics for a Free Choice.[38] After the Vatican instructed religious who signed the statement to issue public retractions, Sister Donna Quinn told *Time* magazine, "We believe we have the right to speak out when we have a differing opinion, and this is something European men do not understand."[39]

In 1986, NCAN gave its "national medal of honor" to Frances Kissling "for her prophetic leadership in reclaiming for women the decision-making for their own bodies".[40] The January 1986 NCAN newsletter called on retired Catholic bishops to ordain women to the priesthood, since, NCAN reasoned, the retired bishops had nothing to lose, "not promotion to positions of higher jurisdiction, nor to a red hat". In 1987, NCAN endorsed "individual choice" in sexual ethics, saying that "individuals should be allowed to make their own decisions in the area of homosexuality. . . . Individuals have a right to choose how they fulfill the divine command to love one another."[41]

NCAN celebrated its twenty-fifth anniversary in October 1994 in Rome with picketing in Saint Peter's Square and a Sisters Synod during the World Synod of Bishops, which was meeting on the topic of consecrated life. The NCAN newsletter announced that members were invited to join the protest in Saint Peter's Square to demonstrate their message of "Enough already, of 'big daddy-o's who have all decision-making in the Church."[42] Sponsors of the Sisters Synod included Catholics for a Free Choice; 8th Day Center for Justice, Women's Issues; Corpus Association of Married Priests, Seattle; New Ways Ministry; Institute of Women Today; Catholics Speak Out, Quixote Center;

[38] NCAN Newsletter, May & June 1986, CARW 39/42, UNDA.
[39] *Time*, January 7, 1985, 83.
[40] NCAN Newsletter, Fall 1986, CARW 39/42, UNDA.
[41] *If Anyone Can, NCAN*, 72.
[42] NCAN Newsletter, January 1994.

the Women's Office of the Sisters of Charity of Chicago; and the BVM Network for Women's Issues of California.[43] In 1996, NCAN joined the We Are Church coalition, profiled later in this chapter.

NCAN continued the same agenda into the twenty-first century, with a small but vocal leadership. The NCAN group issued an open letter to Catholic voters in 2006 as an alternative to voter education efforts by church hierarchy. It counseled "respect for the moral adulthood of women" and stated that they "will choose legislators who will recognize the right of women to make reproductive decisions and receive medical treatment according to the rights of privacy and conscience." The letter also called for people in "committed relationships" to have adoption rights.[44]

NCAN was equally critical of the 2009–2011 apostolic visitation of US sisters. Its August 16–18, 2010, board meeting issued this statement: "We cannot help but feel that this investigation is an attempt on the part of the Vatican to control U.S. nuns and to silence dissenting voices." The statement claimed that recent polls showed that "the majority of Catholics believe that women religious should follow their consciences and make public statements concerning church and society even when those statements run counter to those voiced by the bishops."[45] Sister Jeannine Gramick also weighed in on the CDF doctrinal assessment of the LCWR on MSNBC, saying: "We women come from a different conception of 'church' from the Vatican. We are following ... the Second Vatican Council which in the 1960's talked about the 'church' as a community. And in a community, people disagree. But in a totalitarian institution, there is no disagreement. This is the clash that we are seeing."[46]

In spite of attention in the media, NCAN has represented the views of very few American sisters since its founding in 1969. Only a handful of NCAN supporters show up at NCAN-orchestrated events, and membership is open to any person, religious or lay. Contrary to what

---

[43] NCAN Newsletter, October 1994.

[44] Hilary White, "American Nuns' Group Voter's Guide Favors Abortion, Homosexuality", *LifeSiteNews*, November 3, 2006, http://www.lifesitenews.com/news/archive/ldn/2006/nov/06110306# (accessed September 5, 2012).

[45] *National Catholic Reporter*, September 8, 2010.

[46] Jeannine Gramick, SL, quoted in "Comments on LCWR Action from National Catholic LGBT Organization", *New Ways Ministry Bondings 2.0*, April 22, 2012, http://newwaysministryblog.wordpress.com/tag/second-vatican-council (accessed September 5, 2012).

its name implies, NCAN is really not a group of American nuns; it is an international organization composed of some women religious as well as laymen and laywomen, amounting to between 500 and 1,500 members. As with the NAWR, NCAN's radical views have unfairly impugned the image and reputation of many American women religious who support the authority and teachings of the Catholic Church.

Network

Network is a Washington, DC, lobbying organization controlled by sisters and defined as "a national task force to facilitate the process of political education and action for American religious women and their organizations in ministry for social justice".[47] It was started in 1971 by several individuals, including Sister Marjorie Tuite of the NAWR, Sister Mary Luke Tobin, and Sister Margaret Cafferty. Network was endorsed in 1972 by a LCWR resolution. A LCWR representative sits on the Network board, its coordinating council and its advocacy committee.[48]

Sister Catherine Pinkerton, longtime Network lobbyist, noted the close relationship between LCWR and Network in 2006 when she accepted the LCWR annual Outstanding Leadership Award. "I have never doubted that for me Network was a natural progression from LCWR. In truth, we two entities are inextricably linked. LCWR has always been a part of NTW's Board, helping to set its direction", Sister Catherine said, adding, "Too, LCWR and Network are revolving doors. Network has been blest by both past and future LCWR on its staff." [49]

Here are some of the sisters who have worked with Network and also held office in the LCWR: Sisters Mary Luke Tobin (LCWR president, 1964–1966), Bette Moslander (LCWR president, 1981), Catherine Pinkerton (LCWR president, 1983, who became a full-time lobbyist for Network), Margaret Cafferty (LCWR president, 1984, and executive director, 1993–1997), Immaculate Heart of Mary Sister Carol Quigley (LCWR president, 1986), and Nancy Sylvester (LCWR president, 1999).

[47] *National Catholic Reporter*, September 29, 1972.
[48] According to *LCWR Annual Report 2007–2008*, 16.
[49] Catherine Pinkerton acceptance speech posted on www.lcwr.org.

Even though Network is primarily controlled by women religious, its membership is open to any interested individuals. Dominican Sister Carol Coston was Network's first executive director, and she traveled extensively to give workshops for nuns on the legislative and political process. Network's lobbying efforts over the years have focused on some laudable, albeit nonecclesial, causes, such as economic justice, immigration reform, health care, peacemaking, ecology, released prisoners, and the environment.[50]

However, Network has remained silent on the topic of abortion and has been heavily involved in some women's liberation issues that do not equate with the position of the hierarchy. Network supported the Equal Rights Amendment (ERA), which the US bishops did not endorse over concerns it would further abortion rights. In 1983, Network stood firmly behind Sister Agnes Mary Mansour in the dispute with the Vatican over her appointment as director of Social Services for the State of Michigan, which administers funding for abortions. Network regularly sponsors a booth at meetings of Church-reform organizations such as the Women's Ordination Conference and Call to Action.[51]

However, those skirmishes with Church authorities were minor compared with the events of 2010–2012, when Network openly challenged the teaching authority of the Catholic bishops.

Network had taken a strong interest in the Patient Protection and Affordable Care Act, also known as Obamacare. So, too, had the US bishops, who had long worked for access to good health care for everyone. As details of Obamacare began to emerge, however, the bishops became concerned that the bill expanded abortion funding and failed to protect conscience rights. Some Catholic congressmen were conflicted between their desire to reform health care and their concern about abortion, and their reticence threatened to hold up passage of the Senate version of the bill in the House of Representatives.

The Catholic Health Association and other Catholic groups countered the moral objections over abortion by arguing that conscience rights could be resolved after the bill was passed. Cardinal Francis George of Chicago, however, then president of the USCCB, issued a statement on March 15, 2010, explaining the bishops' lack of confidence

---

[50] See Network website: www.networklobby.org.
[51] *Network*, November / December 1995, 16.

in this outcome: "The bishops ... judge that the flaws are so fundamental that they vitiate the good that the bill intends to promote.
Assurances that the moral objections to the legislation can be met
only after the bill is passed seem a little like asking us, in Midwestern
parlance, to buy a pig in a poke." [52]

Two days later, on Saint Patrick's Day, Network released an open
letter to Congress urging "a life-affirming 'yes' vote" on Obamacare.
The accompanying press release (cited earlier in this chapter) claimed
that the letter was "from organizations and communities representing
tens of thousands of Catholic Sisters", although the letter had been
signed by only about fifty individual religious and a few "leadership
teams". The following day, the USCCB issued a press release noting
that Network had "grossly overstated" the numbers who were represented by the signatures.

Nevertheless, the Network letter and support from the Catholic
Hospital Association were sufficient, as one analyst observed, to give
"moral cover" to the Catholic congressmen who had been on the
fence. The bill passed the House and was signed into law on March
23, 2010. Rep. Tim Ryan of Ohio said, "There was a huge momen-
tum shift when Network came over and really gave everybody a lot of
confidence.... The last six to eight pro-life members of Congress were
comfortable [supporting the legislation]." [53] At an event honoring
women religious for their contributions to health care reform, Rep.
Nancy Pelosi said the support of Catholic sisters "made a tremendous
difference" in passage of the historic health care law. [54]

The fear of the bishops became a reality in August of 2011 when
Health and Human Services secretary Kathleen Sebelius issued a mandate under the PPACA that requires all employers to provide insurance that covers sterilizations, contraceptives, and drugs that can induce
an abortion. The only exception given was for churches themselves
and their institutions that serve and employ primarily members of their
own church. This, of course, meant that Catholic schools, hospitals

[52] Cardinal Francis George, March 15, 2010, http://old.usccb.org/comm/archives/2010/
10-043.shtml (accessed September 5, 2012).

[53] See http://www.youtube.com/watch?v=_tgtSiGtXbo (accessed September 5, 2012).

[54] Network press release, January 31, 2011, http://www.networklobby.org/news-media/
press-release-sr-simone-campbell-honored-healthcare-reform-role (accessed September 5,
2012).

and social services were subject to the mandate. The US bishops and multiple other entities and individuals objected vigorously to this blow against religious liberty, but Network did not join in their objection.

When in 2012 the Congregation for the Doctrine of the Faith issued the results of its four-year doctrinal assessment of the LCWR, the CDF named Archbishop J. Peter Sartain of Seattle to oversee a thorough "renewal" of the organization (treated comprehensively in chapter 17). As part of that renewal, the CDF said, the LCWR "links" with Network and the Resource Center for Religious Institutes should be reviewed. Network obviously was not pleased to be named in the document and issued a press release on June 1 supporting an LCWR board statement on the same day. That LCWR statement had said the "assessment was based on unsubstantiated accusations and the result of a flawed process that lacked transparency." The Network statement praised and affirmed the "powerful" LCWR statement, calling the CDF assessment "scandalous". Further, Network objected to being named in the assessment, saying that "Network was *never* [emphasis in original] asked to provide information about our mission or activities. This is just one of the many errors in the assessment and process by which it was put together." [55]

As Network executive director Sister Simone Campbell would reveal a few days later, the group decided to respond publicly to the Vatican in their own way. A June 6 Network press release announced that sisters would take a nine-state bus tour from June 18 to July 2, allegedly to highlight damage that would be done to poor people if the budget proposed by Rep. Paul Ryan and passed by the House of Representative were to take effect. [56] In reality, the Ryan budget was virtually dead, as the Democratic-controlled Senate had made clear that it would never approve the plan, and in fact Congress had not approved any budget in over three years. Not coincidentally, the US bishops had previously announced a two-week campaign of prayer, education, fasting, and action to preserve religious liberty in the face of the onerous HHS Mandate. Called the Fortnight for Freedom, the bishops' campaign was scheduled to run from June 21 to July 4.

[55] Network press release, June 1, 2012, http://www.networklobby.org/news-media/press-release-network-applauds-lcwr-statement (accessed February 7, 2013).

[56] Network press release, June 6, 2012, www.networklobby.org/news-media/nunsonbus (accessed September 20, 2012).

The Nuns on the Bus campaign immediately became a media sensation in spite of the fact that only two sisters made the entire trip—Sister Simone Campbell and another Sister of Social Service, Diane Donoghue. Other sisters joined them along the way for a few hours or a day or two. Nevertheless, their bus with its billboard-size signs that proclaimed "Nuns on the Bus: Sisters driving for faith, family and fairness" attracted a media that seems to thrive on disputes within the Catholic Church. It also took the spotlight off the thousands of Catholics—including many more sisters than those on the bus—who were praying in churches for religious freedom as part of the bishops' Fortnight campaign.

Even the secular media read the motives for the Nuns on the Bus trip, however. A June 5 *New York Times* article called the venture a "spirited retort to the Vatican". A June 27 *Washington Post* headline proclaimed, "The Nuns on the Bus Tour Promotes Social Justice and Turns a Deaf Ear to the Vatican". In the article under that headline, Sister Simone alluded to the CDF doctrinal assessment that had cited Network, saying, "Their big mistake was naming us.... With all this attention, we had to use it for our mission." Similarly, a full-page profile of Sister Simone in the July 2 issue of *Time* magazine observed that "at times Nuns on the Bus can seem like Campbell's personal act of retaliation against the Vatican for its virtual takeover of the nuns' LCWR and its rebuke of Network." Indeed, the article quoted Sister Simone: "I've been a faithful woman religious for over 40 years.... And some guy who's never talked to me says we're a problem? Ooh, that hurts." It is unclear whether the "guy" referred to by Sister Simone was CDF Prefect Cardinal William Levada, who issued the CDF assessment, or Pope Benedict XVI, who approved the document.

After Rep. Paul Ryan was named to be the vice-presidential candidate on the 2012 Republican ticket along with Mitt Romney, Network intensified its campaign against him, and Sister Simone accepted an invitation to give a speech at the 2012 Democratic National Convention.[57] She also was invited to be the homilist at the 2012 Call to Action conference liturgy.

---

[57] Cardinal Timothy Dolan of New York, president of the USCCB, accepted invitations from both the Democratic and Republican conventions to appear, but only to offer a prayer at each gathering.

The Women's Ordination Conference

The Women's Ordination Conference (WOC) is not a sisters' organization, but sisters—many of whom were also active in the LCWR, the NAWR, and NCAN—have been instrumental in sustaining it. As noted already, NCAN fostered the beginnings of the Women's Ordination Conference, which was established in 1975. Sister Mary Luke Tobin, who was president of the CMSW from 1964 to 1967, was an influential member of the WOC task force. Even though Archbishop Augustine Mayer, secretary of the Congregation for Religious, asked the LCWR not to be associated with the first Women's Ordination Conference meeting in Detroit in 1975, Sister Mary Daniel Turner, executive director of the LCWR, was a major presenter, along with Sister Marjorie Tuite of the NAWR. Also speaking were Sister Marie Augusta Neal (creator of the Sisters' Survey), talking on "Models for Future Priesthood"; Sister (Thomas Aquinas) Elizabeth Carroll (a former Sister Formation Conference leader and president of the LCWR, 1971–1972), talking on "'The Proper Place' of Women in the Church"; Sister Margaret Farley, on "The Moral Imperatives for the Ordination of Women"; and Sister Anne Carr, a Sister of Charity of the Blessed Virgin Mary, speaking on "The Church in Process: Engendering the Future".[58] Priests addressing the conference included Fathers William Callahan, Carroll Stuhlmueller, and Richard McBrien.[59]

Among those making public endorsements of the 1975 WOC conference were some of the past or future presidents of the LCWR, including Sister Angelita Myerscough, president from 1970 to 1971; Sister Francine Zeller, president from 1974 to 1975; and Sister Theresa Kane, elected president in 1979. The NAWR and several provinces or orders of sisters, including the Sisters of Loretto, Sisters of Saint Joseph of Cleveland, and the general council of the Adrian Dominican Sisters, also offered their endorsement.[60]

The WOC established an office in the Quixote Peace and Justice Center in 1977, with Ruth McDonough Fitzpatrick (a comember of

[58] *National Catholic Reporter*, December 19, 1975.
[59] *National Catholic Reporter*, September 5, 1975.
[60] Flyer, Public Endorsements, Ordination Conference, "Women in Future Priesthood Now: A Call for Action," November 28–30, 1975, Detroit, Mich., CLCW 28/12, UNDA.

the Sisters of Loretto) as the first staff person. The second major meeting of the WOC in 1978 drew about one thousand people and was endorsed by the executive committee of the LCWR. In a letter to the WOC's Sister Mary Luke Tobin, LCWR executive director Sister Mary Daniel wrote, "The executive committee feels we would be doing the LCWR and the entire Church a disservice if we fail to be associated with the upcoming meeting." For good measure, Sister Mary Daniel enclosed an LCWR check for one hundred dollars for the WOC.[61]

In 1984, the WOC honored Sister Theresa Kane as a "prophetic figure" because of her 1979 public challenge to Pope John Paul II on the subject of women's ordination. Feminist theologian Elisabeth Schussler Fiorenza was similarly honored for "working for equality within church and society".[62] According to news reports, only about fifty people attended that awards ceremony. Attendance was not large at the WOC tenth-anniversary meeting in Saint Louis in 1985, either, as that meeting reportedly drew about two hundred people.[63]

Apparently the WOC ran into financial difficulty over the years, for a 1995 letter to "Dear WOC Friend" earnestly requested donations. Internal differences also roiled the organization. The November 10–12, 1995, national meeting—the first one in ten years—drew about one thousand participants although planners had expected about three thousand. There was speculation that some WOC supporters did not attend because they feared reprisals from Catholic employers since Pope John Paul II had ordered an end to discussion about women's ordination in his May 1994 apostolic letter *Ordinatio Sacerdotalis*.[64] (Mercy Sister Carmel McEnroy had been fired on April 26, 1995, from her tenured position at Saint Meinrad Seminary in Indiana because of her public advocacy for women's ordination.)

There were plenty of fireworks at the WOC national meeting, but not because of the pope's letter. Rather, a power struggle between factions inside the WOC became evident. One faction, represented by Professor Diana Hayes of the Theology Department of Georgetown

[61] Sister Mary Daniel Turner letter to Sister Mary Luke Tobin, August 31, 1978, CCPC 2/31, UNDA.
[62] *National Catholic Reporter*, December 28, 1984.
[63] *National Catholic Reporter*, December 1, 1995.
[64] Ibid.

University and Professor Elisabeth Schussler Fiorenza of Harvard Divinity School (author of *Discipleship of Equals: A Critical, Feminist Ekklesialogy of Liberation*) advocated dropping their goal of ordination in favor of reconstructing the Catholic Church. Schussler Fiorenza argued that the gospel vision of equality cannot be realized in a male-dominated church based on a Roman imperial model. WOC board member Karen Schwarz was quoted as saying: "WOC will demonstrate that the mere ordination of women does not solve anything. Nothing short of major deconstruction of clericalism, patriarchy and hierarchy will do." [65]

Peter Steinfels of the *New York Times* reported:

> The meeting's planners presented an elaborate program proposing that the group's goal should now be a "discipleship of equals," a concept of a church without hierarchy, and without priests ordained for life and bestowed with special power to administer sacraments.
>
> This model of the church is associated more with New Testament times, with the radical wing of the Protestant Reformation and with movements like the Quakers rather than with Catholicism. [66]

The other faction was represented by WOC board members Sisters Maureen Fiedler and Jeannine Gramick. Sister Maureen observed, "I love the ideal of a discipleship of equals, but if it means we don't seek ordination in the Roman Catholic church, I don't buy one syllable of it."

Sister Jeannine said that the WOC mission statements of 1991 and 1994 incorporated the vision of "discipleship of equals" but also included the goal of "ordination to a renewed priestly ministry". Sister Jeannine had written meeting coordinator, Loretto Sister Agnes Ann Schum, in May of 1995 about her concern that meeting planners were moving in an either-or direction. Silvia Cancio, president of the WOC board, acknowledged that the board had agreed the meeting would include both options, but the meeting had taken on "a life of its own". [67]

---

[65] Ibid.
[66] *New York Times*, November 14, 1995, A17.
[67] *National Catholic Reporter*, December 1, 1995, 9–11.

One month after the tumultuous national meeting, WOC national coordinator Ruth McDonough Fitzpatrick resigned, saying the group's board had violated her contract by interfering with her management. She also said she felt she was being made "the scapegoat for the financial deficit of the WOC Gathering '95", estimated by the *National Catholic Reporter* to be around $100,000.[68] A 1996 mailing from new national coordinator Andrea Johnson solicited new members to keep alive the discussion of women's ordination and to "help birth a more inclusive church". The WOC never achieved a large membership, though it claims that the majority of Catholics support the ordination of women.

Mary's Pence

Mary's Pence is an organization that also includes laywomen but was started by mostly sisters. Mary's Pence was incorporated in 1987 as a feminist alternative to Peter's Pence, the traditional collection for support of the Vatican. The idea behind Mary's Pence was to provide an agency for Catholic donation that would be independent of hierarchical control. Women were encouraged to put "wooden nickels" in the collection basket for Peter's Pence to demonstrate that they had given their money to Mary's Pence instead. According to one of the founding board members of Mary's Pence, feminist theologian Rosemary Radford Ruether, "This allows Catholics who are distressed and alienated by the way the institutional Church is using its resources to channel their contributions into a Catholic fund that will support the sort of empowerment of women and poor people that is closer to the liberation model of church."[69] Many of the founding board members had also been active in organizations already discussed in this chapter. They included Sister Mary Luke Tobin (former president of the CMSW and active in Network and Center of Concern); Sister Jane-Marie Luecke (an author in *The Changing Sister*); Immaculate Heart of Mary Sister Amata Miller (of Network); Sister Margaret Ellen Traxler (of NCAN); Yolanda Tarango of the Congregation of the Sisters of Charity of the

---

[68] *National Catholic Reporter*, December 29, 1995 / January 5, 1996.

[69] Rosemary Radford Ruether, "Mary's Pence: Promoting Women's Ministries", *Cross Currents* (Spring 1989): 98.

Incarnate Word; Sister of Notre Dame de Namur Teresita Weind; and Dominican Sisters Kaye Ashe, Carol Coston (of Network), and Maureen Gallagher.[70]

Mary's Pence has funded social services for poor women and children in fifteen countries. Mary's Pence also has given grants to women attending theological seminaries, a support group for "women facing burn-out from work in service to human and community needs", and New Ways Ministry, which helps "Catholic lesbians to develop a consciousness-raising and support group".[71]

In recent years, Mary's Pence has focused on "justice" grants for women. Its 2012 Annual Report listed fifty-six congregations of sisters that made "special gifts" of at least $1,000 to fund grants totaling $60,000 to $100,000. That same year, Mary's Pence issued a statement of support for the LCWR in dealing with the doctrinal assessment by the CDF, observing on its website: "Mary's Pence history is inextricably linked to the Sisters' communities of LCWR." During the LCWR 2012 annual assembly, Mary's Pence invited all the LCWR members to an open house at the nearby Hilton Hotel in downtown Saint Louis.

Call to Action

Call to Action (CTA) is a Church-reform organization based in Chicago. According to its website, CTA claimed to have fifty-four local chapters and a total of twenty-five thousand members in 2012.[72] The organization has a variety of supporters, with a good number being women religious.[73] The sisters involved in CTA are among the most visible proponents of the reforms being promoted by the group. Speakers at CTA conferences have been former LCWR presidents: Sisters Joan Chittister, Nancy Sylvester, Mary Whited, Theresa Kane, Catherine Pinkerton, and Kathleen Pruitt. Other speakers have been Sisters Sandra Schneiders, Jeannine Gramick, Margaret Farley, Maureen Fiedler, Franciscan Sister of Perpetual Adoration Fran Ferder of Therapy and Renewal Associates, and Medical Mission Sister Miriam Therese

[70] Board member names found on Mary's Pence website: www.maryspence.org.

[71] Ruether, "Mary's Pence: Promoting Women's Ministries", 98.

[72] See www.cta-usa.org.

[73] *Call to Action News*, December 1995 / January 1996.

Winter, as well as Sisters Simone Campbell and Carol Coston of Network and Sister of Saint Joseph Christine Schenk of FutureChurch, who appears almost yearly.

CTA draws its name from an October 1976 meeting in Detroit sponsored by the US bishops as part of the American bicentennial celebration. Sister Margaret Cafferty, president of the LCWR in 1984 and executive director of the conference from 1992 to 1997, planned and coordinated the 1976 "A Call to Action" conference for the bishops.[74] However, the similarity between that 1976 event sponsored by the bishops and the contemporary CTA organization is in name only. Before the 1976 conference took place, the late Cardinal Joseph Bernardin, then president of the USCCB, called the conference "an effort to consult the church at large in the United States on a broad range of issues relating to justice in the church and society". But the conference seemed to take on a life of its own, for some of the 1,350 delegates approached the conference determined to promote their own special interests. (Some of the conference facilitators and group chairwomen—including some leaders of women religious—had also attended the first Women's Ordination Conference in 1975, titled "Women in Future Priesthood Now: A Call for Action", and they took the women's ordination agenda to the 1976 conference sponsored by the bishops.) By what some conference observers called a manipulation of the political process, several controversial resolutions were approved by the body of delegates, which reportedly passed every resolution that came out of committees. After the conference, Cardinal Bernardin observed:

> First, in retrospect, it seems that too much was attempted. Any one of the eight large topics considered [humankind, personhood, nationhood, ethnicity and race, the church, neighborhood, the family and work] would have provided more than enough work for the limited time available. All of them together overwhelmed the conference. The result was haste and a determination to formulate recommendations on complex matters without adequate reflection, discussion and consideration of different points of view.
>
> Second, special interest groups advocating particular causes seemed to play a disproportionate role. These groups had a right to be present

[74] From biographical material enclosed in LCWR August 18, 1993, press release.

and make their views known. However, their actual role went beyond this and, in my judgment and that of others, dominated the conference as a whole. The result was a process and a number of recommendations which were not representative of the church in this country and which paid too little attention to other legitimate interests and concerns.[75]

The recommendations from the conference were lengthy and wide ranging, covering every one of the eight topics addressed. Many of the recommendations were well reasoned and within the authority of the bishops to address, such as appropriate training of leaders involved in family ministry, availability of Natural Family Planning classes, and fostering of vocations to the priesthood. But there also were several controversial recommendations well beyond the authority of a bishops' conference, including the following:

The local church must be involved in the selection of bishops and pastors.
    That the United States Conference of Catholic Bishops take affirmative action to respectfully petition the Holy Father . . . to allow married men to be ordained to the priesthood and that they also initiate dialogue on this topic with such national groups as National Federation of Priests' Councils, Corpus, Fellowship and Padres.
    That the United States Conference of Catholic Bishops initiate dialogue with Rome to . . . allow women to be ordained to the diaconate and priesthood.
    That the church, bishops, priests, religious, laity affirm their commitment to the validity of personal sexual fulfillment in married life while at the same time engaging in continuing dialogue with each other and with other persons who are expressing their sexuality in a variety of lifestyles on matters related to the human and spiritual significance of human sexuality.
    That the church in the United States acknowledge that it is living in a state of conflict and anguish arising from tension between the common understanding of church teaching on contraception and the current practice of many Catholics, and that this state of conflict produces intense pastoral and human problems which, in justice, the church is obliged to face.
    The American bishops should use the present pastoral leadership to affirm more clearly the right and responsibility of married people to form their own consciences and to discern what is morally appropriate

---

[75] Archbishop Joseph Bernardin, "Archbishop Sees Mixed Results from Justice Conference", *Origins*, November 4, 1976, 324.

within the context of their marriage in view of historic church teaching including *Humanae Vitae*, and contemporary theological reflection, biological and social scientific research; and those factors influencing the spiritual and emotional qualities of their marital and family lives. . . .

. . . That the church leaders publicly address the request of the divorced who have remarried to receive, under certain conditions, the sacraments of the church.[76]

In response to the recommendations, a 1977 statement by the US bishops noted that some of the recommendations departed from official Church positions, specifically recommendations related to contraception, homosexual activity, divorce, priestly celibacy, and ordination of women. But the statement also pointed out that all recommendations were being referred for study to committees of the bishops' conference and that implementation of appropriate recommendations would be considered.[77]

This ended the formal relationship of the US bishops with the conference "A Call to Action". But some people dedicated to Church reform instead saw this event as a beginning, not an end. According to the CTA February–March 1991 newsletter, *Churchwatch*:

The 800,000 people who fed ideas into Detroit [in 1976], and the delegates who voted there, trusted that the bishops really wanted to listen to them. So they raised issues of reform in the church as well as justice in society. Many bishops didn't want to hear about church reform. The resolutions were not acted upon.

Chicago-based Call to Action was organized the following year by people who didn't want the Detroit issues to die. Many of those issues— women's ordination, hearing lay people's experiences on sexual issues, a lay voice in decision-making, multicultural leadership—are still on "our" agenda and are reiterated in our Call for Reform in the Catholic Church. Most of all, the process of listening to the people begun in Detroit is the way we want our church to do business again!

An Ash Wednesday 1990 ad in the *New York Times* titled "A Call for Reform in the Catholic Church" carried the CTA platform, which

[76] "Justice in the Church" conference resolutions passed at CTA conference, *Origins*, November 4, 1976, 311–19.

[77] US bishops' pastoral statement, "A Response to the Call to Action", *Origins*, May 19, 1977, 757–64.

was reaffirmed by CTA in 1996 after the pope and the Congregation for the Doctrine of the Faith stressed in 1994 and 1995 that the matter of women's ordination was not open to debate. CTA announced in the December 1995–January 1996 issue of its newsletter that "CTA and FutureChurch are launching a 1996 National Dialogue on the priest shortage crisis and the availability for ordination of qualified, spirit-called women and married men." Some other issues still being promoted in that platform included popular election of bishops; return of resigned priests to ministry; consultation with the laity on sexual issues; more dialogue, academic freedom and due process; and financial openness by the Church.

CTA bills itself as an organization of mainstream Catholics, but its positions have been extreme on many issues. CTA founded and coordinates an umbrella organization called Catholic Organizations for Renewal (although some of these organizations are Catholic in name only and have members who are not Catholic). Among the member groups of that coalition are: Catholics for a Free Choice (now called Catholics for Choice), Catholics Speak Out (Quixote Center), Celibacy Is the Issue, Chicago Catholic Women, Conference for Catholic Lesbians, DignityUSA, FutureChurch, Friends of Creation Spirituality (Matthew Fox), Friends of Vatican III on Church and Democracy, Loretto Women's Network, NCAN, New Ways Ministry, Women-Church Convergence, and the Women's Ordination Conference.[78] Most of these organizations also were involved in the We Are Church movement, which was coordinated by Sister Maureen Fiedler.

At the 1996 CTA conference in Detroit, the group's annual award was presented to sisters who, according to conference promotional material, "have played a key role in bringing the U.S. Church to a new threshold of renewal in 1996".[79]

The 2002 CTA Leadership Award went to Sister Christine Vladimiroff, who the year before had refused a Vatican order to prohibit Sister Joan Chittister from speaking at the First World Women's Ordination Conference.

Sister of Charity Louise Akers was invited to be the keynote speaker at the 2009 CTA conference after she had been dismissed from her

---

[78] See http://www.cta-usa.org/COR.html (accessed September 5, 2012).
[79] Call to Action 1996 National Conference promotional tabloid.

teaching position in the Archdiocese of Cincinnati because she refused to withdraw her public support of women's ordination. She told the conference that "women's ordination is a justice issue. Its basis is the value, dignity and equality of women. I believe this to my very core. To publicly state otherwise would be a lie and against my conscience." At the same conference, Sister Christine Schenk of FutureChurch referred to the apostolic visitation of US women's congregations and said that "the issue of the denial of women's ordination by the Vatican has taken on a whole new life as a result of the investigation of the women religious. . . . It's the injustice of both that's becoming increasingly clear to many." [80]

The program for the CTA November 9–11, 2012, conference advertised an "inclusive liturgy" celebrated by "Roman Catholic Womenpriests". Featured speakers were to include Matthew Fox, who became an Episcopalian priest after being dismissed from the Dominicans; and Patricia Fresen, described by CTA as a former Dominican sister who had to leave her order when she was "ordained".

We Are Church

We Are Church was a coalition of groups that organized in 1996 to gather the signatures of at least one million Catholics to promote democracy and broad reforms in the Catholic Church. The coalition was modeled after the 1995 national petition drives in Germany and Austria that called for ordination of women, optional priestly celibacy, and a voice for the laity in choosing hierarchy and defining Church doctrine.

Most groups in the We Are Church coalition were made up of laity as well as some religious and priests, but sisters were heavily involved, with Sister Maureen Fiedler serving as the national coordinator.

The reforms called for by We Are Church were very similar to the CTA platform: lay participation in selecting pastors and bishops; ordination of women to the diaconate and the priesthood; optional celibacy for priests; primacy of pastoral care over canon law; respect for "primacy of conscience in all moral decision making" (i.e., on sexual issues); and a Church welcome for "those who are divorced and remarried, married priests, theologians and others who exercise freedom of speech".

---

[80] *National Catholic Reporter*, November 9, 2009.

Archbishop Anthony Pilla of Cleveland, president of the USCCB in 1996, observed that the We Are Church referendum challenged long-standing Church teaching and ignored the views of Catholics who do not agree with the opinions of the sponsoring groups. He also pointed out that being Catholic means sharing a common religious heritage and moral vision. "It is not something purely subjective, radically private and self-constructed. It is a system of religious teachings and moral imperatives which are to be freely embraced and faithfully handed on to the next generation." [81]

Yet, some sisters who were in the forefront of the We Are Church movement expressed their certitude that they are more qualified than the Church's Magisterium to interpret the movement of the Holy Spirit and that even Church dogma should be open to question or endless "dialogue". Loretto Sister Virginia Williams, who took it upon herself to try to gather the signatures of Loretto sisters in Missouri for the We Are Church petition, told the Saint Louis Post Dispatch that the We Are Church campaign was "a public way to let 'good Catholics' who differ with the Vatican on some issues know they are not isolated. . . .

"We want to give heart to many to practice their faith. . . . The Holy Spirit moves at will. We cannot box the Spirit in, or out. Everyone who is a child of God, female or male, has a mandate to be open to the movement of the Spirit." [82]

We Are Church national coordinator Sister Maureen Fiedler said she expected the referendum to "make church reform and renewal a household word in the United States". [83] However, when the petition fell far short of its goal, We Are Church faded away but maintained a presence on the Internet, with former priest Anthony Padovano of CORPUS as a contact person. [84]

Through these various groups, the most visible and vocal American sisters have professed a vision of the Catholic Church and of religious life that is in sharp contrast to actual Church teaching and the desire of the majority of women religious to use their feminine gifts to build

[81] Bishop Anthony Pilla, "Will Referendum Campaign Create New Polarization?", Origins, June 6, 1996, 36–38.

[82] Saint Louis Post Dispatch, May 25, 1996.

[83] National Catholic Reporter, May 31, 1996.

[84] See http://we-are-church.org/us/, (accessed on August 27, 2012).

up the Church. Additionally, these high-profile sisters have shown their disdain for Church authority and for the reputation of their own religious institutes. They have made it clear that they have a great deal to tell the Church but that the Church has little of value to tell them. As a result, the image of every American sister has suffered considerably. Rather than giving sisters a corporate presence and a voice in the affairs of the Church and society, these organizations have further delineated the differences between sisters who accept the authority of the Church and those who reject it.

The image of sisters is not the only thing that has suffered, however. Many sisters themselves have been harmed by unfettered changes and by leaders who have failed to recognize and to correct mistakes, as detailed in the next chapter.

PART III

WHERE DO SISTERS GO FROM HERE?

15

Vocations, Finances, and the Elderly

Why are we continuing on the road away from the Catholic Church?[1]

— Sister Gerald Hartney, CSC

Two distinct models of religious life for women evolved in the United States after Vatican II. About 15 to 20 percent of US sisters belong to orders that fall into the traditional category: they follow the classical model of life and prayer in common, a corporate apostolate exercised in the name of the Church, and strong fidelity to Church teachings and authority. The leaders of these traditional institutes tend to be affiliated with the Council of Major Superiors of Women Religious.

The other orders can be described as change-oriented, and most of these orders are affiliated with the LCWR. Both of these models of religious life for women share some common problems in the twenty-first century, but the future of the traditional orders looks much brighter than the future of the change-oriented orders, for most of the new vocations are attracted to traditional orders, which have a lower percentage of elderly than the LCWR-affiliated congregations.

---

[1] Gerald Hartney, CSC, response to her CSC superiors regarding a congregational survey, as sent to the author in a letter from Sister Gerald, April 10, 1998.

Difficulties of the Orders in Decline

In contrast to the traditional religious institutes that are attracting new vocations, the institutes of women religious that carried experimentation and renewal to extremes that were neither intended nor authorized by the Second Vatican Council are in decline. Statistics show that these change-oriented institutes have lost a greater percentage of their membership than the traditional institutes, for their average age is in the seventies. In these institutes, the lifestyle of the sisters evolved to a point at which it became impossible to distinguish sisters from their lay professional counterparts. Some sisters are connected to their orders only by way of a tax exemption for their income and occasional community mailings and meetings.

A myriad of problems have arisen in aging orders, including retirement funding, building maintenance, and even decisions about continuing the existence of the institute. Still, as these problems escalated in the twenty-first century, many leaders of women religious continued to be more willing to accept the inevitable demise of their institutes than to admit that they had made mistakes.

The population of sisters most adversely affected by this unraveling of women's religious communities has been the elderly. Some of these elderly sisters helped promote the ill-advised, rapid deconstruction of their orders, but most of them had no role in the remaking of their communities; in fact, many of them tried to advocate more moderate, gradual renewal. Some of these sisters are still trying to prevent the demise of their once-great orders.

Financial Crises

Regardless of what philosophy motivated them, many orders of women religious encountered dire financial straits because so many sisters were retired and so few younger sisters were available to work. In 1988 the bishops instituted an annual appeal, the Retirement Fund for Religious, administered by the Tri-Conference Retirement Office. That office eventually became the National Religious Retirement Office of the USCCB.

The Retirement Office reported in 2011 that the largest age cohort of sisters was the 70–79 group, followed by the 80–89 group, followed by the 60–69 group, with the 90–99 age group being the fourth largest.[2] The *Recent Vocations to Religious Life* CARA study reported that 91 percent of sisters were over the age of 60 in 2009. Thus, retirement programs for religious are suffering from a problem similar to that of the Social Security System—a decreasing percentage of younger workers to support an increasing percentage of retirees.

For years, the only retirement program many women's institutes had was the practice of relying on large numbers of young workers to support their elderly population. Dioceses traditionally provided retirement benefits to their diocesan priests, but not to the religious working in their institutions. In addition, religious were not eligible to enter the Social Security system until the law was changed in 1972; consequently, in 2012 the average retired sister received only about $4,800 in Social Security benefits, compared with the $14,000 received by the average lay beneficiary.

The 2012 annual cost of care for sisters seventy and older, however, was $37,000.[3] Medicare and even Medicaid have helped with health care costs, but sometimes sisters in need of skilled nursing are placed in secular nursing homes because their orders do not have licensed facilities that would qualify for government assistance. In some cases, orders that do have licensed health facilities willingly accept the elderly of other orders so that the sisters can live in a religious environment.

The annual national collection for the Retirement Fund for Religious has helped fill the gap between the retirement benefits and the cost of caring for aging sisters. Since its inception in 1988, the fund has distributed over six hundred million dollars to religious orders to help care for their elderly. Also assisting are private individuals and groups such as the Support Our Aging Religious (SOAR) fund, which has contributed nearly ten million dollars since 1986.[4] Even with such generous assistance, most orders of women still have an underfunded

[2] National Religious Retirement Office Statistical Report August 2012, http://www.usccb.org/about/national-religious-retirement-office/nrro-statistics.cfm (accessed September 4, 2012).

[3] Ibid., http://www.usccb.org/about/national-religious-retirement-office/upload/Statistical-Report.pdf (accessed September 5, 2012).

[4] According to www.soar-usa.org.

retirement liability, and the gap between income and expenses continues to widen.[5]

Are Existing Funds Well Managed?

While most Catholics love and respect sisters for everything they have done for the Church and society, fund-raising personnel are encountering resistance from a number of lay Catholics who are unhappy with the image projected by some sisters. Many laypeople who are struggling to support their own families do not understand why so many sisters live alone or in pairs in expensive apartments when a convent with empty rooms is nearby. They wonder if it is necessary for so many sisters to own their own cars and to have wardrobes that rival those of the best-paid professional laywomen. They wonder if it is financially responsible for religious institutes to continue supporting members who spend year after year after year taking university courses or conducting research projects instead of requiring those sisters to hold down jobs and provide income for their institute. Laypeople— who cannot afford to take lengthy vacations themselves—wonder if it is financially responsible for religious institutes to allow many of their members to forego gainful employment for the sake of lengthy sabbatical projects or six-month retreats to "discern where the spirit is leading" them. Laypeople wonder if it is necessary for religious to travel as far and as frequently as some of them do. They wonder if extensive bureaucracies and frequent meetings that consume a large portion of the annual budget are necessary. And potential donors have withheld funds because they do not approve of some of the projects sisters are spending their money on, money that instead could have gone toward care of the elderly.

Some elderly sisters resent the fact that, as one sister told the author, "elderly are used as bait" in general fund-raising efforts for their communities. She observed that whenever her institute wanted to launch a fund drive for any reason, the leaders would choose a couple of the elderly sisters who still wear a habit and "parade" them before the media. Predictably, the laypeople who remember how much the sisters did for them respond positively when they see sisters in habit, she

---

[5] Per the National Religious Retirement 2012 statistics.

said, noting that this is the only time the leadership of her community sees any benefit to the religious habit.

Similar tactics are being used by other orders, some of which are now offering to put former students in touch with their retired teachers or asking former students to recount tales of how much the sisters meant to them. One fund-raising letter received by the author—accompanied by the photo of an elderly sister in habit praying in the chapel—invited donors to send their prayer requests along with their donations so that the retired sisters could include the intentions in their "power-house of prayer". The letter also assured donors that steps were being taken to "decrease by half" the expenses of caring for retired sisters. It would seem that most donors who wish to support the elderly sisters would prefer that the budgets of religious institutes be cut elsewhere. Furthermore, the fund-raising letter and the return envelope offered no indication that the donations being solicited in the name of the elderly would indeed go toward care of the elderly. Many sisters—active as well as retired—recommend that those who wish to contribute toward the care of retired and infirm religious specify that when they donate.

Mergers: A Blessing or a Curse?

Some orders have attempted to deal with their financial deficiencies and membership decline by joining two or more orders together into a new entity. This practice is called amalgamation or union, and thus far it has occurred usually with orders that were founded under the same rule. For example, in 1995, three different Dominican congregations in Massachusetts and New York merged into the new Dominican Sisters of Hope. Many other institutes have done the same thing. During the 1980s, for example, Sisters of Saint Joseph in Superior, Wisconsin, merged with the Saint Joseph sisters in Saint Paul, Minnesota. Franciscan sisters in Maryville, Missouri, merged with others in Saint Louis. In 2007, seven independent communities of Sisters of Saint Joseph, comprising about 750 nuns in various states, formed into a single congregation.

While merging sounds like a practical solution to financial and personnel problems, it is not without difficulties. Communities that were founded under the same rule often have no more in common than an early founding principle. In practice, sisters whose communities are named after the same tradition can be radically different from each other in philosophy, lifestyle, apostolate, and spirituality.

Canon law requires that the majority of members of an institute must agree to such a merger or union, but there isn't much latitude for any minority dissenting members. For all practical purposes, they have only three choices, and two of them hardly qualify as choices: (1) they can find another religious institute that is willing to accept them as a transfer, (2) they can leave religious life and live on their own, or (3) they can go along with the whole merger deal whether they like it or not. In practice, the first two choices are not viable for a sister who is elderly or infirm, as most orders would not accept them. Unless an elderly or infirm sister had a wealthy family willing to support her, she could not afford to strike out on her own. Since most such sisters take their vows quite seriously, they would not consider their own personal discomfort with lifestyle or spirituality changes to be adequate grounds to ask for dispensation from their vows.

There is one other alternative for a sister who does not want her order to merge with others—formation of a new institute—but the author was able to find only two cases in which this was accomplished. The first occurred in 1991 after several autonomous congregations of Mercy Sisters worked toward forming a single institute.[6] Twelve sisters, however, did not want to join the new group, and Bishop Joseph Gerry of Portland, Maine, agreed to establish them as a diocesan institute. A financial settlement with the order was reached, and the Holy See gave permission for the Diocesan Sisters of Mercy of Portland. Likewise, in 2009, when the new congregation of the Dominican Sisters of Peace was formed by joining seven formerly independent Dominican congregations, a group of those sisters who did not approve of the decision were established as a diocesan order, the Dominican Sisters of Our Lady of the Springs, of Bridgeport, Connecticut.[7]

---

[6] Catherine C. Darcy, RSM, *The Institute of the Sisters of Mercy of the Americas* (Lanham, Maryland: University Press of America, Inc., 1993), 170–72. Merging orders were: The Sisters of Mercy of Albany, Auburn, Belmont, Brooklyn, Buffalo, Burlingame, Burlington, Cedar Rapids, Erie, Hartford, Merion, Pittsburgh, Plainfield-Watchung, Portland, Rochester, Windham, and the Union, which had nine provinces: Baltimore, Chicago, Cincinnati, Detroit, New York, Omaha, Providence, Saint Louis, and Scranton.

[7] See the website of the new order: http://dominicanvocations.org.

The Vatican is very cautious about approving new religious institutes but apparently accepted the new Portland and Bridgeport congregations because they both had a supportive bishop, were able to make financial agreements with their original congregation, and had a varied age span among a sizable group of sisters.

Unselfishness or Pathological Denial?

Several sociologists have observed that declining organizations normally stop taking outside risks and direct their attention inward. Most declining institutes of women, however, have taken the unexpected course of downplaying or ignoring their own demise and concentrating on exterior works, such as finding additional ministries for their few remaining active members. Some observers have attributed this behavior to the typical unselfishness of women religious; others consider it to be the result of either stupidity or denial. In any event, the choices some orders are making put at risk the sisters who depend on their continuation.

Sociologist Helen Rose Fuchs Ebaugh reported in *Women in the Vanishing Cloister* that declining orders tended to allocate most of their resources to external goals. "Most notably, in line with their ideological stance of 'opting for the poor,' many orders have encouraged their members to take jobs working with the poor, jobs that frequently provide very low pay and poor benefits. As a result, the order has to subsidize these members from its general fund, a practice that has contributed to the severe financial crisis in most orders today."[8]

Likewise, sociologist Sister Patricia Wittberg has observed that

far from evincing an unwillingness to risk, an inward-looking focus on turf battles and boundary maintenance, and an attempt to alter the environment to one more favorable to their organizational existence, women's religious communities are doing the opposite—celebrating risk-taking, blurring the boundaries of their orders in solidarity with the poor, and committing their resources toward systemic change, not for their own survival, but for the empowerment of the most oppressed.

[8] Ebaugh, *Vanishing Cloister*, 33.

But Sister Patricia cautioned that "an extroverted focus and a willing-ness to risk may actually be dysfunctional for organizational survival. During the same period that congregations have been moving toward risk-taking and solidarity with the poor, there has also been ... a cor-responding de-emphasis on internal concerns such as membership recruitment or maintaining a distinct group identity." She added that several studies have shown that a major reason for decline in vocations is that religious no longer actively try to recruit young people. "Rather than squander valuable, and increasingly scarce, human resources in outside positions, the organization could enhance its power, including its power to serve the poor, by utilizing the efforts of all its members to strengthen its own institutions." [9]

According to the LCWR 2007 Annual Report, "Our gatherings of the national board have revealed the energy and creativity of our regions and members who continue to stand with and for the poor, to address the issues of our time—trafficking, sustainability, immigration, vio-lence, and war—even as they deal with the challenge of restructuring and diminishment [within their own orders]."

It seems not to have occurred to such orders that their own large elderly population may fit the description of poor or oppressed people.

Transforming Religious Life Preoccupies Sisters

Among religious there are widely divergent opinions about why voca-tions have declined so dramatically. Some believe that the renewal pro-cess begun after Vatican II is still just that—a process. Some sisters think that the Church is in a second, or ongoing, stage of renewal, and that religious must continue to search and experiment until they hit on the right combination, which will cause everything to fall into place. In fact, many sisters compare their situation to that of the Old Testament Hebrews who wandered in the desert for forty years after the Exodus from Egypt. In her August 4, 2008, presidential address at the LCWR annual assembly, Sister Mary Whited used that metaphor, saying: "We leave behind our familiar motherhouses, provinces, struc-tures that have served us well, and ways of living and ministering that deter us from being together.... Amid the 'letting go's,' we risk the

---

[9] Wittberg, "Outward Orientation in Declining Organizations", in *Claiming Our Truth*.

exodus journey. Drawn forward by the Mysterious Presence, we are led into the desert, the place of ultimate trust."

Indeed, the LCWR refers constantly to its task of "transforming religious life", yet it never seems to hit on an acceptable formula for doing so and clearly does not accept the one that has developed over the centuries in the Church. It is almost as if any practice or understanding that predated Vatican II is, as Sister Joan Chittister observed, "suspect" [10] and ripe for transformation, even though the actual Council documents reinforced and praised the Church's longstanding definition of religious life.

One of the five-year goals adopted at the LCWR 1994 and 2000 assemblies was to transform religious life. The October 2007 LCWR newsletter *Update* observed that the group's board recognizes that "leaders spend most of their time facilitating the transformation of their own institutions".

Feminist theologian Sister Elizabeth Johnson has written: "In fact, the very effort to keep alive forms of religious life that have for the most part run their historical course may well be counterproductive to the evangelical following of Jesus. Rather, what is needed is vigilant patience, profound prayer and the ability to act boldly toward that future where new forms of evangelical life will develop." [11]

Other sisters seem to feel that the problem is with the young people, who are simply too materialistic and selfish to consider a religious vocation. Certainly there is some truth to that speculation, but trusted studies on the topic prove that the very aspects that attracted young people to religious life in the past—self-sacrifice, a sense of belonging to a community, a clear sense of identity, a specific corporate ministry— are the very things that most religious institutes deconstructed after Vatican II.

Few religious institutes seem willing to admit that they have brought on their own demise by the decisions they have made. Some sisters believe that religious life is dying a natural death that should not be mourned, so they see no point in inviting new candidates into their institutes. Sister Sandra Schneiders hinted at this position when she

---

[10] Chittister, *Fire in These Ashes*, 34.

[11] Elizabeth Johnson, CSJ, "Between the Times: Religious Life and the Postmodern Experience of God", *Review for Religious* (January / February 1994): 24.

told the ninth National Congress of the Religious Formation Conference, "We must resolutely commit ourselves to risk-taking. . . . Religious must not allow diminished resources to call the shots. The Spirit is calling religious to something. Maybe to end religious life. But that's not a foregone conclusion." [12]

Sociologist Helen Ebaugh found some sisters who believe that "people don't live forever and neither do organizations. There was a time when we were needed in the Church, but perhaps that is not the case anymore. Perhaps other types of groups will take over those needs. Our job is to die gracefully and not hold on to something that is no longer needed." In a case study of one order, Ebaugh found that individualism had taken priority.

> For many members, survival of the order is no longer a major concern. More important is the sense that one's own meaningful work contributes to the Church and the modern world. As long as membership in the order promotes and sustains this goal, people stay. If however, the order jeopardizes or challenges what individuals value, then some members are prepared either to leave the order or simply to refuse to comply. Presently, the order has virtually no mechanisms of social control over members, other than in the area of budget requests. Because the order depends upon the salaries of these members, the risk of alienating and losing members, especially those drawing high salaries, is too risky. For those reasons, the demise of the order in time seems almost inevitable. [13]

This tension between individual desires and congregational needs was alluded to by Sister Margaret Cafferty, when she was executive director of the LCWR. She reported that a conference study of ministry found "the experience of individual members is currently a stronger factor in ministry decisions than corporate commitments of the congregations. This finding may suggest a need to find a new balance between the common good and reverence for individual rights of community members." [14]

Sister Joan Chittister wrote in 1989 that "we need to get over the numbers game. Numbers are not the essential witness to either the

---

[12] *Saint Louis Review*, October 20, 1995.
[13] Ebaugh, *Vanishing Cloister*, 132, 150.
[14] "On File", *Origins*, September 10, 1992, 222.

value or the beauty of the life. The numbers game, in fact, is surely the residue of a culture that operates always as if bigger were automatically better in everything."[15]

Ironically, it is these leaders of the change-oriented orders with rapidly declining populations who seem least concerned about vocations. These leaders seem to be unable to step back far enough to see that the "new paradigms of religious life" their institutes have created are exactly what has brought them to the tenuous position they are in today. As Father Albert DiIanni observed, "The center has not held" because these sisters took "the religious heart out of things" and deconstructed their congregations so completely that even they themselves see little difference between the religious vocation and the lay vocation.[16]

On the other hand, religious orders that identify themselves with the essentials of religious life espoused by the Church continue to expend a good deal of energy on recruitment, and many of them use the "best practices" identified in the 2009 study *Recent Vocations to Religious Life*. Even though some of these traditional institutes have been relatively successful in attracting new members, it still is difficult for religious orders of women to overcome the public image of sisters that has evolved during the last forty to fifty years, and sisters came to be viewed as the most rebellious group within the United States Catholic Church.[17] As one sister observed, regarding the public image projected by some sisters: "It's no wonder that the people don't love us any more."

The Plight of the Elderly

In spite of the retirement shortfall, most retired sisters seem to be receiving good physical care from their institutes, although there is legitimate concern about continuing to fund this level of care in the future as the number of working sisters declines every year. Some sisters report that their leaders are asking them to tighten their belts and reduce their budgets, and anecdotal reports indicate that some orders even are calling apartment-dwelling members back to community houses to reduce housing costs.

[15] *National Catholic Reporter*, May 19, 1989, 1.
[16] DiIanni. *Religious Life as Adventure*, 153–54.
[17] Burns, *Frontiers*, 131.

A larger problem affecting the retired sisters is both spiritual and psychological. Many retired sisters feel that the philosophy of religious life adopted by their institutes makes it difficult for them to sustain their spiritual life and to be faithful to their vows. For example, one sister reported that her congregation built a beautiful new retirement home for the sisters, but did not include a chapel in the facility. She noted that there is a beauty shop in the building, but if a sister wants to attend daily Mass, she must go outside to another building, not an easy task for the elderly or the infirm.

Sister Gerald Hartney, who had been an officer and councilor in her congregation for many years, shared with the author a 1996 questionnaire response she had sent her leadership.[18] She was eighty-five at the time, and she thanked her leadership for the "magnificent efforts" in caring for the well-being of the elderly sisters, but she lamented the fact that her leadership seemed resigned to the dying of her congregation. And she wrote of "a very grave concern at the ever-growing drift toward Protestantism led by LCWR." And "Concern: We look to LCWR rather than to our highest superior, the Roman Pontiff. . . . Why are we continuing on the road away from the Catholic Church?"

In some places, sisters regularly leave their convents to attend Mass at other locations because at the convent Mass, sisters or other non-ordained persons read the Gospel, preach the homily, and perform other functions reserved to priests or deacons by canon and liturgical law. In her questionnaire response discussed above, Sister Gerald remarked, "We went for years without the Nicene Creed at Sunday Mass."

Other liturgical aberrations in convents have included improper reservation of the Blessed Sacrament and illicit changes in the language of the Sacramentary and the Lectionary, as noted in previous chapters. As one sister wrote, many women Religious "are repulsed by rituals that center on shells and stones, streams and twigs, windmills and waterfalls and at which so fundamental a Christian symbol as the cross of Jesus Christ is often noticeable only by its absence."[19]

In a 1985 statement to the United States bishops, the national board of the LCWR reflected a disturbing attitude about liturgy:

---

[18] Hartney, letter to the author with her responses to a congregational survey enclosed, April 10, 1998.

[19] McDonough, "The Past Is Prologue: Quid Agis?" *Review for Religious* (January/February 1992): 96.

The exclusion and / or negation of women in liturgy and worship is one of the most demoralizing experiences which women sustain. This is particularly true because of the church's longstanding assertion that liturgy (especially the eucharist) is the "center of our lives." If one is *de facto* invisible in something said to be "the center," one is, quite literally, displaced or alienated.

Women may not, given the church's prohibition of their ordination, preside; the ritualization, symbols and language of liturgy and worship are more often than not sexist; concelebrated liturgies multiply the presence of males (especially hard to take when the congregation is exclusively or primarily female as is the case in religious communities and organizations of women); qualified women are not permitted to preach (except through subterfuges like giving the homily a different name and dislocating it); God is addressed and referred to in language and images which identify the deity as male, manlike, possessing male traits. Some liturgical roles are barred to women; others they may experience but cannot be formally installed in.[20]

Liturgical practices also were cited in the 2012 doctrinal assessment of the LCWR, and part of the mandate to Archbishop Sartain was: "To review and offer guidance in the application of liturgical norms and texts. For example: The Eucharist and the Liturgy of the Hours will have a place of priority in LCWR events and programs."

Renovation or Iconoclasm?

In addition to a feminization of the liturgy, in countless congregations the leadership also has completely renovated the convent chapel or church, removing pews, altars, statutes, and stained glass, erasing nearly every vestige of the sacred that had inspired the elderly sisters for most of their years in religious life.[21] The result in many of these cases is a

[20] "LCWR Board Urges Change of Course" at pastoral on women hearings, *Origins*, March 21, 1985, 653.

[21] The author was an adjunct instructor at Saint Mary's College when the Holy Cross sisters "renovated" their church in 1992. Almost all of the original stained-glass windows were removed, as well as most of the statuary and the pews. Sisters told the author that the sisters had little input into the renovation and, in fact, were told not to talk about it. Students also reported that some sisters quietly approached them to ask for their help. The students responded by vocalizing their own opposition to the renovation, but were told that the renovation was in accord with Vatican II. The story of that renovation was reported by the author in "Costly Renovation of Campus Church Stirs Protest", *Our Sunday Visitor*,

"modern liturgy space" that is not designed for eucharistic adoration, a customary occupation of many elderly and infirm Religious. Critics of such renovations have argued that the finished product of these renovations is more suitable for holding community meetings than for any liturgical ceremonies that are intended to invoke the transcendent. One sister even told the author she believed that these renovations of chapels have been orchestrated precisely so that the elderly will not be able to spend so much of their time in prayer and eucharistic adoration. And some observers of these "renewed" chapel configurations have suggested that some renovations are intended for the explicit purpose of de-emphasizing the presider role of the priest-celebrant. For example, in some convent chapels, the sanctuary space is not delineated in any way—not even by one raised step; the altar has become a small, movable table placed in the middle of the congregation; and the presider's chair is placed in the midst of the assembly. The author has attended Mass in one of the convent "worship spaces" and has observed that in this configuration, the priest blends in with the congregation. Sisters have explained the purpose of this configuration is to diminish the "pain" of women's exclusion from the priesthood.

In any event, regardless of how good the intentions of the change-oriented orders might be, the fact is that many of the elderly—and some not-so-elderly—sisters have suffered immeasurably and continue to suffer from many of the practices and theologies that have entered their orders since the end of the Second Vatican Council.

First of all, sisters who entered religious life prior to 1970 did so under an entirely different set of circumstances from those of sisters who prevail in a change-oriented institute today. In orders that based their renewal on the Vatican II documents, changes in religious life may have been difficult for some of the elderly and even younger members who were resistant to change. But when Church guidelines were followed, and change was implemented intelligently and slowly,

---

April 26, 1992, 3–4. The following year, Bishop John M. Darcy issued a fourteen-page pamphlet correcting errors that had appeared in a brochure the Holy Cross Sisters had published about their "renewed" church. He ordered that the CSC brochure be removed from the church because it presented "an understanding of the Holy Eucharist that is flawed and does not do justice to the teachings of the Church". See Ann Carey, "Controversy Continues Over Church Renovations", *Our Sunday Visitor*, August 8, 1993, 17.

and essentials of religious life were maintained, the sisters could be reassured that they were complying with the mind of the Church simply by reading the documents of Vatican II, papal communications, and decrees from the Congregation for Religious.

In orders that totally transformed the whole concept of religious life and tried to reengineer a new definition, however, many of the elderly feel totally disenfranchised. Some simply were not consulted about sudden and massive changes that affected the very heart of their communities. Others were coerced to give their tacit approval to sweeping changes or to remain silent about actions they could not and would not approve. And many of these sisters disapprove of what they perceive to be their leaderships' open disrespect for the hierarchy, traditions, and teachings of the Catholic Church.

In general, these sisters take very seriously the vows they made, and they are disturbed not only that religious life has been fundamentally restructured in their own communities, but even more alarmed that in the restructured model, it is difficult, if not impossible, for them to live out the vows they made to God. And many of them are very troubled when they see that their leadership either rejects or ignores directives from the Vatican, apparently with impunity, for most bishops seem reluctant to intervene, even in areas where bishops do have authority.

One elderly sister explained, "We are refugees in our own communities." She said that her community's leadership considers the elderly well cared for if their physical needs are met. But, she said, the spiritual and emotional needs of the elderly are not understood. The active members of her community give more of their time and attention to the prisoners in the local jail than they give to their own sisters in the community, she observed. Also, many sisters who do not need nursing-home care find themselves living a solitary existence in apartments because there simply are no other community living facilities left in their orders, which have sold off convent and motherhouse properties.

Certainly, this treatment of the elderly is contrary to what Pope John Paul II promoted in *Vita Consecrata*, in which he wrote that care and concern for elderly religious should be derived from a "clear obligation of charity and gratitude" as well as "an awareness that their witness greatly serves the church and their own institutes". Further, he wrote that the mission of the elderly is "worthwhile and meritorious" even after age or infirmity causes them to retire from their apostolates: "The elderly and sick have a great deal to give in wisdom and experience to the community, if only the community can remain close to them with concern and an ability to listen." The pope also noted that the elderly live out their vocation by persevering in prayer, by accepting their condition, and "by their readiness to serve as spiritual directors, confessors or mentors in prayer" (44).

Indeed, the Church's elderly nuns are the sisters who literally built the Catholic parochial school system. These are the sisters who founded and sustained most of our Catholic hospitals and other social-service institutions. Yet, in spite of this legacy, their voices are seldom heard in the ongoing debate over religious life. Their voices are not being heard by many of their leaders who are prepared to see their institutes die rather than admit that many of the decisions they made since Vatican II should be reevaluated.

For many years, it seemed that Church officials overlooked the unraveling occurring in religious orders of women, many of which now celebrate more funerals than any other occasion. However, that picture changed when the Vatican announced in 2009 an apostolic visitation of American sisters, which is discussed in the next chapter.

16

The Apostolic Visitation of US Sisters[1]

My hope is that the Apostolic Visitation will not only provide the Holy See with a thorough analysis of the condition of religious life in the United States, but also be a realistic and graced opportunity for personal and community introspection, as major superiors and sisters cooperate with this study.[2]

— Cardinal Franc Rodé, CM, November 3, 2009

The year 2009 was extremely significant for American sisters. First, it was announced on January 30 that the Congregation for Religious was going to conduct an apostolic visitation of all US orders of women. Three months later, it was revealed that the CDF was doing a doctrinal assessment of the LCWR, which will be discussed in the next chapter. Both of these unprecedented Vatican initiatives demonstrated the Holy See's concern for the four hundred–plus orders of sisters in this country.

[1] Some of the material in this chapter originally appeared in articles by the author in *Catholic World Report*: "How Is It Going", January 2011; "In Denial", November 2009; "Post-Christian Sisters", July 2009; "An Update on Challenges to the Apostolic Visitation of Sisters", January 2011.

[2] Cardinal Franc Rodé, CM, "Statement of the Prefect of the Congregation of Institutes of Consecrated Life and Societies of Apostolic Life, Card. Franc Rode, C.M., on the Apostolic Visitation of Institutes of Women Religious in the USA", November 3, 2009, www.apostolicvisitation.org/en/news/CardRodeMsg.html (accessed November 15, 2009).

An Apostolic Visitation Is Requested by Sisters

The first public mention of a possible apostolic visitation of US sisters was made on September 27, 2008, at a symposium on religious life cohosted by Cardinal Seán O'Malley, a Capuchin friar and the archbishop of Boston, and Bishop George Coleman of Fall River. The theme of the event at Stonehill College in Easton, Massachusetts, was "Religious Life Since Vatican II: Recovering the Treasure". The symposium was open to any women or men religious who wished to come. Organizers expected about 250 participants for the day-long event. Instead, nearly 700 religious were present.[3]

Cardinal O'Malley invited nine speakers. The keynote addresses were given by Cardinal Franc Rodé, a Vincentian who was then prefect of the Congregation for Religious, and Sister Sara Butler, a theologian and a Missionary Servant of the Most Blessed Trinity who wrote *The Catholic Priesthood and Women: A Guide to the Teaching of the Church*. The other speakers were Bishop Robert Morlino of Madison, Wisconsin; Sister Elizabeth McDonough, a canon lawyer and professor at the Josephinum Pontifical Seminary; Loretto Sister Gill Goulding, a theologian at Regis College in Toronto; Dominican Father Kurt Pritzl, dean of the School of Philosophy at the Catholic University of America; Jesuit Father Joseph Lienhard, theology professor at Fordham University; Father Hugh Cleary, superior general of the Congregation of Holy Cross; and the author, who was invited to give the viewpoint of a layperson.[4]

In her morning keynote, Sister Sara told the symposium and Cardinal Rodé that most religious were aware that "all is not well" in religious life and "that something has been lost and must be reclaimed". She identified some of the problems that have arisen since Vatican II: (1) abandoning some of the "ascetical practices that gave public witness to their quest for holiness of life"; (2) obscuring "identity as publicly consecrated, ecclesial persons"; (3) diluting the meaning of the vows and emptying them of "their specific objects and obligations";

---

[3] *Boston Pilot*, October 3, 2008.

[4] The talks at the symposium were posted on the Stonehill College website, www. stonehill.edu. Those by clergy and religious were published in Richard Gribble, CSC, ed., *Apostolic Religious Life in America Today: A Response to the Crisis* (Washington, D.C.: Catholic University of America Press, 2011). Quotations from the talks in this chapter were taken from the Stonehill website.

(4) becoming "indistinguishable from generous lay persons whose good works are motivated by faith"; (5) abandoning common life; and (6) giving up traditional apostolates and focusing "so resolutely on the world's agenda and global issues" while giving "so little attention to the needs of the Church". She suggested that "if an institute has abandoned practices the Holy See identifies as 'essential' to religious life, for example, one must ask whether it should plan to reclaim that element, or whether it may now belong to some other category of consecrated life."

Sister Sara noted a regrettable polarization in the Church that also had affected relationships within and between religious orders, as well as relationships of religious with priests, bishops, and the Holy See. She called this polarization "more than regrettable; it is a cause of scandal, a counter-sign". She also identified "a crisis of faith with respect to the origin, structure, and authority of the Church that has affected the relations between apostolic religious and the hierarchy—the 'institutional Church'". These "different ecclesiologies", she said, are "a major source of our malaise".

Cardinal Rodé praised the contributions religious have made to this country: "The history of the Church in the United States of America is rich with the contributions of consecrated men and women who have left an indelible mark on the culture." He also, however, echoed Sister Sara: "Despite this past greatness and present vitality, we know— and it is one of the major reasons we are gathered here today—that all is not well with religious life in America."

This was not the first time Cardinal Rodé had talked about problems in religious life. In a 2006 interview with Catholic News Service, he said that Pope Benedict XVI, like his predecessor John Paul II, desired an "in-depth reform of consecrated life" as an important element in revitalizing the faith of the Church. Reform was needed to recover "apostolic dynamism" and to overcome "excessive secularism".[5]

Addressing the thirty-fifth general congregation of the Society of Jesus in Jaunary 2008, Cardinal Rodé said that many other religious as well as laity look to the Jesuits as role models. He expressed "sorrow and anxiety" about the state of the order, which has been shifting its

---

[5] John Thavis, "Vatican Official: Spiritual Reform Must Begin with Religious Orders", Catholic News Service, February 22, 2006.

thinking away from the mind of the Church and distancing itself from the hierarchy. "The Church is waiting for a light from you to restore the *sensus Ecclesiae* [an awareness of being in and of the Church]", he said.[6]

Two months later, Cardinal Rodé told Vatican Radio of his concern about a "secularized mentality" that had seeped into religious congregations. The solution to this problem, he said is "to flee from this worldly spirit, therefore, and to put the emphasis on life in community, on fraternal life, on prayer, on poverty, on obedience, on chastity lived in the joy of the heart and in interior liberty. It is this that we should recover, that we should live intensely." He added that the only way to solve the "crisis situation" in religious life is to live the "charism intensely" and to return to "the authenticity of religious life". He struck an upbeat note when he talked about the "great admiration and joy" people experience when they meet young religious representing their vocation "in joy and peace of heart". These joyful new vocations, he continued, give "very convincing, very believable testimony"; their very existence is "an invitation".[7]

While making many of these same points in his Stonehill talk, Cardinal Rodé identified various types of religious communities in the United States. The first two varieties were growing, he said, and he predicted that they had a "promising future". The growing communities were (1) new ones, "many of which are thriving and whose individual statistics are the reverse of the general trends", and (2) older communities "that have taken action to preserve and reform genuine religious life in their own charism."

Two types of orders have a less promising future, he said, those that (1) "accept the present situation of decline" and "the disappearance of religious life or at least of their community" and (2) "have opted for ways that take them outside communion with Christ in the Catholic Church, although they themselves may have opted to 'stay' in the Church physically." A fifth type of institute, he added, is attempting to reverse the downward trend but might not be able to do so in time.

---

[6] Homily of Cardinal Franc Rodé to 35th General Congregation of the Society of Jesus, January 7, 2008, www.lifesitenews.com/news/archives/ldn/2008/jan/08010 7b (accessed September 21, 2012).

[7] "Cardinal Rode Calls for Renewal of Religious Life", Zenit, March 19, 2008, www.zenit.org/article-22107?l=english (accessed September 21, 2012).

Two sisters at the symposium, each from a different order, asked the cardinal for an apostolic visitation of women's communities in the US. The audience responded with spontaneous applause. Cardinal Rodé replied that there were too many orders of women religious in this country for a visitation; consequently, most people were surprised by the subsequent announcement that it would take place.

The Apostolic Visitation Begins

On January 30, 2009, a press conference at the Basilica of the National Shrine of the Immaculate Conception in Washington, DC, was convened to announce the apostolic visitation of women's orders in the United States. The visitation was to involve only those orders engaged in apostolic works and did not include cloistered, or contemplative, nuns. Mother Mary Clare Millea of Connecticut, superior general of the Apostles of the Sacred Heart of Jesus, was named apostolic visitator. A canon lawyer and fluent in several languages, Mother Mary Clare had been the leader of her international congregation since 2004 and had worked for years in the Vatican.

A December 22, 2008, decree from Cardinal Rodé stated that the visitation was being undertaken to "look into the quality of life of religious women" in the United States. Information on the apostolic-visitation website cited "challenging times" for religious life as a motivation for the initiative: "The Congregation for Consecrated Life is aware that many new congregations have emerged in the United States while many others have decreased in membership or have an increased median age. Apostolic works have also changed significantly because of societal changes. These and other areas need to be better understood and assessed in order to safeguard and promote consecrated life in the United States." [8]

The announcement of the apostolic visitation was a surprise to virtually everyone, and reactions were mixed. An initial statement from the LCWR on February 2 said it welcomed receiving additional information about the visitation and encouraged members "to participate in

---

[8] Unless otherwise indicated, quotations of officials connected to the apostolic visitation, as well as documents from the apostolic visitation office, were taken from the apostolic visitation website, www.apostolicvisitation.org.

the process as fully as possible". A follow-up statement on February 20 by the LCWR national board was a bit more specific, saying that "the planned visitation comes as a surprise to the conference and its purpose and implications for the lives of US women religious remain unclear." [9] The LCWR board also indicated that women religious already were "aware of their individual, community and ecclesial strengths and challenges" and sought to understand how the visitation would "augment the significant discernment and study processes already inherent in religious life". The "unanticipated news of the visitation", the statement continued, "has evoked a variety of responses in women religious, has generated many questions on what the visitation might involve and has prompted deliberations on how best to proceed with it".

The CMSWR welcomed the visitation in its statement: "The Council welcomes the visitation and we ask our membership to pray for this endeavor and to cooperate in whatever way necessary in order that the visitation will be a fruitful outcome for all women religious in the United States for the sake of the Church." [10]

A Four-Phase Plan

Mother Mary Clare established a four-phase plan that was expected to take two years to complete. Phase One was to solicit input from superiors about their hopes, joys, or concerns regarding their orders. Phase Two was to gather empirical data about the orders as well as observations from their superiors. Phase Three would involve on-site visits to various orders across the United States by teams of religious made up mainly of representatives of the orders nominated by their superiors. Individual sisters of visited congregations would have the opportunity to speak privately with a visitator, and sisters were invited to write the visitation office about their experiences with religious life. All such individual contacts were to be treated confidentially. During Phase Four a comprehensive report would be prepared and delivered to the prefect of the Congregation for Religious.

---

[9] Unless otherwise indicated, quotations from the LCWR or its officers were taken from the LCWR website, www.lcwr.org.

[10] CMSWR statement of Mother Quentin Sheridan, RSM, chairperson, April 23, 2009, www.cmswr.org.

Push-back from Sisters

Almost immediately after Cardinal Rodé and Mother Mary Clare invited women's superiors to participate in Phase One, some prominent sisters denounced the visitation as an out-of-bounds intrusion into their lives. Sister Sandra Schneiders was among the first to speak out in an e-mail she circulated to friends and eventually allowed to be published in the February 27 issue of the *National Catholic Reporter*. She wrote:

> I do not put any credence at all in the claim that this is friendly, transparent, aimed to be helpful, etc. It is a hostile move and the conclusions are already in. It is meant to be intimidating. . . .
>
> We cannot, of course, keep them from investigating. But we can receive them, politely and kindly, for what they are, uninvited guests who should be received in the parlor, not given the run of the house.[11]

She explained that religious congregations like those represented in the LCWR were "birthing a new form of religious life" that was not yet recognized in canon law.

Sister Sandra went on to write a series of essays on the meaning of modern religious life that were published in the *National Catholic Reporter* and eventually collected, along with her original e-mail, in her 2011 book, *Prophets in Their Own Country: Women Religious Bearing Witness to the Gospel in a Troubled Church*.

Sister Joan Chittister also commented on the visitation in the *National Catholic Reporter*. In a February 16, 2009, column, she extolled the many noteworthy accomplishments of women religious, claiming that the sisters had worked for the past fifty years "without support or approval or understanding or encouragement in those efforts from the church". She warned, "After all, if religious life for women disappears—or, conceivably, begins to function outside the boundaries of the institutional church—it will not only affect religious women—it will also definitely affect the church in the modern world."

[11] Sandra Schneiders, IHM, "We Have Given Birth to a New Form of Religious Life", *National Catholic Reporter*, February 27, 2009.

In spite of opposition, Mother Mary Clare proceeded with her mission. In the first four months she personally talked with 133 sisters and received written responses from fifty superiors.[12] In May, she invited the superiors to nominate sisters to serve on the visitation teams.

As the visitation progressed, change-oriented orders continued to criticize it. An August 17 press release from the LCWR reported the group's recent discussion of it at their annual assembly:

> The leaders noted that while their orders have always been fully accountable to the church and plan to collaborate with the Vatican in these studies, they request that those conducting the inquiries alter some of the methods being employed. Among the expressed concerns are a lack of full disclosure about the motivation and funding sources for the studies. The leaders also object to the fact that their orders will not be permitted to see the investigative reports about them that are being submitted directly to the Vatican.
>
> Throughout the assembly, the leaders emphasized that their orders have remained faithful to the reform and renewal of their communities called for by the Second Vatican Council that urged women and men religious to adapt their lives, prayer and work so they may most effectively fulfill their mission. They reclaimed their commitment to what they believe is the unique and needed role of religious life which includes serving at and speaking from the margins of the Catholic Church.[13]

A September 1 editorial in the *National Catholic Reporter* used the visitation as an opportunity to attack the hierarchy: "A way to make sense of the Vatican investigations of US women religious is to concede that in the church of the 21st century we will still tolerate an exclusively male monarchy that operates by its own rules, believes itself accountable to virtually no one, understanding that it can act against groups and individuals with impunity and in secret".

About this time, the visitation office sent a two-part questionnaire to all the orders, soliciting information about finances and properties,

---

[12] Kathryn Jean Lopez, "Head of Visitation See Opportunities for Dialogue", *Our Sunday Visitor Newsweekly*, October 24, 2010.

[13] LCWR press release, August11, 2009, https://lcwr.org/sites/default/files/media/files/LCWRassembly09.pdf (accessed September 21, 2012).

governance, ministries, spiritual and common life, and observance of liturgical norms. The Center for Applied Research in the Apostolate (CARA) helped design and implement the questionnaire. CARA assured participants that individual information was to be kept confidential, while general information would be used to contribute to a "composite analysis".

That questionnaire, however, was met with resistance by some sisters, who said that they did not wish to disclose financial or property information, as well as certain demographic and occupational data. Wild accusations also circulated that Church authorities wanted to inventory sisters' property so it could be confiscated to pay for debts incurred in the clergy sex-abuse crisis.

Sister Mary Waskowiak, president of the Sisters of Mercy of the Americas, the largest order of women in the United States, told the Associated Press that she did not answer all the questions because some were inappropriate and too legalistic. She added that many other superiors had done the same thing. (Sister Mary had been LCWR president in 1997.) The AP quoted Sister Mary Ann Zollman, president of the Sisters of Charity of the Blessed Virgin Mary, saying that she did not complete the questionnaire but instead sent a copy of her order's constitution.[14] (Sister Mary Ann also had been president of LCWR, in 2002.)

Some sisters told the author that canon lawyers engaged by some of the orders had said that the superiors need not comply with the request to fill out the questionnaire. The lawyers recommended that superiors send Mother Mary Clare their constitutions with the explanation that since their sisters were living by their constitutions, they need not provide further information.

Archbishop Joseph Tobin, a Redemptorist priest who had become the secretary for the Congregation for Religious in the middle of the apostolic visitation, observed that some "unscrupulous canonical advisers exploited" rumors that the Vatican was going to replace the leaders in some orders or cause some orders to be dissolved.[15]

---

[14] Eric Gorski, "Catholic Sisters Decline to Fully Answer Vatican-Ordered Inquiry, Question True Motivations", Associated Press, December 4, 2009.

[15] Cindy Wooden, "Vatican Aims to Regain Trust of U.S. Religious Women, Official Says", Catholic News Service, August 10, 2011.

Cardinal Rodé Weighs In

With all the fuss over the questionnaire, more details about the Vatican's motivation for the apostolic visitation emerged. In a November 3, 2009, press statement, Cardinal Rodé said:

> For many years this dicastery had been listening to concerns expressed by American Catholics—religious, laity, clergy and hierarchy—about the welfare of religious women and consecrated life in general, and had been considering an Apostolic Visitation as a means to assess and constructively address these concerns.
>
> The multitude and complexity of these issues were made clear by speakers and participants at the Symposium on Religious Life at Stonehill College in September 2008. This helped me understand that such an evaluation of the challenges facing individual religious and their congregations could benefit the Church at-large as well as the sisters and institutes involved. My hope is that the Apostolic Visitation will not only provide the Holy See with a thorough analysis of the condition of religious life in the United States, but also be a realistic and graced opportunity for personal and community introspection, as major superiors and sisters cooperate with this study.

Two days later, Mother Mary Clare sent a letter to the superiors repeating the goal of the apostolic visitation. Quoting Cardinal Rodé, she wrote that "this apostolic visitation hopes to encourage vocations and assure a better future for women religious." Mother Mary Clare also reported that a number of completed questionnaires had already arrived at the visitation office, and they exhibited the "deep commitment" of religious congregations to the mission of the Church, as well as a "profound love for religious life and for the individual sisters". With the deadline for returning the questionnaire drawing near, she stressed the importance of "wholehearted cooperation with the Holy See on the part of each institute".

In that same November 5 letter, Mother Mary Clare also acknowledged that some superiors had expressed concern about protecting "privileged" information about their congregations. She explained that canon and civil lawyers had determined that the Holy See had the right to all the information requested, but she agreed to drop three sections from the questionnaire because of the complaints she had received. Those sections included a list of each sister with her age, address, and type of ministry; a list of properties owned or sponsored; and a complete copy of the most recent independent audit or the last internal financial statement if an external audit was not made.

This decision to delete the questions was an effort by Mother Mary Clare to preserve goodwill, but this concession may also have emboldened the sisters resisting the visitation while limiting its scope. Furthermore, dropping the financial questions prevented Church authorities from assessing the overall condition of the orders at a critical time when the aging of their sisters began presenting huge challenges.

Four days after the November 20 deadline for returning the completed questionnaire, the *National Catholic Reporter* stated:

> The vast majority of U.S. women religious are not complying with a Vatican request to answer questions in a document of inquiry that is part of a three-year study of the congregations. Leaders of congregations, instead, are leaving questions unanswered or sending in letters or copies of their communities' constitutions.
>
> "There's been almost universal resistance," said one women religious familiar with the responses compiled by the congregation leaders. "We are saying 'enough!' In my 40 years in religious life I have never seen such unanimity."

Mother Mary Clare again wrote the superiors on January 12, 2010:

> When I recently met with Cardinal Rodé, he assured me that the Holy Father continues to show his interest in and support of the Apostolic Visitation. The Cardinal was pleased to hear about the wholehearted and genuine responses of many congregations to the Questionnaire.
>
> However, I also shared with him my sadness and disappointment that not all congregations have responded to this phase of dialogue with the Church in a manner fully supportive of the purpose and goals of the Apostolic Visitation. He encouraged me to ask those who have not yet fully complied to prayerfully reconsider their response. I take this opportunity, then, to once again invite all major superiors who have not responded fully to the Questionnaire to do so.

Phase Three Begins

In her January 12 letter, Mother Mary Clare also announced that the third phase of the visitation would begin in April with on-site visits to "a representative sample of institutes". The visitors would be "many fine religious nominated by superiors general and others and represent a variety of congregations and areas of expertise".

Mother Mary Clare fleshed out some more details about the visitation in a February 18 interview with the *National Catholic Reporter*. She said nearly every congregation had eventually responded to the visitation office, though not every one answered all the questions. About one hundred congregations had been chosen for an on-site visit, she reported, not because they exhibited problems, but because she wanted to look at as much variety as possible with visits to both progressive and traditional congregations. Mother Mary Clare said that about eighty sisters would serve on the visitation teams, and the visitors would give their reports to her. In Phase Four she then would do a report on each congregation that had contact with the visitation office, whether or not it had had an on-site visit. Her reports then would be sent to the Congregation for Religious, and individual congregations would receive feedback from that curial office.

Training for the visitation teams took place February 26–28, 2010, with on-site visits set to begin April 11 and end in December. Sisters began to contact the author about how the visitation was being handled in the communities that were to be visited. Some said that their leadership approached the visitation with a fear that was fed in part by LCWR leadership and other outspoken women religious, as well as by misinformation in the media and questionable canonical advice. This fear, in turn, caused anxiety among many sisters. So did preparatory "informational meetings" that seemed more like indoctrination sessions. Some sisters said they felt intimidated by leaders who warned them not to answer certain questions from the visitors, not to say anything negative about the order, and not to tell anyone about the visitation, even as these leaders continued to disparage the visitation publicly.

Some orders also conducted meetings after the visit for sisters to report what they said and heard during their appointments with a visitator and to discuss how they felt about the visitation experience. One sister told the author that the announcement of these meetings before the visitation made her feel that her conversations with the visitators would not be confidential, as she would be required afterward to report on them to her superiors. To guard their identity and to ensure confidentiality, some sisters instead opted to send their input in writing to the visitation office.

The Push-back Continues

As the on-site visits took place during 2010, the criticism continued and was given a platform by secular media accustomed to playing up disputes within the Catholic Church. For example, a CNN *Belief Blog* television segment on September 17 was entitled "American Nuns Take on the Vatican". It featured Loretto Sister Maureen Fiedler, speaking on WAMU radio in Washington, DC. who said that the Vatican wanted to control sisters "in every aspect of their lives", silencing sisters and forcing them back into habits and behind convent walls. In the same segment, Sister Marlene Weisenbeck, past president of the LCWR, complained that the Vatican was testing the "authenticity and integrity" of sisters and that many sisters were alarmed by so-called intrusive questions posed by the all-male hierarchy.

In an October 18 cover story produced by WGN television, Sister Patricia Crowley, prioress of the Benedictine Sisters of Chicago and a member of the LCWR national board, said there was no clear rationale for the visitation. "I don't know of anybody that's too happy about it", she said, adding that sisters were offended by the intrusion because they were simply doing what they were supposed to be doing.

That same WGN story repeated another common but erroneous complaint about the visitation: that sisters would not get feedback. While it was true that the report written on each order by Mother Mary Clare would not be shared with anyone but the Congregation for Religious in order to protect the confidentiality of sisters who spoke to visitators, each order would indeed receive feedback.

Campaigns to petition Church authorities to leave the American sisters alone also were launched by publications and groups, with some people suggesting that the sisters' resistance to oversight by the hierarchy could be a model for laity, too.

In spite of all the hand-wringing and protestations about the on-site visits, no complaints about the visitation teams ever emerged. To the contrary, all reports that were made public indicated that the visitators were nonjudgmental and open to learning about the orders they visited. In the end, all the challenges and negativity were no match for the actual visitation experience of US sisters, for the on-site visits went very smoothly by all accounts and evoked abundant goodwill. Even some sisters who continued to be suspicious of the process praised the seventy-four visitors, who were all Americans, members of religious orders themselves, and mostly sisters (contrary to erroneous reports that Vatican priests conducted the on-site visits).

LCWR past president Sister Marlene Weisenbeck was asked in an August 30 interview in the *National Catholic Reporter* if the "energy" that the Vatican "investigations" had sparked in sisters would prompt her to see the projects in a positive light. She responded: "You know, I think we're quite a ways along the road to that being true already. There was anger at first, but as people are having better experiences with the visits, the mood has been changing."

An unnamed Immaculate Heart of Mary sister from Monroe, Michigan, wrote on the "IHM Calling" website on September 28 that she had felt "ambivalent" about her order's visitation, but she praised the actual visitors: "There is a warm, 'sisterly' spirit about the way our visitors have interacted with us. They seem open and appreciative about who we are."

In an October interview with *Our Sunday Visitor*, Mother Mary Clare spoke about the positive impact of the visitation so far:

> It's certainly understandable that the first reaction of many, religious and non-religious alike, was one of fear and even suspicion about the underlying motives of the initiative. I think that the voices of the sisters who have experienced an on-site visit can attest to the reverent atmosphere and respectful dialogue that has marked them. Several congregational leaders have told me that although they initially resisted the visitation, they have already noticed a renewed interest in communal reflection on the core values of religious life, coupled with a search for greater authenticity in the areas that are less fully lived.[16]

The apostolic visitators finished their on-site visits in December, having gone to nearly a hundred women's communities, comprising about one-fourth of the sisters in the United States. A final workshop for the visitators took place March 4–6, 2011, giving Mother Mary

---

[16] "Head of Visitation Sees Opportunities for Dialogue", *Our Sunday Visitor Newsweekly*, October 24, 2010.

Clare an opportunity to hear about the visitators' impressions, even though they had already submitted written reports to her. She planned to spend 2011 writing the reports for the Vatican.

New Personnel at the Congregation for Religious

Somewhat complicating the apostolic-visitation picture was the turn-over of top personnel at the Congregation for Religious. Archbishop Joseph Tobin, an American who had been superior general of the Redemptorist Order from 1997 to 2009, had been named the new secretary of the congregation on August 2, 2010. In January of 2011, Archbishop João Bráz de Aviz of Brazil was named to replace as prefect the retiring Cardinal Rodé, who was one year past the normal retirement age.

The new leadership at the Congregation for Religious caused jubilation for some sisters who resented the visitation but consternation for others who welcomed it. Archbishop Bráz was not a religious himself, and both he and Archbishop Tobin gave interviews early in their tenures that indicated little support for the apostolic visitation and even implied criticism of Cardinal Rodé's handling of it.

Archbishop Bráz said that when he came to the Congregation for Religious, "there was little trust on the part of the religious, on account of some positions taken previously. Now, the focal point of the work is precisely that of rebuilding a relationship of trust." Regarding the visitation he said: "That, too, has not been an easy matter. There was mistrust and opposition. We've spoken with them, and their representatives have come here to Rome. We've started to listen again. That's not to say there aren't problems, but we have to deal with them in a different way, without preemptive condemnations and by listening to people's concerns." [17]

Archbishop Tobin said that the Vatican should acknowledge the "depth of anger and hurt" caused by the visitation and that a "strategy of reconciliation" was needed.[18] He also said that there was "real harm done at the beginning" of the visitation process, and "I believe a

[17] Allen, "Vatican's Point Man for Religious Life: 'We've Started to Listen Again'" *National Catholic Reporter*, July 5, 2011.

[18] Allen, "Vatican Must Hear 'Anger and Hurt' Of American Nuns, Official Says", *National Catholic Reporter*, December 7, 2010.

visitation has to have a dialogical aspect, but the way this was structured at the beginning didn't really favor that." [19]

John Allen of the *National Catholic Reporter* summed up the new situation this way: "Under Brazilian Cardinal João Bráz de Aviz and American Archbishop Joseph Tobin, the Congregation for Religious has attempted in the last couple of years to calm anxieties generated by a wide-ranging apostolic visitation of women's religious communities in the United States, which recently reached conclusion. Leaders in religious life who have met the two prelates say they were told that the Congregation for Religious now wants dialogue, not confrontation." [20]

The Visitation Summary Goes to the Vatican

On January 9, 2012, the apostolic visitation office issued a statement saying that Mother Mary Clare had presented a summary of her findings to the Congregation for Religious. She also submitted most of the four hundred individual reports for each of the religious institutes she had contact with, whether or not they had an on-site visit. The rest of the individual reports were submitted in early 2012, thus bringing an end to Phase Four of the apostolic visitation and an end to Mother Mary Clare's involvement.

The Congregation for Religious then took on the task of reading the summary and all of the individual reports and formulating a response for each of the orders. This was a monumental job for the congregation, which reportedly had few English speakers on staff. Complicating matters was the October 18, 2012, appointment of Archbishop Tobin to lead the Archdiocese of Indianapolis, thus leaving a key vacancy at the Congregation for Religious at the very time the visitation results were being studied. Archbishop Tobin himself indicated surprise at his new appointment, and some commentators speculated that he had such a short tenure at the Congregation for Religious because Vatican officials were displeased with his negative comments about the visitation.

---

[19] Wooden, "Vatican Aims to Regain Trust of U.S. Religious Women".

[20] Allen, "LCWR Crackdown More Complicated Than 'Rome vs. America'", May. 3, 2012.

Pope Francis filled the Tobin vacancy with his first curial appointment on April 6, 2013, choosing Father Jose Rodriguez Carballo of Spain, head of the worldwide Franciscan Order.

No timeline ever was given for when orders might expect a response from the Congregation for Religious, and as this book went into publication, no news had emerged about the results of the visitation. However, some of the information gathered in the apostolic visitation apparently had been circulating around the Vatican by early 2012, for when the Congregation for the Doctrine of the Faith released the results of its four-year doctrinal assessment of the LCWR on April 18, reference to the apostolic visitation was made in its document, which will be covered in the next chapter.

17

The Doctrinal Assessment of the LCWR

The teaching and interpretation of the faith can't remain static and really needs to be reformulated, rethought, in light of the world we live in and new questions, new realities as they arise.[1]

— Sister Pat Farrell, OSF, LCWR president

On April 14, 2009, the *National Catholic Reporter* broke the story that the Vatican's Congregation for the Doctrine of the Faith (CDF) was conducting a formal doctrinal assessment of the LCWR. This news exploded like a bombshell, for it came just two months after the apostolic visitation of women religious had been announced, and many sisters were still reeling from that news.

The *Reporter* had learned of the assessment from an April 2 letter that had been sent by officers of the LCWR to its fifteen hundred members. The letter stated that Cardinal William Levada, prefect of the CDF, had written the group about an upcoming doctrinal assessment.

In his letter to the LCWR, Cardinal Levada reminded the group that the CDF had warned their leaders during a 2001 meeting in Rome about several doctrinal problems in official LCWR statements and publications. These problems included positions on women's ordination, homosexuality, and the identity of Jesus Christ at odds with official Church teaching. Since the LCWR had not addressed these problems,

[1] Pat Farrell, OSF, "An American Nun Responds to Vatican Criticism", National Public Radio, July 17, 2012, http://www.npr.org/templates/transcript/transcript.php?storyId=156858223 (accessed July 18, 2012).

Cardinal Levada explained, the CDF was launching a formal doctrinal assessment.[2]

The LCWR Reacts

The LCWR initially reacted cautiously to the news that the CDF was undertaking a doctrinal assessment. The organization issued a statement saying that LCWR "faces this process with confidence, believing that the conference has remained faithful to its mission of service to leaders in congregations of women religious as they seek to further the mission of Christ in today's world".[3]

LCWR leaders were already scheduled to meet with the CDF on April 22 as part of their annual visit to the Vatican, so the LCWR was tight-lipped until after that meeting took place. In a prepared April 23 statement by the group's officers, little was revealed about that meeting. However, the sisters said they were "disappointed" to learn from a *National Catholic Reporter* article[4] the speculation that "some US bishops and / or members of the Committee on Doctrine of the US Conference of Catholic Bishops may have requested a doctrinal assessment of LCWR by the Vatican's Congregation for the Doctrine of the Faith." The statement went on to say that the LCWR had always been "open to dialogue with our US bishops" and continues "to remain open to conversation with the Committee on Doctrine and any bishop who would be interested in speaking to us".[5]

As the doctrinal assessment was being conducted by Bishop Leonard Blair of Toledo, a member of the US Bishops' Committee on Doctrine appointed by the Holy See to oversee the study, the CDF would not comment on the process. Bishop Blair and staff of the CDF quietly met with LCWR leaders on several occasions, but very little information about these meetings leaked out.

---

[2] Thomas C. Fox, "Vatican Investigates U.S. Women Religious Leadership", *National Catholic Reporter*, April 14, 2009.

[3] Nancy Frazier O'Brien, "Vatican Orders 'Doctrinal Assessment' of Group Representing US Nuns", Catholic News Service, April 16, 2009.

[4] Allen, "Women Religious Meet Vatican Accusers in Rome", *National Catholic Reporter*, April 22, 2009.

[5] LCWR Officers Statement on Doctrinal Assessment of LCWR, April 23, 2009, https://lcwr.org/media/april-23-2009-lcwr-officers-statement-doctrinalassessment-lcwr (accessed September 21, 2012).

Exhibit "A" for the Defense: The Good Works of Sisters

The LCWR leaders also were relatively quiet about the assessment as it was taking place, but they were very public about promoting public support for their members and all US sisters. In 2009 they had mounted an impressive traveling museum exhibit called "Women & Spirit: Catholic Sisters in America" that collected artifacts from women's religious orders and told the story of women religious in this country. The LCWR said it conceived of the exhibit to celebrate its fiftieth anniversary. The traveling exhibit cost four million dollars. Donations to cover the cost came from the Catholic Health Association, which gave half a million dollars; the Hilton Foundation, which gave one million dollars; and other Catholic health organizations, religious orders, and outside donors.[6] Between May 2009 and June 2012, the exhibit attracted over one million visitors at venues in Cincinnati; Dallas; Washington, DC; Cleveland; New York; Dubuque, Iowa; Los Angeles; South Bend, Indiana; and Sacramento.

While most Americans recognize and appreciate the good works of sisters, some observers speculated that the exhibit had been conceived by LCWR leaders to build up public support for the organization in the event that the CDF announced it had strayed from Catholic doctrine. Mercy Sister Dolores Liptak, a historian specializing in American Catholic Church history, wrote that such exhibits rightly honor the many accomplishments of sisters. However, she continued, "when the discussion of 'questioning' the sisters comes up, their history seems to be viewed as an argument to stop inquiries about present concerns of loss of numbers. This is a diversionary tactic."[7]

National campaigns of support for the LCWR and US sisters also were launched by groups depicting a "war on nuns", with sisters being portrayed as innocent victims of an abusive all-male hierarchy.

Meanwhile, it was business as usual for LCWR, with only occasional public reference to the doctrinal assessment, and those references made it clear that the LCWR leaders did not intend to back down. Speaking to a reporter at the LCWR 2009 annual assembly,

---

[6] Suzy Farren, "Traveling Exhibit Showcases Catholic Sisters Meeting Needs", *Health Progress* (September–October 2009): 58.

[7] Dolores Liptak, RSM. "The *Origins* of the 'New Nun'", *Catholic World Report*, May 1, 2011.

Sister J. Lora Dambroski, a Franciscan, said the doctrinal assessment coupled with the apostolic visitation would be "an opportunity to be who we are and to speak our truth, not to back away from that, and to understand what our common response will be". She added, "It's a good chance for the sisters to be honest and to tell the story of who we are without fear."[8]

The July 2009 LCWR newsletter *Update* published a reflection by Sister Lora, who said that the CDF doctrinal assessment and apostolic visitation of women religious presented a "unique and historical challenge". She referred to "conversations" that depicted the Vatican actions as "meddling" and as "investigations". The visitation was "a procedure without precedent in religious life in a particular nation", she wrote, and the doctrinal assessment of the LCWR was "an unusual approach to evaluation of adherence to Church teaching".

The August / September 2009 LCWR *Update* carried this reflection by outgoing past president Sister Mary Whited: "As I attend to an apostolic visitation of my congregation and doctrinal assessment of LCWR, I am deeply saddened by initiatives that do not build on common ground and indicate that the contributions of women religious are not valued by some in the church. To carry this pain has been the most difficult part of my service to the conference."

In an August 17 press release, LCWR leaders reported their disappointments with the doctrinal assessment and the apostolic visitation. "While their orders have always been fully accountable to the church and plan to collaborate with the Vatican," stated the release, the LCWR had concerns about some of the Vatican's methods. For example, on the part of the Vatican there had been "a lack of full disclosure about the motivation and funding sources for the studies." The conference also objected to the fact that they would not be permitted to read the reports about their orders that were being submitted directly to the Vatican.[9]

The October 2009 *Update* reported on that year's LCWR assembly:

> Throughout the assembly, the leaders emphasized that their orders have remained faithful to the reform and renewal of their communities called

[8] Chris Granger, "1,500 Catholic Sisters Convene in New Orleans", *The New Orleans Times-Picayune*, August 11, 2009.

[9] LCWR press release, August 17, 2009, https://lcwr.org/sites/default/files/media/files/LCWRassembly09.pdf (accessed September 21, 2012).

for by the Second Vatican Council that urged women and men religious to adapt their lives, prayer, and work so they may most effectively fulfill their mission. They reclaimed their commitment to what they believe is the unique and needed role of religious life which includes serving at and speaking from the margins of the Catholic church.

The LCWR 2009–2010 Annual Report referred to the doctrinal assessment and the apostolic visitation as "a formidable experience of chaos". They hastened to add, however, "We women religious are not afraid of chaos."

The LCWR Complicates Its Position

As the doctrinal assessment continued, the LCWR complicated its situation by taking a public position on the Patient Protection and Affordable Care Act (known as Obamacare), in direct opposition to the US bishops.[10] The bishops had consistently supported universal health care but were opposing the bill being proposed by the Obama administration because it would mandate insurance coverage for abortion and would not provide adequate conscience protection. The bishops made their position very clear and very public, but the first signature on a March 17, 2010, letter asking Congress to pass the bill was that of Sister Marlene Weisenbeck, as president of LCWR. The letter was organized by the sisters' lobbying organization, Network, and was later credited with helping to gather the needed votes from Catholic lawmakers to push the bill through Congress (see chapter 14).

When the LCWR leaders visited the CDF in April 2010, the doctrinal assessment and the LCWR support for Obamacare reportedly were the two items on the agenda. Based on a letter from the LCWR leaders to its members, the *National Catholic Reporter* stated that LCWR leaders told Cardinal Levada they do not support abortion but felt a "moral imperative" to support the universal health care bill. The sisters said they simply were exercising their "rights, duties and obligations as citizens." Cardinal Levada reportedly told the LCWR leaders that their

[10] The LCWR officers also supported the so-called "compromise" to the HHS mandate requiring all employers to provide insurance to employees that covers contraceptives, abortifacient drugs, and sterilization that had been rejected by the USCCB. See LCWR February 10, 2012, statement: https://lcwr.org/media/statement-white-house-resolution-healthcare-coverage-and-conscience-protection.

actions were perceived as public disunity within the Church and "undercut the perception of the Church as one, holy, catholic, and apostolic".

Regarding the doctrinal assessment, the sisters complained to Cardinal Levada that some of the LCWR materials that had been requested by the Vatican went beyond the scope of a doctrinal assessment.[11]

Bishop Blair finished his report on the doctrinal assessment of LCWR and submitted it to the Vatican in July 2010.[12] In the July 2011 LCWR *Update* newsletter, president Sister Mary Hughes related: "We have finished our parts in the apostolic visitation and we await word on the doctrinal assessment. We hold mixed feelings of grieving, of relief, of anticipation, perhaps some anger, and yes, some exhaustion. We welcome this 'down time' feeling as though we both need and deserve a break."

The Vatican Orders a Reform of LCWR

During their 2012 visit to the CDF, LCWR leaders learned the findings of the doctrinal assessment: With the approval of the Pope Benedict XVI, the CDF was ordering a sweeping reform of their organization. Simultaneously, in Washington, DC, the USCCB released the eight-page assessment document,[13] which outlined the reforms to be made under the supervision of Archbishop J. Peter Sartain of Seattle, with the assistance of two other bishops—Leonard Blair and Thomas Paprocki of Springfield.

The team of bishops was charged with taking up to five years to revise LCWR statutes; review LCWR plans, programs, and publications; create new LCWR programs to assist members in a deeper understanding of the Church's doctrine; review and guide application of liturgical norms and texts, particularly so that the Eucharist and the Liturgy of the Hours had a "place of priority in LCWR events and programs"; and review LCWR links with Network and the "Resource Center for Religious Life", which actually is named the Resource Center for Religious Institutes and is located in the same building as the LCWR.

---

[11] Thomas Fox, "Vatican Officials, US Women Religious Meet", *National Catholic Reporter*, July 6, 2010.

[12] "Timeline of Vatican Relations with US Women Religious Since 1950s", Catholic News Service, April 27, 2012.

[13] See appendix.

The LCWR presidents reacted to the assessment with an April 19 statement:

> The presidency of the Leadership Conference of Women Religious was stunned by the conclusions of the doctrinal assessment of LCWR by the Congregation for the Doctrine of the Faith. Because the leadership of LCWR has the custom of meeting annually with the staff of CDF in Rome and because the conference follows canonically-approved statutes, we were taken by surprise.
>
> This is a moment of great import for religious life and the wider church. We ask your prayers as we meet with the LCWR National Board within the coming month to review the mandate and prepare a response.[14]

However, it turns out that the LCWR leaders had not been as surprised by the assessment as the above statement implies. Cardinal Levada had written to them in advance about what was coming. Someone must have objected to the accusation that the CDF had ambushed the LCWR leaders with the results of the assessment, for the group quietly changed their statement a couple of days later. The second sentence of the above statement was replaced with this: "We had received a letter from the CDF prefect in early March informing us that we would hear the results of the doctrinal assessment at our annual meeting; however, we were taken by surprise by the gravity of the mandate."[15]

The assessment document's cover letter from Cardinal Levada explained that the CDF wanted to foster "a patient and collaborative renewal of this conference of major superiors in order to provide a stronger doctrinal foundation for its many laudable initiatives and activities." He said that the first step would be a personal meeting between the CDF and the officers of the LCWR "for the opportunity to review the document together in a spirit of mutual respect and collaboration,

---

[14] This statement was sent to the author by e-mail on April 19, 2012, by Sister Annmarie Sanders, LCWR director of communications, and posted on the LCWR website. The statement also is cited in Joshua J. McElwee, "LCWR 'Stunned' by Vatican's Latest Move", *National Catholic Reporter*, April 19, 2012.

[15] Undated "LCWR Statement from Presidency on CDF Doctrinal Assessment", https://lcwr.org/media/lcwr-statement-presidency-cdf-doctrinal-assessment (accessed September 21, 2012).

hopefully thereby avoiding possible misunderstandings of the document's intent and scope".

The scope of the assessment document was comprehensive, but also precise, detailing doctrinal problems found in LCWR assemblies, workshops, and publications. The "serious doctrinal problems that affect many in Consecrated Life" included a distortion of the role of Jesus in the salvation of the world and an undermining of "the revealed doctrines of the Holy Trinity, the divinity of Christ, and the inspiration of Sacred Scripture". Also, the document noted "policies of corporate dissent" involving unacceptable positions on the Eucharist, the nature of religious life, women's ordination, human sexuality, and ministry to homosexual persons.

Groups Defend the LCWR

Public support for the LCWR and denunciation of the Vatican ramped up as soon as the assessment results were released. Sensational headlines appeared, such as the following: "Nuns Gone Wild! Vatican Chastises American Sisters",[16] "Vatican Waging a War on Nuns",[17] and "Guess Who the Vatican Is Picking on Now".[18] A common theme in much of the media coverage of the CDF action was that the out-of-touch men in the Vatican were unfairly criticizing the most faithful and hardworking members of the Church, even though the CDF document had specifically praised the work of US sisters and made it clear the document concerned only the fifteen-hundred-member LCWR and not all consecrated women.

Nevertheless, many people ignored such facts, raising doubts that they had even read the CDF document that had been prominently placed on the USCCB website. The *National Catholic Reporter* launched a "Sisters under Scrutiny" section on its website, a "one stop site" for

[16] Barbie Latza Nadeau, "Nuns Gone Wild! Vatican Chastises American Sisters", *The Daily Beast*, April 20, 2012, http://www.thedailybeast.com/articles/2012/04/20/nuns-gone-wild-vatican-chastises-american-sisters.html (accessed April 21, 2012).

[17] Carol Marin, "Vatican Waging a War on Nuns", *Chicago Sun-Times*, April 20, 2012, *http://www.suntimes.com/news/marin/12026003-452/vatican-waging-a-war-on-nuns.html* (accessed April 21, 2012).

[18] Sandy Hingston, "Guess Who the Vatican Is Picking on Now", *Philly Post*, April 23, 2012, http://blogs.phillymag.com/the_philly_post/2012/04/23/nuns-catholic-church-vatican/ (accessed April 24, 2012).

all the news about the CDF assessment of the LCWR. Also, a "Support Our Catholic Sisters" Facebook page was created so that people could post short essays, photos, and videos about sisters and report on prayer services, vigils, and letter-writing campaigns supporting the LCWR in its struggle with the CDF.

In the May 6 issue of the Springfield Diocese's *Catholic Times*, Bishop Thomas Paprocki, one of the bishops delegated to oversee the reform of the LCWR, responded to some of the criticism by explaining the doctrinal assessment to his diocese:

> It is important to note that the doctrinal assessment of LCWR does not deal with the faith and life of the 57,000 women religious in the United States. This has been the task of the recent apostolic visitation conducted by the Congregation for Institutes of Consecrated Life and Societies of Apostolic Life. The doctrinal assessment is not meant to call into question the faith and witness of so many dedicated and faithful women religious throughout the country. In fact, the Congregation for the Doctrine of the Faith affirmed them in its doctrinal assessment of the LCWR, saying, "The Holy See acknowledges with gratitude the great contribution of women religious to the church in the United States as seen particularly in the many schools, hospitals, and institutions of support for the poor which have been founded and staffed by Religious over the years."

Bishop Paprocki explained that the doctrinal assessment revealed "serious doctrinal problems" within the LCWR and focused on three areas of concern: (1) addresses given during the annual assemblies that had "problematic statements and serious theological, even doctrinal errors"; (2) "policies of corporate dissent" in which leadership teams of some communities of sisters, among them LCWR officers, "have protested the Holy See's actions regarding the question of women's ordination and of a correct pastoral approach to ministry to homosexual persons. These sisters collectively take a position not in agreement with the church's teaching"; and (3) "a prevalence of certain radical feminist themes incompatible with the Catholic faith in some of the programs and presentations sponsored by the LCWR, including theological interpretations that risk distorting faith in Jesus and his loving Father who sent his Son for the salvation of the world."

Bishop Paprocki ended by writing that the purpose of the doctrinal assessment was to "work collaboratively" to renew the LCWR and to "strengthen the doctrinal foundations that should guide the organization's many important initiatives and efforts." He also asked for prayers for success of the initiative.

Three weeks later, the LCWR's twenty-one-member national board held a special meeting to plan a response to the CDF. It was the first time since the assessment was formally announced that the national board had met. A June 1 LCWR press release reported:

> The board members raised concerns about both the content of the doctrinal assessment and the process by which it was prepared. Board members concluded that the assessment was based on unsubstantiated accusations and the result of a flawed process that lacked transparency. Moreover, the sanctions imposed were disproportionate to the concerns raised and could compromise their ability to fulfill their mission. The report has furthermore caused scandal and pain throughout the church community, and created greater polarization.

That same press release signaled that the LCWR embraced the support it was receiving from laity who either perceived the sisters as victims or who wanted changes in the Church that they thought could be spearheaded by LCWR:

> The board recognizes this matter has deeply touched Catholics and non-Catholics throughout the world as evidenced by the thousands of messages of support as well as the dozens of prayer vigils held in numerous parts of the country. It believes that the matters of faith and justice that capture the hearts of Catholic sisters are clearly shared by many people around the world. As the church and society face tumultuous times, the board believes it is imperative that these matters be addressed by the entire church community in an atmosphere of openness, honesty, and integrity.

In an interview the same day, LCWR president Sister Pat Farrell said that many people inferred from the CDF document that LCWR members were "unfaithful and not in communion with the church". She said the sisters did not see themselves that way, but rather as asking "genuine questions" that are shared by many laity and are a sign of deep faith in the Church. Unfortunately, she continued, the "climate" for dialogue on these questions is not always present. Sister Pat also took the opportunity to restate the LCWR desire to reform the Church, saying that the doctrinal assessment calls for renewal of the LCWR, but the LCWR hoped that out of the dialogue process, a renewal of the US Catholic Church would occur.[19]

Dueling Statements and Interviews

The CDF and the bishops delegated to conduct the assessment apparently realized they had to respond to the criticisms and misrepresentations about the CDF initiative instead of allowing the LCWR to control the message. On June 1, Archbishop Sartain issued a response to the LCWR statement of that same day and had it e-mailed to all the journalists, including the author, who had received the earlier LCWR statement. He said he was "wholeheartedly committed to dealing with the important issues raised by the doctrinal assessment and the LCWR Board in an atmosphere of openness, honesty, integrity and fidelity to the Church's faith", adding that he looked forward to the meeting at the CDF on June 12 with the LCWR president and executive director. And he emphasized that "the Holy See and the Bishops of the United States are deeply proud of the historic and continuing contribution of women religious—a pride that has been echoed by many in recent weeks."

On June 8, Bishop Blair wrote a letter published in his diocesan newspaper, *Catholic Chronicle*, which was posted on the diocesan website and subsequently read by him in a video posted on YouTube. Titled "Reality Check", the letter was written, the Bishop said, to respond to public "distortions and misrepresentations of the facts" related to the CDF doctrinal assessment of LCWR. "The biggest distortion of all is the claim that the CDF and the bishops are attacking or criticizing the life and work of our Catholic sisters in the United States", the Bishop wrote. He went on to explain that the CDF action concerned only the LCWR, and while the LCWR members led most of the religious sisters in this country, "that does not mean that criticism of the LCWR is aimed at all the member religious communities, much less all sisters."

Bishop Blair said the "fundamental question" posed by the CDF to the LCWR leaders was why the "LCWR constantly provides a one-

[19]Joshua J. McElwee, "LCWR President Speaks of Pain and Process", *National Catholic Reporter*, June 1, 2012.

sided platform—without challenge or any opposing view—to speakers who take a negative and critical position *vis-à-vis* church doctrine and discipline and the church's teaching office." Bishop Blair went on to note that:

> LCWR speakers also explore themes like global spirituality, the new cosmology, earth-justice and eco-feminism in ways that are frequently ambiguous, dubious or even erroneous with respect to Christian faith. And while the LCWR upholds Catholic social teaching in some areas, it is notably silent when it comes to two of the major moral challenges of our time: the right to life of the unborn, and the God-given meaning of marriage between one man and one woman.

Bishop Blair also explained that people who do not hold the teachings of the Catholic Church or Catholics who dissent from those teachings are attacking the CDF and the bishops for the conclusions of the assessment. On the other hand, he continued, "a person who holds the reasonable view that a Catholic is someone who subscribes to the teachings of the Catholic Church will recognize that the Catholic Bishops have a legitimate cause for doctrinal concern about the activities of the LCWR, as evidenced by a number of its speakers and some of its resource documents." In spite of those controversies, misunderstandings, and misrepresentations, Bishop Blair expressed his hope that "if the serious concerns of the CDF are accurately represented and discussed among all the sisters of our country, there will indeed be an opening to a new and positive relationship between women religious and the church's pastors in doctrinal matters, as there already is in so many other areas where mutual respect and cooperation abound."

Four days after Bishop Blair's letter was published, the LCWR president and executive director met at the Vatican with Cardinal Levada and Archbishop Sartain. An LCWR press release that same day said that the meeting was an "open" meeting and that the sisters "were able to directly express" their concerns to Cardinal Levada and Archbishop Sartain.

A statement from the Vatican Press office the same day reported an atmosphere of "openness and cordiality" and reaffirmed that canon law directs that a superiors' conference is under "the supreme direction of the Holy See in order to promote common efforts among the individual member institutes and cooperation with the Holy See and the local conferences of bishops". Further, "the purpose of the doctrinal assessment is to assist the LCWR in this important mission by promoting a vision of ecclesial communion founded on faith in Jesus Christ and the teachings of the Church as faithfully taught through the ages under the guidance of the Magisterium."

Then, in a highly unusual move, Cardinal Levada gave a rare media interview on June 12, the same day that he had met with LCWR president Sister Pat Farrell and executive director, Sister of Saint Joseph Janet Mock. In that interview with John Allen of the *National Catholic Reporter*, Cardinal Levada "strongly rejected" the LCWR charges that the assessment report contained "unsubstantiated accusations" or lacked transparency.

The cardinal also reaffirmed that the assessment was not a surprise, for it had been going on for four years and was based not on some secret accusations, but rather on the content of the LCWR assemblies and website as well as what the members "do or don't do." Cardinal Levada also said he thought the reform of the LCWR could work, but he was concerned that the CDF's four-year interaction with LCWR leaders risked being a "dialogue of the deaf" because the LCWR had done things that demonstrated it had not taken the CDF concerns seriously. He named some of the LCWR actions that he said showed their lack of concern: publishing in the LCWR Winter 2011 *Occasional Papers* an interview with Father Charles Curran, who had been censured by the Vatican for his views on sexual morality; inviting Barbara Marx Hubbard, a New Age "futurist" to give the keynote at the 2012 LCWR assembly; and awarding its annual Outstanding Leadership Award to Sandra Schneiders, a frequent critic of the Vatican.

Six days later, on June 18, the LCWR issued a press release reporting on the June 12 meeting at the CDF. It confirmed that LCWR leaders had been able to express their concerns but said, "The meeting was difficult because of the differing perspectives the CDF officials and the LCWR representatives hold on the matters raised in the report." Some Vatican officials and bishops had "publicly claimed" that the assessment report was not a reflection on all US sisters, but was directed only to the LCWR, the release said. However, "the board noted that the actions of CDF are keenly felt by the vast majority of Catholic sisters who have elected, and therefore feel a close identity with, their leaders." The release also highlighted support for the LCWR from men religious and sisters in other countries. And it stated that "letters and petitions from thousands of lay supporters worldwide, indicate that many others are also concerned about how to live as people of faith in the complexities of these times. The concerns they have shared with LCWR will be part of the conference's discernment of its response to the CDF report."

In the midst of all this activity, Cardinal Francis George was a guest on the EWTN *World Over* program on June 21 for a Fortnight for Freedom special. Cardinal George said the bishops wanted to be supportive of both the Holy See and of the sisters, for "if the unity of the church is destroyed by this, it is a pastoral concern and the bishops are interested." The cardinal said he had spoken to Sister Pat Farrell when the CDF report was first issued, but "she made it very clear to me that this is a conversation between the Holy See and the sisters and therefore the bishops should not interfere."

On July 16, *America* magazine published "The Journey of Women Religious Since Vatican II" by Sister Nancy Sylvester, who had been both a president of LCWR and a national coordinator for Network. She also founded the Institute for Communal Contemplation and Dialogue. Sister Nancy wrote that women religious throughout the world had changed and had "altered how we see ourselves, the Gospel, our church, our world and most importantly how we understand our God".

That change, she continued, "is shaking the very foundations of what continues to be a church seemingly caught in an earlier time and place". What is needed for the postmodern world, she said, is a faith "that comes from a stance of openness and understanding of the changes that our evolutionary development has brought us. It cannot be a faith that comes from a position of condemning modernity. It will be a faith that has been tested in the crucible of our time and has emerged with new insights and new interpretations of how we can love one another as Jesus did."

LCWR president Sister Pat Farrell took to the airwaves one day later to continue to make the group's case publicly. On National Public Radio's *Fresh Air*, Sister Pat said she saw three options for the LCWR regarding the CDF mandate: (1) comply; (2) don't comply and either see what the Vatican does or remove the LCWR from canonical oversight and form a separate organization, or (3) find a "third way" that "refuses" to define the issues in "such black and white terms". Sister Pat expressed her preference for that "third way".

Interviewer Terry Gross asked Sister Pat about the CDF report's conclusion that the LCWR had taken a position on human sexuality that was contrary to Church teaching. Sister Pat replied that the LCWR had "in good faith" been raising concerns about some Church teaching on human sexuality because "the teaching and interpretation of the faith can't remain static and really needs to be reformulated, rethought, in light of the world we live in and new questions, new realities as they arise." Since women religious work so closely with people "at the margins", she said, sisters see people coping with "painful, difficult situations" in their everyday lives. Later in the interview, she said that many people in the Church see a need to reexamine the topic of human sexuality and "to give interpretations that fit the situation of our time and real-life people".

In commenting on the LCWR position on abortion, Sister Pat insisted that the works of LCWR members were pro-life, but the sisters would question "any policy that is more pro-fetus than actually pro-life. You know, if the rights of the unborn trump all of the rights of all of those who are already born, that is a distortion too, if there's such an emphasis on that."

The "essential question" Sister Pat identified was "Can you be Catholic and have a questioning mind?" She went on to say that one of LCWR's "deepest hopes" was that, by the way the organization handled the doctrinal assessment, it could create "a safe and respectful environment" in which ordinary Catholics could engage with Church leaders to ask questions and "search for truth freely" on complex and shifting contemporary issues. However, she added, the climate for such an environment does not presently exist in the Church. Putting bishops in charge of the LCWR reform, she continued, caused "pain" and "anger" and looked more like "shutting down dialogue" than creating the environment for it.[20]

The following week, on July 25, Bishop Blair was interviewed by Terry Gross on *Fresh Air* as part 2 of the program's coverage of the doctrinal assessment. When Gross questioned Bishop Blair about the CDF's criticism of the LCWR for being silent on the issue of abortion

---

[20] Farrell, "An American Nun Responds to Vatican Criticism".

and challenging Church teaching on homosexuality, she reminded him that many people believe "gay marriage" is acceptable and that the Church is "out of step" on the topic. The bishop agreed that indeed many people don't agree with Catholic teaching on moral issues. "But", he said, "we would expect that a group of religious sisters who are Catholic nuns would accept the teaching of their Church." He also added that the Church teaching on the sanctity of marriage between one man and one woman was not something recently dreamed up, but had always been "the God-given nature of human sexuality and marriage".

When Gross used the term "cracking down" to characterize the doctrinal assessment, Bishop Blair said that was not the correct description, but rather that the assessment was an effort to work with the LCWR "to remedy what we feel are serious doctrinal concerns". Gross told Bishop Blair that Sister Pat Farrell wanted to "dialogue" about the questions, but that the assessment asked not for dialogue but for "conformity". Bishop Blair responded, "If by dialogue they mean that the doctrines of the Church are negotiable and that the bishops represent one position and the LCWR presents another position, and somehow we find a middle ground about basic Church teaching on faith and morals, then no. That's—I don't think that's the kind of dialogue that the Holy See would envision." True dialogue, he continued, would be about how the LCWR could inform and assist sisters to appreciate and accept Church teachings and about how to "heal" some of the concerns sisters have about those teachings.

Bishop Blair explained that there are objective truths and teachings of the faith that come from revelation and are interpreted by the Church, with the guidance of the Holy Spirit. Those teachings are not negotiable, he continued. Though one could dialogue about understanding the teachings, "it's not new understandings that then change the faith ... that's what really gets to the heart of all that we find in this assessment, that they are promoting, unilaterally, new understandings, a new kind of theology that is not in accordance with the faith of the Church."

Regarding the CDF discussions with the LCWR about the doctrinal problems, Bishop Blair said that so far there had been "denial" by the LCWR and a refusal to recognize that the organization has problems that should be of concern to the bishops and the Holy See. It creates a "grave difficulty", he said "if someone will not even acknowledge that this is a problem". He said he would like to see the situation resolved by the LCWR leadership's acknowledging that the questions raised in the assessment "had merit", adding that the CDF could then help the group "to appreciate and accept the teachings of the Church".[21]

The LCWR Decides How to Respond

As the 2012 LCWR annual assembly approached, all of the recent media attention fueled speculation about how the sisters would decide to respond to the doctrinal assessment. Archbishop Sartain offered to attend but was told by the leadership that his presence "would not be helpful".[22]

The strain in the relationship between the LCWR and the hierarchy, as well as anticipation over the sisters' decision, drew an unprecedented number of media representatives to cover the event (including the author, reporting for the *National Catholic Register*). About nine hundred members of the LCWR attended, more than the usual number, and only those members were admitted to the executive sessions during which a response to the doctrinal assessment was discussed. Indeed, members were cautioned by the leadership not to discuss the doctrinal assessment with any of the media present. LCWR president Sister Pat Farrell even told members that since it was such a "critical moment" for the group, confidentiality was necessary: "If in your own conscience you cannot understand or perceive confidentiality as anything other than total transparency, we ask you to think about not coming to the executive sessions, not in the interest of ever excluding anyone, but in creating the kind of environment we need to really discern with each other in freedom and openness."[23]

The open sessions that media were able to attend did not touch directly on the assessment, but reporters were alert for hints about what was

[21] "Bishop Explains Vatican's Criticism of U.S. Nuns", National Public Radio, July 25, 2012, www.npr.org/templates/transcript/transcript.php?storyId=157356092 (transcript accessed July 26, 2012).

[22] Per August 14, 2012, telephone conversation between the author and Sister Mary Ann Walsh, RSM, director of Media Relations for the USCCB.

[23] From notes taken by the author at the LCWR Annual Assembly, August 8, 2012, Millennium Hotel, Saint Louis, Missouri.

being discussed behind closed doors. The "prayer services" that took place every morning seemed designed to bring the membership to a consensus about their pending decision regarding the doctrinal assessment. Sisters were repeatedly urged to set aside their own opinions and judgments to be open to where "the spirit" was leading them.

Such language hinted that the leadership was leaning in the direction of the "risky" path of refusing to cooperate with the CDF's mandate to reform the organization. However, conflicting messages were sent on other occasions during the meeting. When Thomas Fox, publisher of the *National Catholic Reporter*, suggested during a panel discussion that the sisters should "just say 'no'" to the Vatican, many sisters reacted with audible groans of disapproval.

In her presidential address on August 10, Sister Pat Farrell also sent mixed messages about which direction the LCWR would take. She made it clear that the members believed they were speaking for many people in the Church: "Clearly they share our concern at the intolerance of dissent even from those with informed consciences, the continued curtailing of the role of women."

"Creative Fidelity"

Sister Pat said that in their orders, members had moved from a "hierarchically structured lifestyle" to a "more horizontal model", which she said had been "empowering, lifegiving." This evolution, she said, had changed the sisters' understanding of obedience, thus affecting their response to the CDF assessment. "A response of integrity to the mandate needs to come out of our own understanding of creative fidelity", Sister Pat said. Questions that members should ask, she said, included the following: "Is this doctrinal assessment process an expression of concern or an attempt to control? ... Does it allow us the freedom to question with informed consciences? Does it really welcome feedback in a Church that claims to honor the *sensus fidelium*, the sense of the faithful?"[24]

The much-anticipated response to the doctrinal assessment was announced at an afternoon press conference on the last day of the

[24] Quotations of Sister Pat Farrell are from a copy of the text of her presidential address provided to the press by LCWR media personnel.

assembly, August 10. The decision, however, did not live up to the hype that had preceded the assembly for weeks, because it was that "third way" Sister Pat Farrell had talked about; the group would continue "dialoguing" with the assessment team led by Archbishop Sartain. In a prepared statement, Sister Pat said that LCWR members wanted to maintain the official role in the Church as a recognized superiors' conference even though they had "deep disappointments with the CDF report". She also made it clear that the LCWR leaders would pursue "dialogue" on their own terms: "The officers will proceed with these discussions as long as possible, but will reconsider if LCWR is forced to compromise the integrity of its mission." [25]

Journalists at the press conference asked Sister Pat what the LCWR wanted to get out of the dialoguing, and she responded, "What we want is ... to be recognized and understood as equals in the Church, that our form of religious life can be respected and affirmed. Really we do want to come to the point of having an environment not just for us, but for the entire Catholic Church, of the ability to ... search for truth together, to talk about issues that are very complicated." Regarding her perception of the bishops and whether they were being fair, she responded that "there is a power differential between the bishops and ourselves, and there is not right now a climate of openness and dialogue in general in the church", and she added that the LCWR hoped to contribute to moving the Church in that direction.

Archbishop Sartain reacted to the LCWR decision in a statement issued later that day, saying that he, along with LCWR members, was "committed to working to address the issues raised by the doctrinal assessment in an atmosphere of prayer and respectful dialogue". He said that the parties must work to clear up any misunderstandings and that he was "hopeful" they could work together "without compromising Church teaching or the important role of the LCWR."

The following day, August 11, Archbishop Sartain met with the twenty-one-member LCWR national board. The LCWR issued the following statement about that meeting:

> The LCWR board members believe they were able to express both their concerns and their feelings about the CDF report with great openness and honesty, and that Archbishop Sartain listened carefully. The

[25] LCWR press release provided to media at LCWR assembly, August 10, 2012.

archbishop asked for assistance from LCWR to learn more about the conference and about the members' experience and understandings of religious life. LCWR will provide Archbishop Sartain with resources they believe will be helpful, and its officers plan to meet with him again later in the fall.

... The LCWR assembly, which closed the day before the board met with Archbishop Sartain, had charged the board to conduct their conversation with the archbishop from a stance of mutual respect, careful listening and open dialogue. The expectation of the LCWR members is that open and honest dialogue may lead not only to increasing understanding between the church leadership and women religious, but also to creating more possibilities for the laity and, particularly for women, to have a voice in the church. Furthermore, the assembly instructed the board to articulate its belief that religious life, as it is lived by the women religious who comprise LCWR, is an authentic expression of this life that must not be compromised.[26]

After the 2012 LCWR assembly, little was said publicly about the dialogue between the CDF and the LCWR. When Pope Benedict announced in February of 2013 that he would resign, speculation swirled about whether the next pope would continue the CDF mandate to reform the LCWR. That speculation swiftly ended when the LCWR made its annual spring visit to the Vatican. On April 15, CDF prefect Archbishop Gerhard Ludwig Müller told the sisters that "he had recently discussed the Doctrinal Assessment with Pope Francis, who reaffirmed the findings of the Assessment and the program of reform for this Conference of Major Superiors."[27]

As this edition of *Sisters in Crisis* went into publication, the "dialogue" was continuing. However, if the "dialogue" does not succeed in helping the LCWR members to embrace the Church's teachings and to understand that their vow of obedience applies to rightful Church authorities, LCWR's future as a Vatican-approved entity will be in serious jeopardy, for canon lawyers agree that there is no possible appeal beyond the CDF to a higher body at the Vatican.

---

[26] LCWR August 13 press release, https://lcwr.org/media/lcwr-statement-meeting-archbishop-sartain (accessed September 21, 2012).

[27] "Communique of the Congregation for the Doctrine of the Faith Concerning a Meeting with the Presidency of the Leadership Conference of Women Religious in the USA", April 15, 2013, http://attualita.vatican.va/sala-stampa/bollettino/2013/04/15/news/30807.html, accessed April 15, 2013.

18

Denial and Demise or Hope for the Future?

It would make no sense to say religious life is dying. What's dying is the American experiment with the '6os. And let it go, I say. There is no call for keeping the '6os alive; it's over.[1]

—William Coulson, psychologist

When the first edition of this book was published in 1997, many religious orders of women were in chaos, and the voices of doom were predicting the end of religious life for women in the United States. The ensuing years have been eventful, however, and now there is greater hope for the revitalization of religious life than at any time since the Second Vatican Council closed in 1965.

As William Coulson has observed, the tumultuous decades of the 1960s and 1970s that wrought so much havoc in the Church and in society are over. Many people now realize and bemoan the disastrous results of deconstructing institutions, rejecting traditional authority, and discarding long-held social norms.

In those decades, strong instruction in the Catholic faith often gave way to simplified, even erroneous religious education texts and classes that tended to dwell more on relating to one's neighbor than on the entire content of the faith. Dissident theologians often attracted large followings of Catholics who uncritically accepted their erroneous positions. And even official representatives of the Catholic Church

[1] William Coulson in telephone interview with author, March 13, 1995. See chapter 9 for his experiences working with renewal of religious orders.

sometimes misrepresented Church teachings. These influences also crept into religious orders, with disastrous results.

The Leadership of Popes John Paul II and Benedict XVI

Both John Paul II and Benedict XVI expressed deep concerns about the post-conciliar turmoil that caused division in the Church and a dilution of the faith. They commented on the modern rejection of universal moral norms, which has damaged the Church and society at large.

Pope John Paul II identified "a world which has experienced marvelous achievements but which seems to have lost its sense of ultimate realities and of existence itself". And he called for more in-depth catechesis of Catholics as well as evangelization of nonbelievers in order to help cure an ailing society: "Particularly in countries with ancient Christian roots, and occasionally in the younger Churches as well, where entire groups of the baptized have lost a sense of the faith, or even no longer consider themselves members of the Church, and live a life far removed from Christ and his gospel. In this case what is needed is a 'new evangelization' or a 're-evangelization'." [2]

Pope Benedict echoed this theme by calling for a "re-proposing of the Gospel to those regions awaiting the first evangelization and to those regions where the roots of Christianity are deep but who have experienced a serious crisis of faith due to secularization".[3] He emphasized throughout his pontificate the damage done to the faith and to society by the "dictatorship of relativism" that acknowledges no objective truth: "Today, a particularly insidious obstacle to the task of education is the massive presence in our society and culture of that relativism which, recognising nothing as definitive, leaves as the ultimate criterion only the self with its desires. And under the semblance of freedom it becomes a prison for each one, for it separates

---

[2] Pope John Paul II, *Redemptoris Missio*, December 7, 1990, 33, www.vatican.va/holy_father_john_paul_ii/encyclicals/documents/hf_jp-ii_enc_07121990_redemptoris-missio_en.html (accessed September 21, 2010).

[3] Pope Benedict XVI, "Homily of First Vespers on the Solemnity of the Holy Apostles Peter and Paul", June 28, 2010, www.vatican.va/holy_father/benedict_xvi/homilies/2010/documents/hf_ben-xvi_hom_20100628_vespri-pietro-paulo_en.html (accessed September 21, 2012).

people from one another, locking each person into his or her own ego."[4]

However, neither of the two popes tried to take the Church back to pre–Vatican II days, as their critics often charged. Rather, both have called for adherence to the actual teachings of the Council rather than to some nebulous "spirit of Vatican II" that many reformers in religious orders had assumed gave legitimacy to their proposals. What is needed is deeper study and understanding of Vatican II documents, as Pope John Paul II recommended in his 1994 apostolic letter *Tertio Millennio Adveniente*:

> The reflection of the faithful in the second year of preparation ought to focus particularly *on the value of unity* within the Church, to which the various gifts and charisms bestowed upon her by the Spirit are directed. In this regard, it will be opportune to promote a deeper understanding of the ecclesiological doctrine of the Second Vatican Council as contained primarily in the Dogmatic Constitution *Lumen Gentium*. This important document has expressly emphasized that the unity of the Body of Christ *is founded on the activity of the Spirit*, guaranteed by the Apostolic Ministry and sustained by mutual love (cf. *1 Cor* 13:1–8). This catechetical enrichment of the faith cannot fail to bring the members of the People of God to a more mature awareness of their own responsibilities, as well as to a more lively sense of the importance of ecclesial obedience.[5]

Even before he became pope, Benedict XVI had sounded this theme, as quoted in *The Ratzinger Report*:

> To defend the true tradition of the Church today means to defend the Council. It is also our fault if we have at times provided a pretext (to "right" and "left" alike) to view Vatican II as a "break" and an abandonment of the tradition. There is, instead, a continuity that allows neither a return to the past nor a flight forward, neither anachronistic longings nor unjustified impatience. We must remain faithful to the

---

[4] Pope Benedict XVI address to the participants in the Ecclesial Diocesan Convention in Rome, June 6, 2005, www.vatican.a/holy_father/benedict_xvi/speeches/2005/jne/documents/hf_ben-xvi_spe_20050606_convegno-famiglia_en.html (accessed September 21, 2012).

[5] Pope John Paul II, *Tertio Millennio Adveniente*, November 10, 1994, 47, www.vatican.va/holy_father//john_paul_ii/apost_letters/documents/hf_jp-ii_apl_10111994_tertio-adveniente_en.html (accessed September 21, 2012).

today of the Church, not the yesterday or tomorrow. And this today of the Church is the documents of Vatican II, without *reservations* that amputate them and without *arbitrariness* that distorts them.[6]

Benedict XVI proclaimed as a Year of Faith the period from October 11, 2012, the fiftieth anniversary of the opening of the Second Vatican Council, to the solemnity of Christ the King in November 2013. The pope explained in his apostolic letter *Porta Fidei* that this year would be "a good opportunity to usher the whole Church into a time of particular reflection and rediscovery of the faith".

Benedict noted that the last Year of Faith had been announced by Pope Paul VI in 1967 as a way for the entire Church to reappropriate knowledge of the faith. The "great upheavals" of 1967, he explained, "made even more evident" the need for such a Church-wide celebration:

> In some respects, my venerable predecessor saw this Year as a "consequence and a necessity of the postconciliar period", fully conscious of the grave difficulties of the time, especially with regard to the profession of the true faith and its correct interpretation. It seemed to me that timing the launch of the Year of Faith to coincide with the fiftieth anniversary of the opening of the Second Vatican Council would provide a good opportunity to help people understand that the texts bequeathed by the Council fathers, in the words of Blessed John Paul II, "have lost nothing of their value or brilliance. They need to be read correctly, to be widely known and taken to heart as important and normative texts of the Magisterium, within the Church's Tradition.... I feel more than ever in duty bound to point to the Council as the great grace bestowed on the Church in the twentieth century: there we find a sure compass by which to take our bearings in the century now beginning." I would also like to emphasize strongly what I had occasion to say concerning the Council a few months after my election as Successor of Peter: "if we interpret and implement it guided by a right hermeneutic, it can be and can become increasingly powerful for the ever necessary renewal of the Church." [7]

---

[6] Joseph Cardinal Ratzinger and Vittorio Messori, *The Ratzinger Report* (San Francisco: Ignatius Press, 1987), 31.

[7] Pope Benedict XVI, *Porta Fidei*, October 17, 2011, 5, *Origins*, October 27, 2011.

The Popes' Influence on Religious Life

The teaching and example of John Paul II and Benedict XVI have had a profound effect on the Church. Many Catholics, whether laity, clergy, or religious, are discovering anew the richness of the faith as well as of the documents of Vatican II. Furthermore, many of the young people recently drawn to the priesthood or religious life have cited in particular the influence of these two popes, and many have related that they heard their vocation call while attending a World Youth Day. Religious who have started new religious orders also have spoken of the inspiration they had received from the pontiffs, and some long-existing orders have embraced the popes' teachings with enthusiasm.

Just three days after Pope Benedict announced that he would resign at the end of February 2013, he met with the parish priests and clergy of the Diocese of Rome and talked about the Second Vatican Council, which he had attended. The media saw the Council as a political struggle for power between different currents in the church, he explained, and the media took the side "of whatever faction best suited their world". This "virtual" Council interpreted through the media "created many calamities, so many problems, so much misery, in reality: seminaries closed, convents closed, liturgy trivialized", he said.

"But the real strength of the Council was present and slowly it has emerged and is becoming the real power which is also true reform, true renewal of the Church", he continued. "It seems to me that 50 years after the Council, we see how this virtual Council is breaking down, getting lost and the true Council is emerging with all its spiritual strength. And it is our task, in this Year of Faith, starting from this Year of Faith, to work so that the true Council with the power of the Holy Spirit is realized and the Church is really renewed." [8]

Unfortunately, many orders of women have continued to pursue a path that is leading them further and further from the faith and the life of the church. This path has led to a rejection of central teachings of the Church and conflict with the magisterial authority responsible for explaining and preserving those teachings. It has caused division

---

[8] Pope Benedict XVI, talk to parish priests and clergy of Rome, February 14, 2013, http://en.radiovaticana.va/news/2013/02/14/pope_to_rome's_priests:_the_second_vatican_council,_as_i_saw_it/en1-664858 (accessed February 14, 2013).

among US sisters and the implosion of once-great orders. Yet, many consecrated women remain convinced that this is the right path to be on and that only they have the ability to discern the direction they should follow.

As this edition went to press, the results of the apostolic visitation of US sisters and the doctrinal assessment of the LCWR were still pending. While some sisters have been angered by this interference from the Vatican, others have breathed a sigh of relief. As one sister remarked about the visitation, "This is the first time anyone from the Vatican ever asked me how I'm doing."

The moves by the Holy See have prompted some religious orders to reassess themselves, and many sisters expect that this process will bear much fruit.

Into the Future

Sociologist Sister Patricia Wittberg has pointed out there will always be people who want to live out the universal call to holiness in a more radical manner than the lifestyle pursued by the ordinary lay-person.[9] And in *Vita Consecrata* Pope John Paul II stressed that "the profession of the evangelical counsels indisputably belongs to the life and holiness of the church" and will always be an essential character-istic of the Church (29).

Hopefully some of the change-oriented religious orders will be able to reform themselves and begin attracting young vocations once again. Many of them, however, will not survive long in the twenty-first cen-tury, for they have large populations of elderly and few young sisters. Many of these orders recognize their plight, and some are making plans to hand off their properties and their works to lay associates when the last remnant of sisters is unable to function. This is indeed a sad situation, given the rich contributions those orders have made to the Catholic Church. Another sad situation is faced by those sisters who, in spite of leaders who have rejected Church teachings, remain faithful to the Church and their vows under difficult circumstances. These women persist in their determination to imitate Jesus, to be a sign to the world that the ultimate goal of every person is union with

---

[9] Carey, "Why 'People on Fire' Fizzled Out", 5.

God. This is exactly what John Paul II asked of sisters in "sad situations of crisis":

> By persevering faithfully in the consecrated life, consecrated persons confess with great effectiveness before the world their unwavering trust in the Lord of history, in whose hands are the history and destiny of individuals, institutions and peoples, and therefore also the realization in time of his gifts. Sad situations of crisis invite consecrated persons courageously to proclaim their faith in Christ's death and resurrection that they may become a visible sign of the passage from death to life.[10]

Though the total number of US sisters will decline precipitously for the next several years because of current demographic trends, this does not mean that religious life for women is over in this country.

Indeed, there is much good news to celebrate. Some well-established religious orders are thriving with the infusion of new vocations, and many new foundations are doing likewise, though some of those are still small and fragile.

There likely will never again be nearly two hundred thousand sisters serving the Church in the United States, as there were in 1965, for both society and the Church have changed. Nevertheless, the future is bright for the more than one hundred religious orders of women in this country that live the classical model of religious life. They are attracting serious, faith-filled young women who want to give themselves to the Lord with an undivided heart.

These dedicated and inspirational women, and those who follow them, are a gift to the Church and to the world as they continue the beautiful legacy of all the sisters who have gone before them.

[10] *Vita Consecrata*, 63.

APPENDIX

Doctrinal Assessment of the
Leadership Conference of Women Religious

I. Introduction

The context in which the current doctrinal Assessment of the Leadership Conference of Women Religious in the United States of America is best situated is articulated by Pope John Paul II in the Post-Synodal Apostolic Exhortation *Vita consecrata* of 1996.

Commenting on the genius of the charism of religious life in the Church, Pope John Paul says:

> In founders and foundresses we see a constant and lively sense of the Church, which they manifest by their full participation in all aspects of the Church's life, and in their ready obedience to the Bishops and especially to the Roman Pontiff. Against this background of love towards Holy Church "the pillar and bulwark of truth" (1 Tim 3:15), we readily understand ... the full ecclesial communion which the Saints, founders and foundresses, have shared in diverse and often difficult times and circumstances. They are examples which consecrated persons need constantly to recall if they are to resist the particularly strong centrifugal and disruptive forces at work today. A distinctive aspect of ecclesial communion is allegiance of mind and heart to the Magisterium of the Bishops, an allegiance which must be lived honestly and clearly testified to before the People of God by all consecrated persons, especially those involved in theological research, teaching, publishing, catechesis and the use of the means of social communication. Because consecrated persons have a special place in the Church, their attitude in this regard is of immense importance for the whole People of God. (46)

The Holy See acknowledges with gratitude the great contribution of women Religious to the Church in the United States as seen particularly in the many schools, hospitals, and institutions of support for the poor which have been founded and staffed by Religious over the years. Pope John Paul II expressed this gratitude well in his meeting with Religious from the United States in San Francisco on September 17, 1987, when he said:

> I rejoice because of your deep love of the Church and your generous service to God's people. . . . The extensive Catholic educational and health care systems, the highly developed network of social services in the Church—none of this would exist today, were it not for your highly motivated dedication and the dedication of those who have gone before you. The spiritual vigor of so many Catholic people testifies to the efforts of generations of religious in this land. The history of the Church in this country is in large measure your history at the service of God's people.

The renewal of the Leadership Conference of Women Religious which is the goal of this doctrinal Assessment is in support of this essential charism of Religious which has been so obvious in the life and growth of the Catholic Church in the United States.

While recognizing that this doctrinal Assessment concerns a particular conference of major superiors and therefore does not intend to offer judgment on the faith and life of Women Religious in the member Congregations which belong to that conference, nevertheless the Assessment reveals serious doctrinal problems which affect many in Consecrated Life. On the doctrinal level, this crisis is characterized by a diminution of the fundamental Christological center and focus of religious consecration which leads, in turn, to a loss of a "constant and lively sense of the Church" among some Religious. The current doctrinal Assessment arises out of a sincere concern for the life of faith in some Institutes of Consecrated Life and Societies of Apostolic Life. It arises as well from a conviction that the work of any conference of major superiors of women Religious can and should be a fruitful means of addressing the contemporary situation and supporting religious life in its most "radical" sense—that is, in the *faith* in which it is *rooted*. According to Canon Law, conferences of major superiors are an expression of the collaboration between the Holy

See, Superiors General, and the local Conferences of Bishops in support of consecrated life. The overarching concern of the doctrinal Assessment is, therefore, to assist the Leadership Conference of Women Religious in the United States in implementing an ecclesiology of communion founded on faith in Jesus Christ and the Church as the essential foundation for its important service to religious Communities and to all those in consecrated life.

II. The Doctrinal Assessment

The decision of the Congregation for the Doctrine of the Faith (CDF) to undertake a doctrinal Assessment of the Leadership Conference of Women Religious (LCWR) was communicated to the LCWR Presidency during their meeting with Cardinal William Levada in Rome on April 8, 2008. At that meeting, three major areas of concern were given as motivating the CDF's decision to initiate the Assessment:

- **Addresses at the LCWR Assemblies.** Addresses given during LCWR annual Assemblies manifest problematic statements and serious theological, even doctrinal errors. The Cardinal offered as an example specific passages of Sr. Laurie Brink's address about some Religious "moving beyond the Church" or even beyond Jesus. This is a challenge not only to core Catholic beliefs; such a rejection of faith is also a serious source of scandal and is incompatible with religious life. Such unacceptable positions routinely go unchallenged by the LCWR, which should provide resources for member Congregations to foster an ecclesial vision of religious life, thus helping to correct an erroneous vision of the Catholic faith as an important exercise of charity. Some might see in Sr. Brink's analysis a phenomenological snapshot of religious life today. But Pastors of the Church should also see in it a cry for help.
- **Policies of Corporate Dissent.** The Cardinal spoke of this issue in reference to letters the CDF received from "Leadership Teams" of various Congregations, among them LCWR Officers, protesting the Holy See's actions regarding the question of women's ordination and of a correct pastoral approach to ministry to homosexual persons, e.g. letters about New Ways Ministry's conferences. The

terms of the letters suggest that these sisters collectively take a position not in agreement with the Church's teaching on human sexuality. It is a serious matter when these Leadership Teams are not providing effective leadership and example to their communities, but place themselves outside the Church's teaching.

- **Radical Feminism.** The Cardinal noted a prevalence of certain radical feminist themes incompatible with the Catholic faith in some of the programs and presentations sponsored by the LCWR, including theological interpretations that risk distorting faith in Jesus and his loving Father who sent his Son for the salvation of the world. Moreover, some commentaries on "patriarchy" distort the way in which Jesus has structured sacramental life in the Church; others even undermine the revealed doctrines of the Holy Trinity, the divinity of Christ, and the inspiration of Sacred Scripture.

Subsequently, in a letter dated February 18, 2009, the CDF confirmed its decision to undertake a doctrinal Assessment of the LCWR and named Most Rev. Leonard Blair, Bishop of Toledo, as the CDF's Delegate for the Assessment. This decision was further discussed with the LCWR Presidency during their visit to the CDF on April 22, 2009. During that meeting, Cardinal Levada confirmed that the doctrinal Assessment comes as a result of several years of examination of the doctrinal content of statements from the LCWR and of their annual conferences. The Assessment's primary concern is the doctrine of the faith that has been revealed by God in Jesus Christ, presented in written form in the divinely inspired Scriptures, and handed on in the Apostolic Tradition under the guidance of the Church's Magisterium. It is this Apostolic teaching, so richly and fully taught by the Second Vatican Council, that should underlie the work of a conference of major superiors of Religious which, by its nature, has a canonical relationship to the Holy See and many of whose members are of Pontifical right.

Most Rev. Leonard Blair communicated a set of doctrinal *Observations* to the LCWR in a letter dated May 11, 2009, and subsequently met with the Presidency on May 27, 2009. The LCWR Presidency responded to the *Observations* in a letter dated October 20, 2009. Based on this response, and on subsequent correspondence between the

Presidency of the LCWR and the Delegate, Bishop Blair submitted his findings to the CDF on December 22, 2009.

On June 25, 2010, Bishop Blair presented further documentation on the content of the LCWR's *Mentoring Leadership Manual* and also on the organizations associated with the LCWR, namely *Network* and *The Resource Center for Religious Institutes*. The documentation reveals that, while there has been a great deal of work on the part of LCWR promoting issues of social justice in harmony with the Church's social doctrine, it is silent on the right to life from conception to natural death, a question that is part of the lively public debate about abortion and euthanasia in the United States. Further, issues of crucial importance to the life of Church and society, such as the Church's Biblical view of family life and human sexuality, are not part of the LCWR agenda in a way that promotes Church teaching. Moreover, occasional public statements by the LCWR that disagree with or challenge positions taken by the Bishops, who are the Church's authentic teachers of faith and morals, are not compatible with its purpose.

All of the documentation from the doctrinal Assessment including the LCWR responses was presented to the Ordinary Session of the Cardinal and Bishop Members of the CDF on January 12, 2011. The decision of that Ordinary Session was:

1. The current doctrinal and pastoral situation of the LCWR is grave and a matter of serious concern, also given the influence the LCWR exercises on religious Congregations in other parts of the world;
2. After the currently-ongoing Visitation of religious communities of women in the United States is brought to a conclusion, the Holy See should intervene with the prudent steps necessary to effect a reform of the LCWR;
3. The Congregation for the Doctrine of the Faith will examine the various forms of canonical intervention available for the resolution of the problematic aspects present in the LCWR.

The Holy Father, Pope Benedict XVI, in an Audience granted to the Prefect of the Congregation for the Doctrine of the Faith, Cardinal William Joseph Levada, on January 14, 2011, approved the decisions of the Ordinary Session of the Congregation, and ordered their implementation. This action by the Holy Father should be understood in virtue of the mandate given by the Lord to Simon Peter as the rock on which He founded his Church (cf. Luke 22:32): "I have prayed for you, Peter, that your faith may not fail; and when you have turned to me, you must strengthen the faith of your brothers and sisters." This Scripture passage has long been applied to the role of the Successors of Peter as Head of the Apostolic College of Bishops; it also applies to the role of the Pope as Chief Shepherd and Pastor of the Universal Church. Not least among the flock to whom the Pope's pastoral concern is directed are women Religious of apostolic life, who through the past several centuries have been so instrumental in building up the faith and life of the Holy Church of God, and witnessing to God's love for humanity in so many charitable and apostolic works.

Since the Final Report of the Apostolic Visitation of women Religious in the United States has now been submitted to the Holy See (in December, 2011), the CDF turns to the implementation of the above-mentioned decisions approved by the Holy Father as an extension of his pastoral outreach to the Church in the United States. For the purpose of this implementation, and in consultation with the Congregation for Institutes of Consecrated Life and Societies of Apostolic Life (CICLSAL) and the Congregation for Bishops, the Congregation for the Doctrine of the Faith has decided to execute the mandate to assist in the necessary reform of the Leadership Conference of Women Religious through the appointment of an Archbishop Delegate, who will—with the assistance of a group of advisors (bishops, priests, and women Religious)—proceed to work with the leadership of the LCWR to achieve the goals necessary to address the problems outlined in this statement. The mandate given to the Delegate provides the structure and flexibility for the delicate work of such implementation.

The moment for such a common effort seems all the more opportune in view of an implementation of the recommendations of the recent Apostolic Visitation of women Religious in the United States, and in view of this year's 50th anniversary of the beginning of the Second Vatican Council, whose theological vision and practical recommendations for Consecrated Life can serve as a providential template for review and renewal of religious life in the United States, and of the mandate of Church law for the work of this conference of major superiors to which the large majority of congregations of women Religious in the United States belong.

III. Implementation: Conclusions of Doctrinal Assessment and Mandate

1) Principal Findings of the Doctrinal Assessment

LCWR General Assemblies, Addresses, and Occasional Papers   One of the principal means by which the LCWR promotes its particular vision of religious life is through the annual Assemblies it sponsors. During the Assessment process, Bishop Blair, in his letter of May 11, 2009, presented the LCWR Presidency with a study and doctrinal evaluation of keynote addresses, presidential addresses, and Leadership Award addresses over a 10 year period. This study found that the talks, while not scholarly theological discourses *per se*, do have significant doctrinal and moral content and implications which often contradict or ignore magisterial teaching.

In its response, the Presidency of the LCWR maintained that it does not knowingly invite speakers who take a stand against a teaching of the Church "when it has been declared as authoritative teaching." Further, the Presidency maintains that the assertions made by speakers are their own and do not imply intent on the part of the LCWR. Given the facts examined, however, this response is inadequate. The Second Vatican Council clearly indicates that an authentic teaching of the Church calls for the religious submission of intellect and will, and is not limited to defined dogmas or *ex cathedra* statements (cf. *Lumen gentium*, 25). For example, the LCWR publicly expressed in 1977 its refusal to assent to the teaching of *Inter insigniores* on the reservation of priestly ordination to men. This public refusal has never been corrected. Beyond this, the CDF understands that speakers at conferences or general assemblies do not submit their texts for prior review by the LCWR Presidency. But, as the Assessment demonstrated, the sum of those talks over the years is a matter of serious concern.

Several of the addresses at LCWR conferences present a vision or description of religious life that does not conform to the faith and practice of the Church. Since the LCWR leadership has offered no clarification about such statements, some might infer that such positions are endorsed by them. As an entity approved by the Holy See for the coordination and support of religious Communities in the United

States, LCWR also has a positive responsibility for the promotion of
the faith and for providing its member Communities and the wider
Catholic public with clear and persuasive positions in support of the
Church's vision of religious life.

Some speakers claim that dissent from the doctrine of the Church is
justified as an exercise of the prophetic office. But this is based upon
a mistaken understanding of the dynamic of prophecy in the Church:
it justifies dissent by positing the possibility of divergence between the
Church's magisterium and a "legitimate" theological intuition of some
of the faithful. "Prophecy," as a methodological principle, is here directed
at the Magisterium and the Church's pastors, whereas true prophecy
is a grace which accompanies the exercise of the responsibilities of the
Christian life and ministries within the Church, regulated and verified
by the Church's faith and teaching office. Some of the addresses at
LCWR-sponsored events perpetuate a distorted ecclesiological vision,
and have scant regard for the role of the Magisterium as the guarantor
of the authentic interpretation of the Church's faith.

The analysis of the General Assemblies, Presidential Addresses, and
Occasional Papers reveals, therefore, a two-fold problem. The first consists in positive error (i.e. doctrinally problematic statements or formal
refutation of Church teaching found in talks given at LCWR-
sponsored conferences or General Assemblies). The second level of
the problem concerns the silence and inaction of the LCWR in the
face of such error, given its responsibility to support a vision of religious life in harmony with that of the Church and to promote a solid
doctrinal basis for religious life. With this Assessment, the CDF intends
to assist the LCWR in placing its activity into a wider context of
religious life in the universal Church in order to foster a vision of
consecrated life consistent with the Church's teaching. In this wider
context, the CDF notes the absence of initiatives by the LCWR aimed
at promoting the reception of the Church's teaching, especially on
difficult issues such as Pope John Paul II's Apostolic Letter *Ordinatio
sacerdotalis* and Church teaching about homosexuality.

*The Role of the LCWR in the Doctrinal Formation of Religious Superiors and
Formators* The program for new Superiors and Formators of member
Communities and other resources provided to these Communities is

an area in which the LCWR exercises an influence. The doctrinal Assessment found that many of the materials prepared by the LCWR for these purposes (*Occasional Papers, Systems Thinking Handbook*) do not have a sufficient doctrinal foundation. These materials recommend strategies for dialogue, for example when sisters disagree about basic matters of Catholic faith or moral practice, but it is not clear whether this dialogue is directed towards reception of Church teaching. As a case in point, the *Systems Thinking Handbook* presents a situation in which sisters differ over whether the Eucharist should be at the center of a special community celebration since the celebration of Mass requires an ordained priest, something which some sisters find "objectionable." According to the *Systems Thinking Handbook* this difficulty is rooted in differences at the level of belief, but also in different cognitive models (the "Western mind" as opposed to an "Organic mental model"). These models, rather than the teaching of the Church, are offered as tools for the resolution of the controversy of whether or not to celebrate Mass. Thus the *Systems Thinking Handbook* presents a neutral model of Congregational leadership that does not give due attention to the responsibility which Superiors are called to exercise, namely, leading sisters into a greater appreciation or integration of the truth of the Catholic faith.

The Final Report of the Apostolic Visitation of Religious Communities of Women in the United States (July, 2011) found that the formation programs among several communities that belong to the LCWR did not have significant doctrinal content but rather were oriented toward professional formation regarding particular issues of ministerial concern to the Institute. Other programs reportedly stressed their own charism and history, and/or the Church's social teaching or social justice in general, with little attention to basic Catholic doctrine, such as that contained in the authoritative text of the *Catechism of the Catholic Church*. While these formation programs were not directly the object of this doctrinal Assessment, it may nevertheless be concluded that confusion about the Church's authentic doctrine of the faith is reinforced, rather than corrected, by the lack of doctrinal content in the resources provided by the LCWR for Superiors and Formators. The doctrinal confusion which has undermined solid catechesis over the years demonstrates the need for sound doctrinal formation—both initial and ongoing—for women

Religious and novices just as it does for priests and seminarians, and for laity in ministry and apostolic life. In this way, we can hope that the secularized contemporary culture, with its negative impact on the very identity of Religious as Christians and members of the Church, on their religious practice and common life, and on their authentic Christian spirituality, moral life, and liturgical practice, can be more readily overcome.

2) The Mandate for Implementation of the Doctrinal Assessment

In the universal law of the Church (Code of Canon Law [C.I.C.] for the Latin Church), Canons 708 and 709 address the establishment and work of conferences of major superiors:

> Can. 708: Major superiors can be associated usefully in conferences or councils so that by common efforts they work to achieve more fully the purpose of the individual institutes, always without prejudice to their autonomy, character, and proper spirit, or to transact common affairs, or to establish appropriate coordination and cooperation with the conferences of bishops and also with individual bishops.
>
> Can. 709: Conferences of major superiors are to have their own statutes approved by the Holy See, by which alone they can be erected even as a juridic person and under whose supreme direction they remain.

In the light of these canons, and in view of the findings of the doctrinal Assessment, it is clear that greater emphasis needs to be placed both on the relationship of the LCWR with the Conference of Bishops, and on the need to provide a sound doctrinal foundation in the faith of the Church as they "work to achieve more fully the purpose of the individual institutes."

Therefore in order to implement a process of review and conformity to the teachings and discipline of the Church, the Holy See, through the Congregation for the Doctrine of the Faith, will appoint an Archbishop Delegate, assisted by two Bishops, for review, guidance and approval, where necessary, of the work of the LCWR. The Delegate will report to the CDF, which will inform and consult with the Congregation for Institutes of Consecrated Life and Societies of Apostolic Life and the Congregation for Bishops.

The mandate of the Delegate is to include the following:

1. To revise LCWR Statutes to ensure greater clarity about the scope of the mission and responsibilities of this conference of major superiors. The revised Statutes will be submitted to the Holy See for approval by the CICLSAL.

2. To review LCWR plans and programs, including General Assemblies and publications, to ensure that the scope of the LCWR's mission is fulfilled in accord with Church teachings and discipline. In particular:

   • *Systems Thinking Handbook* will be withdrawn from circulation pending revision.
   • LCWR programs for (future) Superiors and Formators will be reformed.
   • Speakers/presenters at major programs will be subject to approval by Delegate.

3. To create new LCWR programs for member Congregations for the development of initial and ongoing formation material that provides a deepened understanding of the Church's doctrine of the faith.

4. To review and offer guidance in the application of liturgical norms and texts. For example: The Eucharist and the Liturgy of the Hours will have a place of priority in LCWR events and programs.

5. To review LCWR links with affiliated organizations, e.g. Network and Resource Center for Religious Life.

The mandate of the Delegate will be for a period of up to five years, as deemed necessary. In order to ensure the necessary liaison with the USCCB (in view of Can. 708), the Conference of Bishops will be asked to establish a formal link (e.g. a committee structure) with the Delegate and Assistant Delegate Bishops. In order to facilitate the achievement of these goals, the Delegate is authorized to form an Advisory Team (clergy, women Religious, and experts) to assist in the work of implementation. It will be the task of the Archbishop Delegate to work collaboratively with the officers of the LCWR to achieve the goals outlined in this document, and to report on the progress of this work to the Holy See. Such reports will be reviewed with the Delegate at regular interdicasterial meetings of the CDF and the CICLSAL. In this way, the Holy See hopes to offer an important contribution to the future of religious life in the Church in the United States.

SELECTED BIBLIOGRAPHY

Beane, Marjorie Noterman. *From Framework to Freedom: A History of the Sister Formation Conference.* Lanham, Md.: University Press of America, Inc., 1993.

Becker, Joseph M., SJ. *The Re-Formed Jesuits.* San Francisco: Ignatius Press, 1992.

Bernstein, Marcelle. *The Nuns.* Philadelphia: Lippincott, 1976.

Bunson, Matthew, ed. *Our Sunday Visitor's Encyclopedia of Catholic History.* Huntington, Ind.: Our Sunday Visitor Publishing Division, Our Sunday Visitor, Inc., 1995.

Burns, Gene. *The Frontiers of Catholicism: The Politics of Ideology in a Liberal World.* Berkeley and Los Angeles: University of California Press, 1992.

Caruso, Michael P., SJ. *When the Sisters Said Farewell.* Lanham, Md.: Rowman & Littlefield Education, division of Rowman & Littlefield Publishers, Inc., 2012.

Caspary, Anita M. *Witness to Integrity: The Crisis of the Immaculate Heart Community of California.* Collegeville, Mn.: The Liturgical Press, 2003.

Center for Applied Research in the Apostolate. *Recent Vocations to Religious Life.* August 2009.

Chittister, Joan, OSB, et al. *Climb Along the Cutting Edge: An Analysis of Change in Religious Life.* New York: Paulist Press, 1977.

Chittister, Joan, OSB. *The Fire in These Ashes: A Spirituality of Contemporary Religious Life.* Kansas City: Sheed & Ward, 1995.

Congregation for Catholic Education. *Consecrated Persons and Their Mission in Schools: Reflections and Guidelines.* Origins, January 23, 2003.

Congregation for Institutes of Consecrated Life and Societies of Apostolic Life. *Essential Elements in the Church's Teaching on Religious Life as Applied to Institutes Dedicated to Works of the Apostolate.* Origins, July 7, 1983.

——. *Fraternal Life in Community.* February 19, 1994. Executive Summary. *Origins,* March 24, 1994.

——. *The Service of Authority and Obedience. Origins,* June 12, 2008.

——. *Starting Afresh from Christ: A Renewed Commitment to Consecrated Life in the Third Millennium. Origins,* July 4, 2002.

Consortium Perfectae Caritatis. *"Widening the Dialogue . . . ?"* Huntington, Ind.: Our Sunday Visitor, Inc., 1974.

Courtois, Abbé Gaston, ed. *The States of Perfection According to the Teaching of the Church: Papal Documents from Leo XIII to Pius XII.* Westminster, Md.: The Newman Press, 1961.

Creek, Mary Immaculate, CSC. *A Panorama: 1844–1977, Saint Mary's College Notre Dame, Indiana.* Notre Dame: Saint Mary's College, 1977.

Daley, Robert J., SJ, et al., eds. *Religious Life in the American Church.* New York: Paulist Press, 1984.

Darcy, Catherine C., R.S.M. *The Institute of the Sisters of Mercy of the Americas: The Canonical Development of the Proposed Governance Model.* Lanham, Md.: University Press of America, Inc., 1993.

DiIanni, Albert, SM. *Religious Life as Adventure: Renewal, Refounding or Reform?* Staten Island, N.Y.: Alba House, 1994.

Doely, Sarah Bentley, ed. *Women's Liberation and the Church: The New Demand for Freedom in the Life of the Christian Church.* New York: Association Press, 1970.

Ebaugh, Helen Rose Fuchs. *Out of the Cloister: A Study of Organizational Dilemmas.* Austin: University of Texas Press, 1977.

——. *Women in the Vanishing Cloister: Organizational Decline in Catholic Religious Orders in the U.S.* New Brunswick, N.J.: Rutgers University Press, 1993.

Felknor, Laurie, ed. *The Crisis in Religious Vocations: An Inside View.* New York: Paulist Press, 1989.

Fleming, David L., SJ, and Elizabeth McDonough, OP, eds. *The Church and Consecrated Life.* Saint Louis: Review for Religious, 1996.

Florence, Mother Mary, SL, ed. *Religious Life in the Church Today: Prospect and Retrospect.* Notre Dame: University of Notre Dame Press, 1962.

Foley, Nadine, OP, ed. *Claiming Our Truth: Reflections on Identity.* Washington: LCWR, 1988.

Gaillardetz, Richard R., ed. *When the Magisterium Intervenes: The Magisterium and Theologians in Today's Church.* Collegeville, Mn.: Liturgical Press, 2012.

Gleason, Philip. *Contending with Modernity: Catholic Higher Education in the Twentieth Century*. New York: Oxford University Press, 1995.

Gribble, Richard, CSC, ed. *Religious Life in America Today: A Response to the Crisis*. Washington, D.C.: Catholic University of America Press, 2011.

Grollmes, Eugene E., SJ, ed. *Vows But No Walls: An Analysis of Religious Life*. Saint Louis: B. Herder Book Co., 1967.

John Paul II. "Renewal and Rebirth of the Consecrated Life". June 13, 1998. *Origins*, August 13, 1998.

———. *Vita Consecrata* (On Consecrated Life). March 28, 1996. *Origins*, April 4, 1996.

Kauffman, Christopher J. *Ministry and Meaning: A Religious History of Catholic Health Care in the United States*. New York: The Crossroad Publishing Company, 1995.

Kelly, Rosemary Skinner, and Rosemary Radford Ruether, eds. *Encyclopedia of Women and Religion in North America*. Bloomington, Ind.: Indiana University Press, 2006.

King, Margot H., ed. *A Leaf from the Great Tree of God: Essays in Honour of Ritamary Bradley*. Toronto: Peregrina Publishing Company, 1994.

Kolmer, Elizabeth, ASC. *Religious Women in the United States: A Survey of the Influential Literature from 1950 to 1983*. Wilmington, Del.: Michael Glazier, Inc., 1984.

LCWR. *Widening the Dialogue*. Ottawa: Canadian Religious Conference; Washington, D.C.: LCWR, 1974.

Leddy, Mary Jo. *Reweaving Religious Life: Beyond the Liberal Model*. Mystic, Conn.: Twenty-Third Publications, 1990.

Morey, Melanie M., and John J. Piderit, SJ. *Catholic Higher Education*. New York: Oxford University Press, 2006.

Muckenhirn, Sister M. Charles Borromeo, CSC, ed. *The Changing Sister*. Notre Dame: Fides Publishers, 1965.

Murray, Mary Cecilia, OP. *Other Waters: A History of the Dominican Sisters of Newburgh, N.Y.* Old Brookville, N.Y.: Brookville Books, 1993.

NCAN. *If Anyone Can, NCAN: Twenty Years of Speaking Out*. Chicago: NCAN, 1989.

Neal, Marie Augusta, SND. *Catholic Sisters in Transition: From the 1960s to the 1980s*. Wilmington, Md.: Michael Glazier, 1984.

———. *From Nuns to Sisters: An Expanding Vocation.* Mystic, Conn.: Twenty-Third Publications, 1990.

Nygren, David, CM, and Miriam Ukeritis, CSJ. "Executive Summary of Study on the Future of Religious Orders in the United States." *Origins,* September 24, 1992.

O'Connor, David F., ST. *Witness and Service: Questions about Religious Life Today.* New York: Paulist Press, 1990.

Pacwa, Mitch, SJ. *Catholics and the New Age: How Good People Are Being Drawn into Jungian Psychology, the Enneagram, and the Age of Aquarius.* Ann Arbor: Servant Publications, 1992.

Philibert, Paul J., OP, ed. *Living in the Meantime: Concerning the Transformation of Religious Life.* New York: Paulist Press, 1994.

Quinonez, Lora Ann, CDP, and Mary Daniel Turner, SNDdeN. *The Transformation of American Catholic Sisters.* Philadelphia: Temple University Press, 1992.

Quinonez, Lora, CDP, ed. *Starting Points: Six Essays Based on the Experience of U.S. Women Religious.* Washington, D.C.: LCWR, 1980.

Ratzinger, Joseph Cardinal and Vittorio Messori. *The Ratzinger Report.* San Francisco: Ignatius Press, 1987.

Sanders, Helen, SL. *More Than a Renewal: Loretto Before and After Vatican II: 1952–1977.* Nerinx, Ky.: Sisters of Loretto, 1982.

Schneiders, Sandra M., IHM. *New WineSkins: Re-imagining Religious Life Today.* New York: Paulist Press, 1986.

———. *Prophets in Their Own Country: Women Religious Bearing Witness to the Gospel in a Troubled Church.* Maryknoll, N.Y.: Orbis Books, 2011.

Sommers, Christina Hoff. *Who Stole Feminism? How Women Have Betrayed Women.* New York: Simon & Schuster, 1994.

Stewart, George. *Marvels of Charity: History of American Sisters and Nuns.* Huntington, Ind.: Our Sunday Visitor Publishing Division, Our Sunday Visitor, Inc., 1994.

Synod of Bishops General Secretariat. *The Consecrated Life and Its Role in the Church and in the World: "Lineamenta" for the 1994 Synod of Bishops. Origins,* December 10, 1992.

Vatican Council II. *The Decree on the Renewal of Religious Life of Vatican Council II (Perfectae Caritatis).* Translated by Austin Flannery, O.P. Glen Rock, N.J.: Paulist Press, 1966.

Ware, Ann Patrick, SL, ed. *Midwives of the Future: American Sisters Tell Their Story.* Kansas City: Leaven Press, 1985.

———. *Naming Our Truth: Stories of Loretto Women*. Inverness, Calif.: Chardon Press, 1995.

Weber, Msgr. Francis J. *His Eminence of Los Angeles: James Francis Cardinal McIntyre*. Mission Hills, Calif.: Saint Francis Historical Society, 1997.

———. *Magnificat: The Life and Times of Timothy Cardinal Manning*. Mission Hills, Calif.: Saint Francis Historical Society, 1999.

Werner, Sister Maria Assunta, CSC. *Madeleva: Sister Mary Madeleva Wolff, CSC, A Pictorial Biography*. Notre Dame: Congregation of the Sisters of the Holy Cross, 1993.

Wittberg, Patricia, SC. *Pathways to Re-Creating Religious Communities*. New York/Mahwah: Paulist Press, 1996.

———. *The Rise and Fall of Catholic Religious Orders: A Social Movement Perspective*. Albany: State University of New York Press, 1994.

INDEX

Collins, Sister Mary, OSB, 231
comembers, 214–15
Commission on Religious Life and
Ministry, 92
common life, 43, 151, 225–26, 230,
341, 347, 392
Commonweal, 251–52, 293–94
communities, religious,
community life, 42, 56, 79, 184, 196,
229–30, 247, 258, 264
disintegration of community life,
63–64, 225–27, 234, 277
"fraternal life in", 149, 286
inclusivity and intentionality in,
116
pre-Vatican II, 185
witness, community, 287
See also common life; *Fraternal Life in
Community;* orders; prayer
"community without walls", 64, 196
Concannon, Sister Isabel, CSJ, 166
Conference of Major Religious
Superiors of Women's Institutes
(CMSW), 17–18, 23, 53, 69, 71–72
1965 assembly, 73–74
1966 assembly, 74–75
1967 assembly, 53, 75–76, 175
1968 assembly, 75, 77, 179
1969 assembly, 79–81
1970 assembly, 55, 86–89, 91–94,
98–99, 137–38, 292
1970 special assembly, 84–86,
100–101
1971 assembly (name changed to
LCWR), 18, 97–98, 100–107,
143, 199
bylaws, 101–3, 105–7
early years, 71–71
evolution of, 72, 83, 91–97
membership, 18, 72
statutes, 18
See also Leadership Conference of
Women Religious; *specific topics*,
e.g., Sisters' Survey

Conference of Major Superiors of Men
(CMSM), 71, 92–93, 126n40, 129,
136, 155–56, 158, 215n, 268–69
Confraternity of Catholic Clergy, 140
Congar, Yves Cardinal, OP, 166, 177
Congregation for Catholic Education,
21, 228, 245
Congregation for Institutes of
Consecrated Life and Societies of
Apostolic Life (CICLSAL), 15, 343,
364, 384, 388, 392
See also Congregation for Religious
Congregation for Religious, 15, 19–21,
28–31, 139
Experimenta Circa, 58–60
new personnel at, 353–54
See also apostolic visitation of US
women religious; Congregation
for Institutes of Consecrated Life
and Societies of Apostolic Life;
*Essential Elements on Church
Teaching in Religious Life; Fraternal
Life in Community; Service of
Authority and Obedience, The;
Starting Afresh from Christ: A
Renewed Commitment to Consecrated
Life in the Third Millennium; specific
topics*, e.g., teaching sisters
Congregation for the Doctrine of the
Faith (CDF), 20
dialogue between LCWR and, 375
Doctrinal Assessment of LCWR, 22,
355–75, 383–94
doctrinal problems discussed with
LCWR, 123–26
Gramick-Nugent notification, 119–21
mandate to reform LCWR, 375
Responsum ad Dubium, 118
See also *specific topics*
Congregation of Religious and Secular
Institutes (SCRIS), 15, 61, 93, 228,
244
Congregation of the Humility of Mary,
94, 197

departures from orders. *See under*
religious life: departures from
dialogue,
　between LCWR and CDF, 375
　maintaining, 124
　between sisters' groups, 143–46
Diekmann, Father Godfrey, OSB, 193
DiIanni, Father Albert, SM, 187, 333
DiNardo, Daniel Cardinal, 134
Diocesan Sisters of Mercy of Portland,
　328–29
"discipleship of equals", 311
*Discipleship of Equals: A Critical, Feminist
　Ekklesialogy of Liberation* (Fiorenza),
　311
dissent,
　at Catholic universities, 192–93
　as love and loyalty, 121–23
　"most radical act" of, 126–28
　See also corporate dissent
divorce, 134, 300, 316, 318
doctrinal formation, 390–92
Dolan, Timothy Cardinal, 308n
Dominic, Sister Mary, OP, 98
Dominican Sisters, 14–15, 33, 211,
　276n20, 309, 313, 327–28
Dominican Sisters of Hawthorne, 14
Dominican Sisters of Hope, 327
Dominican Sisters of Our Lady of the
　Springs, Bridgeport, Connecticut,
　328–29
Dominican Sisters of Peace, 328
Dominican Sisters of Saint Cecilia, 14
Dominican Sisters of the Congregation
　of the Most Holy Rosary in
　Sinsinawa, Wisconsin, 14–15
Dominus Jesus, 21
Donoghue, Sister Diane, SSS, 308
Donovan, Sister Mary Ann, SC,
　117–18, 283
Downing, Sister Mary Omer, SC, 79
Dries, Sister Angelyn, OSF, 195
Dubay, Father Thomas, SM, 77, 211,
　279–80, 285

"Earth Spirit Rising" conference, 186
"earth-honoring" theology, 186
Ebaugh, Helen Rose Fuchs, 16, 48,
　329, 332
Ecclesiae Sanctae, 17, 44, 46–48, 58, 60,
　165, 167, 238, 241, 250, 264
Ecclesial Role of Women Committee,
　110–11
ecclesial role of women religious, 131,
　133
"ecofeminist" theology, 186
ecology; ecological future of the planet,
　72, 125, 187, 305
education,
　Catholic, 50, 249, 255, 288, 295, 384
　Catholic Higher Education (Morey and
　　Piderit), 226–27
　dissent at Catholic universities, 192–93
　National Catholic Educational
　　Association (NCEA), 190–91
　of sisters, 29, 35, 189–204
　See also Congregation for Catholic
　　Education.; parochial school
　　system; sister formation programs;
　　teaching sisters
"Education of Sister Lucy, The", 190
Egan, Monsignor Jack, 291
Eichten, Sister Beatrice, OSF, 128
elderly sisters, 36, 209–11, 213, 288,
　323–28, 330, 333–38, 381
election maneuvering, 208–12
encounter groups, 183–84
enneagram, 185–86, 203
Equal Rights Amendment (ERA), 72,
　110–11, 199, 203, 301, 305
　National Catholic Coalition for the
　　Equal Rights Amendment, 203
"equality feminists", 38
*Essential Elements on Church Teaching in
　Religious Life (Essential Elements)*, 19,
　60–63, 137, 145, 148, 157, 205,
　262–88 *passim*
*Ethical and Religious Directives for Catholic
　Health Care Services*, 41